Inclusive

FINTECH

Blockchain, Cryptocurrency
and ICO

Other Related Titles from World Scientific

Electronic Trading and Blockchain: Yesterday, Today and Tomorrow
by Richard L Sandor
ISBN: 978-981-3233-77-5

Trade, Currencies, and Finance
by Morris Goldstein
ISBN: 978-981-4749-57-2

Contemporary Issues in the Post-Crisis Regulatory Landscape
by Imad A Moosa
ISBN: 978-981-3109-28-5

Inclusive

FINTECH

Blockchain, Cryptocurrency and ICO

David LEE Kuo Chuen
Linda LOW

Singapore University of Social Sciences, Singapore

W&S World Scientific

NEW JERSEY · LONDON · SINGAPORE · BEIJING · SHANGHAI · HONG KONG · TAIPEI · CHENNAI · TOKYO

Published by

World Scientific Publishing Co. Pte. Ltd.

5 Toh Tuck Link, Singapore 596224

USA office: 27 Warren Street, Suite 401-402, Hackensack, NJ 07601

UK office: 57 Shelton Street, Covent Garden, London WC2H 9HE

Library of Congress Cataloging-in-Publication Data

Names: Lee, David (David Kuo Chen), author. | Low, Linda, author.
Title: Inclusive fintech : blockchain, cryptocurrency and ICO /
    David Kuo Chuen Lee (Singapore University of Social Sciences, Singapore),
    Linda Low (Singapore University of Social Sciences, Singapore).
Description: New York : World Scientific, [2018] | Includes bibliographical references and index.
Identifiers: LCCN 2018012983 | ISBN 9789813238633 (hardcover) |
    ISBN 9789813272767 (softcover)
Subjects: LCSH: Finance--Technological innovations. | Blockchains (Databases) |
    Bitcoin. | Electronic funds transfers.
Classification: LCC HG173 .L3796 2018 | DDC 332.1/78--dc23
LC record available at https://lccn.loc.gov/2018012983

British Library Cataloguing-in-Publication Data
A catalogue record for this book is available from the British Library.

For any available supplementary material, please visit
http://www.worldscientific.com/worldscibooks/10.1142/10949#t=suppl

Desk Editor: Jiang Yulin

Typeset by Stallion Press
Email: enquiries@stallionpress.com

Printed in Singapore

Contents

Foreword

When Professor Barry Marshall, Nobel Laureate in Physiology or Medicine, contacted me some months ago regarding my knowledge on cryptocurrencies, I had to confess that I did not know much, if at all, on the matter. I decided I would instead bring along my good friend and former colleague, Professor David Lee, to discuss the subject together. Sure enough, when we met over dinner, the night was spent not chatting about health and medicine, nor economic growth and recession. Instead, we deliberated over cryptocurrencies, and Professor David Lee, as expected, answered every question that Professor Marshall brought up.

Inclusive FinTech is a consolidation of Professor David Lee's and Professor Linda Low's knowledge and expertise on this new and emerging topic. Not much has been written about the subject and it is a timely book that elucidates the cryptocurrency market, and the linkages to large FinTech companies.

New financial instruments will continue to develop in the financial markets of tomorrow, and while this might be easier for the newer generations to understand as they are well-acquainted with the digital economy, it is perhaps more difficult for the older and in-between generations.

The key question is: Are cryptocurrencies here to stay? There are costs and benefits, and it requires a great deal of changing mind-sets and deeper understanding for investors, financial institutions and policy regulators. For example, regulating cryptocurrencies is difficult as it does not fall under the jurisdiction of any country. Regulation could strip away the attractiveness to investors. The value of cryptocurrencies is also highly volatile and dependent on market sentiments. Yet, there are also benefits such as the potential for microfinancing developing countries which lack access to formal credit markets. Nevertheless, we continue to observe that cryptocurrency hedge funds are increasingly being formed, and it only seems like cryptocurrencies are here to stay.

This book is a useful reference to complement classic financial textbooks, with a modern take and the business perspectives of financial technologies, describing with clarity the concepts of new finance, trends in FinTech, blockchain, as well as Initial Crypto-Token Offerings. It provides a systematic and logical presentation of the key cryptocurrencies today, and sieves out the myths and misconceptions from the realities of the subject. The book covers applications in the context of China, US, Australia, India, ASEAN, Japan, and Singapore. It is an insightful and practical resource, and an enjoyable read for experts and the general public alike.

Professor Euston Quah

President
Economic Society of Singapore

Professor and Head of Economics
Director, Economic Growth Centre
Nanyang Technological University, Singapore

Editor
Singapore Economic Review

Preface

"Banks must be trusted to hold our money and transfer it electronically, but they lend it out in waves of credit bubbles with barely a fraction in reserve. We have to trust them with our privacy, trust them not to let identity thieves drain our accounts. Their massive overhead costs make micropayments impossible."[1]

— Satoshi Nakamoto

"The Times 03/Jan/2009 Chancellor on brink of second bailout for banks."[2]

— Satoshi Nakamoto

The word "FinTech" is an invention in 2014 in response to the failure of traditional financial institutions to innovate despite the huge capital and technology at their disposal. The onset of the Global Financial Crisis (GFC) saw the emergence of bitcoin, a new centralised e-cash by the accumulated efforts of cryptographers, and invented by an anonymous group or a person by the name Satoshi Nakamoto. A few years before that in 2004, a centralised form of digital cash online payment was already born and mass adopted in China going by the name Alipay. The Chinese invented the term "Internet Finance" and that was 10 years before "FinTech" was first

---

[1]http://p2pfoundation.ning.com/forum/topics/bitcoin-open-source
[2]https://imgur.com/pGYXHJh

used. Financial Technology (FinTech) has its root in China with a
social objective of serving those who were excluded in the financial
system dominated by state-owned enterprises (SOEs) and financial
institutions. Chinese banks were serving mainly the SOEs and the
micro, small and medium enterprises (MSMEs) and individuals were
primarily neglected.

Outside China, financial institutions thrived on lightly regulated
environment to foster financial invention and engineering to increase
their revenue prior to the GFC. Since the crisis, regulators have
tightened regulation in many financial activities. Stricter requirements in financial and technical requirements have been instituted
and regulators view negatively those innovations that are susceptible
to rent seeking. The inability and unwillingness of traditional
institutions in providing services to the needy have been the major
issues for policy makers. There are still too many that are excluded
from the financial system with the imposition of barriers such as high
remittance charges despite the efforts of international organisations,
for example, the World Bank. However, all that are changing with
the availability of digital devices and decentralised technology.

The Rise of Satoshism

In 2008, a group or a Cypherpunk[3] that believed privacy was sacred
decided that it was time to use technology to change the world
instead of the physical occupation of Wall Street. There was an
earlier discussion about the concept of Bit-Gold by Nick Szabo[4]
before Satoshi Nakamoto's 2018 white paper.[5] Satoshi held the view
that decentralised Peer-to-Peer (P2P) cryptographic-based electronic
cash system would address some of the issues of the current financial
system. The Bitcoin cash system was created to address issues such
as credit-cycle bubbles and financial exclusion caused by a centralised
banking system. Quotations listed at the end will give readers a

---

[3]Cypherpunks are futuristic as they author science fiction and are very conversant
with cryptography.
[4]http://nakamotoinstitute.org/bit-gold/
[5]https://bitcoin.org/bitcoin.pdf

flavour of what were in the mind of Satoshi and many of the like-minded early adoptors of Bitcoin. Hopefully, the thinking behind the invention of Bitcoin will kindle the interest in finding out what FinTech really means.

Satoshi discussed his invention publicly online after he became a member of P2P Foundation on 11 February 2009 and on Bitcoin Forum on 19 November 2009. The activity log showed that the postings were late into the evening in California.

Satoshi Nakamoto is now a member of P2P Foundation

Feb 11, 2009

◀ Welcome Them!

Source: http://p2pfoundation.ning.com/forum/topics/bitcoin-open-source

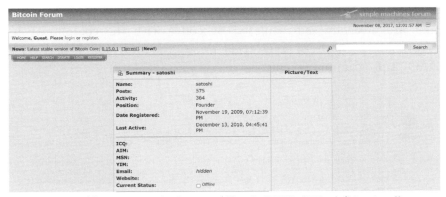

Source: https://screenshots.firefox.com/ChgxbzJBVJcOPLvA/bitcointalk.org

Satoshi's most notable quote is on the power of central authority:

"Governments are good at cutting off the heads of a centrally controlled networks like Napster, but pure P2P networks like Gnutella and Tor seem to be holding their own."

— Satoshi Nakamoto

This quote is perhaps the powerful concept of Satoshi that centralised regulatory system is weakened if there were no legal entity

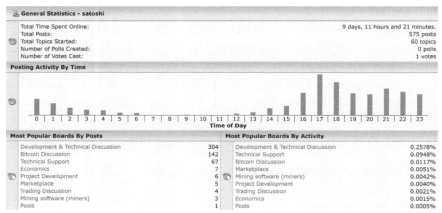

Source: https://screenshots.firefox.com/HLoIohvtgJHPeReA/bitcointalk.org;
https://bitcointalk.org/index.php?action=profile;u=3;sa =statPanel

that is being held accountable with a bunch of software codes. This gives rise to the decentralised autonomous organisations (DAOs) that are basically self-regulated by codes with the community as stakeholders. With bitcoin, it is programmable money and with DAO, a programmable entity.

∞ Reply by Satoshi Nakamoto on February 15, 2009 at 16:42

Could be. They're talking about the old Chaumian central mint stuff, but maybe only because that was the only thing available. Maybe they would be interested in going in a new direction.

A lot of people automatically dismiss e-currency as a lost cause because of all the companies that failed since the 1990's. I hope it's obvious it was only the centrally controlled nature of those systems that doomed them. I think this is the first time we're trying a decentralized, non-trust-based system.

▶ Reply

Source: https://screenshots.firefox.com/uyRMThe3QkaPKKns/p2pfoundation.
ning.com

The aforementioned quote would give an idea of the very unique feature of bitcoin and the motivation of creating a system that bypasses regulatory system or is too costly to regulate. Satoshi disappeared in 2010 and on 7 March 2014, there was a message posted from the account saying that he was no Dorian Nakamoto, someone who lived near Hal Finney — one of the well-known computer scientists.[6,7]

 ∞ Reply by Satoshi Nakamoto on March 7, 2014 at 1:17
I am not Dorian Nakamoto.

▶ Reply

Source: https://screenshots.firefox.com/0BwZ36Ms1xpW7NdB/p2pfoundation. ning.com

The aforementioned are information and background on the rise of Satoshism with decentralised and distributed innovation. The invention of Bitcoin triggered the ideas surrounding FinTech. Perhaps we can better understand that FinTech is just not a combination of the use of capital and technology to have efficient cost structure alone just as the banks and financial institutions are thinking about. The search for a sustainable business model that serves the community is the more powerful ultimate motivation. This was indeed what happened in China four years before Satoshi Nakamoto released his white paper on Bitcoin in 2008. China, with a social objective, has been allowing TechFin[8] companies to flourish.

The Rise of Chinese Finance

Out of the top 10 FinTech companies in the world, five are from China. In 2016, Ant Financial raised USD4.5 billion in one of the largest funding rounds for a private Internet company, P2P lending and online wealth management company Lufax raised USD1.2 billion, online direct sales JD.com's subsidiary JD Finance raised USD1 billion, and installment e-commerce firm Qudian (known as

---

[6]https://www.forbes.com/forbes/welcome/?toURL=https://www.forbes.com/sit es/andygreenberg/2014/03/25/satoshi-nakamotos-neighbor-the-bitcoin-ghostwrit er-who-wasnt/&refURL=https://www.google.com.sg/&referrer=https://www.go ogle.com.sg/
[7]https://www.forbes.com/sites/andygreenberg/2014/03/25/satoshi-nakamotos-neighbor-the-bitcoin-ghostwriter-who-wasnt/#289e37ea4a37
[8]Defined as those companies using technology to design new business models to serve the underserved.

Qufenqi prior to this exercise) raised USD449 million. In September 2017, China's first Internet-only insurer ZhongAn Online Property and Casualty Insurance Co Ltd announced its intention to raise USD1.5 billion in Hong Kong's biggest ever FinTech IPO. ZhongAn was formed in November 2013 by Alibaba Executive Chairman Jack Ma, Tencent Chairman Pony Ma and PingAn Insurance Group Co of China Ltd (2318.HK) Chairman Peter Ma. The appetite for FinTech, especially inclusive FinTech, from the investment community has been large and there are good reasons to be so. For these companies, the technology strategy is about the use of ABCD (Artificial Intelligence, Blockchain, Cloud and Data Analytics) or BASIC (Blockchain, Artificial Intelligence, Security, Internet of Things, and Cloud Computing).

Since the GFC, we have seen the balance sheet of some central banks increase by as much as four folds. Unconventional monetary easing has not rekindled inflation and increased lending to MSMEs as expected. There have been many controversies surrounding quantitative easing (QE). Some argue that the increased liquidity has not channelled to productive sectors as much as economic theory has suggested, but into speculative activities and investable asset classes such as real estate, bonds and equities. The Federal Reserve Bank (FED) has raised rates four times since December 2015 as part of a normalisation of monetary policy from near zero rates, reversing an earlier trend of increasing the balance sheet from USD0.9 trillion in 2007 to a high of USD4.516 trillion in Jan 2015. As at end Aug 2017, it was USD4.452 trillion. Meantime, others have commented that many other countries such as China have employed innovative backdoor QE methods by introducing new lending instruments.

Despite the slowing down of the advanced economies from 2.1% in 2015 to 1.7% in 2016 according to International Monetary Fund (IMF) statistics, the Standard & Poor (S&P) had returned −0.73% in 2015 and 9.84% in 2016. The MSCI World Index had similar performance with −0.35% for 2015 and 8.15% for 2016. While the growth of emerging markets and developing economies was fairly constant at 4.3% for both 2015 and 2016, the MSCI Emerging Markets returned −14.60% in 2015 and 11.60% in 2016.

The Bloomberg Barclays Global Aggregate Unhedged Index returned
-3.15% in 2015 and 2.09% in 2016, a very similar picture. If one
were to observe the correlations of economic activities, equities and
bonds, there remained more questions than answers viewed from
the perspective of fundamental analysis. Since the GFC, the long-
term risk adjusted returns of traditional as well as alternatives
have suffered as demonstrated by the real and perceived decrease
in expected returns and increased in volatility.

An almost full employment economy with slowing momentum
tends to see a decline in corporate profit margins. This is indeed
the case of many countries especially the US which is at the mature
state of the business cycle and according to Societe Generale SA,
we are close to 80% completion of this business cycle. Furthermore,
the complexity of products has also become an issue for regulators,
increasing the liabilities of the managers, thus increasing the costs
of investment with more compliance and complicated regulation. All
these are symptoms of an over-leveraged market with a focus on high
profit margin and complex investment products.

More interestingly, three-quarters of large investors were disappointed by the performance of their alternative investment, especially
hedge funds, in 2016 (Merle, 2017). There was an increase in the
level of frustration with hedge fund returns, up from two-thirds of
investors who felt disappointed by the asset class in 2015. The returns
of 5.6% for hedge funds in 2016 was less than the 9.84% gain of the
S&P 500 Index. But what is at odds is that according to J.P. Morgan
Survey of 234 institutions, 90% intend to increase or maintain their
current allocation to hedge funds in 2017. However, it was observed
that investors redeemed USD70 billion from hedge funds in 2015.
There is evidence to suggest that capacity is an issue given that too
many managers were chasing the same limited trading opportunities.
The excess funds from QE have been channelled to the market rather
than the real economy, triggering the fear in policy makers that
bubbles are forming in the asset markets, especially the real estate
sector. With increased correlation and a potential bubble in asset
markets, there is disquiet of where the market will be heading when
there is a reversal in the policy of central banks.

One of the obvious side effects of the innovative QE is the concentration of investment portfolio on asset classes that concentrate on serving the Top of the Pyramid. Given the uneven growth and uneven distribution of wealth, the asset bubbles only serve to enhance the wealth of those who have invested in these asset classes. Those at the bottom who have a higher marginal propensity to consume seem to find it difficult to get a long-term job with higher unemployment rates, thus lowering the actual consumption even further. The displacement of jobs by artificial intelligence (AI), robotics and other technologies will contribute to a further loss of confidence in the economy. With many excluded from the financial, economic and social system globally, the largest source of risk from the investors' viewpoint may come from global investable assets that may have already benefitted and captured most of the returns from the massive liquidity.

Any global tightening of central bank balance sheets or natural disasters may impact the market adversely. There is a disquiet about the possibility that most large investors are exposed heavily to a single risk factor, i.e., asset classes such as equities, bonds, commodities, alternatives are all focused on serving the top of the pyramid with huge downside risk. Meanwhile, the middle and the bottom of the pyramid are experiencing a fear of having their jobs displaced by disruptive technology. There are signs that investors are seeking not just alternative investments, but a completely new class of negatively correlated investment known as FinTech, the term that never existed before 2014. But the search for the new FinTech class started much earlier when the confidence in the USD was shaken during the GFC. It is not by chance that bitcoin, as a digital currency, was invented in 2008 and started distribution in 2009.

This book is written for the "FinTech and Innovation" course at the Singapore University of Social Sciences (SUSS). It compiles all the work since 2013 when David Lee was teaching in the course "Alternative Investment" in Singapore Management University and executive courses in the same university. Many of these chapters were developed from research papers and PowerPoint presentations at Stanford and Singapore Management University for the World Bank,

IMF, CAIA (San Francisco, Korea, Hong Kong, Singapore), Sim Kee Boon Institute for Financial Economics, Tsinghua University, Shantou University, Jiao Tong University, SUSS, Singapore government departments, financial institutions and many other public talks, media articles, podcasts and television programmes. Many of these talks and speeches were a peek into the future with implications for business and public policies. While many of the ideas went into five edited books,[9] there were still many uncompiled ideas. The course at SUSS was an opportunity to gather some of these thoughts, though not all were presented, in the form of teaching notes that resulted in this book. Linda Low assisted in getting the work going with tremendous help from Lo Swee Won and other researchers that are mentioned in the acknowledgement section.

In 2013, there were a lot of scepticisms about FinTech and a few main line of thoughts that these lectures were ahead of its time:

(1) Cryptocurrency and especially bitcoin would be an important asset class in the future;

(2) Blockchain, as a trust machine and relationship efficiency enhancer, would have a lot of applications in finance and beyond;

(3) Banks were innovating too slowly as regulations were unintentionally protective of their markets;

(4) Banks that are too big to collaborate will disappear in the future;

(5) The Rise of Chinese Finance would dominate the FinTech scene and disrupt the financial sector;

(6) Financial Inclusion and Impact Investment would be the sought-after asset classes of the future;

(7) Centralised sharing economy with services alone is a false sharing economy that would lead to a concentration of power of wealth;

---

[9]The five edited books refer to *Handbook of Digital Currency: Bitcoin, Innovation, Financial Instruments, and Big Data*; *Handbook of Blockchain, Digital Finance, and Inclusion, Volume 1: Cryptocurrency, FinTech, InsurTech, and Regulation*; *Handbook of Blockchain, Digital Finance, and Inclusion, Volume 2: ChinaTech, Mobile Security, and Distributed Ledger*; *Handbook of Asian Finance: Financial Markets and Sovereign Wealth Funds*; *Handbook of Asian Finance, Volume 2: REITs, Trading and Fund Performance*.

(8) The most powerful feature of decentralised technology with blockchain is the fractional ownership of digital assets that would lead to a more equitable and just society;

(9) The gradual convergence of profit motives and social mission to create the new class of post-capitalist enterprises.

The Rise of ASEAN Financial Inclusion

Few were receptive to these ideas, and it was difficult to foresee a country like Singapore who had been focusing on multi-national companies (MNCs) and wealth management. As conditions change, Singapore has moved from pushing for Funds Passport Scheme to be managed from Singapore since a decade ago, to start embracing financial inclusion as one of the leading activities of the financial regulator. With the Alliance for Financial Inclusion (AFI) headquartered in Kuala Lumpur, it is interesting to see that Singapore is among the rare few countries in the Association of Southeast Asian Nations (ASEAN) to not be a part of the organisation. This is however, not an exception, with financial cities such as New York, London, Japan, Zurich and Hong Kong in the same category. There was just not enough motivation to be part of the financial inclusion space or to further embrace impact investment. Joining organisations such as AFI and Global Impact Investment Network was not a trend, but that would all be changing shortly. On the other hand, there were those that were advocating businesses that only served the bottom of the pyramid. The business world seemed to be dichotomous with those serving the top or the bottom, with either the sole objective of rent-seeking or sole purpose of charity. All these started to change when the Chinese, with a socialist mentality, believed that all should be served rather than being selective. Digital finance provided the solution via the use of a smartphone to bring down the business cost of serving those excluded. Convergence of top and bottom services was possible with many gaps in the markets. By leaving those that bridge the gaps alone, the policy makers have gotten their wish to fill the gaps, making the market more efficient. These are not all without risk-taking on the part of regulators that are afraid of financial and social instability.

However, digital finance has forged the convergence of profit motives with social objectives creating a class of large FinTech companies. Good examples are Baidu, Ant Financial, Tencent and JD.com (known as BATJ), as well as Lufax, CreditEase, DianRong and other that serve hundreds of millions via their platforms through the Internet and digital devices. We are glad to be teaching and researching in a financial city with a group of dedicated policy makers pushing the agenda of inclusive growth via a more open financial system. The Financial Technology and Innovation Group at the Monetary Authority of Singapore has to be commended for their relentless efforts in pushing the needle to make financial inclusion and impact investment as an essential part of a viable global policy to reboot the financial system. Special mention of Sopnendu Mohanty and his team that have inspired many to do the impossible and they present a good case study for many regulators. As described in this book, the next growth area will be ASEAN with many low hanging fruits among the underserved with a population size of 660 million people.

The Rise of Decentralisation FinTech (DFinTech)

It is with this book that the authors hope to dispel a lot of the misconceptions about blockchain and cryptocurrencies (especially bitcoin and initial crypto-token offering or ICO), as well as the idea that businesses can be sustainable without a social dimension going forward. It is written for those who are looking for a switch from their careers to something more meaningful and sustainable. It is also written for those who want a deeper understanding of where to search for business opportunities. But most important of all, it is written to change the mindset of a whole new generation that is familiar with digital economy and is yearning for a world that is more just and equitable.

Going forward, many will realise that a sharing economy without the sharing of asset ownership is not truly sharing and will be unsustainable. The combination of Decentralisation and FinTech will give rise to a new concept of Decentralised FinTech or DFinTech that will lead to fractional ownership of digital asset for a more equitable and sustainable economy. Decentralised and distributed innovation will be the future for Finance.[10] Perhaps the 10th point is

(10) The future development of DFinTech, a combination of decentralisation autonomous technology and FinTech, will be interesting.

A Textbook to Capture Evolving Thoughts and Events

FinTech has arrived from China as BAT (Baidu–Alipay–Tencent) in Singapore with its Report of the Committee on the Future Economy (CFE). The designated future is digital, including a cashless society. As much as there are advantages and benefits in efficiency from digital transactions, there is the need to weigh the flipside of using cryptocurrencies. Blockchain-transactions create cryptocurrencies just as coupons, vouchers, tokens and other forms of exchange that enable transactions, but on a much larger scale. Cryptocurrencies created by blockchain-transactions are unregulated in contrast to currencies issued by central banks as legal tender as part of their monetary policies.

As a revolution, FinTech is still evolving and like an infant, this textbook designed for teaching is thus a pioneer to capture the essence, implications and nuances as perceived until measured by more empirical evidence. The book attempts to capture the existing literature in tandem, but it needs to be emphasised again, features and events are still evolving.

This book is a standard text with additional readings along the way to complement and supplement, especially with contributions from practitioners and regulators over time. Any revised editions or sequels need not abrogate the usefulness of this basic textbook. All users and readers would expect this, just as there is no fully captured and scripted literature on the Fourth Industrial Revolution yet to

---

[10]Lee, David Kuo Chuen (2017), "Decentralisation and Distributed Innovation", Presented to Stanford APARC Innovation Conference, Stanford.

fully replace the First or subsequent revolutions as passé, that is, completely replaced by the new.

Indeed, the book is a learning curve as authors, lecturers, students and other professional experts contribute to its journey as FinTech evolves and matures over time. There is a need for much more exchanges from academicians to practitioners and central banks as regulators. Equally important are views from users of cryptocurrencies from consumers to producers across countries, without exchange rates complications. Thus, the authors writing this book have much excitement and desire to be on the learning with all on board.

Acknowledgement

Since this is a book that is compiled with work and ideas from 2013, there are many to express our appreciation. Many research assistants have contributed to this book. Special mention should also go to Master's students from Singapore Management University and Nanyang Technological University. To all of you, thank you very much.

I cannot end this without thanking our creator and express gratitude for His providence. May this work be able to help and encourage others to make this a better world.

Notable Quotes of Satoshi Nakamoto

1. On the invention

"I've developed a new open source P2P e-cash system called Bitcoin. It's completely decentralized, with no central server or trusted parties, because everything is based on crypto proof instead of trust."[11]

2. On P2P

"I've been working on a new electronic cash system that's fully peer-to-peer, with no trusted third party."[12]

---

[11] http://p2pfoundation.ning.com/forum/topics/bitcoin-open-source

[12] http://www.metzdowd.com/pipermail/cryptography/2008-October/014810.html

3. On monetary policy

"The root problem with conventional currency is all the trust that's required to make it work. The central bank must be trusted not to debase the currency, but the history of fiat currencies is full of breaches of that trust."[13]

4. On decentralisation

"A purely peer-to-peer version of electronic cash would allow online payments to be sent directly from one party to another without going through a financial institution."[14]

5. On investment psychology

"It might make sense just to get some in case it catches on."[15]

6. On investment incentives

"Eventually at most only 21 million coins for 6.8 billion people in the world if it gets really huge."[16]

7. On behavioural finance

"A rational market price for something that is expected to increase in value will already reflect the present value of the expected future increases. In your head, you do a probability estimate balancing the odds that it keeps increasing."[17]

8. On consensus and blockchain

"It is a global distributed database, with additions to the database by consent of the majority."[18]

---

[13]http://p2pfoundation.ning.com/forum/topics/bitcoin-open-source
[14]http://nakamotoinstitute.org/bitcoin/
[15]http://www.metzdowd.com/pipermail/cryptography/2009-January/015014.html
[16]https://bitcointalk.org/index.php?topic=44.msg267#msg267
[17]https://bitcointalk.org/index.php?topic=57.msg415#msg415
[18]http://p2pfoundation.ning.com/forum/topics/bitcoin-open-source?commentId=2003008%3AComment%3A9562

9. On economic incentives for why miners should help to maintain the ledger and facilitate transactions

"I'm sure that in 20 years there will either be very large transaction volume or no volume."[19]

10. On individual security and burned coin

"Lost coins only make everyone else's coins worth slightly more. Think of it as a donation to everyone."[20]

11. On financial inclusion

"Bitcoin would be convenient for people who don't have a credit card or don't want to use the cards they have."[21]

12. On crowdsourcing wisdom

"Being open source means anyone can independently review the code. If it was closed source, nobody could verify the security. I think it's essential for a program of this nature to be open source."[22]

13. On massive electricity consumption

"The heat from your computer is not wasted if you need to heat your home. If you're using electric heat where you live, then your computer's heat isn't a waste. It's equal cost if you generate the heat with your computer."[23]

14. On location of mining

"Bitcoin generation should end up where it's cheapest. Maybe that will be in cold climates where there's electric heat, where it would be essentially free."[24]

---

[19]https://bitcointalk.org/index.php?topic=48.msg329#msg329

[20]https://bitcointalk.org/index.php?topic=198.msg1647#msg1647

[21]https://bitcointalk.org/index.php?topic=671.msg13844#msg13844

[22]https://bitcointalk.org/index.php?topic=13.msg46#msg46

[23]http://satoshi.nakamotoinstitute.org/posts/bitcointalk/337/#selection-33.0-33.155

[24]https://bitcointalk.org/index.php?topic=721.msg8431#msg8431

15. Rare comment!

"If you don't believe it or don't get it, I don't have the time to try to convince you, sorry."[25]

References and Further Readings

Merle, R. (May 20, 2017). Once considered the titans of Wall Street, hedge fund managers are in trouble. Retrieved from https://www.washingtonpost.com/business/economy/once-considered-the-titans-of-wall-street-hedge-fund-managers-are-in-trouble/2017/05/29/61049f1e-34ce-11e7-b373-418f6849a004_story.html?noredirect=on&utm_term=.5eccc0655a44

---

[25] https://bitcointalk.org/index.php?topic=532.msg6306#msg6306

Chapter 1

Overview

1.1 What Is FinTech?

FinTech or financial technology refers to the new solutions which demonstrate innovation in the development of applications, processes, products or business models in the financial services industry using technology. FinTech should have four features. They need to be highly innovative, pioneering, disruptive and customer-focused. Technology will include the use of artificial intelligence (AI), big data, computational power, Internet of Things (IoT) or others. These solutions can be differentiated in at least five areas by customer segments like financial services or products built upon technology in the banking and insurance sectors shown in Table 1.1.

We have earlier defined FinTech to be as general as possible to embody a broad range of technology applications and to include payments, investment, financing, insurance, advisory, cross-processed (bank/insurer/non-bank/non-insurer) and infrastructure services. There is no one definition agreed by all. Some may define FinTech as technology that increases efficiency and creates new financial business models that utilise some or all of the followings: AI, Blockchain, Cloud and Data Analytics. Others have defined FinTech companies as those applying emerging technologies to alter the current financial landscape, while TechFin companies are those that utilise technology to enhance existing financial capabilities. Still, others have viewed FinTech companies as those driven by the desire to use emerging technologies to disrupt the financial landscape, while

Table 1.1.   **Coverage of FinTech.**

Sector	Business process	Customer segment	Interaction form	Market position
✦ Bank	✦ Payments	✦ Retail banking	✦ C2C	✦ Bank/insurer
✦ Insurer	✦ Investments	✦ Corporate banking	✦ B2C	✦ Non-bank/insurer – bank/insurer-cooperation
	✦ Financing (e.g. crowdfunding)	✦ Private banking	✦ B2B	✦ Non-bank/insurer – bank/insurer-competition
	✦ Insurance (e.g.risk management)	✦ Life insurance		
	✦ Advisory	✦ Non life insurance		
	✦ Cross-process (e.g. big data analytics and predictive modeling)			
	✦ Infrastructure (e.g. security)			

Source: By authors; Alt and Pushchmann (2012).

TechFin companies are those using technology to enable efficiency improvements, preferring a less disruptive and a more incremental approach.

However, Jack Ma, the founder of the world's largest e-commerce platform Alibaba, has given an entirely different definition for TechFin. To Ma, FinTech takes the original financial system and improves its technology (Zen, 2016), and TechFin is to rebuild the system with technology and solve the problem of *a lack of inclusiveness*.

Before the use of the word FinTech, there were discussions in China between the utilisation of the two terms: Internet Finance and Internet Banking. These two concepts in the Chinese language are (i) *Internet Finance* (互联网金融) that focuses on providing innovative financial services via the Internet to the masses and (ii) Finance on the Internet (金融互联网) that provides traditional financial services on the Internet. The former uses AI, big data, and computing power to lower credit risk and provide innovative online and offline services, while the latter uses the Internet to provide old economy financial services. If that is not confusing enough, there is also the use of the terms Digital Banking, Virtual Banking, Online Banking, Mobile

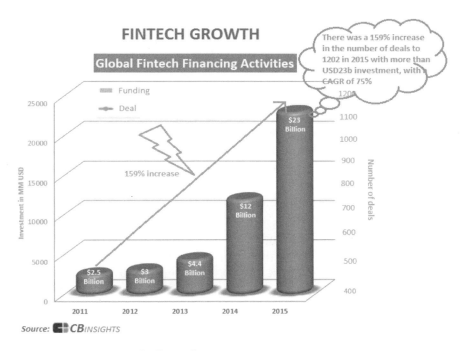

Figure 1.1. **FinTech Growth: 2011–2015.**
Source: By authors; CBInsights.

Banking, Social Banking in Europe that describe business models with digital or online services without any physical branches.

These debates on the use of the terms are fuelled by an exponential increase in the investment into FinTech start-ups and companies. Regarding FinTech growth in the world according to CB Insights, there was an estimated 260% increase in the number of deals from 2008 to reach 730 in 2014 with more than USD12 billion investment. By 2015, Figure 1.1 shows there was an increase of 159% in the number of deals to 1,202 in 2015, with more than USD23 billion in investment, with a compound average growth rate (CAGR) of 75%.

1.1.1 *FinTech and Silicon Valley*

Silicon Valley has a start-up culture that is unmatched elsewhere. To understand FinTech, we need to understand the ecosystem and the underlying "3C" philosophy. In the Silicon Valley ecosystem, the three Cs are Community, Compassion and Creativity. Moreover, the *raison d'etre* for FinTech is three-pronged. One is the repression of the Financial Services Industry which offers the potential for FinTech, resulting in massive customer demand as yet to be met by the traditional financial industry. The second reason for the rapid commercial technology advances is providing tools for innovation as by mobile Internet, big data, cloud computing, and blockchain. In turn, rapidly changing customer behaviour is an impetus for innovation as customers want to have a decisive role in choosing financial services. The unmatched mindset of Silicon Valley, sometimes termed the Left Coast Culture, is supplemented by deep skills of those taking up the technology and start-ups' challenges in the Bay Area. However, without the massive capital to fund the development of the ecosystem that sees 80% to 90% failure rates, it will be difficult for the deep skill and mindset to evolve. It is not the community alone that supports the ecosystem, but it is also the compassionate spirit that grows the investment culture into one that prides itself for buying into failures. However, more importantly, the creative culture is the consequence of the right environment to acquire the right skill set, the right mindset and the resilience of fundraising capabilities despite high rates of failures.

1.1.2   *FinTech and corporate culture*

FinTech is not only attractive to financial institutions, but it is also attracting the attention of non-financial services as shown in three different technological businesses represented by the three companies Google, Intel and Salesforce (the primary activity of the companies is in parenthesis): namely:

(1) Google has invested in OnDeck (loans and credit), Robinhood (investment), rippleLabs (payment), digit (finance tracking), puddle (L&C), Upstart (L&C), CircleUp (investment), Abacus (accounting), LedgerX (trading), Kensho (analytics);

(2) Intel has invested in iZettle (payment), fortumo (billing), technisys (banking), mFoundry (retail banking solutions), FundersClub (investment);

CORE DIFFERENCE: LIABILITY VERSUS MISSION ACCOUNTING

Traditional Financial Services   Fintech

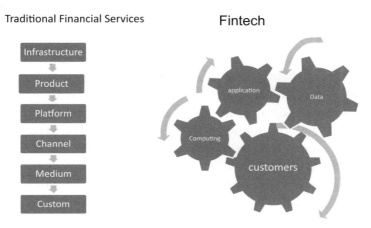

Figure 1.2. **Core Difference between Traditional Financial Services and FinTech.**

Source: By authors.

(3) Salesforce has invested in nCino (Cloud SaaS), Financial-Force.com (Cloud ERP), Moneytree (expenditure management).

Corporate venture capital in financial services includes Citi Services with one to ten new deals per year and with median deal size of USD19 million. Corporate venture capital backs about half of such ventures. As shown in Figure 1.2, the core difference between traditional financial services and FinTech is of respectively, block and silo structure to a flat and interconnected structure. In conventional finance, processes are organised along infrastructure, product, platform, channel, medium and custom. In FinTech, it is a flat organisation structure that drives application, cloud and custom. The latter is smooth, interconnected and with few pain points.

Whereas traditional banks act openly to engage with technology solutions early and have their own intellectual property to generate new ideas, they also need to collaborate to co-innovate within the industry and engage with start-ups too. They do venture investing in start-ups.

However, traditional banks are matrix organisations, working according to marketing lines (investment, corporate, retail, wealth management, etc). They are sub-divided into product lines (loans, deposits, equity, fixed income, derivatives, structured, etc). A dotted line (indirect) and solid line (direct) reporting structure are super-imposed on existing structure.

In terms of their corporate governance and compliance as sacred, there is minimum discretion to prevent "mistakes". The paper trail is essential for accountability of adherence. Incentives exist to encourage competition and innovation within the rules to maximise profits. Conflict of Interest and Interested Party Transactions are frowned upon. Whistleblowing to expose inefficiency and violations is the practice. Liability accounting means mistakes, not sunk cost, but the beginning of witch-hunting with punishment.

In Google Insurance Tech, for instance, it moves around invest-ments (collective Health, OSCAR, Gusto, The Climate Corporation) and partnerships (American Insurance, CoverFund, Liberty Mutual Insurance, VSP and AXA). There is an increasingly diverse cast of tech

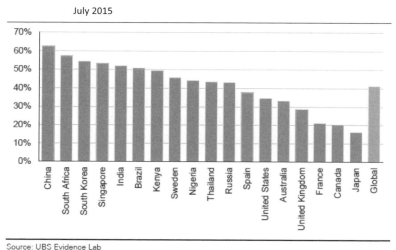

MOBILE (INTERNET) BANKING PENETRATION

July 2015

Source: UBS Evidence Lab

Figure 1.3.   Mobile and Internet Banking Penetration.

Source: UBS Evidence Lab.

MOBILE BANKING CUSTOMERS AT THE TOP 12 GLOBAL BANKS

Forbes rank	Bank	HQ location	Mobile banking customers	annual mobile growth	Online banking customers	Total customers	Mobile percentage of customers
1	Industrial and Commercial Bank of China	China	100 million +	49.5%	390 million	432 million	23.2%
2	China Construction Bank	China	117 million	38.9%	150 million	291 million	40.2%
3	Agricultural Bank of China	China	83.0 million	N/A	110.9 million	320 million	25.9%
4	JPMorgan Chase	USA	16.4 million	24%	35.0 million	N/A	N/A
8	Wells Fargo & Company	USA	12.5 million	23%	23.8 million	70 million	17.9%
9	Bank of China	China	52.1 million	24.6%	101.1 million	N/A	N/A
13	Bank of America	USA	14.4 million	19.8%	30.0 million	50 million	28.8%
14	HSBC Holdings	UK	2.5 million	N/A	N/A	60 million	4.2%
16	Citigroup	USA	N/A	N/A	N/A	100 million	N/A
24	BNP Paribas	France	1 million	N/A	N/A	N/A	N/A
37	Mitsubishi UFJ Financial	Japan	N/A	N/A	N/A	N/A	N/A
43	Banco Santander	Spain	2.6 million	N/A	11.6 million	106.6 million	2.4%

Source: Banks 2013 annual reports
Except JPM and WFC: Q1 2014 report.   Via © mobiThinking

Figure 1.4.   Mobile Banking Customers at the Top 12 Global Banks.
Source: Banks 2013 annual reports.

players, stretching from the US in early-stage of insurance tech deals, to Germany, the UK and lately to India and China among others.

1.1.3   *FinTech and mobile banking*

For mobile (Internet) banking penetration, by July 2015, Figure 1.3 shows the fast catch-up is by China of over 60%, followed by South Africa (near 60%) and South Korea (55%) while the US lags (35%) behind even the global as 45%.

Figure 1.4 shows for mobile banking customers at the top 12 global banks in 2013, China also excels, with top three from China, namely, Industrial and Commercial Bank of China (over 100 million mobile banking customers), China Construction Bank (117 million) and Agricultural Bank China (83.0 million).

1.2   The Economics of Financial Inclusion

The economics of financial inclusion is evident with the global emergence of mobile technology to play a significant role in enabling

ACTIVE MOBILE-BROADBAND
SUBSCRIPTIONS PER 100 INHABITANTS:
DEVELOPED VS. DEVELOPING COUNTRIES
+ WORLD ACG. 2007-2017+

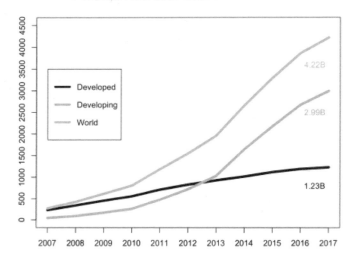

Figure 1.5.   The Economics of Digital Inclusion Active Users.

Source: By authors; ITU World Telecommunication/ICT Indicators Database.

financial inclusion. Through mobile and other smart devices, many unbanked and underbanked segments of the world will be able to gain access to financial services. Figures 1.5 and 1.6 show the growth in trends of financial inclusion by active mobile subscriptions in developed and developing countries, in 2007–2014. The potential in the developing countries is enormous to catch up with the developed.

FinTech companies work on the economics of financial inclusion which by nature involves financial technologies which are disruptive. They are quintessentially a form of disruptive technology involving interplay of groups of individuals, thus termed as terminators, destroyers and disruptors. Terminators are excellent executors and by the book, but mark the end of careers and traditionalists as well as conformists. Destroyers come out from witch-hunting without fresh ideas and are unhappy with current conditions. Disruptors are non-conforming problem solvers with alternative or out-of-the-box ideas, as mission driven. Once the idea is sold to them, there is no looking back.

ACTIVE MOBILE-BROADBAND
SUBSCRIPTIONS PER 100 INHABITANTS:
DEVELOPED VS. DEVELOPING COUNTRIES
+ WORLD ACG. 2007-2017+ (percentage)

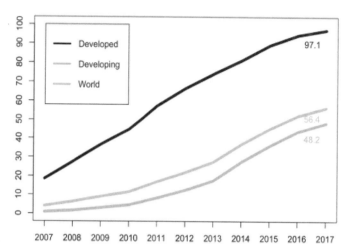

Figure 1.6. The Economics of Digital Inclusion Active Users (percentages).

Source: By authors; ITU World Telecommunication/ICT Indicators Database.

Financial Technologies will play a significant role in redefining finance. First, business costs (capital adequacy requirements and compliance) are rising for traditional financial institutions. Second, with financial technology, business costs can be lowered to serve a large segment of those not currently served by the financial institutions (Bottom of the Pyramid or BoP). Finally, serving the unbanked and underbanked or BoP (known as financial inclusion) can be sustainable FinTech business with scalable growth potential.

Lower margin businesses like microfinance and micro-insurance will become not only viable but profitable. Additional services such as credit rating, e-commerce, O2O (Online–Offline), LBS (Location Based Services) can enhance stickiness and profitability. Consumers will be attracted by the low costs and convenience that these new technologies will bring. Traditional financial institutions with substantial assets and significant fixed costs will be disrupted due to

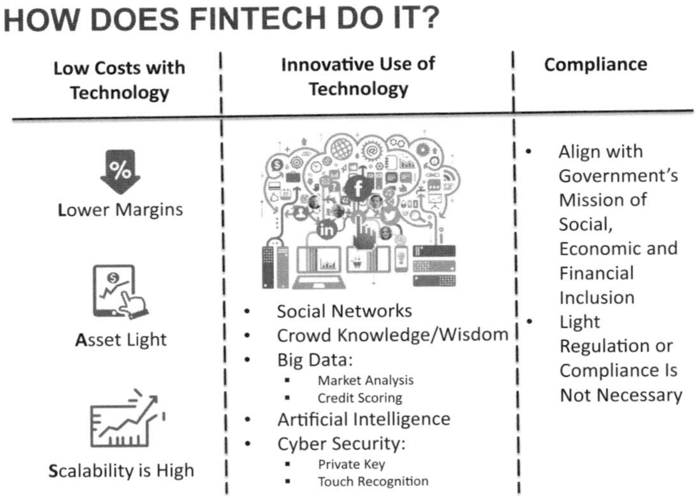

Inclusive FinTech

HOW DOES FINTECH DO IT?

Low Costs with Technology	Innovative Use of Technology	Compliance
Lower Margins		• Align with Government's Mission of Social, Economic and Financial Inclusion

Asset Light	• Social Networks
	• Crowd Knowledge/Wisdom
	• Big Data:
	  ▪ Market Analysis
	  ▪ Credit Scoring
	• Artificial Intelligence
	• Cyber Security:
		• Light Regulation or Compliance Is Not Necessary

Scalability is High	▪ Private Key ▪ Touch Recognition	

Figure 1.7.   How Does FinTech Do It?

Source: By authors.

the ability to respond to disruptions. Compliance cost and political resistance will be lower by aligning with the governments' social, economic and financial inclusion agendas with skills future job creation as a priority.

Figure 1.7 combines low costs with technology and innovative use of technology, to sum up how FinTech works.

1.3   Unbundling the Bank with FinTech

Why is unbundling a trend? First, let us define terms as Millennials, Gen Y, and Gen X. Millennials (also known as Generation Y) are the demographic cohort following Generation X. Generation X, or Gen X, is the demographic cohort following the baby boomers and preceding the Millennials. There are no precise dates for when these Gen Y or Gen X cohorts start or end; demographers and researchers typically use the early 1980s as starting birth years and the mid-1990s to early 2000s as ending birth years for Gen Y. For Gen X, birth years ranging from the early-to-mid 1960s to the early 1980s. As shown in Figure 1.8, one reason has to do with Millennials demanding

Figure 1.8. Unbundling of a Bank.

Source: CBInsights, https://www.cbinsights.com/research/disrupting-banking-FinTech-startups/

personal control and transparency of their financial interactions from banking to insurance. Also, less than half of Millennials (46%) see themselves staying with their current financial services companies over the next few years. Lastly, some of affluent Millennials (76%) would seek information about personal investing on a social network, as opposed to just 18% of the affluent Gen Xers.

1.4   Successful Tech Companies

Successful tech companies are of a flat structure with little hierarchy. They have interconnected wheels that propel and synchronise with each other and innovation is sacred. They seek user experience (UX) to compete to reduce pain points and encourage good designs as well as seek collaboration: to reduce friction via alignment of interest and sharing of expertise, knowledge, information, network etc. Their mission in accounting is to see mistakes as a sunk cost and move on with error correction mechanism to reach the ultimate goal.

The underserved in the world turn to non-traditional forms of alternative financial services such as those provided by cheque cashers, loan sharks and pawnbrokers. For example, illegal workers in the US cash cheques via agents such as cashing depots or convenience stores. To reach the economics of financial inclusion, the global picture of the unbanked and underbanked as even more skewed needs to be addressed. Only 50% of adults in the world have an individual or joint account at a formal financial institution (Demirrguc-Kunt and Klapper, 2012).

There are 2.5 billion adults in the world with no formal bank accounts in 2012, most of them in developing countries. Financial exclusion does not just exist in developed countries as 7% of US households are also unbanked, and 20% are underbanked.

1.5   Why Use FinTech?

Consumers choose these FinTech institutions instead of trusted banks for many reasons. They include lower fees and better rates, lower thresholds for investments, lower thresholds for loans, ease of use and convenience. Some have argued that as regulations catch up with the FinTech companies, these advantages will disappear. Others have argued that the new FinTech business models are more cost effective and therefore these advantages will stay.

The banking sector is plagued by a risk adverse culture, dominated by amply staffed regulatory departments and a financial control ethos. None of these characteristics screams innovation or disruption. While the old bank culture needs to change, FinTech companies are running ahead to innovate, explore and recalibrate their offerings rapidly. User data as new money implies that data availability as extremely valuable. Apps that have high user commitment or access to a part of a community have high switching costs, are more customer sticky and collect richer data. Digital services or apps that have huge captive user bases can generate enormous amounts of valuable data.

Before plumbing deeper into the FinTech paradigm as non-bank as a start to the evolution of new banking services, the new business models and principles need to be defined.

1.6 New Business Models and Principles

The necessary changes in the business model for FinTech are from high to low margin. In the past, companies with high margins were attractive destinations for capital. Their features were thus large margin with barrier of entry and no disruption from technology. Now, companies that attract capital are innovative, have low margins and low barrier of entry, and possess potential for high scalability to enable FinTech businesses to focus on customer stickiness instead of cash flow.

1.6.1 *CLASSIC characteristics*

The common characteristics abbreviated as EY's CLASSIC were discovered by one of the four audit firms EY. Referring to Figure 1.9, **C** is for customer-centric with simple-to-use and high-convenience products and services with needs-focused propositions designed around particular consumer use cases and pain points. There is thus a high degree of customer engagement. **L** stands for being legacy-free

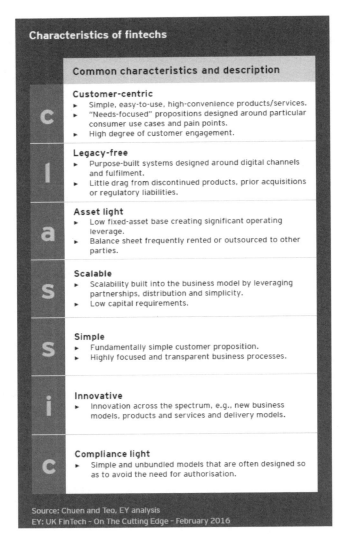

Figure 1.9.   EY's CLASSIC Model.

Source: Lee and Teo (2015); EY (2016b).

with purpose-built systems designed around digital channels and fulfilment. There is little drag from discontinued products, before acquisition or regulatory liabilities. **A** stands for asset-light as in small fixed asset base to create significant operating leverage. As a result, balance sheets are frequently rented or outsourced to other parties. **S** stands for scalability. Scalability is built into the business model by leveraging partnerships, distribution and simplicity with resulting low capital requirements. The next **S** also stands for a fundamentally simple customer proposition as highly focused and transparent in business processes. **I** stand for innovative with innovation across the spectrum in the new business model, products, services and delivery modes. Finally, the last **C** stands for compliance light as simple, unbundled models that are often designed to avoid the need for approval. This EY model was built upon an earlier model developed by Lee and Teo Model (Lee and Teo, 2015).

1.6.2 *LASIC principles*

A shorter version of the new business model is dubbed as LASIC (Lee and Teo, 2015) in Figure 1.10, with the abbreviations denoting low margins, asset light, scalable, innovative and compliance easy. Small margins as FinTech companies starting low to attract and build a critical mass as well as to prevent competition. Asset light means to ride on existing infrastructure as e-commerce and telecom companies. Scalability is achieved by being expandable without exponential costs as technology allows for large scale changes. Being innovative is using technology such as social media to find untapped markets while being disruptive and inclusive (not exclusive) to solve real issues/problems. Finally, compliance easy means the great likelihood for government support in a lowly regulated way as the government sees the rise and promise of FinTech.

The financial system is being disrupted, first by innovative competitors operating on sleek business models and offering new alternative services are entering at the bottom of the market, where gross margins are low and latent demand is high. Moreover, financial services and banking still enjoy robust margins, but this is more a function of regulatory protection than the actual value they create.

Tightening regulation has encumbered large complex, financial institutions, probably as a response to the Global Financial Crisis (GFC) since 2007. This silo mentality and burdensome physical infrastructure make it ripe for digital disruption.

LASIC PRINCIPLES

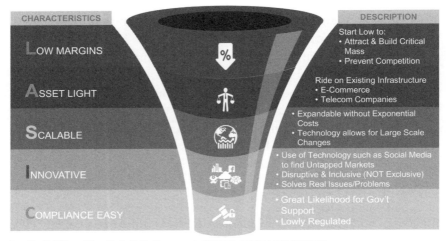

Lee, David K.C. and Teo, Ernie G. S., Emergence of Fintech and the Lasic Principles (September 30, 2015). Available at SSRN: http://ssrn.com/abstract=2668049

Figure 1.10. LASIC Principles.

Source: Lee and Teo (2015).

The World Bank's 2014 Global Findex Report sets the trend of mobile banking led by non-banks. Low penetration of high-speed mobile broadband in developing countries features worldwide adults with financial deposits ranging from 51% in 2010 to 62% in 2014. The report also notes that telecom, Internet and e-commerce companies are leading this change. With unbanked and underbanked in low-income countries considered too risky and too poor, mobile communications technology has allowed massive networks with extraordinary scale making possible, servicing these markets with low margin models. This is the beginning of the acceleration of disruption with growth in FinTech investment.

1.7 Smart Nation

From new business models and principles, the emergence of FinTech services creates the fundamentals for a Smart Nation (See Chapter 8 on Singapore). The main features are in payment services as the backbone and an integral part of a smart city. With the Internet of Things (IoT), digital information and digital assets/currency will be merged to be a single channel. It allows all individuals, including those who are excluded because of age, health or wealth, to be connected and included in the economy. Thus, connectivity inclusion is accomplished. More cases of smart nations will be observed in ensuing country chapters. The trade-off is legal and regulatory control.

1.8   What Are the Types of FinTech?

Types of FinTech services go beyond traditional banking services as unbundled. Traditional Bank services which can be amplified and done faster include money transfer/remittance, equity funding/crowdfunding, P2P(Peer-to-Peer)/marketplace lending and others. The one that provides the most value-added will be mobile Payments/eWallets. Added on this list of services are trading platforms, financial advice, data analytics, especially of big data, credit scoring, insurance and others. FinTech companies are more than banks as even traditional insurance services are subsumed.

FinTech companies are versatile and capable first because they incorporate low costs with technology. This is manifested in lower margins, asset-light nature and high scalability. Second is their intense use of technology as including onboarding, social networks, crowd knowledge/wisdom, big data with the requisite analytics for market analysis and credit scoring. The use of AI with the requisite cybersecurity as in the use of a private key and touch recognition are equally important to ensure customer trust.

Having unbundled the bank (Figure 1.8), FinTech companies continue to rebundle the banking services (Figure 1.11). Some FinTech companies expand into other financial services after their initial success. Next, we look at some examples of how this re-bundling occurs in three areas, namely, Telecom FinTech (M-PESA) Social Media FinTech (Fidor) and e-commerce FinTech (Alibaba Group).

Figure 1.11.   Rebundling the Bank.

Source: By authors.

Table 1.2.   Mobile Money Subscribers in Kenya, April 2014.

	December 2013	December 2012
Total mobile subscribers	31.31 million	30.43 million
Mobile money subscribers	26.02 million	21.41 million
Number of Agents	93,689	62,300

Source: Communications Commission of Kenya (CCK), http://ca-go.
ke/index.php/statistics

1.8.1   *Telecom FinTech: M-PESA*

Mobile penetration rates are increasing all over the world. In developing countries where Internet services and smart devices are not widespread, simple mobile technology such as Short Message Service (SMS) can be used as a means to transfer money. M-PESA from Kenya is one such successful example as Table 1.2 shows.

M-PESA was launched in 2007. M-PESA (Pesa meaning money in Swahili) is a mobile money transfer service introduced by Safaricom (a telecommunications provider in Kenya). It drives financial

M-PESA

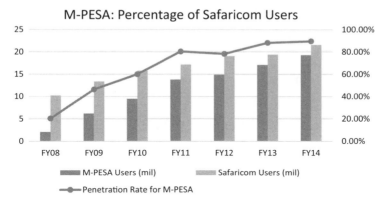

Figure 1.12. M-PESA Percentage of Safaricom Users.

Source: By authors; Annual Reports of Safaricom; M-PESA.

inclusion by providing money transfer services, local payments and international remittance services.

M-PESA started as an "SMS payments as a corporate social responsibility (CSR)" project. Mobile phone platform facilitates payments, money transfers, deposits and withdrawals communicated via text message. Cash withdrawals and deposits can simply be made through Point-of-Sales locations at vendors and kiosks. In Kenya of 46 million people, 5 million have bank accounts, and 19 million have M-PESA accounts.

In Figure 1.12, as of 2014, M-PESA has 81,025 agents, 122,000 registered merchants (24,137 active) and 19.3 million registered customers (12.2 million active). It accounted for 18% of Safaricom revenue and had penetrated 90% of Safaricom's customers.

M-PESA customers are only charged for "doing something". Transaction fees are kept low and stable. Agents are attracted to join, as a store can earn USD5.70 per day (with 60 transactions), which is double the prevailing wage for a clerk in Kenya. The agent system works well and does not require infrastructure investment. With an established consumer, merchant and agent network, it can start expanding to more than payments.

M-PESA has since expanded to Tanzania, Afghanistan, South Africa, India and Eastern Europe. It has also expanded into more products to include M-Shwari, a paperless banking platform with loan services, Lipa Na M-PESA, payment for goods and services, Lipa Kodi, rental payments to landlords, payment of bills, public transport, insurance premiums as well as receipt of pension or social welfare handouts.

1.8.2 *Social Media FinTech: Fidor*

In Social Media FinTech, Fidor Bank was established in Germany in 2007. It is the world's first online-only bank that operates through the Internet and using social media. In 2014, Fidor had more than 300,000 people registered and 250,000 community members with EUR200 million worth of deposits. Its lending totals about EUR160 million, employing only 34 staff and it has no branches. The cost is EUR20 to set up a customer with full banking. The overheads are low compared with traditional banks that may be 10 times more.

Fidor Bank is a leader in innovative banking processes with several awards including being the most Innovative Bank for Social Media-Germany (2013, Global Banking and Finance Review Award) as well as being the most Innovative Bank-Germany (2013, International Finance Magazine) and winning the Bank Innovation Award (2013, Bankinnovation.net).

There are many ways for Fidor Bank to engage customers as through social media and the Internet community, enabling customers to rate products and rate bank advisors. Figures 1.13 and 1.14 show that the more "like" one can generate, the lower the rates of financing. Products as shown in Figure 1.15 include emergency money, P2P lending through SMAVA.

Fidor's strategy is based on two distinguishing concepts; both centred on openness. One is community banking where members can share advice on forums and collaborate on product development. Two is "app store" banking with Fidor Bank operating an open platform that hosts independent services from third parties.

In Fidor TecS (Figure 1.16), fidorOS is an open middleware software on top of local core banking systems and provides

FIDOR BANK

• Ways they engage customers through social media

Figure 1.13.   Fidor Bank: Social Media Banking.

Source: Fidor Bank, https://www.fidor.com

Fidor Bank

• Ways they engage customers through internet community
• Rate Products, Rate Bank Advisors

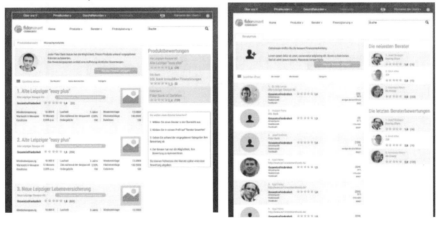

Figure 1.14.   Fidor Bank: Engaging Internet Community to Rate Products and Advisor.

Source: Fidor Bank, https://www.fidor.com

Fidor Bank

- Products

Figure 1.15.   Fidor Bank: Emerging Money and Peer to Peer Loan Products.

Source: Fidor Bank, https://www.fidor.com

Fidor TecS

Fidor TecS AG

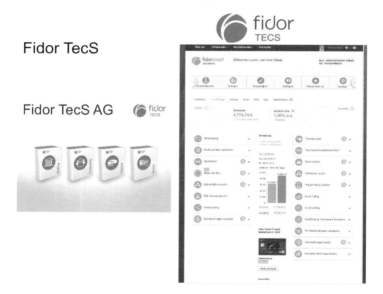

Figure 1.16.   Fidor TecS: Open Middleware.

Source: Fidor Bank, https://www.fidor.com

next-generation community, payment, and banking service solutions. It is also a middleware written specifically for modern banking which enables. It can send money instantly to friends via Twitter, Email or mobile number for lending among other purposes. Moreover, fidorOS also features social trading, social lending and crowdfinance with both funding and investing.

An application programming interface (API) is a set of subroutine definitions, protocols and tools for building application software. It is a set of clearly defined methods of communication between various software components. Using public APIs, Fidor seeks Business-to-Business (B2B) clients to do banking as what Apple does for mobile applications with iTunes. Fidor creates an entirely new technology that is not tied to any legacy code. It is flexible enough to be used in nearly any core banking system and powerful enough to be used by banks as a white label. The full white label means looking and feeling can be customised. White label partner can define the content of In-Account App-Store.

1.8.3   *E-commerce FinTech: Alibaba Group*

In the final area of e-commerce FinTech, the crown goes to the Alibaba Group as Alibaba and Alipay (Lee and Teo, 2017). Amazon Lending was started in the last quarter of 2012 with the company providing loans to online merchants. Amazon provided loans to small-sized merchants, enabling them to purchase inventory. The loans take only four days for approval, and interest rates are lower than small-business credit cards. This increased revenue for Amazon as merchants were able to expand inventory and make more sales.

However, three years before Amazon Lending, Alibaba in 1999 had already started offering financial services in China and later through Alipay under Ant Financial. The Alibaba Group is a Chinese e-commerce company started in 1999 by Jack Ma. It provides Consumer-to-Consumer (C2C), Business-to-Consumer (B2C) and B2B sales services via the Internet.

In 2004, Alipay was established as a payment platform and provided an escrow service. It quickly expanded to include movie, plane and lottery tickets, ordering of takeaways, insurance and payment of utility bills. Later, it is used as a Point-of-Sales (POS) system by small businesses. However, the payment platform was just the beginning with options to pay at Kentucky Fried Chicken (KFC) or pay the fishmonger.

In April 2010, Alibaba Microfinance started lending to merchants dealing with Taobao and TMall. As of end June 2013, it had extended a cumulative total of over RMB100 billion to more than 320,000 micro-enterprises and individuals. The default rate on its micro-loans, of which lending amount never exceeds RMB1 million, is only 0.87% of its total portfolio. The loan terms are usually short and ranging from a few days to several months.

Using big data analysis on small and medium-sized enterprises (SMEs) to assess their creditworthiness, Alibaba can grow its loan books to USD16 billion in three years. It also raised USD87 billion to be the largest fund manager in China by offering 15 times higher than the standard saving rates. It captured 20% of all new RMB deposit only nine months after launch.

Alibaba launched a new financial product Yu'E Bao in June 2013 as a money market fund and allows Alipay's account holders to invest their excess cash in the fund. Accounts holders are allowed to redeem the fund at any time to pay for their online purchase on Alibaba. They can handle all transactions online through personal computers and via Alipay Wallet-enabled smartphones.

Yu'E Bao accounts can be used to shop, pay utility bills, buy lottery and train tickets, book holidays, and pay off credit cards, among other services. Other financial services which Alibaba subsidiaries have branched into include retail and SME P2P lending, crowdfunding, micro-insurance and a whole range of other funds such as gold exchange-traded funds (ETFs).

Alipay was rebranded as Ant Financial Services on 16 October 2014. The rebranding of the Alipay unit, whose legal name is Zhejiang Ant Small and Micro Financial Services Group Co (see Figure 1.17), is part of a strategy by Alibaba and its affiliated companies to accelerate development of the financial business. The name "Ant" was chosen to symbolise the potential strength of a number of smaller brands working together.

Figure 1.17.   Ant Financial and Its Brands in 2017.

Source: By authors; Ant Financial.

From unbundling, FinTech has continued in rebundling with many lessons learnt. The phenomenal progress of FinTech has shown that institutions with large existing consumer bases have the most potential. With various tools leading to the integration of social networks, another lesson is that innovation with technology is crucial. The provision for innovative and specialised FinTech products through large trusted entities is as clear. Finally, the whole process is agent-based, risk capital based or insurance based. Figure 1.18 shows the growth of mobile payment in China at the beginning of 2010s.

The new FinTech investment paradigm is based on stickiness. In 2013, Facebook bought WhatsApp for USD22 billion despite WhatsApp's net loss of USD138.1 million. The 400 million active WhatsApp users can be potentially integrated into a FinTech platform. Logistic companies that manage valuable customer data are being "acquired" too, e.g. Alipay has invested and increased its stakes in a Singapore listed company Singpost, previously Singapore Post Office.

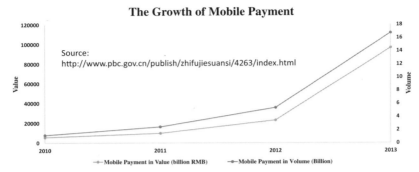

The Growth of Mobile Payment

Source: http://www.pbc.gov.cn/publish/zhifujiesuansi/4263/index.html

Year	Mobile Payment in Volume (Billion)	Growth Rate	Mobile Payment in Value (billion RMB)	Growth Rate
2010	1.18	77.08%	5700	102.01%
2011	2.47	109.32%	9900	73.68%
2012	5.35	116.46%	23100	132.39%
2013	16.74	212.86%	96400	317.56%

David Lee: The Game of Dian Fu

Figure 1.18.   The Growth of Mobile Payment in China 2010–2013.

Source: People's Bank of China, http://www.pbc.gov.cn/publish/zhifujiesuansi/4263/index.html; BOC News, http://www.boc.cn/en

1.9   FinTech beyond Payments

FinTech is beyond payments. E-commerce companies are expanding their business beyond simple payment, delivery and settlement services. These companies are partnering with social media companies to provide many services including lending, micro-credit, investment products, insurance, crowdfunding and much more.

The online-only insurance company, ZhongAn was launched in February 2013 in China. It is a joint venture (JV) between Alibaba and Tencent partnering PingAn, China's largest insurer. Lucrative insurance premiums were generated on small margins. On 11 November 2014, Alibaba had sales of more than USD9 billion of which RMB100 million was generated through online insurance premiums like ZhongAn which sold 50-cent insurance policies covering package delivery.

Beyond payments, FinTech is converting bit and byte to profits. The information advantage provides Internet companies with intimate information of the consumers. FinTech companies with this information can better forecast customers' potential financial risk than traditional banks to lend and insure at a lower cost. Cost is further reduced and passed on to more customers on a low margin but fast-moving model due to the scalability of the technology and no need for brick and mortar branches.

FinTech companies serve the masses in many different ways. Profit is secondary, FinTech companies grow by reaching out to the masses, diversifying service offerings and disrupting further up the value chain, attracting more capital in the process. For example, Alibaba has been offering low-cost loans to merchants and have branched out to micro-loans to consumers. Using an e-wallet like Alipay as the mode for transactions, Alibaba can quickly assess an individual's cash flow in real time and approve low interest rate short-term loans in 24 hours.

1.10 New FinTech Banking Services

Morphing from payments to beyond as noted earlier, FinTech focus is on customers' needs and the ability to raise funds. Compliance costs are low when fractional reserve banking is not involved. P2P lending democratises the lending process and allows borrowers to get access to credit within hours while lenders can earn returns more than most coupon rates. For example, Lending Club, an online P2P lending service facilitates unsecured personal loans of up to USD35,000 and delivers a solid return to lenders while spreading the risk across multiple borrowers. This model allowed Lending Club to raise USD900 million in 2014. Similar services are also provided by Singapore-based Capital Match which matches individual lenders to SMEs.

FinTech companies also enable democratisation and opportunity to tap the masses. Cross-border remittances that charge for less than the traditional fees have been gaining popular usage. TransferWise provides remittance facilities at 0.5% which is much lower than the typical money transfer services charge of 5%. This is achieved through crowdsourcing the fund flow, allowing it to bypass traditional banking and payment networks which lets it to avoid currency conversion. Instead of facilitating a direct transfer from a sender to a recipient, TransferWise reroutes payments from a sender to a recipient of another transfer, which is simultaneously taking place but going in the opposite direction. The disruption is happening from the bottom up.

1.11 FinTech and Digital Finance

This digital revolution in finance would not have been possible without the use of handphone. The use of mobile phone is the key reason for growth in Kenya and China. Figures 1.19 and 1.20 show the speed of penetration of mobile phone and Internet usage in China. This is important to note as other countries in Association of Southeast Asian Nations (ASEAN) such as Myanmar are also at the beginning of the digital finance cycle. There are opportunities at the bottom of the pyramid and in countries that can leapfrog the economy.

The number of Internet users (Figure 1.21) in China is huge, and the economies of scale can set in fairly quickly for any online business. The game is to build a sticky user base in the shortest possible time with payment and then followed by taking advantage of the network effect. These large number of users will allow economies of scale to take shape with new financial services.

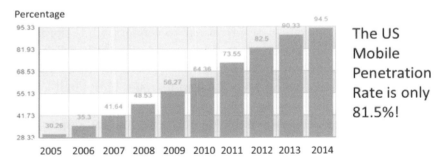

Figure 1.19.   Mobile Phone Penetration Rate in China.

Source: National Bureau of Statistics of China, http://data.staff.gov.cn/

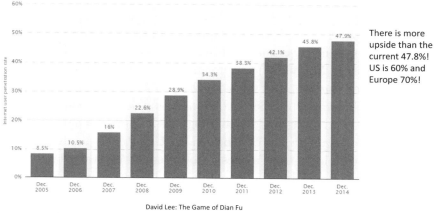

Penetration rate of internet users in China from 2005 to 2014

David Lee: The Game of Dian Fu

Figure 1.20.   Internet Penetration Rate in China.

Source: Statista, https://www.statista.com

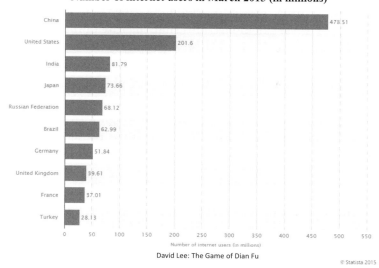

Number of internet users in March 2015 (in millions)

David Lee: The Game of Dian Fu

Figure 1.21.   Number of Internet Users in March 2015.

Source: Statista, https://www.statista.com

1.12   Decentralisation

Decentralising control by FinTech companies enables a programmable sharing economy. It is a powerful trend towards financial disintegration and eventually, towards a completely distributed financial system. Many of the arguments were presented in a paper by Lee (2017) at the Stanford Asia-Pacific Innovation Conference that conjecture that many of the developing countries will leapfrog with decentralised and distributed technology with appropriate infrastructure. Further examination of blockchain (Chapter 2) as distributed database technology that makes public ledger of transactions for cryptocurrencies and beyond possible, will be discussed.

Suffice to say, a more secure than traditional banking system is achieved as hacking would need to overcome security protocol at each node which is extremely costly to have slight success. While not all will agree, cryptocurrencies (in Chapter 3) can be self-regulating, democratising the function of the central bank and blockchain can remove the need for clearing houses or a custodial bank.

Disruption from the bottom up is evident, from a service sharing to an asset sharing economy. Thomas Piketty's *Capital in the Twenty-First Century* demonstrates that the rate of return on capital is greater than economic growth and people without assets are left behind. Asset inflation driven by quantitative easing worsens the gap between the wealthy and the poor and reduces social mobility. However, one type of asset inherent to all human beings exists, apart from their labour; data generated daily. Although Internet companies get to profit off this data, users can also take ownership and gain monetary benefit by contributing this data, for example through the app Gems.

Adding P2P to CryptoEquity means an asset sharing economy or a complete disruption of the financial system is not far from happening. The continual growth of the sharing economy and the rise of P2P platforms and cryptocurrency are facilitating this disruption. The result: decoupling of the sharing economy from the current economic system, where the asset rather than service sharing economy becomes the dominant system in which control and ownership of the economy are democratised.

To sum up and remind again, disruption from bottom up is the LASIC principle, incorporating low margin, asset light, scalable, innovative and compliance easy. The tip of the FinTech iceberg is being played out in China (Chapter 4) as part impressive and part scary. With over 90% mobile phone penetration, over 60% mobile banking penetration, and a P2P market more than five times the size of the US, China is leading the financial innovation space with banks transforming rapidly with Online-to-Offline (O2O) e-commerce and supply chain financing. Education, government, supply chain, real estate, medicine and law are beginning to be disrupted as seen in China. It is eminently clear that the current service sharing economy world is on the verge of the next disruptive wave of programmable asset sharing economy. Adopting LASIC with connectivity inclusion for those excluded will be the main feature of sustainable FinTech business, just like Alipay and M-PESA.

References and Further Readings

Accenture (2015). The Future of FinTech and Banking: Digitally disrupted or reimagined?. Retrieved from http://www.FinTechinnovationlablon don.net/media/730274/Accenture-The-Future-of-FinTech-and-Banking-digit allydisrupted-or-reima-.pdf

Alt, R., & Puschmann, T. (2012). The rise of customer-oriented banking — electronic markets are paving the way for change in the financial industry. Electronic Markets, 22(4), 203–215.

BOC News. http://www.boc.cn/en

CBInsights. https://www.cbinsights.com/

Communications Commission of Kenya (CCK). http://ca.go.ke/index.php/statistics

Demirrguc-Kunt, A., & Klapper, L. (2012). Measuring Financial Inclusion: The Global Findex Database. Policy Research Working Paper 6025, The World Bank Development Research Group. http://documents.worldbank.org/curated/en/453121468331738740/pdf/WPS6025.pdf

EY. (2016a). Defining FinTech. Retrieved from https://FinTechauscensus.ey.com/Home/Defining-FinTech

EY. (2016b). UK FinTech: On the cutting edge. Retrieved from https://www.gov.uk/government/uploads/system/uploads/attachment_data/file/502996/UK_FinTech_-_On_the_cutting_edge_-_Exec_Summary.pdf

Fidor Bank. https://www.fidor.com

Lee, D. K. C. (2015a). Handbook of Digital Currency. Elsevier.

Lee, D. K. C. (2015b). Handbook of Digital Currency: Bitcoin, Innovation, Financial Instruments, and Big Data. Academic Press ISBN: 0128023511, 9780128023518. Retrieved from http://store.elsevier.com/Handbook-of-Digital-Currency/isbn-9780128021170/

Lee, D. K. C. (2015c). On the edge of disruption. Asian Management Insights, 2(2), 78–83. Retrieved from http://www.emeraldgrouppublishing.com/learn ing/ami/vol2_iss_2/disruption.pdf

Lee, D. K. C. (2017). Decentralisation and Distributed Innovation. Paper presented to Stanford Asia-Pacific Innovation Conference, Stanford.

Lee, D. K. C., & Teo, E G. S. (2015) Emergence of FinTech and the LASIC Principles Journal of Financial Perspectives, (Vols. 33) Retrieved from https://www.gfsi.ey.com/the-journal-x.php?pid=18&id=122

Lee, D. K. C., & Teo, E (2017) The Game of Dian Fu: The Rise of Chinese Finance: Handbook of Blockchain, Digital Finance and Inclusion (Vol. 1). Elsevier.

National Bureau of Statistics of China. http://data.stats.gov.cn/

People's Bank of China. http://www.pbc.gov.cn/publish/zhifujiesuansi/4263/index.html

Piketty, T. (2014). Capital in the Twenty-First Century. (Goldhammer. A., Trans.). Belknap Press.

Statista. https://www.statista.com/

The Global Findex Database. (2014). World Bank. Retrieved from http://www.worldbank.org/en/programs/globalfindex

Zen, S. (2016, December 6). TechFin: Jack Ma coins term to set Alipay's goal to give emerging markets access to capital. South China Morning Post. Retrieved from http://www.scmp.com/tech/article/2051249/TechFin-jack-ma-coins-term-set-alipays-goal-give-emerging-markets-access

Chapter 2

Digital Currency, Bitcoin and Cryptocurrency

2.1 Evolution of Digital Currency as Alternative Currency

Various innovative money payment systems in the market have arrived with smart phones, Internet and digital storage cards. The emergence of this class of digital payment systems has revolutionalised the way values are being transferred. The latest and most interesting form of value transfer was created by Satoshi Nakamoto (2008). Satoshi's Bitcoin is now a well-known system of cross-border value transfer for untrusted parties without a centralised authority. Bitcoin is a medium of exchange, a store of value and a unit of account. Conventionally, the uppercase "Bitcoin" refers to the network and technology, while the lowercase "bitcoin(s)" refers to units of the currency. The currency is also commonly abbreviated to "BTC", although some exchanges use "XBT", a proposed currency code which is compatible with the ISO 4217 standard (Matonis, 2013).

There are still debates about whether bitcoin and other cryptocurrencies are alternative currencies. From 1 April 2017, bitcoin has become a legal payment system in Japan with a potential retail base of 260,000 merchants. The Chinese regulator, on the other hand, has stopped all cryptocurrency trading by unregulated exchanges at the end of September 2017. To understand cryptocurrency, it is important to comprehend the history and development of centralised digital currency to have a good understanding on the philosophy underpinning decentralised cryptocurrency. As bitcoin is the first decentralised cryptocurrency, it is important to understand the features of bitcoin before moving on to discuss cryptocurrency as a whole, initial crypto-token offering (ICO) and blockchain. Up to 20% of the materials in this Chapter is taken from "Introduction to Bitcoin" (Lam and Lee, 2015) from the reference book *Handbook of Digital Currency* (Lee, 2015) with technical details on cryptocurrency and bitcoin.

2.1.1   *Nature and types of digital currency*

There are the many types of alternative currencies other than government issued fiat currency. Hileman (2009) has broadly classified them into two categories: tangible and digital. Tangible currencies, closely associated with "commodity money", derive their value from relative scarcity and non-monetary utility. Digital or virtual seems to be used interchangeably as describing currencies based on an electronic medium. However, they are not synonyms. The term "virtual" has a negative connotation, as signifying what is "seemingly real", but not exactly "real". This is not commonly used when referring to a currency, as pretentious, "falsely created" in literal Chinese (虚拟的) or interpreted as computer generated or simulated. A more neutral term digital currency is generally more common.

In this Chapter, we focus on those digitised currencies for value transfer. We can classify value transfer broadly into four categories.

(a) Centralised, Not Geographically Bounded:
     Examples are loyalty points from financial, telecom or retail companies, air miles from airlines, Second Life's Linden Dollar and World of Warcraft Gold which are closed system with transactions within specific entities. This class of currency also includes crossborder pre-paid phone cards and to some extent, cash value smart cards, pre-paid debit and credit cards. These cards can be physical or virtual on mobile devices. Other examples are Alipay RMB wallet that can be used in different

countries and even for tax refunds with QR (Quick Response) Code or facial recognition. It is more appropriate to think in terms of online (e-wallet) and offline (physical card wallet) digital payments. This is a case of online/offline value transfer and storage unconstrained by location. This class may not be dependent upon governance as in the case of fiat currency and more importantly, it is not geographically bounded.

(b) Centralised, Geographically Bounded:

Digitalised national currency, local or community currencies e-Brixton Pound and Bristol Totnes Pound that is used in England, and eChiemgaue in Germany. The purpose is more specific and usually bounded by some social contracts or agreement such as honouring them for exchange for goods or to limit the supply of goods. The governance is centralised and the value transfer is localised.

(c) Centralised, Cross-Platform:

Flooz and Beenz which are open market systems and can be transacted with other entities. Note that the crypto debit or credit cards such as TenX are built upon a decentralised system of cryptocurrencies and tokens. Smart contracts allow for the exchange of value between different digital currencies and across the network. The governance structure is centralised on top of decentralised and sometimes with smart contracts. The value is transacted digitally across the platform and can be online or offline.

(d) Fully Decentralised or Distributed Currency:

This includes the cryptocurrencies such as Bitcoin, Ether, Qtum, Zcash, Litecoin, Dogecoin and others. They can be transacted with any outside agents, and the governance and technology are both decentralised due to open source software. There is usually no legal entity responsible for the activities, and therefore they fall outside traditional regulation. Value transfer is online.

Cryptocurrency is a Peer-to-Peer (P2P) programmable digital currency. It allows online payments to be sent directly from one party to another without going through an intermediary. The network timestamps transactions cryptographically and in the case of bitcoin, using what is known as Proof-of-Work (PoW). The Proof-of-Work Bitcoin protocol is basically a contest for decoding and acts as an incentive to reward those who participate. The first participant to crack the code will be rewarded with the new bitcoins. A new block of transactions is formed every 10 minutes approximately. The transaction record is almost impossible to change or too costly to change after six blocks of confirmations. It is straightforward to create a cryptocurrency as an alternative currency or as a token for free because most of them are open source. Many altcoins are created to solve the pain points of bitcoin. There are more than 1,000 cryptocurrencies in circulation with 900 trading actively.

As to why cryptocurrencies are gaining traction, various socioeconomic forces drive their demand including:

(a) Bitcoin has become a legal payment system and classified as an asset for accounting purposes in Japan. The Financial Services Agency has also issued 11 bitcoin exchange licenses in September 2017 (See Figure 2.1).
(b) Asset allocators and fund managers are beginning to allocate funds to cryptocurrencies.

Figure 2.1. Bitcoin Is a Legal Payment System in Japan.
Source: By authors.

(c) Demand for cryptocurrencies due to the launch of many ICOs.

(d) Governments are wishing to have a more centralised control over local governments or to prevent corruption, seeking transparency and control via digital currency built on blockchain or distributed ledger, the underlying technology of cryptocurrency.

(e) Technology and Internet as making it much easier to use with improved software and low entry barriers contributing to network effects.

(f) A political economy with disillusionment about inequality, and the notion of traditional banks not willing to embrace financial inclusion.

(g) There is economic uncertainty associated with high debt and quantitative easing with many investors seeking shelter in alternatives.

(h) Environmentalism means ecology concerns and the question of whether we have reached the point of maximum extraction of natural resources seen as the fundamental backing for some currencies.

(i) The inefficiency of financial architectural with the view that financial services are overpriced and the whole financial system is too costly to operate.

(j) Financial freedom from using cryptocurrencies with the advantage of transferring value through the Internet where control is weak.

(k) The ability to bypass capital controls and may provide safe harbour during a fiat currency crisis.

(l) Speculation with the anticipation that there will be a steep price appreciation due to subsequent wider acceptance.

(m) Acceptance that cryptocurrency is an asset class to hedge against the collapse of fiat currency system in a diversified portfolio.

(n) Acting as base currencies to conduct token (coin) sales ICOs globally for innovative projects by passing fiat currency system and control, which is perceived to be too heavily regulated.

(o) Use as a form of tokens to digitise or securitise underlying commodity or ownership rights.

(p) Use as a form of token rights to use the network, to vote, to wrap cash flow, to execute smart contracts or other privileges usually related to the network.

With many alternative cryptocurrencies or altcoins, many will fail and only a few will be globally adopted because of superseding advancements in technology, tighter regulation and insufficient demand.

2.2   eCash and Other Pioneer Cryptocurrencies

The first centralised cryptocurrency was eCash started in 1990s. eCash system was available via various banks and smart cards in various countries and slowly developed into the current form of cryptocurrencies with several refinements. Two papers by DigiCash's founder David Chaum (Chaum, 1983; Chaum, Fiat and Naor, 1992) are the basis for eCash. Both online and offline use cryptographic protocols to prevent double spending. Cryptographic protocols also use blind signatures to protect the privacy of users. The company DigiCash was later sold to eCash Technologies and finally acquired by InfoSpace in 1999. Due to tight regulation on know your customer (KYC), most crypto or tokenised currencies ran afoul of the law and regulation and went out of favour or business.

2.2.1   *Revival of cryptocurrencies since the Global Financial Crisis (GFC)*

Nick Szabo (2008)'s bit gold idea was published in a blog at the beginning of the Global Financial Crisis (GFC). He suggested that gold can be mined and the resulting bit could be a bit recorded on a digital register. The public digital register would resolve the issues of a trusted third party. He suggested an economic incentive scheme of requiring the participants to spend resources to mine the bit gold with no barrier to access the content of the digital register. What differentiated his approach from past failed digital currencies was the timing of the GFC and the distributed nature of the protocol. More ideas were discussed in the literature and technology developed over time, such as Chaum (1983) on DigiCash, Back (1997) on hashcash, Dai (1998) on b-money, Szabo (1999, 2000, 2008) on the concept of money, and Shirky (2000) on micropayment system.

It is interesting to note that the late Hal Finney or Harold Thomas Finney II, a console game developer and employee for PGP Corporation, ran the cypherpunk remailer from late 1992 using cryptography that is multi-jurisdictional. He said

> It seemed so obvious to me; Here we are faced with the problems of loss of privacy, creeping computerisation, massive databases, more centralisation — and Chaum offers a completely different direction to go in, one which puts power into the hands of individuals rather than governments and corporations. The computer can be used as a tool to liberate and protect people, rather than to control them.

Cypherpunk (Eric Hughes' "A Cypherpunk's Manifesto" in 1993, Hughes (1993)) combines the terms of Cypher and Cyberpunk. It is an informal group that aims to achieve privacy and security through the use of cryptography. One of their key thought is perhaps best summarised by Steven Levy (1993):

> The people in this room hope for a world where an individual's informational footprints — everything from an opinion on abortion to the medical record of an actual abortion — can be traced only if the individual involved chooses to reveal them; a world where coherent messages shoot around the globe by network and microwave, but intruders and feds trying to pluck them out of the vapor find only gibberish; a world where the tools of prying are transformed into the instruments of privacy.

> There is only one way this vision will materialise, and that is by widespread use of cryptography. Is this technologically possible? Definitely. The obstacles are political — some of the most powerful forces in government are devoted to the control of these tools. In short, there is a war going on between those who would liberate crypto and those who would suppress it. The seemingly innocuous bunch strewn around this conference room represents the vanguard of the pro-crypto forces. Though the battleground seems remote, the stakes are not: The outcome of this struggle may determine the amount of freedom our society will grant us in the 21st century. To the Cypherpunks, freedom is an issue worth some risk.

As the GFC unfolded, the policy makers responded by quantitative easing (QE).[1] Loose monetary policy was conducted. Even though the fear of hyperinflation was unnecessary, the confidence in the fiat currency system was shaken. Many were looking for alternatives to protect their wealth. A cypherpunk or a group of them using the name Satoshi Nakamoto wrote a white paper and circulated to their community in 2008 for a P2P electronic cash system using cryptography. Despite many efforts, the identity of Satoshi remains unknown to the public. Satoshi in Japanese means "wise" and in Chinese (中本聪) means "the Chinese are clever".

Someone has suggested that the name might be a portmanteau of four technology companies: SAmsung, TSOHIba, NAKAmichi and MOTOrola. Others have noted that it could be a team from National Security Agency in the US or an e-Commerce firm (Wallace 2011). Other suggestions are from David Chaum, the late Hal Finney, Nick Szabo, Wei Dai, Gavin Andresen or the Japanese living in the neighbourhood of Finney by the same surname Dorian Nakamato. More are from suggestions such as Vili Lehdonvirta, Michael Clear, Neal King, Vladimir Oksman, Charles Bry, Shinichi Mochizuki, Jed McCaleb, and Dustin Trammell but most have publicly denied that they are Satoshi. Those who claimed that they were Satoshi had little credibility, and their behaviour was hardly consistent with Satoshi's actions and thoughts.

With the white paper (Nakamoto, 2008), mining of the first decentralised cryptocurrency called bitcoin was born in early 2009. Bitcoin is run using open source software and can be downloaded by anyone from Github. The system runs on a decentralised P2P network. It is meant to be fully distributed in the sense that every node or computer terminal is connected to each other. Each node may leave and re-join as it wishes. The nodes are bounded by a consensus that accepts the longest PoW known as the blockchain as the authoritative record. Each time there is a crisis, the price of bitcoin has a spike.

---

[1]Quantitative easing, also known as large-scale assets purchases, is an expansionary monetary policy whereby a central bank buys predetermined amounts of government bonds or other financial assets in order to stimulate the economy.

The price of bitcoin spiked 57% within a week to USD74 during the 2013 Cypriot property-related banking crisis. With a combination of P2P data sharing and a transfer of value without intermediary, no one could close down the newly created network. There was simply no legal entity in existence, and no one knew who Satoshi was. There was no centralised entity or figure to close it down using legal means. Even if there is a legal way, it will be too costly. The only way to shut it down would have been to cut off all electrical power in the world. A new alternative currency was found and no central authority could close it down unilaterally! The interest on cryptocurrency is back!

2.2.2 *Bitcoin as coined*

Despite the fact that bitcoin has been around since 2009, cryptocurrency is still misunderstood and mysterious for a few reasons. First, few knew who was/were really behind some of these cryptocurrency systems and that the entire system is usually run on a network owned by no one. It was designed so that trust is not needed for the parties who wish to transact. Most of the time, there is no legal entity behind it. Instead, it is just an open source software.

Second, there is confusion over the Bitcoin network and intermediaries. Mt. Gox was a bitcoin exchange based in Shibuya, Tokyo, Japan that filed for bankruptcy proceedings in 2014. Launched in July 2010, it was handling over 70% of all bitcoin transactions worldwide by early 2014. It was the largest Bitcoin intermediary and the world's leading bitcoin exchange. In February 2014, Mt. Gox suspended trading, closed its website and exchange service, and filed for bankruptcy protection from creditors and finally went into liquidation. Many confused the collapse of Mt. Gox in 2014 with a collapse of Bitcoin network. However, "Mt. Gox was merely a financial intermediary" and one of many unregulated exchanges trading in bitcoins. Mt. Gox was not part of the Bitcoin network/software itself. Many thought that the Bitcoin network was hacked or there was a legal entity that had gone bankrupt. Given the decentralised nature of the design with smart contract, these intermediaries such as centralised unregulated exchanges should not even exist in the first place. A peer can search for another peer on the network to transact among them with a smart contract, thus eliminating even the need for a centralised exchange that acts an intermediary. It is difficult to understand when there is no legal entity responsible for the network.

Third, cryptocurrency such as bitcoin involves mining or Proof-of-Work. The use of the word "mining" here refers to the Proof-of-Work that involves cryptography competition and confuses a lot of newcomers. The miners' reward is given to the first who can solve a cryptography problem. The degree of difficulty of the problem will ensure that the timing to solve the problem is approximately 10 minutes for Bitcoin. It cleverly solves the double spending problem so that every cryptocurrency can be spent only once and unlike emails that can be sent to many parties. The common perception is that it is financial technology and it involves financial regulation, but therein lies the difficulty in understanding even for the professionals.

There are implications for public policy such as the effects on money supply, the impact on the current financial systems, the potency of existing regulation against the decentralised network with no clear legal entities, and the role of cryptocurrency in changing social behaviour and business conduct. That is why it is an area of great interest to researchers, regulators, investors, merchants and it is hitting the headlines regularly. These discussions are beyond the scope of this book and some of these are discussed in Lee (2017) and Lee and Deng (2017).

2.2.3   *Some technical terms*

We start off by having a few general terms and more technical terms will be introduced in later chapters.

Open Source: The term "open source" means that something people can modify and share because its design is publicly accessible. This will allow trusted core developers to verify and suggest changes for the code to be adopted by the network.

Centralised Network: This is a network that all users are connected to a single or central server that acts an agent for all communications. The centralised server stores both the communications and user account information. The computing power can be distributed but still a single entity controls the entire network. The consensus is that nodes are altruistic and so it needs only to handle crash faults. Google and Facebook are good examples.

Decentralised Network: This is opposite to centralised computing. In the case of computing, it means that the allocation of hard and software resources and the majority of the associated activities and functions are not carried out, obtained or stored in a centralised location.

Server-based or Private Decentralised Networks: A server-based decentralised network has no single entity that controls the network. The computing power is distributed. There must be a consensus algorithm and it has to handle crashes and faults. Anyone that is permissioned can read and write. Clients can have anonymity but validators will have no anonymity. Examples are Corda and Multichain.

Server-free Fully or Public Decentralised Network: There is no single entity that controls the network and the computing is distributed. The consensus algorithm must be able to handle crashes, Byzantine Faults and Sybil Attacks. There is anonymity for clients and validators. Anyone can read and write with notable examples such as Bitcoin, Ethereum and Zcash.

Distributed Network: This is when computer programming and the data are spread out across computers without a centralised server or control.

Peer-to-Peer: In its simplest form, two or more personal computers are connected and share resources without going through a server computer. A P2P network is created when two or more computers are connected in that way.

The general arguments for a successfully distributed cryptocurrency are:

(1) Open source software: A core group of trusted developers to verify the code and possible changes for adoption by the network;

(2) Decentralised: Even if it is not entirely distributed, it is essential that there is no single point of attack;

(3) P2P: There should be no intermediaries with pools of subnetwork forming;

(4) Global: It is easily available to global talents and users with ease;

(5) Fast: It should be able to handle high transactions per second;

(6) Reliability: It should be non-repudiable with almost instant settlement;

(7) Secure: It should have a good architecture for proof of identity with encryption and yet anonymous transactions;

(8) Sophisticated and cross-chain flexible: The system will be able to communicate with another network for exchange of and support for all types of assets, financial instruments and markets;

(9) Automated: It is designed to execute algorithm for payments and contracts with ease;

(10) Scalable: The system can handle a large number of users and transactions;

(11) Platform for integration and interoperability: It can be designed to integrate digital finance and digital law with an ecosystem to support smart contract with financial transactions. Customised agreements between multiple parties, containing user-defined scripted clauses, hooks and variable; and

(12) Appropriate economic incentive: The interest of all participants are taken care of with the inbuilt balance of interest among parties.

The possible applications will be wide-ranging and include global payment and remittance systems, decentralised exchanges, merchant solutions, online gaming, digital asset management and digital contracting system. Each cryptocurrency is an interesting experiment.

The number of transactions per second, the storage space for the chain of a 10-minute block of transactions (known as blockchain), the speed of confirmation of these transactions are all bottlenecks for the wide adoption of almost all the cryptocurrencies. These are the problems that prevent cryptocurrencies from taking off besides regulatory issues that involve money laundering, terrorist financing and tax evasion.

The technology is in its infancy, but it will eventually disrupt the payment system as we know it because it costs almost little or nothing to transfer payments with short settlement period. Cryptocurrency technology can be an enabling tool to reach out to the unbanked and underbanked if appropriately designed. Cryptocurrency can be an excellent conduit for payments and funds, as well as fractional ownership of assets. Business is being transformed by diminishing the role of middleman, whether it is smart accounting or smart contract. When combined with the Internet of Things (IoT) and other technologies, it can maximise digitalisation with digitisation and digital identity. With decentralisation and democratisation of technology, services, and governance, it can lower cost to a level that allows the underserved and the excluded to enjoy goods and services that previously not available to them.

Financial world will operate differently especially in fundraising and lending. It is possible to do an initial crowd/coin/crypto-token offering (ICO) or crowdlending. The P2P framework eliminates the middleman, especially in financial services providers. It is already having an impact on banking, insurance, trustee, custody, fund management, private equity, and venture capital.

There are risks associated with cryptocurrency such as regulatory, technology, financial and economics. It is unlikely that the entire class of cryptocurrency will be fully embraced by any centralised agency and authority. The degree of decentralisation is inversely related to acceptance by authorities. There will be many cryptocurrencies on the spectrum with different designs and degree of decentralisation in governance and/or technology.

2.3   Bitcoin

As the pioneer in cryptocurrency, we need to understand Bitcoin and bitcoin further as the system and technology as well as the currency, respectively.

2.3.1   *Bitcoin features*

Two features are noted. First, its network and as a digital currency. Bitcoin is a P2P decentralised digital currency network that verifies and processes transactions. Bitcoin technology uses cryptographic proof in its computer software, instead of a trusted third parties, to process and record transactions. A cryptography proof of work is used to verify the legitimacy of bitcoins (Nakamoto, 2008).

Bitcoin is not a fiat currency issued by a central government or an authorised agent of the government. There is no backing as legal tender by any physical commodity. However, like the fiat currency, the value of bitcoin is derived from the relationship between supply and demand rather than the value of the material that the money is made of. The currency unit used in payments on the Bitcoin network is bitcoin which is not a fiat currency. Therefore, Bitcoin in itself is also a digital currency, in the sense that it exists virtually on a computer database or ledger.

The second feature is its genesis and decentralised control. The first bitcoins were mined or created in 2009. The first 10-minute block of transactions after the Bitcoin network started in 2009 was known as the Genesis Block. The PoW is a cryptography problem solving that involves hashed information from the previous block. As the blocks are lined and chained together, the ledger of transactions is known as the blockchain. Due to ill health or fear of being known, Satoshi disappeared from the scene and the project in 2010. His identity largely remains unknown, yet the experiment continues until today. The experiment was largely decentralised in governance[2] to some extent as there is no central agent needed to make a decision. It is because the Bitcoin software protocol is open source, other developers have continued working on it, and the Bitcoin community

---

[2]Most decentralised systems were started with centralised governance and the facilitator decided later to decentralise the system. Others were started with the intention of having a decentralised technology but the governance could remain centralised. Distinction between decentralised technology and governance is important to understand decentralised system.

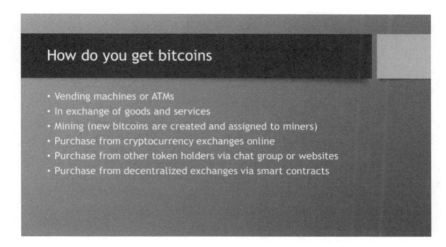

Figure 2.2.   Ways of Getting Bitcoins.

Source: By authors.

flourishes today. It is important to understand that the power to alter the Bitcoin protocol is with the miners and developers. Neither the miners or developers can force a change in the Bitcoin protocol without a fork, i.e., breaking compatibility with the rest of the network.

2.3.2   *Buy and store bitcoins*

Figure 2.2 shows the various ways one can purchase bitcoins. Figures 2.3 to 2.5 show what a vending machine looks like and how it functions.

A wallet is needed to store or transfer bitcoins. There is a private key which is stored in a wallet (CoinDesk, 2014). The private keys are used to access the Bitcoin addresses and sign transactions and therefore must be kept securely to prevent theft. There are a variety of types of Bitcoin wallets, including

(1) desktop (e.g. Jaxx, Blockchain.info, Blocktrail, Multibit, Bitcoin knots, Bitcoin Core, BitGo, Bither, Electrum, Green Address, ArcBit, mSIGNA, Armory);

Figure 2.3.   The Working of Vending Machines.

Source: By authors.

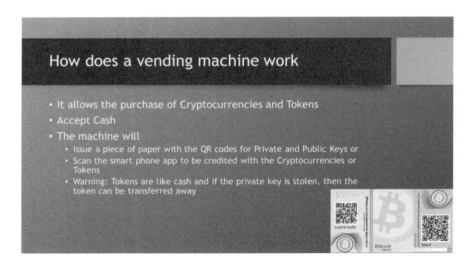

Figure 2.4.   More on Vending Machine.

Source: By authors.

Figure 2.5.   The Ways to Store Cryptocurrencies.

Source: By authors.

(2) online, browser-based or web-based (Blockchain.info, CoinsBank, Jaxx, StrongCoin, BitoEX, Bitgo, Green Address, Coinbase);

(3) mobile (Arcbit, Bither, breadwallet, BTC.com, Coin.Space, Electrum, Green Address, GreenBits, Mycelium, Arbitz, Simple Bitcoin, Bitcoin Wallet, Jaxx, BTC.com, Coinbase, Coin.Space, Green Address, BitGo, Xapo, Coinapult); and

(4) hardware wallets (e.g. ledger, Trezor, Keepkey, Digital Bitbox).

A desktop wallet is installed on the computer. The Bitcoin client software, known as Bitcoin Core, is used to create a bitcoin address. With a bitcoin address, one can then send and receive bitcoins, and to store the corresponding private key for that address.

An online wallet is accessible from anywhere through a browser with an Internet connection, regardless of the device used (CoinDesk, 2014). The online service provider and not the user stores the private keys for a user's Bitcoin addresses in the online wallet. The risk in using an online wallet is that since there is no control over the private key, the vendor or provider can abscond with the bitcoins. Web-based or online wallets offer extra encryption and two-factor authentication for additional security.

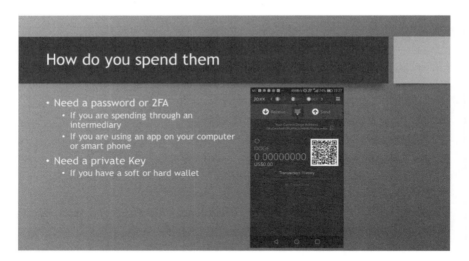

Figure 2.6.   Sending and Spending Cryptocurrencies.
Source: By authors.

Mobile wallets are simply an application which provides for Bitcoin wallet functionality on a mobile phone.

A hardware wallet is a hardware that can hold keys electronically such as a dedicated device. Notable names are Trezor, Nano Ledger HW.1, Ledger Nano, Ledger Unplugged, Pi Wallet, Bwallet Trezor clone, KeepKey, Opendime, CoolWallet, BlochsTech card, BitLox Bitcoin Hardware Wallet, Digital Bitbox, Ledger Nano S, Swiss Bank in Your Pocket, BiSafe, and someone42's original prototype.

A Card or Paper Bit Wallet does not need a battery, Internet connection and is robust. The software on a smart card can be protected, unlike smartphone or computers that are targets for malware. One notable card is TenX. The other type of bit wallet is just a piece of paper with the QR code for public and private keys.[3]

---

[3]Public key cryptography, also known as asymmetrical cryptography, is any cryptographic system that uses pairs of keys: public and private keys. Public keys may be disseminated widely, and private keys are known only to the owner. The public key is used to verify that a holder of the paired private key sent the message. The holder of the paired private key can decrypt the message encrypted

The TenX Wallet

The TenX wallet is the major game changer as it enables a user to spend their blockchain assets through their smartphone or a physical debit card at over 36 million points of acceptance online and offline. The TenX app is downloadable for free both on Android and iOS (iOS available from July 2017 onwards).

Figure 2.7. The TenX Wallet.

Source: By authors; TenX.

Many of these wallets allow the user to hold other cryptocurrencies and crypto assets (tokens). Figure 2.6 shows how to send and spend cryptocurrencies.

It is worth looking at the business model of smart cryptocurrency cards. The TenX wallet shown in Figure 2.7 is the major game changer as it allows a user to spend their blockchain assets through the virtual or physical card in many points of acceptance online and offline. In Figures 2.8 and 2.9, the virtual card is just the smartphone, and the TenX app is downloadable for free from app stores. The cryptocurrency is converted real-time like fiat currency, and the merchants just charge the user fiat currencies. TenX, WireX & Xapo, and TokenCard are all potentials to disrupt the payment industry through the use of existing Point-of-Sales (POS) system.

---

with the public key. Together, they achieve the functions of authentication and encryption.

The user can choose to order a virtual and/or physical debit card directly within the app. As a security measurement, we allow a user to lock and unlock his card in the app. This makes our system more secure than traditional credit and debit card companies.

The user can withdraw his blockchain assets to another wallet without any fees at any time.

Figure 2.8.   Virtual Smart Cryptocurrency Card.

Source: By authors; TenX.

Fees Comparison Table

	TenX	WireX & Xapo	TokenCard
Physical card issuing fee (Incl. shipping & tracking)	$15	$20+	Not applicable
Virtual card issuing fee	$1.5	$3	Not applicable
Physical card annual fee	FREE ($10 if spend less than $1000/year)	$12	Not applicable
Virtual card annual fee	FREE ($10 if spend less than $1000/year)	N/A	$12
Domestic exchange fee	0%	0%	1.5%
Foreign exchange fee	0%	3%	4.5%

Figure 2.9.   A Comparison of Tenx, WireX and TokenCard Charges.

Source: By authors; TenX.

The Point-of-Purchase (POP) or the POS is the time and place where a retail transaction is completed.

2.3.3 *Mining bitcoins*

Some concepts of Mining are being outlined here.

(1) The hard maximum supply of bitcoin is 21 million which was set by Satoshi in the original design. Since the currency is effectively infinitely divisible as long as technology permits, then the precise amount does not matter as long as the limit remains fixed. Bitcoin is designed with a hard limit of 21 million bitcoins, expected to be created by 2040 as shown in Figure 2.10. Until then, bitcoins are generated through mining, during which miners, who are Bitcoin users running the software on specialised hardware, process transactions and are rewarded with new bitcoins for contributing their computer power to maintain the network.

(2) Mining is important and computationally expensive. New bitcoins are mined. The miner who successfully solves the cryptography problem in the last block gets the new bitcoin. It is a necessary process for transactions to be added onto the blockchain and be confirmed approximately after six mined blocks. Mining ensures that only legitimate transactions are verified and recorded onto the blockchain. It is the network which provides the computing power for the transactions to take place and for the transactions to be recorded.

(3) Mining is a mathematical process. The software controls the degree of difficulty of this mathematical problem. As it becomes increasingly more difficult to find the larger numbers, miners have to use special high-performance computers to find them (Tindell, 2013).

Every four years, the number of bitcoins mined is halved. It started with 50 bitcoins approximately every 10 minutes for every 21,000 blocks (approximately four years from 2009 to 2013). Then it halved to 25 for the next 21,000 blocks so that there will be a gradual drop in rewards to the miners. Some argued that the

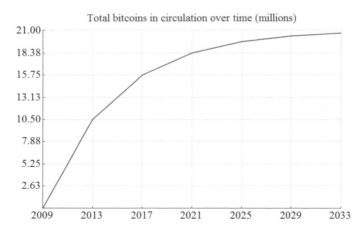

Figure 2.10.   Hard Maximum Number of Bitcoins: 21 Million.
Source: By authors.

design coincided with the commodity cycles, other argued that eight years was when the system was well tested. This decreased reward scheme has fuelled adoption with the expectations that bitcoin will be scarce in the future. Satoshi may or may not have predicted it but the complicated calculation between electricity prices, bitcoin price, miners' collective hash power, and the continuous code enhancements by developers have pushed the price of bitcoin higher. With the experiment being in existence and very robust, the confidence in the network has increased but technology risk associated with SHA-256.[4] and ECDSA.[5] remains.

2.3.4   *Security and cryptography*

(1) The security of the technology is supported using secure hash algorithms and has a good track record. The hash function

---

[4]The SHA (Secure Hash Algorithm) is one of a number of robust cryptographic hash functions. A cryptographic hash is like a signature for a text or a data file and generates an almost-unique, fixed size 256-bit (32-byte) hash. Hash is a one way function that cannot be decrypted back.

[5]Elliptic Curve Digital Signature Algorithm or ECDSA is a cryptographic algorithm used by Bitcoin to ensure that funds can only be spent by their rightful owners. See https://en.bitcoin.it/wiki/Elliptic_Curve_Digital_Signature_Algorithm

mainly used in Bitcoin is SHA-256 (Pacia, 2013), which was incidentally originally designed by the National Security Agency (NSA) in the US. There is no need for suspicion against the NSA because the SHA algorithm is part of the public domain and has been extensively analysed to be secure (Pacia, 2013). SHA-256 is an upgrade from the SHA-1 series and is presently used in Bitcoin for the digital signatures which secure the transactions and blockchain. It forms the basis of the PoW mathematical problem.

(2) Central to Bitcoin technology is public-key cryptography, which with the SHA-256 hash function is used to generate Bitcoin addresses, sign transactions and verify payments. Public-key cryptography is a technique of reliably determining the authenticity of Bitcoin transactions using digital signatures. It uses an asymmetric algorithm which generates two separate but asymmetrically-linked keys: a public key and a private key. The keys are asymmetric in the sense that the public key is derived from the private key but it is computationally impossible to obtain a private key from a public key.

(3) In such a system, the public key is used to verify digital signatures in transactions while the private key is used to sign transactions to produce those very digital signatures. The public key is publicly accessible; in Bitcoin, it is used as the Bitcoin address to and from which payments are sent. The private key, on the other hand, must be kept secret and safe. The beauty of such a system is that transactions can be easily verified using the public key without sharing the private key used to sign the transactions.

2.3.5 *Pseudoanonymity*

A Bitcoin address is an alphanumeric sequence of characters. The sender and recipient of bitcoins are unknown (Brito and Castillo, 2013). Bitcoin is less anonymous than cash as addresses can be traced, and it is not difficult to trace the sender and recipient using digital forensic techniques such as entity merging. Up to 40% of Bitcoin users in a conducted experiment could be easily identified using behaviour-based clustering methods (Androulaki et al, 2012; Brito and Castillo, 2013; Ober, Katzenbeisser and Hamacher, 2013; Reid and Harrigan, 2013). Often with KYC and reporting requirements by intermediaries to collect personally-identifiable information from their customers will increase the probability tremendously.

2.4   Benefits and Risks

Bitcoin as a novel technology that brings a range of benefits and risks as noted below.

2.4.1   *Freedom of payments*

Payments can be processed with little or no fees in theory, with the sender having the option to include a transaction fee for faster confirmation for bitcoin and other cryptocurrencies. For Alipay and other credit card companies, the number of transactions can reach a maximum of 120,000 per second or more. In practice, costs can be high for bitcoin due to only seven transactions per second. However, in the long term, this is unlikely to be an issue as technology advances. When that happens, there is a great potential for remittances given the reduced costs of remittances especially for the underserved and unbanked.

2.4.2   *Merchant benefits*

As an alternative to the other methods of electronic payments accepted by businesses, bitcoin and other cryptocurrencies will be acceptable and free with low fees. At times, such transaction fees seem high, but as technology improves and with more choices of cryptocurrencies, the cost of the transaction is likely to be low enough for mass adoption. This is already happening with many cryptocurrency companies using existing POS with cryptocurrency debit and credit card. Japan's 260,000 businesses may benefit from bitcoin being a legal payment system which triggers the use of other cryptocurrencies as payments system thus lowering cost of transactions.

2.4.3 User control

As each bitcoin transaction can only be effected by the user who has the private key, it puts the user in full control. During a crisis, the traditional financial system may face a bottleneck as untrusted parties rely on banks as a trust agent. Banks may be unlikely to issue a letter of credit or honour other forms of third party transactions as they may not have enough information on counterparties. During crisis where banks are not willing to act as a trusted party, bitcoin or other cryptocurrencies may be the best way for untrusted parties to rely on for payment of goods and other transactions. On the flip side, if the private key is lost, the bitcoin is lost. An incident in 2017 involving poor multisig wallet design left many users vulnerable to crafted malicious software designed to steal cryptocurrencies. Security conscious and personal responsibility with Bitcoin are keys to protecting ownership (Doherty, 2011; Brito and Castillo, 2013; Kaminsky, 2013).

2.4.4 Innovation platform

In its original form, the Bitcoin protocol works as a payment network, but it has the potential for further innovation such as provenance, transfer of data, transfer of digital assets, or act as prediction market (Brito and Castillo, 2013).

2.4.5 Internal change and volatility

The volatility of bitcoin and other cryptocurrencies may increase due to speculation and hype (Doherty, 2011) making it difficult for merchants to convert them into fiat currency very quickly.

2.4.6 Facilitation of criminality and competition to incumbents

Given the techniques in tracing sources of funds are advanced, most of the concerns of criminality may be overdone. However, if there is the slightest suspicion of money laundering and anti-terrorism, financial institutions may overreact to close the accounts of Bitcoin-related businesses. This will be made worse if there are indeed cases of money laundering and when the competition with incumbents heats up, many businesses may find converting bitcoin into fiat currency a challenge.

2.4.7   *Legal and regulatory attitude*

The regulatory risk remains for bitcoin and cryptocurrencies as we have seen with China and Korea clamping down on the intermediaries involved in crypto-related activities such as ICOs. Governments will continue to grapple with the risks and benefits of Bitcoin to their country. However, so far, regulators have been successful in giving clarity and guidance on the treatment of digital currencies. The challenge will come when decentralisation starts to threaten the existence of centralised authority. It is a difficult task for regulators to balance innovation with risk, especially in measures relating to anti-money laundering and the countering of terrorist financing, as well as taxes.

2.4.8   *Economic risks*

The innovative use of Bitcoin is very disruptive to the financial and payments markets. Bitcoin, for example, can scale up to replace money transmission and card payment services, or even stock exchanges. So far, the changes have been slow, But there is a risk at some point that cryptocurrency will destabilise the financial and payments markets, and ultimately price stability in a market. Few cost and benefits analyses of the crypto economy have been done partly due to the complexity of the technology and the difficulties in understanding how the technology can evolve.

2.4.9   *Zcash*

While there are over 1,000 cryptocurrencies, it is worth looking in more detail for Zcash. Another cryptocurrency known as Zcash was created in 2016.[6] based on Bitcoin's code. Zcash's entry seems timely

---

[6]The Economist. (2016, January 26). Known unknown: Another cryto-currency is born. Retrieved from http://www.economist.com/news/finance-and-economics/ 21709329-another-crypto-currency-born-known-unknown

as Bitcoin's capacity reached its limit and many transactions were delayed at the end of 2016. At the same time, Bitcoin community was faced with a governance crisis surrounding the one megabyte blocksize and slow transaction. In 2016, Ethereum recovered somewhat as one of such self-executing business agreements, another venture fund called the DAO proved another bad episode, together with other crises which erupted.

Zcash cryptographers claim its important innovation as being able to mint it more quickly to enable the system to handle more transactions. In turn, Zcash allows for more liquidity and shorter transaction times. Zcash also differs in the way it is governed as an open source project whereby a small group of volunteer developers decides the changes to be made. Zcash as open source is formed as a company with investors bringing in money, with 10% of its 21 million coins issued to be earmarked for founders, investors, employees and a putative Zcash foundation. The objective is to align incentives for all involved which will allow the firm to hire a team to ensure quicker decisions and avert all problems as faced by its rival, Bitcoin.

Moreover, in contrast to Bitcoin blockchain with the ledger keeping track of all the coins, it is open and can be analysed to see the flows of funds as a serious barrier for banks. Zcash can shield transactions using Z addresses while the t addresses remain transparent. Zcash has a scheme based on "zero-knowledge proofs" ("Z" as in its name) as a cryptographic protocol. Quintessentially, Zcash lives up to its name of who owns the coins, but without revealing any other information as size and origin of money. It has sold the idea called "zk-SNARK" (as do not ask) to banks as Zcash itself makes its profit.

New cryptocurrency may not be seen as in competition with earlier version. All are differentiated as representing different trade-offs involving security, complexity, performance, cost and other factors. Each new cryptocurrency will have to find its niche. In fact, there is room for cooperation since their software is open source. This means developers can easily learn and copy from each other as much as they compete. With cooperation (competition plus cooperation) given Zcash's zero-knowledge scheme, if it joins hands with Ethereum or any other crypto's, coders can find ways to connect different blockchains. To go one step further, if such collaboration works with an ÜberCoin to float across all blockchains, the challenge to central bankers may be ameliorated. That is already happening. The value of cryptocurrencies is in its inclusive open design with interoperability standards that allow smart contracts to do many P2P transactions across blockchains. The higher the degree of inclusion, the higher the valuation of an individual network or a huge network of cryptocurrencies!

2.5   Impact of the Digital Currency Revolution

The greatest impact of cryptocurrency will be when there is a convergence of IoT with blockchain, the underlying technology of cryptocurrency. When there is a micro-transfer of value and fractional ownership, the technology will accelerate changes to the world with IoT. There would be a tremendous amount of micro-payments, micro-insurance and micro-asset ownerships happening with the Internet of Everywhere (IoE). In and of itself, IoT and IoE will be a challenge to nations and governments based on hard geographical boundaries. Again, just like trying to regulate cryptocurrencies, some are arguing that centralised authorities may already be at the edge of losing control.

The digital currency will have a lot of impact on the digital and physical world with devices connected to each other. There may not be physical wallets anymore, and cryptocurrencies payments can be executed cross-border with wearable devices and other connected devices. Another development is the sharing economy as another example of using smart contracts. All will be able to share assets such as cars, hard disks, computer memory that are not in use and rent them out to others for a fee. Smart contracts via the distributed P2P network will make all these possible in the future. This will ensure that infrastructure need not increase, with any excess capacity used efficiently.

The desire to own entire assets will be less as more P2P digital assets, or digital trusts can be held by the crowd via blockchain technology. There is also the possibility of time-banking so that the cryptocurrency is stored in hours of work. One can then trade with the time spent in say, palliative care when one is young and then the same person will be entitled to such care when he or she gets older with the hours that have been deposited. While these can be done with a centralised system, a distributed or decentralised blockchain system has unique advantages especially in terms of distributed computing. Cryptocurrency may not replace the fiat currency, but its blockchain technology will certainly have an impact on the welfare of the people and perhaps even out the inequality.

2.6 Conditions for Future Success

Some conditions for future success are required as described below.

2.6.1 *Ecosystem and Bitcoin Cash*

First, there is always the first-mover advantage, and Bitcoin has certainly emerged as the leading cryptocurrency and a base currency in the crypto economy. Bitcoin has a hard fork[7] and Bitcoin Cash was created. Block 478558 was the last common block for both Bitcoin and Bitcoin Cash, and thus the first Bitcoin Cash block was 478559. Bitcoin Cash increases the Max Blocksize Limit parameter of the Bitcoin codebase. While Bitcoin's block size limit remains at one megabyte (allowing for 250,000 transactions per day), Bitcoin Cash has increased the block size limit to eight megabytes (allowing for around 2 million transactions per day). Bitcoin has been successful so far, and an eco-system is up to support its existence. Even though the network effect is kicking in, there is still a long way to go. A successful

---

[7]Hard fork (or sometimes hardfork) is a radical change to the protocol that makes previously invalid blocks/transactions valid (or vice versa), and as such requires all nodes or users to upgrade to the latest version of the protocol software. Hard fork is a permanent divergence from the previous version of the blockchain, and nodes running previous versions will no longer be accepted by the newest version. See http://www.investopedia.com/terms/h/hard-fork.asp#ixzz4xPikczJh

digital currency must be able to ride on its initial success and leverage on the network effect.

2.6.2   *Incentives*

Second, there are incentives because as the mining costs go up with equipment becoming more expensive, mining pools will be formed as miners are usually risk averse and want better odds in winning the race. Of course, there are technical solutions to all these, and some cryptocurrencies have come up with the idea of proof of stake (PoS). PoS may reduce the probability that any single person can use a quantum computer to overwrite the whole system.

2.6.3   *Identification*

Third, there are also cryptocurrencies that are looking into proof of identity to reduce the possibility of using the currency for money laundering or terrorist activities. If the identity problem can be resolved, cryptocurrency has a genuine potential to be very popular for financial inclusion. If a particular cryptocurrency can accept that the government is part of the ecosystem and its community engages with the government meaningfully in creating the ecosystem, that cryptocurrency is likely to become more widely accepted. Given that most of the welfare improvement comes from the bottom of the wealth pyramid, emerging markets have the upper hand in harnessing the low-hanging fruits of cryptocurrency via a decentralised but not necessary distributed system. A cryptocurrency that addresses issues as identified will have a bright future.

2.7   Conclusion and Prospects

Comparison is valid up to a point where Internet is for connectivity and cryptocurrency is about money. Similarities between the growth of the Internet and the growth of cryptocurrency are evident, leading one to postulate that cryptocurrency is going to see exponential growth like the Internet. However, from the business perspective, the growth of Internet has more to do with e-commerce and less to do with finance. On the other hand, with cryptocurrency, for once in the history of humanity, technology is playing a leading role in finance. In the future, one should expect a bank to be a digital or technologically-savvy bank. The disruptive force has now arrived at the doorstep of finance, and the blockchain technology is one of the solutions.

There are also similarities between hedge funds and cryptocurrency at the industry level. When the hedge funds industry was in its infant stage, it was perceived to be disruptive to currency system because hedge fund managers were perceived as the bad guys who took big bets. They were seen to be the mavericks who attacked the currency system and caused stock markets to collapse. Some banks did not want to deal with them as it did not make business sense with the high compliance costs. Start-ups in cryptocurrency today face the same problems that hedge funds then faced.

Understandably, much bad press and misunderstanding in the media exist, regarding cryptocurrency and some banks are unwilling to open accounts with cryptocurrency start-ups because of various reasons. Increasingly, banks' refusal to embrace cryptocurrencies is seen as a fear of competition with little effort spent on developing technology to deter illegal activities. Crime busters seem to have made a lot more progress in this area in terms of technology development and forensic science. Some regulators are also generally uncomfortable at the moment to deal with a financial innovation as complex as Bitcoin or indeed any other cryptocurrency. However, acceptance is on the rise. At the same time, there is a general resistance and reluctance by Main Street to learn about the intricacies of this financial innovation — it is a wait-and-see situation. There are spurs of interest when prices surge but few are willing to learn about the deep technology. That is human nature, and it is always the universities and those who are interested in the technology who will see the opportunities first.

There are many similarities between cryptocurrency and hedge fund strategies that were inherently quantitative and difficult to understand. It was no surprise to anyone that hedge fund strategies were initially embraced by university endowment funds which were less constrained than traditional managers. Again, universities and financial entrepreneurs will be the first to embrace cryptocurrency technology before it spills over to Main Street.

Cryptocurrency is here to stay and will evolve. If Bitcoin loses its popularity for whatever reason, a new cryptocurrency will emerge to replace it with better features. Countries with huge debts have the incentive to create their own cryptocurrency, and those who wish to promote financial integration may also turn to cryptocurrency, simply because the cost is low in creating a decentralised partially distributed system. There will be welfare improvement in a cryptocurrency world which is decentralised but not necessarily fully distributed, with proof of identity, proof of stake and the flexibility to incorporate smart contracts for a sharing economy.

Eventually, it is about the reduction of business cost and new business models. With low-cost new business models, welfare improvement will follow for those at the bottom of the wealth pyramid. All of this will lead to enhanced efficiency in a sharing economy. The outlook on the development of cryptocurrency is much more optimistic because of blockchain technology. It is likely for great leap in its use, with near field communication (NFC) and mobile technology being the driver behind its boom. At the same time, it is difficult to predict if cryptocurrency is the next big thing as there is still much uncertainty in the cryptocurrency world. However, it is a technology that financial institutions cannot ignore.

In conclusion, Bitcoin is a novel invention which is a breakthrough in terms of the payments and decentralised networks. It brings with it various benefits and risks which users should be cognisant with and indeed conversant with should they wish to deal with bitcoins. This Chapter has mainly discussed the main features of Bitcoin and Zcash, but other cryptocurrencies are likely to have similar features, and a clear understanding of Bitcoin will aid in understanding other cryptocurrencies. A good foundation in the knowledge of this amazing new technology that we will be enable its use to its fullest potential without fear.

This Chapter ends by including a few more figures as introduction and development in bitcoin, crypto-tokens and blockchain space. More information by countries will be provided in the next few chapters.

Figure 2.11.   **What Are Cryptocurrency or Crypto Token.**

Source: By authors.

Cryptocurrency and Crypto-Tokens

- Already, Switzerland is a leading centre for Tokens.
- The ticketing system in railways of the country has adopted the Bitcoin ATM functions and Ernst and Young at Switzerland has added a Bitcoin ATM that can be accessed by the public.
- In addition, Australia has also started creating an accounting standard for Bitcoin last year.
- Singapore is a leading centre for Initial Token Sales/Initial Crypto Token Offerings (ITS or ICOs) and Blockchain (Qtum, Ethereum, Digix and many others in the pipeline).
- PSA, Singapore Power, MAS and other private businesses are all using blockchain based on Ethereum or private blockchains.
- Many will purchase ether if they are using the Ethereum network for operation.
- Many will purchase ether or bitcoin for Initial Token Sales.

Figure 2.12.   **Recent Notable Developments in the Token Economy.**

Source: By authors.

Europe

- Germany: On 19 August 2013, the German Finance Ministry announced that bitcoin is now essentially a "unit of account" and can be used for the purpose of tax and trading in the country. It is not classified as a foreign currency or e-money but stands as "private money" which can be used in "multilateral clearing circles", according to the ministry.
- Finland: The court classified bitcoins as payment instruments.
- Norway: The Norwegian Tax Administration stated in December 2013 that they don't define bitcoin as money but regard it as an asset. Profits are subjected to wealth tax. In business, use of bitcoin falls under the sales tax regulation. The Norwegian government stated in February 2017 that they won't tax the use of bitcoin.
- Sweden: The governmental regulatory and supervisory body Swedish Financial Supervisory Authority (Finansinspektionen) have legitimized the fast growing industry by publicly proclaiming bitcoin and other digital currencies as a means of payment.

Figure 2.13.   Development in Europe.

Source: By authors.

Switzerland

- Bitcoin businesses in Switzerland are subject to anti-money laundering regulations and in some instances may need to obtain a banking license.
- On 5 December 2013 a proposal was put forth by 45 members of the Swiss Parliament for digital sustainability (Pardigli), that calls on the Swiss government to evaluate the opportunities for utilization of bitcoin by the country's financial sector. It also seeks clarification on bitcoin's legal standing with respect to VAT, securities and anti-money laundering laws.
- In response to the parliament postulates, the Swiss Federal Council issued a report on virtual currencies in June 2014. The report states that since virtual currencies are not in a legal vacuum, the Federal Council has concluded that there is no need for legislative measures to be taken at the moment.
- In 2016, Zug added bitcoin as a means of paying city fees, in a test and an attempt to advance Zug as a region that is advancing future technologies. Swiss Federal Railways, government-owned railway company of Switzerland, sells bitcoins at its ticket machines.

Figure 2.14.   Development in Switzerland.

Source: By authors.

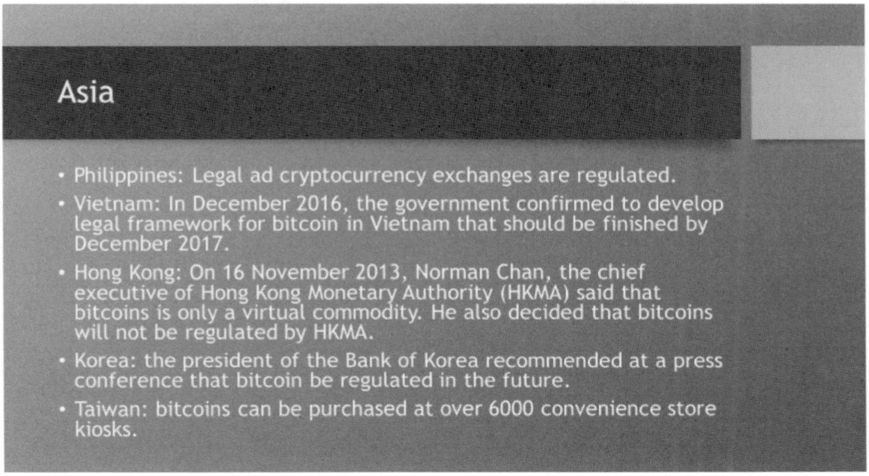

Asia

- Philippines: Legal ad cryptocurrency exchanges are regulated.
- Vietnam: In December 2016, the government confirmed to develop legal framework for bitcoin in Vietnam that should be finished by December 2017.
- Hong Kong: On 16 November 2013, Norman Chan, the chief executive of Hong Kong Monetary Authority (HKMA) said that bitcoins is only a virtual commodity. He also decided that bitcoins will not be regulated by HKMA.
- Korea: the president of the Bank of Korea recommended at a press conference that bitcoin be regulated in the future.
- Taiwan: bitcoins can be purchased at over 6000 convenience store kiosks.

Figure 2.15.   Development in Asia.

Source: By authors.

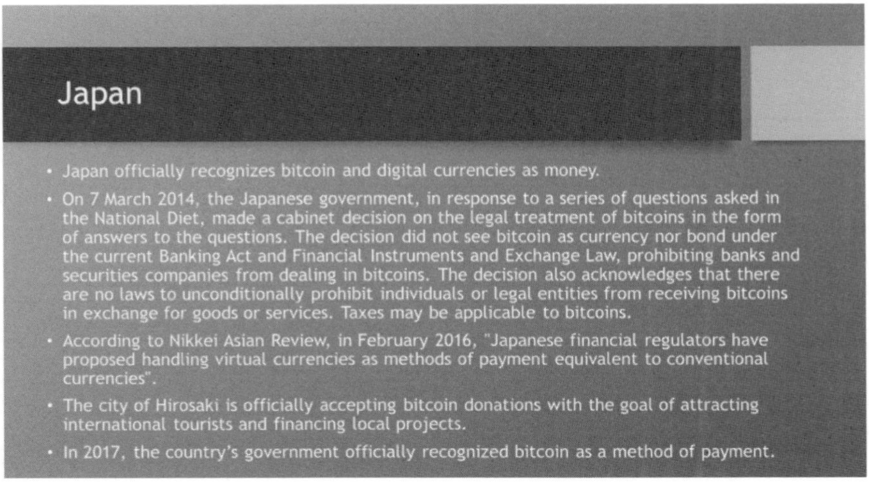

Japan

- Japan officially recognizes bitcoin and digital currencies as money.
- On 7 March 2014, the Japanese government, in response to a series of questions asked in the National Diet, made a cabinet decision on the legal treatment of bitcoins in the form of answers to the questions. The decision did not see bitcoin as currency nor bond under the current Banking Act and Financial Instruments and Exchange Law, prohibiting banks and securities companies from dealing in bitcoins. The decision also acknowledges that there are no laws to unconditionally prohibit individuals or legal entities from receiving bitcoins in exchange for goods or services. Taxes may be applicable to bitcoins.
- According to Nikkei Asian Review, in February 2016, "Japanese financial regulators have proposed handling virtual currencies as methods of payment equivalent to conventional currencies".
- The city of Hirosaki is officially accepting bitcoin donations with the goal of attracting international tourists and financing local projects.
- In 2017, the country's government officially recognized bitcoin as a method of payment.

Figure 2.16.   Development in Japan.

Source: By authors.

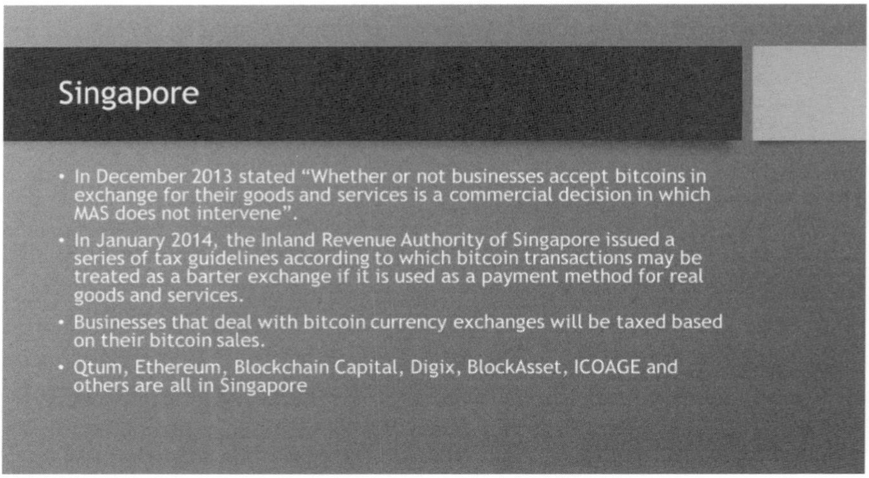

Figure 2.17.   Development in Singapore.

Source: By authors.

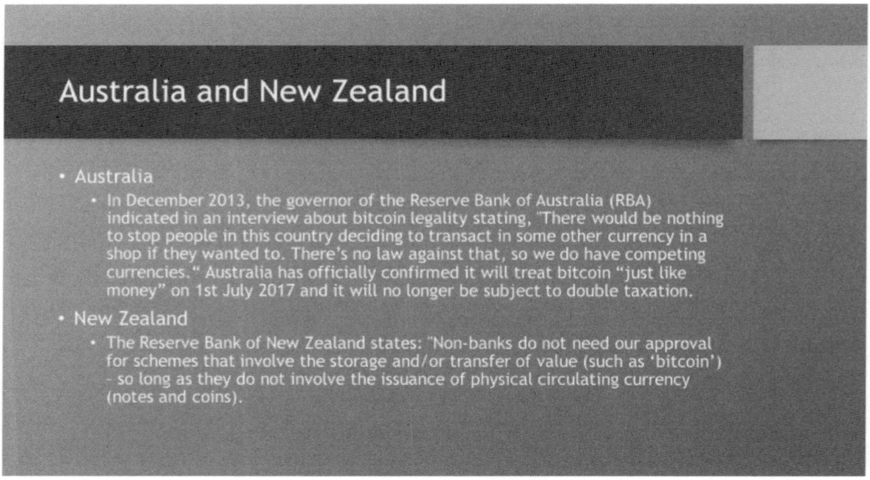

Figure 2.18.   Development in Australia and New Zealand.

Source: By authors.

Regulators on Bitcoin gaining momentum

- Most regulators are friendly to Bitcoin businesses.
- Canada: classified as intangible.
- UK: The government of the United Kingdom has stated that the bitcoin is currently unregulated and is treated as a 'foreign currency' for most purposes, including VAT/GST. Profits and losses on cryptocurrencies are subject to capital gains tax.
- USA:
  - Treasury: a convertible decentralized virtual currency (2013)
  - Commodity Futures Trading Commission: classified as a commodity (Sep 2015)
  - Federal Judge: funds within the plain meaning of the term (Sep 2016)
- Argentina: considered money but not legal currency by National Constitution.

Figure 2.19.   More on Regulation.

Source: By authors.

Digital currency technology

PwC's Vulcan digital asset services is creating opportunities to turn traditional currency into SmartMoney across **four** currency classes:

Central bank money	Commercial bank money	Company rewards	Community currency
The ways that reserve banks issue, use and transfer money	The uses of money for commercial and retail transactions	loyalty points and other incentive schemes	Tokens of value that can be used between groups of people for specific purposes

Figure 2.20.   The Crypto Bank of PWC: Vulcan.

Source: By authors; PwC.

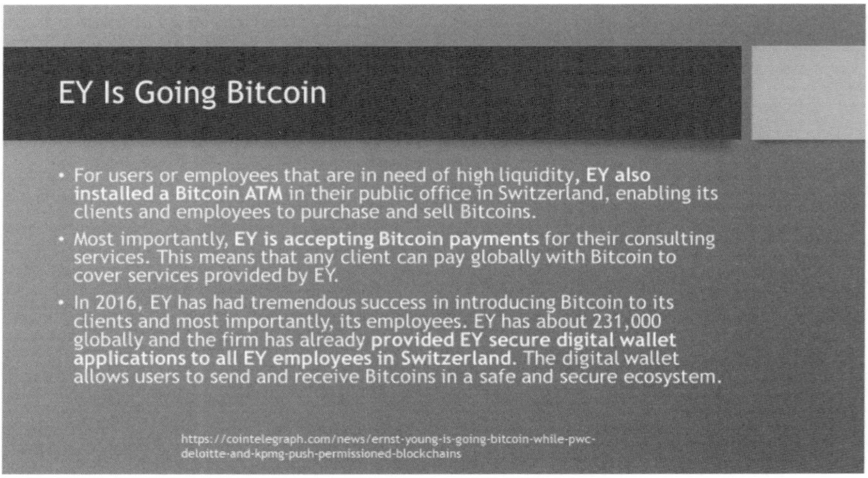

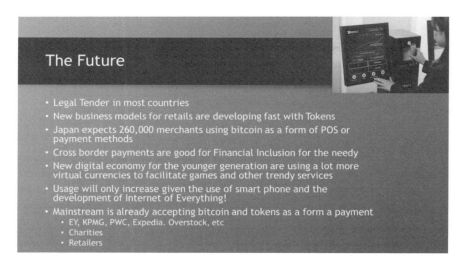

Figure 2.21.   EY Is into Cryptocurrency.

Source: By authors.

Figure 2.22.   The Future of Cryptocurrency.

Source: By authors.

Appendix: More Technical Concepts

This Appendix will discuss technical concepts of cryptocurrency especially bitcoin. As Bitcoin is not perfect, there are many challenges that the network has to overcome before the mass adoption is possible. These challenges include:

(1) block size limit within the network;
(2) the huge storage requirement for the blockchain;
(3) the number of transaction per second;
(4) privacy protection issue;
(5) legality of smart contract and Oracle that gives the true source of external data.

Oracle: An oracle, in the context of blockchains and smart contracts, is an agent that finds and verifies real-world occurrences and submits this information to a blockchain to be used by smart contracts. Oracles will provide the values required by the smart contract in a secure and trusted manner. A particular event will be triggered when pre-determined conditions are met in a smart contract. These pre-conditions are usually defined as a certain value that has to be reached or conditions that have to be met. Since blockchains cannot access data outside their network, a third party data feed is to be provided by Oracles. Oracles are the third party external data provider of data that trigger smart contract executions. The data could be anything from the temperature, rainfall, successful payment, price limits etc.

There are five types of Oracles: Software, hardware, inbound, outbound and consensus-based oracles. Software oracles handle information available online. Hardware oracle is information from the physical world via sensors or other devices. Inbound oracles handle the smart contract with data from the external world. Outbound oracles provide a smart contract with the ability to send data to external. Consensus-based oracles use information from a few other oracles to determine the outcome of an event. Security, especially for online data and sensors, is vital because there are no rollbacks once the smart contract is executed. So it is crucial that trusted and

Challenges
- **Block Size Limit**
- Storage
- Transaction per second
- Privacy
- Legality and Oracle

Block Size Limit
- Bitcoin is currently limited in the number of transactions it can process: up to 1MB of transactions roughly every 10min

Consequences
- Longer transaction time
- Higher fee costs

Figure A2.1.   Bitcoin Blockchain: Challenges.

Source: By authors.

secure information be provided to ensure the smart contracts get trusted information.

The major challenges are shown in Figure A2.1.

The Bitcoin blockchain stores every transaction in a block, after which the block is appended and recorded immutably on the blockchain. At the very beginning, the Bitcoin block size was designed to contain around 36 megabytes of transactions. On the year 2010, the block size was set to one megabyte with the aim to prevent spam and denial-of-service (DoS) attack (Caffyn, 2015), where malicious nodes formulate dust transactions or transactions with a large number of inputs and outputs, causing miners or nodes to spend wasteful amount of computation power to verify the transactions, thereby crippling the network. However, as Bitcoin continues to scale, the blockchain gradually becomes incapable to cope with the number of transactions that it can process per second, and this severely limits its practicality (the Bitcoin blockchain's throughput is around four to seven transactions per second). As the number of transactions pending confirmation starts piling up, miners become selective and will prioritise transactions offering higher transaction fees (Madeira, 2017). This is detrimental and would likely force regular users out of the network.

An intuitive solution would be to increase the block size to accommodate more transactions. The BIP101 (Andersen, 2015) proposal by Gavin Andresen in May 2015 sought a 20-megabyte hard limit, which was rejected by Chinese miners who expressed concern due to the country's limited bandwidth (van Wirdum, 2015a). The Bitcoin Unlimited project (Bitcoin Unlimited, 2017) proposes a solution that allows miners and nodes to vote on increasing the block size as and when required. This solution is favoured by the miners as it gives them control to set transaction fees, which will be important as Bitcoin is approaching its supply limit. However, the concern of having bigger block size limit is the higher data storage cost. A drastic increase of block size limit will mean that fewer users will be willing to operate full nodes, and the blockchain would rely on an exclusive group of nodes (or supercomputers) with the capability to operate and handle bigger blocks.

Segregated Witness

The Segregated Witness (SegWit) was proposed in BIP141 (Lombrozo, Lau and Wuille, 2015) specifically to address the Bitcoin blockchain scaling issue. The idea was first presented in 2015 by Pieter Wuille, who believes that the signature of a transaction (to prove that the sender has the authority to spend the input(s)) "can be reasonably considered expendable after a certain amount of time has passed" (van Wirdum, 2015b); all that matters were the transaction ID that records the essential details such as the sender, the receiver and the amount of Bitcoin sent. Therefore, SegWit was proposed to *segregate* the *witness*, i.e., the signature, from a transaction, thereby reducing the size of a transaction and allowing more transactions to be contained within a block.

SegWit increases the effective block size without increasing the block size limit. This is achieved in two steps. Firstly, in a standard non-SegWit transaction as shown in Figure A2.2, the sender's signature proving authorisation to spend an input is placed at the centre part of the transaction (the scriptSig). In a SegWit transaction, the scriptSig is encapsulated as the *witness data* and it is placed at the end of the structure, as specified in BIP143 (Lau and

T: 706b335514c44e6311439db679f049788122689a21bd40a1b73306c8ff33f894

```
{
"txid": "706b335514c44e6311439db679f049788122689a21bd40a1b73306c8ff33f894",
"size": 225,
"version": 2,
"locktime": 0,

"in": [
{
"txid": "fa53f5c75a28274f3ae029238b4dd03daf2adbaf79bdf221c925958a7c3d8a27",
"n": 1,
"scriptSig": "304402201730eba212e9c8370b9aa571ca184d3c31d4aa329b840291227e96bd620b687c02204572c0ea5bf529781f8f1d
3d53e5263a5ebb784302fb7d638d1b2452709f95f001 02e13d9fab3c4730183d14208163e532de1b61e9b79c8b102a686ac0b8e57b076d"
}
],
"out": [
{
"value": "0.12134079",
"n": 0,
"scriptPubKey": "OP_DUP OP_HASH160 1HJjNPksrnqW374Hb7GhtaKUysDQcvnF1K OP_EQUALVERIFY OP_CHECKSIG",
},
{
"value": "0.05933405",
"n": 1,
"scriptPubKey": "OP_DUP OP_HASH160 1GKQwKx54ahKQFQ4rya54nG5f9w1C8pCYt OP_EQUALVERIFY OP_CHECKSIG"
}
],
}
```

Figure A2.2.   An Example of a Standard Non-SegWit Bitcoin Transaction.

Source: Romano and Schmid (2017).

Wuille, 2016). When sending a SegWit transaction to legacy nodes (i.e., nodes that do not upgrade to support SegWit), the witness data is stripped in the sense that scriptSig is now an empty field, and the *witness data* is encapsulated in a network message with a market byte set to zero (as specified in BIP144), which will not be parsed as a valid transaction by a parser that does not support the BIP (i.e., the legacy node)(Lombrozo and Wuille, 2016). Essentially, legacy nodes ignore the witness data but they would still verify the transaction as valid, because transaction with an empty scriptSig field is regarded as an "Anyone Can Spend" transaction. On the other hand, SegWit nodes will look for a message containing the witness data, and verify the transaction as per the standard verification consensus.

The implication of this design is that the size of a SegWit transaction is significantly smaller than a non-SegWit transaction since the scriptSig data occupies around 65% of the entire transaction size. Therefore, a one-megabyte block would now be able to carry more transactions and effectively increases the throughput of the

Bitcoin blockchain. Furthermore, the transaction ID is now computed without the scriptSig data, allowing both legacy and new nodes to still agree on the makeup of blocks, and thus the entire blockchain. This concurrently solves the transaction malleability problem as will be detailed later.

Secondly, to ensure that blocks containing SegWit transactions would not exceed the block size limit of one-megabyte and can be implemented as a soft fork, a new type of maximum block size is defined in terms of "Block Weight". Essentially, the block size limit of 1,000,000 bytes is converted into a block weight limit of 4,000,000 units. Each transaction has a "weight" which is defined as (Song, 2017):

$$Weight = transaction\ size\ without\ witness\ data^*3 \\ + transaction\ size.$$

Using the aforementioned calculation, a non-SegWit transaction (with a non-empty scriptSig) has a weight of exactly four units whereas for SegWit transaction, its weight will always be less than four units because its witness data is "stripped off" before it is transmitted to the legacy nodes. For SegWit nodes, the actual block size will be greater than one megabyte. Suppose all transactions are SegWit transactions, it is expected the actual block size to be around two megabytes, and in the worst case, up to four megabytes of data per block (Blockgeeks, 2017).

It is also vital to note that although SegWit separates the signature from the transaction, it is still important to embed the signature information in the blockchain to serve as a proof. SegWit does so by creating a Merkle Tree out of all witness data to mirror the Merkle Tree of the transactions. The witness data Merkle Root is included in the input field of the coinbase transaction (which is used by miners to record the rewards obtained from mining the block)(van Wirdum, 2015a).

Soft fork vs. hard fork

A soft fork is defined as a rule change that is backward compatible, i.e., old nodes would still validate blocks created under the new rules. On the other hand, a hard fork is defined as a rule change to the software that requires a compulsory upgrade on all nodes. A hard fork is not backward compatible and it is a permanent split from the legacy rules.

The design of Segregated Witness is commonly considered as a breakthrough as it allows blocks containing SegWit transactions to still be recognised by legacy nodes as valid, at the same time increases the effective block size to around two megabytes. Hence, it can be implemented as a soft fork to the Bitcoin blockchain. However, it is important for a large majority of nodes to agree with the implementation of SegWit to ensure that the SegWit-enabled chain will remain the longest chain on the network.

On the other hand, a hard fork, if not implemented correctly, results in a split. In August 2017, Bitcoin is hard forked because 15–20% of mining power rejected SegWit and resulted in the Bitcoin Cash (BCH) (BitcoinCash, 2017) mining blocks of eight megabytes in size. When a chain is hard-forked, data from the block immediately preceding the fork-point is replicated on the two different chains immediately after, so for cryptocurrencies, wallet entries are replicated, and users will end up with two sets of coins post-fork. This would dilute the mining power and thus a hard fork is normally undesirable.

Transaction malleability

Apart from increasing the on-chain capacity of the Bitcoin blockchain, SegWit also solves the transaction malleability problem. Transaction malleability happens when a transaction ID is changed by modifying the format of the transaction signature without invalidating it (and commonly without knowledge of the sender), resulting in two identical transactions but with different transaction ID. The transaction malleability weakness was exploited in an attack on the Bitcoin exchange MtGox (Decker and Wattenhofer, 2014), but even then, the problem was never properly addressed. The implication of a transaction malleability attack is that the modified transaction may get confirmed on the blockchain first. If the sender is unaware of the balance in his or her wallet, he or she may be tricked into sending the fund multiple times to the receiver.

PUSHDATA 48		48
signature (DER)	sequence	30
	length	45
	integer	02
	length	20
	X	539901ea7d6840eea8826c1f3d0d1fca7827e491deabcf17889e7a2e5a39f5a1
	integer	02
	length	21
	Y	00fe745667e444978c51fdba6981505f0a68619f0289e5ff2352acbd31b3d23d87
SIGHASH_ALL		01
PUSHDATA 41		41
public key	type	04
	X	6c4ea0005563c20336d170e35ae2f168e890da34e63da7fff1cc8f2a54f60dc4
	Y	02b47574d6ce5c6c5d66db0845c7dabcb5d90d0d6ca9b703dc4d02f4501b6e44

Figure A2.3.   The Original Transaction with PUSHDATA 48, Which Pushes 48 Bytes of Data.

Source: By authors.

The root cause of transaction malleability lies in the format of a signature which can be changed without invalidating it. Before SegWit was implemented, the signature is included as part of the calculation of transaction ID. Figures A2.3 and A2.4 extracted from Shirriff (2014) show an example of transaction malleability attack. Both transactions perform identical operations and they are equally valid, but with different transaction IDs.

Lightning Network

The fact that SegWit solves the transaction malleability problem paves the way for Lightning Network. The Lightning Network (Poon and Dryja, 2016) is an off-chain solution that uses smart contract functionality in the blockchain to enable instant payments across a network of participants. Specifically, two parties will create a multisignature account and broadcast this information to the blockchain, after which subsequent transactions happen off-chain.

OP_PUSHDATA2 0048		4d 48 00
signature (DER)	sequence	30
	length	45
	integer	02
	length	20
	X	539901ea7d6840eea8826c1f3d0d1fca7827e491deabcf17889e7a2e5a39f5a1
	integer	02
	length	21
	Y	00fe745667e444978c51fdba6981505f0a68619f0289e5ff2352acbd31b3d23d87
SIGHASH_ALL		01
OP_PUSHDATA2 0041		4d 41 00
public key	type	04
	X	6c4ea0005563c20336d170e35ae2f168e890da34e63da7fff1cc8f2a54f60dc4
	Y	02b47574d6ce5c6c5d66db0845c7dabcb5d90d0d6ca9b703dc4d02f4501b6e44

Figure A2.4.   The Modified Transaction with OP_PUSHDATA2 0048, Which Pushes 0048 Bytes of Data.

Source: By authors.

Hashed Timelock Contract (HTLC) with bi-directional payment channels is created among the parties, which allows payments to be securely routed across multiple P2P payment channels.

Ethereum's scaling solutions

Compared to Bitcoin, Ethereum blockchain has a significantly larger storage requirement due to its smart contract functionality. There have been several solutions proposed to solve Ethereum's scaling problem. One of them is through sharding. Sharding is designed with the rationale that a blockchain cannot process more transactions than a single node can. Thus, instead of having all nodes processing the same transaction at the same time, sharding attempts to split the addresses into different shards. Each shard has its own group of nodes; the transaction history and the effect of transactions is limited within the shard itself. Several challenges to the sharding solution are: cross shard communication (can transactions on one shard trigger events on other shards?), single-shard-takeover attacks (attacker takes over the majority of the nodes in a shard) and the method to detect the attacks, data availability problem (what if data is missing from the shard?). Buterin (2017) is suggested for further reading.

The Raiden Network (Raiden Network, 2017) is an off-chain solution for Ethereum network that is essentially similar to Bitcoin's Lightning Network. In Raiden Network, the payment channel between two parties is represented by a smart contract which specifies the rules for channel operation that are agreed up-front by both parties. The token value as escrow is to back off-chain payments, and rules in case of disputes. The smart contract will be broadcasted on the Ethereum blockchain, after which both parties perform off-chain value transfers.

The Ethereum founder, Vitalik Buterin, along with the author of Lightning Network, Joseph Poon, have jointly proposed a new solution called Plasma (Poon and Buterin, 2017). Plasma can be regarded as Ethereum's version of SegWit. It eliminates unnecessary data in smart contracts and only broadcasts completed transactions to the public Ethereum blockchain. Leveraging on Ethereum's smart contract functionality, Plasma extends the idea of off-chain payment channels to cover more complex computations and operations.

References and Further Readings

Andresen, G. (2015). BIP101: Increase maximum block size. Retrieved from https://githumb.com/bitcoin/bips/blob/master/bip-0101.mediawik

Androulaki, E., Karame, G. O., Roeschlin, M., Scherer, T., & Capkun, S. (2013, April). Evaluating user privacy in bitcoin. In International Conference on Financial Cryptography and Data Security (pp. 34–51). Berlin, Heidelberg: Springer. Retrieved from http://fc13.ifca.ai/proc/1-3.pdf

Back, A. (1997). A partial hash collision based postage scheme, s.l.: s.n. Retrieved from http://www.hashcash.org/papers/announce.txt. Accessed on January 25, 2015.

Back, A. (2002). Hashcash — A denial of service counter-measure, s.l.: s.n. Retrieved from http://www.hashcash.org/papers/hashcash.pdf. Accessed on January 25, 2015.

BBC News. (2013, May 27). Liberty Reserve digital money service forced offline. Retrieved from http://www.bbc.co.uk/news/technology-22680297

BitcoinCash. (2017). Bitcoin Cash — Peer-to-peer electronic cash. Retrieved from https://www.bitcoincash.org/

Bitcoin.org. (2014). Choose your bitcoin wallet. Retrieved from https://bitcoin.org/en/choose-your-wallet

Bitcoin Project. (2014). Frequently asked questions. Retrieved from https://bitcoin.org/en/faq

Bitcoin Unlimited. (2017). Retrieved from https://www.bitcoinunlimited.info/

Blockgeeks. (2017). What is Segwit? Retrieved from https://blockgeeks.com/guides/what-is-segwit/

Brito, J. (2013). The top 3 things I learned at the bitcoin conference. Mercatus Center. Retrieved from http://mercatus.org/expert_commentary/top-3-things-i-learned-bitcoin-conference

Brito, K. & Castillo, A. (2013). Bitcoin: A primer for policymakers. Mercatus Center. Retrieved from http://mercatus.org/publication/bitcoin-primer-policymakers

Buterin, V. (2017). On sharding blockchains. Retrieved from https://github.com/ethereum/wiki/wiki/Sharding-FAQ

Caffyn, G. (2015). What is the Bitcoin block size debate and why does it matter? Retrieved November 9, 2017, from https://www.coindesk.com/what-is-the-bitcoin-block-size-debate-and-why-does-it-matter/

Chaum, D. (1983). Blind signatures for untraceable payments. In Chaum, D., Rivest, R. L., & Sherman, A. T. (Eds.), Advances in Cryptology. In Proceedings of Crypto, vol. 82. Springer, 199–203. Retrieved from http://link.springer.com/chapter/10.1007%2F978-1-4757-0602-4_18

Chaum, D., Fiat, A., & Naor, M. (1990). Untraceable electronic cash. Adv. Cryptol CRYPTO' 88 (403), 319–327.

Chen, A. (2011, June 1). The undergroundwebsite where you can buy any drug imaginable. Gizmodo. Retrieved from http://gawker.com/5805928/the-underground-website-where-you-can-buy-any-drug-imaginable

CoinDesk. (2014, July 22). How to store your bitcoins. CoinDesk. Retrieved from http://www.coindesk.com/information/how-to-store-your-bitcoins/

Dai, W. (1998). b-money, s.l.: s.n.

Decker, C. & Wattenhofer, R. (2014). Bitcoin transaction malleability and MtGox. Cryptography and Security.

Doherty, S. (2011, June 16). All your bitcoins are ours ... Symantec Blog. Retrieved from http://www.symantec.com/connect/blogs/all-your-bitcoins-are-ours

Finney, H. (2004). RPOW — Reusable Proofs of Work, s.l.: s.n. Retrieved from http://cryptome.org/rpow.htm. Accessed on January 25, 2015.

Hileman, G. (2014). From bitcoin to the Brixton pound: History and prospects for alternative currencies (poster abstract). In Böhme, R., Brenner, M., Moore, T., Smith, M. (Eds.), Berlin: Springer, 163–165.

Hughes, E. (1993). A Cypherpunk's Manifesto. Retrieved from https://w2.eff.org/Privacy/Crypto/Crypto_misc/cypherpunk.manifesto

Kaminsky, D. (2013, April 12). I tried hacking bitcoin and I failed. Business Insider. Retrieved from http://www.businessinsider.com/dan-kaminsky-highlights-flaws-bitcoin-2013-4

Kaplanov, N. M. (2012). Nerdy money: Bitcoin, the private digital currency, and the case against its regulation. Retrieved from http://ssrn.com/abstract1/42115203

Lam, P. N. & Lee, D. K. C. (2015). Introduction to Bitcoin. Handbook of Digital Currency. Elsevier.

Lau, J. & Wuille, P. (2016). BIP143: Transaction Signature Verification for Verstion 0 Witness Program. Retrieved from https://github.com/bitcoin/bips/blob/master/bib-0143.mediawiki

Lee, D. K. C. (2015). Handbook of Digital Currency. Elsevier.

Lee, D. K. C. (2017). Decentralised and Distributed Innovation. Paper presented at the Stanford APARC Innovation Concerence.

Lee, D. K. C., & Deng R. (2017). Handbook of Blockchain, Digital Finance and Inclusion. Elsevier.

Levey, S. (1993). Crypto Rebels. Wired. Retrieved from https://www.wired.com/1993/02/crypto-rebels/

LocalBitcoins. (2014). Buy and sell bitcoins near you. Retrieved from https://localbitcoins.com/

Lombrozo, E., & Wuille, P. (2016). BIP144: Segregated Witness (Peer Services). Retrieved from https://github.com/bitcoin/bips/blob/master/bip-0144.mediawiki

Lombrozo, E., Lau, J., & Wuille, P. (2015). BIP141: Segregated Witness (Consensus Layer). Retrieved from https://github.com/bitcoin/bips/blob/master/bip-0141.mediawiki

Madeira, A. (2017, September 28). What is the block size limit. Retrieved from CryptoCompare, https://www.cryptocompare.com/coins/guides/what-is-the-block-size-limit/

Matonis, J. (2013). Bitcoin gaining market-based legitimacy as XBT. Retrieved from http://www.coindesk.com/ bitcoin-gaining-market-based-legitimacy-xbt/

May, T. (1992). The Crypto Anarchist Manifesto. s.l.: s.n. Retrieved from http://www.activism.net/cypherpunk/crypto-anarchy.html. Accessed on January 25, 2015.

Nakamoto, S. (2008). Bitcoin: A P2P electronic cash system. Retrieved from https://bitcoin.org/bitcoin.pdf

Ober, M., Katzenbeisser, S., & Hamacher, K. (2013). Structure and anonymity of the bitcoin transaction graph. Future Internet 5(2), 237–250. Retrieved from http://www.mdpi.com/1999-5903/5/2/237

Pacia, C. (2013). Bitcoin mining explained like you're five: part 2 — mechanics. Escape Velocity. Retrieved from http://chrispacia.wordpress.com/2013/09/02/bitcoin-mining-explained-like-youre-five-part-2-mechanics/. Accessed on September 2, 2013.

Poon, J. & Buterin, V. (2017). Plasma: Scalable autonomous smart contracts. Retrieved from https://plasma.io/plasma.pdf

Poon, J., & Dryja, T. (2016). The Bitcoin Lightning Network: Scalable off-chain instant payments. Retrieved from https://lightning.network/lightning-network-paper.pdf

Raiden Network. (2017). Retrieved from http://raiden-network.readthedocs.io/en/stable/spec.html

Reid, F., & Harrigan, M., 2013. An analysis of anonymity in the bitcoin system. In Altshuler, Y. et al, (Eds.), Security and Privacy in Social Networks. New York: Springer. Retrieved from http://arxiv.org/pdf/1107.4524v2.pdf

Romano, D., & Schmid, G. (2017). Beyond Bitcoin: A critical look at blockchain-based systems. Cryptography, 1(15), 1–31.

Shirky, C. (2000). The case against micropayments. O'Reilly Media, Inc. Retrieved from http://www.openp2p.com/pub/a/p2p/2000/12/19/micropayments.html. Accessed on January 25, 2015.

Shirriff, K. (2014). Bitcoin transaction malleability: Looking at the bytes. Retrieved November 8, 2017, from http://www.righto.com/2014/02/bitcoin-transaction-malleability.html

Song, J. (2017). Understanding Segwit block size. Retrieved from https://medium.com/@jimmysong/understanding-segwit-block-size-fd901b87c9d4

Szabo, N. (1999). The God Protocols. IT Audit, 15 November.

Szabo, N. (2002). Shelling Out — The origins of money, s.l.: s.n. Retrieved from http://szabo.best.vwh.net/shell.html. Accessed on January 25, 2015.

Szabo, N. (2008). Bit gold, s.l.: s.n. Retrieved from http://unenumerated.blogspot.com/2005/12/bit-gold.html. Accessed on January 25, 2015.

The Economist. (2016, January 26). Known unknown: Another cryto-currency is born. Retrieved from http://www.economist.com/news/finance-and-economics/21709329-another-crypto-currency-born-known-unknown

Tindell, K. (2013). Geeks love the bitcoin phenomenon like they loved the internet in 1995. Business Insider. Retrieved from http://www.businessinsider.com/how-bitcoins-are-mined-and-used-2013-4. Accessed on April 5, 2013.

Van Wirdum, A. (2015a). Chinese exchanges reject Gavin Andresen's 20MB block size increase. Retrieved from https://cointelegraph.com/news/chinese-exchanges-reject-gavin-andresens-20-mb-block-size-increase/

Van Wirdum, A. (2015b). Segregated Witness, Part 1: How a clever hack could significantly increase Bitcoin's potential. Retrieved from https://bitcoinmagazine.com/articles/segregated-witness-part-how-a-clever-hack-could-significantly-increase-bitcoin-s-potential-1450553618/

Wallace, B. (November 2011). The rise and fall of Bitcoin. Wired (23).

Chapter 3

Introduction to Initial Crypto-Token Offering (ICO)

Written Jointly with Yu WANG

3.1 What Is an ICO

Token Sales or sometimes known as initial crypto-token offering (ICO) is a swap of newly created tokens with liquid cryptocurrencies that enable blockchain start-ups to execute their experimental community projects. ICOs, sometimes also known by other names such as initial coin offerings, are a borderless and mostly unregulated[1] form of sourcing for a stated amount of one or a variety of cryptocurrencies to fund mostly open source projects that enhance the eco-system of the decentralised network. The most common example is to send a certain amount of bitcoin or Ether to an assigned public address in exchange for a fixed amount of new tokens. At the end of September 2017, the all-time cumulative ICO access to funds reached a high of USD2.377 billion (see Figure 3.1).

Given the success of ICO and its resemblance to an IPO (initial public offering), ICOs have emerged as a way to raise funds for securities or securitised assets globally with cryptocurrencies instead

---

[1]Some ICOs subject themselves to regulation and others are subject to existing regulation because they involved the issue of securities or securities-like tokens. See https://www.sec.gov/oiea/investor-alerts-and-bulletins/ib_coinofferings

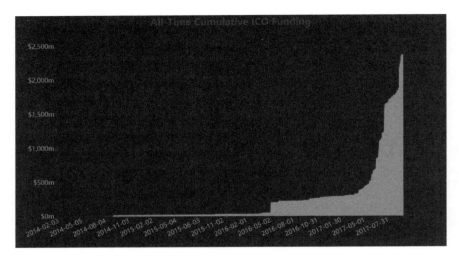

Figure 3.1. All-Time Cumulative ICO Funding Reached USD 2377.68 Million at the end of September 2017.

Source: Coindesk, https://www.coindesk.com/ico-tracker/

of jurisdiction based fiat currencies. The advantage of ICOs over IPOs is that the crowdfunding reach of ICOs is global. ICOs have been transformed into an alternative form of crowdfunding, raising cryptocurrency instead of fiat currencies for legal entities beyond blockchain-based projects. Some of these are not decentralised software projects, and some are not even private blockchain projects. The only link to the fundraising project to blockchain is the issue of a new token or the ERC20[2] compliant or compatible tokens, a new coin created on the Ethereum network.

Financial centres such as those in the US, England, Canada, Australia, Hong Kong, Dubai and Singapore are issuing warnings and advisory notes to the public to warn them that some, if not all, of these ICOs, will need to conform to the existing security

---

[2]The ERC-20 defines a common list of rules for all Ethereum tokens to follow, meaning that this particular token empowers developers of all types to accurately predict how new tokens will function within the larger Ethereum system. See http://www.investopedia.com/news/what-erc20-and-what-does-it-mean-Eth ereum/#ixzz4xVREsJpj

regulation. Depending on the structure of the ICO and if it does not involve the issue of securities, a certain structure of the ICO can be launched with no restrictions in some countries such as Singapore and Switzerland provided that anti-money laundering, anti-terrorism and tax compliant rules are observed. These warnings are reminders to those involved in token sales that there are fiduciary duties in using ICO as access to funding even though there is no regulation, and as reminders to those participating in taking responsibility for their own investment actions.

3.2 An ICO Is a Token Swap

In an ICO, investors swap the newly created crypto-tokens using established cryptocurrencies such as bitcoin and Ethereum. A bitcoin, an Ether, a Zcash, a Litecoin or other chosen coins will swap for the new token at a different ratio. An ICO is not the same as an IPO, despite the similarity of the two terms. In an IPO, investors are being offered the equities or debts of the company in the form of a security. In an ICO, investors are swapping their cryptocurrencies for new tokens that entitle them to certain rights. Whether these tokens are deemed as securities will depend on the regulation of the jurisdiction of the company or the foundation that is contracted to design and build the software, app or network. Investors are not buying the shares of the legal entity but the tokens that are to be created by the software. Therefore, more people are referring to it as Token Sales. However, the terms ICO, initial crypto-token offering, initial coin offering, initial token sales, token sales, crypto crowdsale, and crypto crowdfunding are used interchangeably. This makes reading and understanding the terminology for non-specialists even harder and confusing. In the strictest sense, token sales are not fundraising but access to funding. It is an innovative way to swap tokens in order to have access to funding and indirectly to fiat currencies. This is because the bitcoins, Ethers, Zcashs, Litecoins or other cryptocurrencies that are gathered will be kept as working capital and only a portion is converted to fiat currencies in reputable projects. An ICO often happens before the official launch of the project to cover the costs of development or further development of the project and other expenses that may occur in order to list the coins on the exchanges.

In the event that the project tokens are not ready to be issued by the software, investors may be issued with a temporary token that entitles them a one-to-one exchange for the project token. Such tokens can be issued using the smart contracts on Ethereum, and they are termed ERC-20 compatible or compliant tokens. The advantage of ICO is that as soon as the ERC-20 tokens are issued, trading can start on any unregulated exchanges that are willing to "list" them. Angel investment is usually full of risk because the investment is highly illiquid, with very long horizon and subject to non transparent risk. But, ICO has injected liquidity into angel investment by providing a secondary liquid market, shorter investment horizon and transparent software codes. This is why ICO is seen as a disruptor for traditional venture capital (VC) as it allows access to international funding as well as immediate liquidity after investment. A few of the projects raised hundreds of millions in a matter of a few days or a few hours.

Another emerging trend is the pre-ICO token sale, where a project launches one or more rounds of crowdsale before the official ICO. In most cases, investors invest with a discounted price or were given a bonus for being early investors. For example, in the pre-crowdsale phase of Rialto, investors were awarded a bonus of 15–25% based on the amount purchased; in its second phase called priority pass, the bonus was 10% whereas there was no bonus for next phase which was the official crowdsale (RIATO.AI, 2017).

3.3   How Does It Work

First, a group of reputable technologists in the community start to work on an idea to deal with the programming details. Prior to the token sale, platform prototypes or alpha versions are often released, along with a white paper[3] and an official website introducing the project such as schedules, technical details and programming codes.

---

[3]A white paper for ICO is prepared by a party or facilitator prior to launching a new currency or project. It details commercial, technological and financial details of a new coin or project. There may be several white papers including economic, technical and others.

Next, the technologists will announce the project online and publish all the related information. Platforms include online forums such as *Reddit, Bitcointalk* and the official websites. Prior to the crackdown in China, WeChat was the most popular platform for the Chinese investors. After the crackdown, most chat groups moved to Telegram. Many of the ICOs "underwriters" in China have their own websites and teams to initiate the token sales as intermediaries. Some projects even have an ICO website or section used specifically for the ICO events. Regardless of the forms, the website will state the schedule for ICO, including the number, dates, and duration of the phases, the price and supply of the tokens, and the amount of fund to be raised. There will be official and unofficial social media and chat groups on WeChat, Telegram, Facebook, Slack and WhatsApp to keep the investors informed and to allow interested parties to interact with each other. AMA (Ask Me Anything) sessions are regularly conducted, and video updates are posted on YouTube and Tencent Media to inform investors of the progress of ICOs and the software experiment. Assigned chat-group-secretary will handle all investors' activities and requests for information. Due to the unregulated and lucrative environment, scammers are very innovative and always actively scheming to stealing coins and information from unsuspected investors.

Prior to the launch of the ICO, information will be provided to the investors on the website or through online articles/blogs about how and where to purchase the crypto-tokens. Registration with the cryptocurrency exchanges or a website will allow for a whitelist, a list consisting of all investors who complied with their know your customer (KYC) processes. Investors would have to purchase designated cryptocurrencies to be able to swap for the new tokens when the ICO begins. After crediting their e-wallets with the cryptocurrencies accepted for the ICO, usually bitcoin or Ether, investors are ready to participate in the ICO by sending the coins to their addresses. For example, the ICO facilitator requests the investors to send bitcoin, Ethereum or Litecoin to a wallet address, and then emails the proof of transaction to the ICO email account. In most projects, investors will receive the tokens after the ICO ends and store the tokens in the wallet. Immediately after the official launch of the project, the new token will likely be able to trade on those exchanges that accept the tokens. In order to exchange the new tokens for cash, a reverse of the process is needed. This usually involves the swap of new tokens to bitcoin, Ether, Zcash or other cryptocurrencies, before a conversion to fiat currency is possible.

New tokens are generally stored in two ways:

(1) The more common way is to store the token on top of an existing blockchain, either as a coloured coin on Bitcoin's blockchain or as a token held as ERC-20 compliant or compatible tokens in a smart contract on Ethereum's blockchain.

(2) The other method is to issue a token in an entirely new blockchain, just as what founders of Ethereum did.

In the case of Qtum, the Qtum ERC-20 compatible tokens were first issued on Ethereum and later swap for Qtum tokens on Qtum network after it went live in late September 2017. This has the advantage of allowing investors first to trade the Qtum ERC-20 tokens, reducing the period of initial investors having to wait for the new network. The risk is transferred or shared with investors from the secondary market, and this has led to more participation in pre-ICOs and ICOs, as risks were shared among more investors. The market has become more speculative, investors who are not familiar with ICO and its technology may subject themselves to high risks. It is therefore important that those who are not technically savvy should not be involved in ICOs since these are usually unregulated.

3.4   Characteristics of ICOs and the Cypherpunk Philosophy

3.4.1   *Technology-based project*

Usually, the ICO projects are technology-based experiments related to enhancing the cryptocurrency, blockchain, or decentralisation ecosystem. These projects are targeted at investors that are from the community with knowledge of the mechanism of cryptocurrencies or have already invested in the cryptocurrency market with the intent to support these initiatives. The facilitators or those behind these projects are usually developers or thought leaders in the blockchain and cryptocurrency community.

In practice, more and more speculators without technical knowledge are showing an interest in these ICOs with profit being the only motive. There is also a tendency for many of the projects from the non-blockchain community to be packaging securities as an ICO in order to have access to funds. The telltale signs are projects without anyone associated with or from the community, or without team members that have knowledge of blockchain or cryptocurrency, or hastily packaging security-like products with the sole intention of fundraising without real contribution to the technology or community.

3.4.2   *Disclosure before the sale*

There is currently no requirements or standards on what the project should disclose in order to initiate a token sale. In general, ICOs are launched through a website, a white paper, and/or a post of online forums related to cryptocurrency.

3.4.3   *Identities*

It is also worth mentioning that the identities of both the developers and investors are not necessarily clear. Rare but the project facilitators can make the decision not to reveal their identities. Though few, there are projects that will not perform identity checks on their investors, nor on the source of the incoming funds. The cypherpunk's philosophy is deeply ingrained in ICO culture with privacy being the utmost importance. Privacy in the cypherpunk's language means the following[4]:

> "Privacy is necessary for an open society in the electronic age. Privacy is not secrecy. A private matter is something one doesn't want the whole world to know, but a secret matter is something one doesn't want anybody to know. Privacy is the power to selectively reveal oneself to the world."
>
> — In *A Cypherpunk's Manifesto* by Eric Hughes

---

[4]http://nakamotoinstitute.org/static/docs/cypherpunk-manifesto.txt

3.4.4 *Token raised*

One unique point of ICO is that it usually comes with an upper limit, expressed as a maximal number of tokens to be sold before it starts, sometimes even a lower limit (Lewis, 2017). However, some are confusing fundraising with token sales. If the minimum amount is not met, they will refund the existing buyers and discontinue the project. Besides, owing to the nature of blockchain, records of investing in ICOs can be easily traced via the public ledger. Therefore, the amount of token raised during the sale is public, but not the identity of buyers.

3.5 History of ICOs

Mastercoin (renamed as Omni), a meta-protocol built on top of the Bitcoin blockchain providing additional features, is deemed the first documented use of ICO. The crowdsale happened on *Bitcointalk* forum and allowed investors buy Mastercoin tokens using bitcoins. It took place in mid-2013 and raised over 5,000 bitcoins worth about USD500,000 at the time (Hajdarbegovic, 2013). This was followed by a series of ICOs, among which was Ethereum.

Table 3.1 shows some well-known ICO projects. After the token sale of Mastercoin, NXT started its ICO in September 2013. NXT is the first cryptocurrency that uses purely Proof-of-Stake (PoS) consensus mechanism, and it has a static total supply of 1 billion coins. In the ICO, it raised 21 bitcoins that were worth roughly USD17,000. As of September 2, 2017, the price of NXT was around USD0.12, making it the most profitable investment cryptocurrency with a return on investment (ROI) of over 669 times.

Shortly, Ethereum began its ICO in July 2014. It raised an unprecedentedly total amount of USD18.4 million during the 42 days' ICO period. It is an open source smart contract and decentralised application platform. Many projects have been and are being built on Ethereum Virtual Machine (EVM), leading to a surge in its price, with a market capitalisation of more than USD30 billion, second only to Bitcoin. With the smart contract system, Ethereum opened the door for a new generation of ICOs.

Table 3.1.   Major ICO Projects in the History as at 2017.

ICO start date	Project	Amount raised (USD)	Features	ROI since ICO
Jul-13	Mastercoin	$0.5 Million	A meta-protocol built on top of the Bitcoin blockchain that provides additional features	Not available
Sep-13	NXT	$16,800	The first cryptocurrency that uses purely Proof-of-Stake scheme	669638%
Apr-14	MaidSafeCoin	$7 Million	Designed for the SAFE (Secure Access For Everyone) network and intended to make users' data safe and secure	Not available
Jul-14	Ethereum	$18 Million	A blockchain-based platform that runs smart contract and is still one of the most successful ICOs and widely used cryptocurrencies	115266%
Mar-16	Lisk	$6 Million	A decentralised and public blockchain application platform with the aim to enable every application to run on its own separate sidechain	9016%

(Continued)

Table 3.1.   (*Continued*)

ICO start date	Project	Amount raised (USD)	Features	ROI since ICO
Apr-16	The Dao	$160 Million	Short for Decentralised Autonomous Organisation, developed based on Ethereum smart contract and attacked by the hackers shortly after its ICO	Not applicable
Jun-16	Waves	$16 Million	A blockchain-based platform that enables users to launch their own customised cryptocurrencies	2822%
Mar-17	Qtum	$15.5 Million	An open source blockchain application platform that implements the Bitcoin Improvement Protocols and Ethereum Virtual Machine	5731%
Apr-17	Gnosis	$13 Million	An Ethereum-based project that enables advanced smart contracts and uses Dutch Auction for the token sale	586%
Jun-17	Status	$100 Million	A free and open source project based on Ethereum technologies that target mobile client	22%
Jul-17	Tezos	$232 Million	A new decentralised blockchain with a self-governance system while facilitating formal verification	Not available

Source: ICOStats, CoinSchedule, BlockchainHub as of 2 September 2017.

Notably, there are a number of the ICOs that failed to live up to the hype or were pure scams. The Decentralised Autonomous Organisation (DAO)[5] was one such project that was developed based on Ethereum smart contract with the aim to provide a new open source, decentralised business model for both commercial and nonprofit enterprises (Allison, 2016). It raised a record of USD160 million in the ICO, but a few weeks later hackers managed to steal millions of dollars worth of tokens because of errors in the coding of contracts on the Dao platform. As a consequence, Ethereum community had to hard-fork the Ethereum blockchain to restore the funds to investors, which led to a split in the blockchain, where the original unforked blockchain kept running as a "new" cryptocurrency, Ethereum Classic.

In 2017, fundraising records had repeatedly been broken, with Tezos raising USD232 million worth of bitcoins and Ethers, which is the largest ICO to date. Developed in 2014 when the white paper was first published, Tezos is a new decentralised blockchain with a self-governance system where the token holders can make decisions together for the governance and improvement of the platform while facilitating formal verification (Xie, 2017). Most importantly, Tezos supports meta upgrades as the protocols can evolve by amending their own code (Goodman, 2014).

3.6   Classification of ICOs

3.6.1   *Types of ICO structures*

The most common structure used in ICOs is to sell a fixed number of tokens at a fixed priced on a first come, first served basis until all tokens are sold or the ICO period ends as Capped. In most ICOs, "insiders" such as the founders or the development team will be given a certain amount, a fixed percentage under

---

[5]A decentralised autonomous organisation (DAO) or a decentralised autonomous corporation (DAC), is an organisation that is run through rules encoded as computer programs called smart contracts. The financial transaction record and program rules of a DAO are maintained on a blockchain. See https://en.wikipedia.org/wiki/Decentralized_autonomous_organization

the aforementioned scheme, of total token supply (Reuben, 2017). Usually, more than 50% of the total number of tokens will be sold to the investors to encourage participation and to indicate the autonomy of the community with a majority. There are several other approaches, which are summarised together with the first type in Table 3.2.

In fewer cases, the tech start-ups will give an additional discount on the token price to early investors or even in a pre-ICO period. We will not discuss it here as basically this still can be considered as fixed price scheme. Additionally, the time frame is less discussed here as almost all ICOs have a limited time duration. But some projects do raise funds without setting a deadline for the sale. Tau-Chain is a good example as the team decided to run the sale without an end date.

To sum up, each ICO structure is embedded with some features. The best practice is for the developers to think through the objectives they wish to obtain and choose the most suitable one before the ICO starts. For instance, if they aim to sell the tokens at market price, they may choose the Auction structure, with or without a cap, instead of setting a fixed price for the token themselves in the rest four schemes, just as the Gnosis team used a Dutch auction structure for the ICO. In addition, given the idea of enabling all buyers to get some tokens, they may choose the Uncapped or Capped with re-distribution mechanisms, for in the former investors can buy as many tokens as they want and in the latter they will get the amount proportionally, even if that means fewer tokens when the sale is oversubscribed.

3.6.2 *Types of tokens*

Generally speaking, ICOs can also be categorized according to the tokens they generate. For the great variety of tokens, there are three sub-groups (summarised in Table 3.3): usage token that allows investors to use a service, work token that provides the right to contribute work to a decentralised organisation, and traditional asset token that represents a traditional asset cryptographically (Tomaino,

Table 3.2.   Structure Types of ICOs..

Structure type	Cap on the amount raised	Price	Number of tokens sold to investors	Percentage of total token supply assigned to the insiders
Capped	Yes	Fixed (set by developers)	First come, first served basis until all tokens are sold	Fixed
Uncapped	No	Fixed (set by developers)	As many tokens as they desire	Fixed
Capped auction	Yes	Variable (determined by market demand)	A variable number of tokens are actually sold at the lowest successful bid price in proportion with each buyer's pledged total spent	Variable
Uncapped auction	No	Variable (determined by market demand)	Quantity of tokens they bid in descending bidding price order until all tokens are sold	Fixed
Capped with re-distribution	Yes	Fixed (set by developers)	Total number of tokens distributed in proportion to each buyer's pledged total spent	Fixed
Capped with parcel limit	Yes	Fixed (set by developers)	First come, first served basis until all tokens are sold with a limit on the total amount that each buyer can buy	Fixed

Source: By authors.

Table 3.3.   Token Types of ICOs.

Token type	Features	Examples
Usage token	Allowing investors to use a service	Bitcoin, Ethereum, Blocktix, Melon
Work token	Providing the right to contribute work to a decentralised organisation	ORBITS, FirstBlood, Maker
Hybrid token	A combination of the usage token and work token	FIL, ETH (with Casper)
Traditional asset token	Representing a traditional asset cryptographically	USDT, DigixDAO, DC USD

Source: By authors.

2017). The categories are not mutually exclusive as some tokens possess properties of more than one sub-group.

Traditional asset tokens are less commonly seen in the cryptocurrency market. When people refer to crypto-tokens, they usually think of the protocol-based tokens such as Bitcoin, which is governed by a coded protocol enforced by the underlying blockchain technology and generally not linked to any centralised entities or traditional real-world assets (El-isa, 2017). But there is another type of tokens that represent a traditional asset such as fiat money or precious metal. For example, each unit of USDT is (supposedly) backed by USD1 in Tether Limited's reserve account.

Usage tokens, as indicated by the name, can be used to obtain a particular service. Usually, cryptocurrencies are decentralised, and in order to use the service the platforms offer, tokens are required. Some tokens provide payment rights as they are the sole method of payment for the digital services, while others confer access rights, for they are not the only means but small amounts are necessary to use the platform. For example, Blocktix is an Ethereum-based platform for event hosting businesses, and ETH/TIX are the only accepted methods of payment. Majority of tokens fall under this subset as the payment rights, and access rights are an easy and obvious way to use a new digital currency (Chwierut, 2017a). The demand of these tokens relies heavily on the services the platform provides.

Other than the payment and access rights, many tokens offer holders with rights to impact or contribute to the network and system. We call them work tokens. For some work tokens, holders get a portion of fees or revenues generated by the network. A good example will be OBITS, as its owners can share the profits generated by the organisation. Other work tokens enable investors to perform certain actions, including the rights to make impactful decisions for the platforms on matters like additional features, to maintain the network, or to validate block generation. For instance, users of FirstBlood can serve as witnesses to analyse the results of each match with payment for their service, and they are a crucial part of making the decentralised eSport game betting application function.

3.7 Why Is ICO Used

3.7.1 *For tech start-ups*

There is an increase in projects taking part of ICOs for a number of reasons. One is the low costs — ICOs decreases the cost of fundraising to a large extent for start-ups. Compared to traditional VC methods where there are limited investors and thus the funds collected, ICOs are open to the public, allowing the start-ups to raise a large amount of money. Unlike IPOs, ICOs (excluding those falling under the classification of private placement or crowdfunding) do not need to pass any regulatory hurdles such as fulfilling auditing requirement, document preparation or legal clearance.

The second reason ICOs are becoming more popular among start-ups is that they allow the developers to collect the funds without giving up equity or control over the companies. Even with the equity-like tokens where investors can share the profits of the company or help make important decisions for the project, the ownership and control are still at the hand of the start-ups.

On top of getting equity-free funds to kick-start the project, ICOs can provide a way of gauging interest in the project from a wider community, similar to how pre-sales work well for the traditional crowdfunding on Kickstarter (Lea, 2016). The tokens raised can, in turn, help the team to better develop the project to ensure its long-term growth.

3.7.2   *For investors*

There is a high potential for capital appreciation. For example, the price of bitcoin had increased from around USD1,000 at the beginning of 2017 to over USD4,000 in September 2017. Sometimes the surge in price can happen in a short period of time. The market witnessed the price of Ethereum, for instance, increased three times within one month, from less than USD100 in mid-May to nearly USD400 in mid-June 2017.

In addition, the liquidity of cryptocurrencies makes ICO a good solution to the long investment cycle and information asymmetry problems typically seen in traditional VC. ICO projects can successfully launch within months, sometimes even weeks, after the investment. Funds can be transferred in a much easier way and without worrying about borders. Investors simply need to convert the profits into major coins such as bitcoins or Ethers on any of the cryptocurrency exchanges that support them, and then easily change to fiat currency via online services such as Coinsbank or Coinbase (Kastelein, 2017).

Other than liquidity, ICO also offers much more choices for investors and brings benefits to the portfolio through diversification. Although the change in price is often associated with higher volatility, studies have shown that the cryptocurrency can serve as a good alternative investment opportunity as it provides diversification effect to investors' portfolios that consist of mainly traditional asset classes (Lee, Guo and Wang, 2017).

However, the largest risk facing ICOs facilitators and investors are regulatory risks. It is unclear how regulators will deal with cases that are on the borderline. ICOs are inherently cross-border, and that makes compliance to multiple jurisdictions a daunting task. Unlike bitcoin, Ethereum, Zcash and other pioneering cryptocurrencies or tokens, grey-area ICOs and ICOs that are clear violation of security laws and regulations will likely face legal prosecution eventually.

3.8   Status of ICOs

Since the first ICO in 2013, there is an upward trend for the total number of ICOs as well as the amount raised. Based on data from *Coinschedule*, in 2016, over USD96 million were raised, which surpassed the sum of amounts raised for previous three years. While there has been steady growth in the number of ICOs since the beginning, it was not until 2017 that token sales exploded into the mass consciousness. The total number of ICOs has almost tripled since 2016 (Table 3.4). The amount raised surged in the first eight months of 2017 to USD1.5 billion. Furthermore, the scale of the token sales has increased immensely. The largest token sales in 2016 was Waves with USD16 million. In 2017, that number seemed minute as compared to Tezos' USD232 million.

In terms of profitability, as of September 2, 2017, the ROIs of 30 cryptocurrencies have exceeded 1,000% since their ICOs. The highest among them is NXT with 669,638% according to ICOStats.

Historically, VC funding outnumbers ICOs when it comes to funding (see Figure 3.2). In fact, based on the analysis done by Coindesk for the large deals happened in the first quarter of 2017, the amount raised by blockchain ICOs is USD36 million, one-third of the overall blockchain VC investment for the same period (see Figure 3.3). However, another study reveals that ICOs have emerged as the choice of fundraising for early stage blockchain projects by the second quarter of 2017 when taking sales that raised over USD25,000 into consideration, for the token sales so far have outstripped Seed and Series A investment in the industry (Chwierut, 2017b).

3.9   Comparison to Other Fundraising Methods

According to the crypto-focused research group at Smith + Crown, a token sale can be broadly viewed to have the fundraising campaign of a crowdsale, the product maturity of an early-stage angel or VC investment, and the offering of something tradeable like an IPO. Despite the similarities, they differ in many ways, making ICO a class on its own (see Table 3.5).

Table 3.4.   Top Ten ICOs in 2016 and 2017.

Rank	2017^		2016*	
	Project	Amount raised (USD)	Project	Amount raised (USD)
1	Tezos	$232,319,985	Waves	$16,436,095
2	Bancor	$153,000,000	Iconomi	$10,576,227
3	Status	$90,000,000	Golem	$8,596,000
4	TenX	$64,000,000	SingularDTV	$7,500,000
5	MobileGo	$53,069,235	Lisk	$5,700,000
6	Sonm	$42,000,000	Digix DAO	$5,500,000
7	Aeternity	$36,960,594	FirstBlood	$5,500,000
8	Basic Attention Token	$35,000,000	Synereo	$4,700,000
9	Stox	$33,350,320	DECENT	$4,178,357
10	Civic	$33,000,000	Antshares/NEO	$3,608,378
Total Number of ICOs	125		46	
Total Amount Raised		$1,513,379,020		$96,389,917

^Data as of August 20, 2017.
*Data for 2016 exclude "The DAO" that raised USD160 million but was refunded after the smart contract was hacked.
Source: CoinSchedule, https://www.coinschedule.com/

Many perceive ICO for cryptocurrency market as IPO for the stock market, which is only partially true as the differences can easily outweigh the similarities. Buyers invest in ICOs in expectation of a healthy return when there is an increase in the value of the tokens. While it is certain that IPO shares that are not lockup will be traded on the exchanges, tokens given to ICO buyers can only be traded in future, provided that there is a launch of the token. Furthermore, unlike IPOs, regulatory scrutiny over ICOs is yet to grow, as ICOs are easily accessible for both start-ups and investors. There is no disclosure requirement for the fundraisers, nor existence

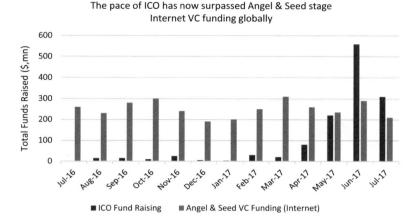

Figure 3.2. ICOs Have More Access to Funds Than Angel & VC Combined.

Source: By authors; CoinSchedule; CB Insights; Goldman Sachs Global Investment Research; CNBC, https://www.cnbc.com/2017/08/09/initial-coin-offerings-surpass-early-stage-venture-capital-funding.html

Figure 3.3. Quarterly Amount of Token Sales Have Crossed USD100 Million.

Source: Smith + Crown, https://www.smithandcrown.com/wp-content/uploads/2017/05/Token-Sale-Market-Overview.png

Table 3.5. Similarities and Differences between ICO and Other Fundraising Methods.

	Crowdfunding	IPO	VC
Similarities with ICOs	— Market campaigns online and via social media — Investing to support a start-up idea	— Investors get a tradeable token (if ICO is successful) — Used to sell a stake and raise money — Have investors who risk the capital to gain a potential profit	— Attempt to earn high-profit margin by engaging in a relatively early stage — Similar risks — Product stage can be similar (business plan or prototype)
Differences with ICOs	— ICO is a mix of donation and investment or risk capital as investors get a tradeable token that has value in a secondary market if the project is successful, while crowdfunding is more like a donation or pre-buy of a product	— Projects are much less mature and usually are not public companies — No requirements for companies to fulfil before initiating an ICO — No (existing) disclosure requirements in ICO — ICOs are open to the general public but mostly supported by investors within the community while IPOs by professional investors — ICOs are not regulated and have no investor verification or protections	— No face-to-face relationship with team when investing in ICOs — Tokens are immediately tradeable — No (existing) disclosure or accredited investor requirements

Source: Smith + Crown; BlockchainHub.

of any screening policies for buyers. ICOs, moreover, are not registered with any governmental organisation, nor do exchanges publish any regulations for the launch of tokens if the project is successful. So, in general, risks associated with ICO are higher, compared to IPO. The price change in cryptocurrency market can fluctuate much, resulting in extremely high returns, but also some huge losses. ICO is simply too "new" to be included in regulatory framework and most regulators are taking a "Wait and Watch" approach.

3.10 Risks Associated with ICOs

3.10.1 *Legal risks*

The legal state of ICOs is mostly undefined or unclear. Token rights may or may not resemble a security. If token rights do not fall under the definition of a security and there are no clear interpretations, it is unclear how to proceed with existing law and regulation. So far, the way to implement the token sale campaign and the procedures are determined solely by the developers. No regulations leads to a lack of standards, which may, in turn, make the surveillance even harder for regulators. Furthermore, it is a chicken-and-egg problem that if no one sets standards, it is unclear who should be the regulator or regulators.

The exchanges where tokens are heavily traded do not have any policies or rules to prevent manipulative and fraudulent acts and to protect investors. Neither periodic disclosure of financial status and risks nor any form of due diligence on the project is in place. What is more, the advantages of ICO compared to traditional fundraising methods may diminish due to the cost and effort to comply with future regulations.

3.10.2 *Lack of transparency*

The success of ICOs or cryptocurrency may have little to do with the services they can provide and how the business model will function in the real world eventually. After all, ICOs are as new experiments. Not all projects will disclose in detail what plan they have with the money raised, how the platform works, what kind of service it provides, what the unique features it possesses, and what problems it can solve. There are some cases that only white paper is published to support the ICO with no elaboration, not even the program code.

In IPOs, companies have to fulfil certain scale requirement which means that they have been operating for quite a while and information of the management team are well disclosed. However, this is not the case for ICOs. A group of technologists who may not know each other can decide to work on a new project as long as they have common interests on certain ideas. Although ICOs are based on the public ledger, blockchains, and the values and amounts of transactions are traceable, the senders or receivers remain anonymous.

3.10.3   *Risk of capital*

Without a proper governance policy to prevent misuse of funds and other misconduct, investors' interests are at risk. For many projects, they raised a large amount of money before they figured out who and how to manage the fund. The absence of external regulations within the cryptocurrency market and disclosure requirements raises the alarm on the need for internal management.

3.10.4   *Loss due to unsuccessful project*

While the number of ICOs goes up, that of projects that made it to a secondary market does not necessarily increase. In fact, based on findings of Smith + Crown, up to mid-May 2017, over 40% of all projects with token sales were active, meaning inactive projects after ICOs accounting for almost 60% of the whole market (Chwierut, 2017b). Therefore, investors should conduct necessary due diligence on the projects to think through before making any decision in pitching in their funds.

3.10.5 *Fraud risks*

There is a potential for project scams and moral hazard. Such projects generally promise the launch of a new cryptocurrency but the intention to deliver falls short. There is little to prevent anyone with bad intention from absconding with the funds they have raised during the token sale.

3.11 State of ICO Regulation

There are a few leading factors, among others, that contribute to the difficulty in regulating ICOs. Regulators will never allow a crisis to develop intentionally and one can expect that there will be regulation for ICOs when necessary. At this moment, there are many regulators who believe it is premature to do so. First of all, there is a lack of consensus on the nature of ICOs. Whether the issuance of such digital tokens are the equivalent to the creation of a new security and thus should come under the oversight and regulation of government or exchanges, remains contentious (Skinner, 2017). In fact, digital tokens share common instruments with all of digital currencies, securities and assets, for it can be used to exchange for certain goods or services like currencies, is viewed as pure investment methods like securities, and has values to perform some special functions like assets. Without the classification, it would be difficult to regulate the market. For example, cryptocurrencies are assets rather than funding or payment instruments according to regulators in Switzerland and Singapore, but there are still no requirements for cryptocurrencies to obtain any approval or license, nor do they regulate the transactions (Keane, 2017).

Another feature of investing in cryptocurrency market also leads to the lack of regulations — no geographic boundary or limits for the investors. Allowing global investors to invest and transact conveniently is one of the important benefits and features of cryptocurrencies. One aspect that makes the jurisdictional lines indistinct is the public and distributed nature of blockchain, involving developers or nodes all around the world under different jurisdictions in the network even though the project itself is located in a certain geography.

Therefore, the cryptocurrency market is pretty much unregulated. In the report published in July 2017 by the FinTech research firm Autonomous NEXT, the author analysed the state of regulation for ICOs in six countries (Lex, 2017).

According to the report, Switzerland and Singapore are the ones that have created a relatively friendly environment and some level of recognition for cryptocurrency market. The Swiss government is exploring the creation of a new regulated entity named "crypto-bank", trying to foster the FinTech and blockchain area. With new phenomenon, a new body is required to deal with the complexity. In Singapore, the Monetary Authority of Singapore (MAS) has set up the Financial Technology and Innovation Group (FTIG). MAS has provided regulatory clarification on digital currencies and crypto-exchanges. FTIG has started projects related to cryptocurrencies and FinTech, one of which is the Project Ubin that will use Distributed Ledger Technology (DLT) to issue Central Bank Digital Money in the first stage and cross-border settlement system in its second stage.

The Financial Conduct Authority in the UK has issued a broad first-stage discussion paper on DLT, but in general, it has taken a neutral approach to DTL as the regulators are waiting to learn from the regulatory Sandbox (Lex, 2017). In other countries, however, cryptocurrencies have not been very welcomed by the authorities.

Russia is planning to shift from being hostile to cryptocurrency historically to making it legal. On 4 September 2017, China's central bank issued a statement and referred to ICO as "a form of unapproved illegal public financing". This is probably due to the speculation by Chinese investors. About half of the ICOs in 2017 took place in China with a sum of RMB2.6 billion or USD398 million (Vincent, 2017). In addition, American regulators have made cryptocurrency companies operation and token issuance difficult.

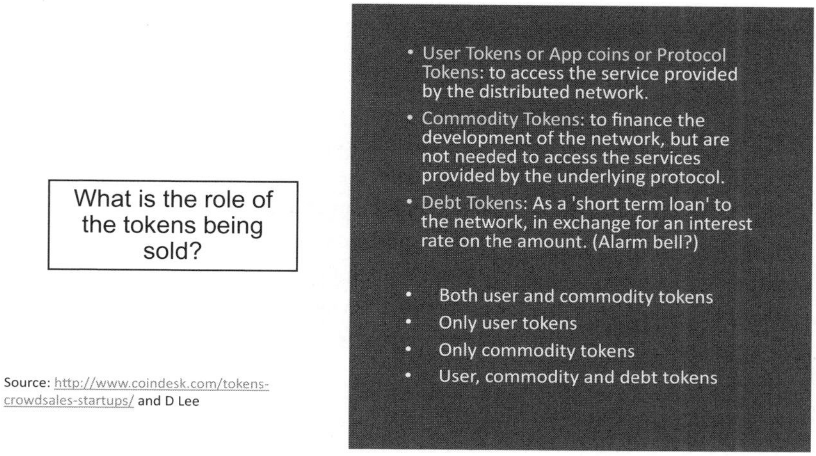

Figure 3.4.   The Role of Tokens.
Source: By authors.

3.12   Discussions

What is the role of the tokens being sold? That is an important question (see Figure 3.4) to determine whether the token sales is a security or a derivative of another security. If they are, then there is likely to have legal implications in violation of security act without proper approval for a public offer. Generally, there are three broad classes of tokens (Breber, 2016):

(1) User Tokens or App Coins or Protocol Tokens: To access the service provided by the distributed network.
(2) Commodity Tokens: To finance the development of the network, but are not needed to access the services provided by the underlying protocol.
(3) Debt Tokens: As a "short-term loan" to the network, in exchange for an interest rate on the amount.

This Chapter has raised some further questions as in Figure 3.5 to highlight that regulating the token economy is complicated. Chwierut (2017a) has given further explanations of what token rights are in

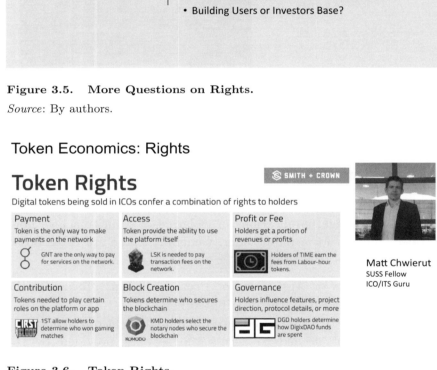

Figure 3.5.   More Questions on Rights.

Source: By authors.

Token Economics: Rights

Figure 3.6.   Token Rights.

Source: Smith + Crown; authors.

Figure 3.6. Tokens may be used as a network payment, as an access right, as an entitlement to profits, as a network contribution, as an entitlement for block creation, or as a voting right. Most of the token rights are associated with access rights as shown in Figure 3.7.

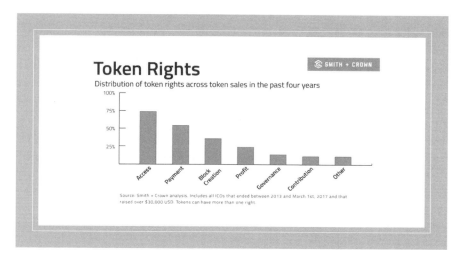

Figure 3.7. Token Rights.
Source: Smith + Crown.

In token economics, a legal air gap is an innovative way to differentiate a security from a non-security. It is delicate. The token design will require professional advice and it is dependent on jurisdictions.

A. In countries where tokens are not securities, the following are noted:

    (1) Award of Contract: A legal entity (e.g. Pte Ltd) awarded a contract by a client (blockchain) to write the code for the blockchain, and subsequently have an ICO/ITS (Initial Crypto-Token Sales/Initial Token Sales) of the resulting blockchain with tokens.

    (2) Commodity Sales: A foundation (e.g. Swiss GmbH-LLC) initiates a sale of a commodity (Fuel/Token) required to run the blockchain on an open source platform.

    (3) CODE: Centralised Organised (CO) legal entity spends the tokens collected from the Decentralised Entity (DE) blockchain ICO/ITS, and the CO also collects the revenue generated after the project of building the app as an example.

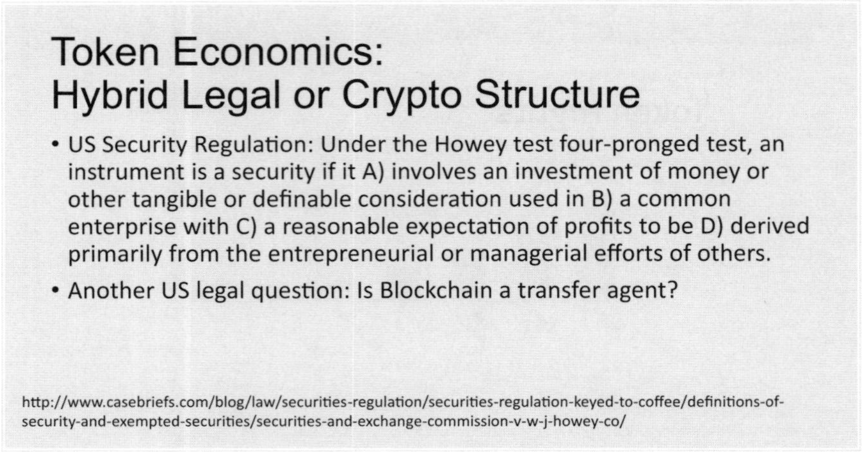

Token Economics:
Hybrid Legal or Crypto Structure

- US Security Regulation: Under the Howey test four-pronged test, an instrument is a security if it A) involves an investment of money or other tangible or definable consideration used in B) a common enterprise with C) a reasonable expectation of profits to be D) derived primarily from the entrepreneurial or managerial efforts of others.

- Another US legal question: Is Blockchain a transfer agent?

http://www.casebriefs.com/blog/law/securities-regulation/securities-regulation-keyed-to-coffee/definitions-of-security-and-exempted-securities/securities-and-exchange-commission-v-w-j-howey-co/

Figure 3.8.   Howey Test.

Source: By authors.

B. Plain Vanilla Token Allocation: Tokens are first mined by allocators and allocated via a computer algorithm that does not specify any specific public addresses to receive funds.

C. Mining: Tokens are simply mined.

Zysman (Zysman, 2017), a practising lawyer in Israel, wrote an interesting article discussing the pros and cons of ICOs. He wrote that in the US, ICO is not all bad because:

(1) Flows of funds are recorded real-time on an open blockchain.

(2) The new JOBS Act Title 3, which opens investment in start-ups to individuals, requires start-ups to publish financials once a year; in contrast, blockchain accounting guarantees their investors financial reporting all year long.

There are also interesting discussions of Howey Test (see Figure 3.11) and he has mentioned the four-pronged tests to determine whether a token is a security. Even if a token is not a security, whether a blockchain is a transfer agent and requires a license to operate is another issue to bear in mind. Some of his arguments and discussions are summarised in Figures 3.9 and 3.10.

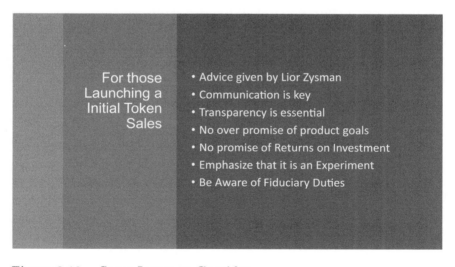

Is ITS Structure all Bad? – Lior Zysman

- The Act also requires businesses to publish a business plan once a year.
- In contrast, some ITS's are powered by transparent open-source code that any machine on a distributed network can run.
- The funds the ITS directs are also published on the blockchain, and the by-laws themselves that determine the relationship between the ICO/ITS participants are embedded in the code.
- The execution of those bylaws and the ITS's accounting don't depend on familiar figures, like the CEO or an auditor, although the status of humans on the edges of the network or curators has never been debated in case law and might be replaced using formal verification methods.
- Given all this, investor expectations, a big concern for lawmakers and regulators, are being met directly by the ITS's code, perhaps for the first time in corporate history.

Amended from https://www.smithandcrown.com/daos-securities-regulation/

Figure 3.9.   Is ITS Structure All Bad?

Source: By authors; Zysman (2016).

For those Launching a Initial Token Sales
- Advice given by Lior Zysman
- Communication is key
- Transparency is essential
- No over promise of product goals
- No promise of Returns on Investment
- Emphasize that it is an Experiment
- Be Aware of Fiduciary Duties

Figure 3.10.   Some Issues to Consider.

Source: By authors.

Figure 3.11.   Issues for Investors.

Source: By authors.

Finally, these are issues of interest to anyone looking at an ICO portfolio (see Figure 3.11). The message is perhaps that while one may wish to participate in financial innovation and sometimes may wish to make hay while the sun shines, bear in mind that FinTech Ponzi is another name of the same to learn and live. One must be afraid to make old mistakes, and must not be afraid to make new mistakes. However, new mistakes must not be so grave to deter one to come back. So one needs to be beware of scams, understand the risk and complexity, invest with restraints, and always diversify.

3.13   Conclusions

ICO has been a popular way for fundraising entities to fuel the blockchain-based projects since 2016. Since the first documented one in 2013, the total number of ICOs launched and the amount raised had surged, to the all-time high in 2017, as a total of USD1.5 billion had been raised for the first eight months in 2017, over 15 times of the total amount raised in 2016. It allows technology start-ups to raise funds more easily at a lower cost within a short period and provides investors with good investment opportunities that are liquid and different from traditional asset classes. Nonetheless, before sending their money to the ICO companies, investors should be aware of the fact that cryptocurrency market is mostly unregulated and the associated risks such as legal risks, potential loss, or fraud risks. The usual caveat emptor[6] applies to ICOs as in any investment.

Some ICOs subject themselves to regulation while others are subject to existing regulation on security issuance. A recent work–around in the US is based on what is called the Simple Agreement for Future Tokens (SAFT) that essentially limits participants in ICOs to "accredited" or "sophisticated" investors, defined as those with an income of at least USD200,000 or net assets above USD1 million.[7] By far, Singapore is among the top three countries that has attracted the most ICOs as the regulation is clear and the regulators are approachable for consultation for those who wish to seek clarity.[8] The general attitude of Singapore towards blockchain and cryptocurrency is more encouraging.[9]

Although regulatory issues and associated risks remain a concern, ICOs show an exciting new frontier, for both types of investors: those who wish to support the innovative world of cryptocurrencies and blockchains; and developers who wish to raise money for the projects. The benefits and features brought by ICOs make the market prominent, and it seems that the trend will continue in the future.

---

[6]The principle that the buyer alone is responsible for checking the quality and suitability of goods before a purchase is made.

[7]https://medium.com/cryptos-today/icos-and-the-saft-why-what-and-how-9dee5 8cc0059

[8]http://www.mas.gov.sg/News-and-Publications/Media-Releases/2017/MAS-cla rifies-regulatory-position-on-the-offer-of-digital-tokens-in-Singapore.aspx

[9]http://www.mas.gov.sg/News-and-Publications/Speeches-and-Monetary-Policy-Statements/Speeches/2017/Economic-Possibilities-of-Blockchain-Technology.aspx

Appendix A: ICO Tabulation

Name	Current price[10]	ICO price[11]	USD raised	Token percentage for investors	First day trading price (USD)	Tokens raised
Tezos	$1.6800	—	232M	90.00%	$0.7894	65,635 BTC; 361,122 ETH
FileCoin	—	—	205M	10.00%	—	—
Bancor	$2.2100	$3.8600	153M	50.00%	$13.7400	396,720 ETH
Status Network Token	$0.0200	$0.0366	102M	41.00%	$0.0618	300,000 ETH
MobileGo	$0.5400	$0.7581	53.07M	70.00%	$2.4500	—
Monetha	$0.1200	—	37M	60.00%	$0.2262	95,000 ETH
Basic Attention Token	$0.2200	$0.0360	36M	66.67%	$0.1682	156,250 ETH
Civic	$0.3900	$0.1000	33M	33.00%	$0.1612	—
ChainLink	$0.2000	$0.0914	32M	35.00%	$0.1565	—
Polybius	$4.9500	$1.7000	31.65M	93.00%	$8.3500	—
Blockmoon Crypto	$0.8000	$1.0000	30M	50.00%	$0.8631	1,142 BT; 73,175 ETH; 32,866 LTC

[10] As at 26 September 2017.
[11] Also known as Average Price.

Storj	$0.5000	$0.4097	30M	17.23%	$0.5221	6,833 BTC
Agrello Delta	$1.1900	—	27.5M	66.60%	$0.4010	148,000 ETH
Stox	$0.5000	$1.8600	27.48M	50.00%	$1.2100	86,206 ETH
Decentraland	$0.0100	—	26.29M	—	$0.0258	117,337 ETH
SONM	$0.0800	$0.0785	26M	74.63%	$0.4167	—
Funfair	$0.0200	$0.0071	26M	21.28%	$0.0174	—
Tierion	$0.0800	$0.0716	25.04M	35.00%	$0.2052	1,732.21 BTC; 71,375.29 ETH
OmiseGo	$10.1100	$0.2738	25M	65.10%	$0.5347	ETH
Monaco	$8.8300	$2.6400	25M	30.00%	$2.2500	71,392 ETH
Aragon	$1.8500	$0.9016	25M	70.00%	$1.4900	275,000 ETH
Aeternity	$1.8500	$0.1950	24.99M	—	$0.6843	1,461.618 BTC; 103,538.569 ETH
Everex	$3.6700	—	22.63M	—	—	45,375 ETH; 1,328 BTC
KickCoin	—	$0.0364	22.34M	74.50%	—	71,837 ETH
Pillar	$0.0700	$0.0416	21.99M	66.00%	$0.0666	113,674.4 ETH
AventCoin	$1.5400	$3.3700	20.20M	60.00%	$4.5200	60,000 ETH
Rivetz	$0.4700	$0.2816	19.71M	35.00%	$0.7347	50,412.77 ETH
MCAP	$2.7600	$3.9800	19.26M	100.00%	$6.7600	—
OpenANX	$0.3800	$0.7503	18.76M	25.00%	$0.3919	52,246 ETH
Ethereum	$292.140	$0.3080	18.5M	83.40%	$2.8300	31,529 BTC
Cosmos	—	$0.1009	17M	—	—	4,870 BTC; 246,890 ETH
Waves	$4.6000	$0.1884	16.01M	85.00%	$1.3300	30,904 BTC

(Continued)

(Continued)

Name	Current price	ICO price	USD raised	Token percentage for investors	First day trading price (USD)	Tokens raised
Qtum	$9.8100	$0.2941	15M	51.00%	$6.4200	11,000 BTC; 75,000 ETH
ATB coin	$1.1800	—	14.98M	—	$1.1300	3,832 BTC; 8,102 ETH; 3,744 LTC; 27 ZCASH
Cofound.it	$0.1400	$0.1184	14.8M	25.00%	$0.2748	56,565 ETH
Propy	$0.5300	$0.4179	14.63M	35.00%	$0.8239	33,991 ETH; 1,019 BTC
Lampix	$0.1000	—	14.61M	50.00%	$0.0804	40,921 ETH
Mysterium	$0.8800	$0.7722	14.4M	57.50%	$2.4500	68,629 ETH
Nimiq Exchange Token	$1.0400	$1.3700	14.4M	5.00%	$1.0300	60,000 ETH
ICOBox	$76.4500	—	14.37M	83.30%	$4.0000	3,290.6216 BTC
TokenCard	$1.6700	$0.5004	12.7M	60.00%	$0.9713	—
Gnosis	$91.2500	$31.2500	12.5M	4.00%	$51.6400	250,000 ETH
DAO.casino	$0.0500	$0.1068	12.5M	70.00%	$0.1386	58,544 ETH
BOScoin	$0.7100	$0.0044	12.2M	55.20%	$0.2360	—
iEx.ec	$0.5500	$0.2027	12.16M	68.96%	$0.3010	2,761.761 BTC; 173,886 ETH
Veritaseum	$78.9000	$6.1200	12M	1.96%	$48.9600	60,000 ETH
Dmarket	—	$0.2576	11.59M	90.00%	—	365 BTC; 26,897 ETH
Substratum Network	—	$0.2157	11.43M	100.00%	$0.4829	—
Primas	$0.2200	$0.2157	11M	51.00%	$0.3759	31,000 ETH

Name						
Viberate	—	$0.0893	10.71M	60.00%	—	—
Iconomi	$1.4900	$0.1257	10.68M	85.00%	$0.1989	—
BitDice	$0.1500	$0.1505	10.23M	68.00%	$0.1105	—
Santiment	$0.3400	$0.2267	10.20M	54.00%	$0.2616	45,000 ETH
Patientory	$0.4700	$0.1453	10.17M	70.00%	$0.6482	46,666.6667 ETH
Blockchain Capital	$1.0100	$1.0000	10M	100.00%	$4.3600	—
Rialto.AI	$0.3500	$0.1333	10M	75.00%	$0.0808	5,936,958 XRP; 25,387.58 ETH; 565.6 BTC
Po.et	$0.0100	$0.0064	10M	50.00%	$0.0215	—
DIMCOIN	—	$3.3200	9.95M	30.00%	—	2,813.51 BTC
Indorse	$0.0800	—	9.61M	35.00%	$0.1991	32,045.413 ETH
district0x	$0.0400	$0.0157	9.41M	60.00%	$0.0187	58,550 ETH
AdEx (ADX)	$0.6100	$0.1130	9.04M	80.00%	$0.2088	40,008.0523 ETH
Populous	$2.6900	$0.2522	9M	67.60%	$2.8100	33,619.7 ETH
Metal (MTL)	$8.8300	$0.4661	9M	29.41%	$1.2200	—
Golem Network Token	$0.2600	$0.0105	8.6M	82.00%	$0.0151	820,000 ETH
Hive	$0.0200	$0.2275	8.53M	75.00%	$0.0135	2,022 BTC
Primalbase	$3,459.6700	—	7.91M	80.00%	$5,344.5000	3,100 BTC
Adtoken	$0.0400	$0.0154	7.70M	50.00%	$0.0595	33,332.9999 ETH
Token as a service	$3.6500	$0.9292	7.57M	100.00%	$0.8199	3,536 BTC; 45,272 ETH; 193,562 USDT
SingularDTV	$0.1800	$0.0150	7.5M	50.00%	$0.0193	—
CoinDash	$0.0400	$1.6300	7.5M	50.00%	$0.0546	—

(Continued)

(Continued)

Name	Current price[10]	ICO price[11]	USD raised	Token percentage for investors	First day trading price (USD)	Tokens raised
BlockCAT	$0.8700	—	7.14M	79.00%	$1.0600	23,799.65 ETH
ZrCoin	$0.9800	$1.4200	7.07M	100.00%	$75.5600	—
Blocktix	$0.1700	$0.1745	6.98M	64.00%	$0.1537	—
iXledger	$0.3100	$0.0695	6.95M	76.92%	$0.0919	—
Social Nexus	$0.2100	—	6.76M	95.00%	$0.3779	21,760.06 ETH
Hubiit	$0.0900	—	6.56M	70.00%	$2.9500	20,125.496 ETH
Maidsafe coin	$0.4900	$0.0142	6.4M	100.00%	$0.0149	26,620 BTC
Wagerr	$0.0700	$0.0375	6.38M	85.00%	$0.0566	—
Lisk	$7.0000	$0.0747	6.35M	85.00%	$2.0400	15,480.52 BTC
True flip Lottery	$0.4900	$0.9122	5.70M	42.50%	$1.3100	1,196.85 BTC; 632.262 LTC; 10,065.340 ETH
Digix DAO	$72.0200	$3.2400	5.50M	85.00%	$31.9000	465,134.95 ETH
Firstblood	$0.3300	$0.0692	5.50M	85.00%	$0.1520	465,312.999 ETH
Time	$18.4200	$8.6400	5.40M	88.00%	$12.8900	—
Exscudo	—	$0.0355	5.35M	62.80%	—	2,314 BTC
Humaniq	$0.1200	$0.0369	5.16M	86.00%	$0.0719	94,500 ETH
Sphre AIR	$0.1800	$0.1887	5.11M	90.00%	$0.1183	2,059 BTC
Mothership	$0.1600	$0.0364	5.10M	70.00%	$0.0401	24,137.4 ETH
Augur	$18.6200	$0.5795	5.10M	80.00%	$1.4700	18,630.8749 BTC; 1,149,880 ETH
Starta	$0.4600	—	5.06M	95.00%	$0.5308	—
DCORP	—	$0.7561	5.05M	82.50%	—	16,907 ETH

Guppy	$0.1800	$0.0833	60.00%	5M	$0.2404	125,000 ETH
Synereo	$0.1600	$0.1587	35.22%	4.7M	$0.0022	—
TrustCoin	$0.3600	$0.0583	80.00%	4.66M	$0.0751	80,092 ETH; 1,048 BTC
EcoBit	$0.0200	—	—	4.50M	$0.0367	—
Peerplays	$3.3800	$4.7000	16.05%	4.50M	$11.2300	—
Presearch	—	$0.0150	30.00%	4.50M		4,500,000 USD
EncryptoTel	$0.0800	$0.0632	70.00%	4.43M	$0.3048	851.84 BTC; 3,742.16 ETH; 2,071,053.30 WAVES
Dent	$0.0000	$0.0005	70.00%	4.20M	$0.0006	21,467.15 ETH
Quantum Resistant Ledger	$0.6500	$0.0790	81.53%	4.16M	$0.7345	—
DECENT	$0.5300	$0.1183	68.00%	4.13M	$0.1102	—
Quantum	$0.1800	$0.0506	33.30%	4.12M	$0.1620	2,417.33 BTC
NVO	$0.3600	$0.2667	50.00%	4M	$0.3931	1,497.22667463 BTC; 765,482 MAID
Crypviser	$0.5000	$0.3862	66.60%	3.87M	$0.3503	86,172,946 BTC; 356,951,631 ETH; 433.423 USD
NEO	$25.8300	$0.3304	23.00%	3.80M	$0.1815	6,119.3 BTC
Bitshares	$0.0800	$0.0110	13.86%	3.60M	$0.0132	5,621 BTC; 415,000 Protoshares

(Continued)

(Continued)

Name	Current price[10]	ICO price[11]	USD raised	Token percentage for investors	First day trading price (USD)	Tokens raised
Lunyr	$8.2800	$1.6100	3.40M	78.00%	$2.4700	47,923 ETH
Skincoin	$0.0200	$0.0371	3.26M	18.00%	$0.0642	14,697 ETH
Melon	$61.0000	$5.8600	2.90M	66.66%	$40.6900	227,000 ETH
MyBit	$2.1600	$1.6600	2.80M	60.00%	$3.3000	10,044 ETH
Suretly	$2.9700	—	2.70M	—	$11.2100	—
Edgeless	$0.9800	$0.0228	2.65M	88.00%	$0.0425	—
ICO OpenLedger	$4.1900	$5.5300	2.61M	100.00%	$0.8066	953 BTC
iDice	$0.4100	$1.2100	2.50M	100.00%	$2.2700	7,400 ETH
CryptoPing	$0.1900	$0.2778	2.50M	90.00%	$0.3192	1,000 BTC
SuperNet	$13.0000	$4.2200	2.41M	70.00%	$5.1702	6,335 ETH
Reality Clash	—	$0.0559	2.41M	43.60%	—	Presale; 1,682 ETH
BitConnect Coin	$118.4300	$0.7143	2.40M	70.00%	$0.1627	—
Mycelium Token	$1,773.0900	$458.5900	2.35M	5.00%	—	5,131.445 BTC
Investfeed	$0.0600	—	2.30M	89.00%	$0.0447	10,420 ETH
COSS	$0.0400	$0.0153	2.30M	75.00%	$0.0353	7,653.1218745453 ETH
Latium	—	$0.2287	2.26M	33.33%	—	1,703.7357 ETH
Corion	—	—	2.01M	51.00%	—	—
Wings DAO	$0.6000	$0.0267	2M	75.00%	$0.0228	—

Legends Cryptocurrency	$1.0800	$1.0000	2M	100.00%	$1.7800	—
Komodo	$1.9500	$0.0220	1.98M	90.00%	$0.1158	2,639 BTC
Intelligent Trading Technologies	—	$0.1256	1.98M	75.00%	—	—
Digital Developers Fund	$0.1500	$0.0073	1.79M	98.80%	$0.2152	6,254 ETH
CounterParty	$10.0800	$0.6622	1.72M	100.00%	$5.8200	2,125.6 BTC
vSlice	$0.7100	$0.0493	1.65M	100.00%	$0.1109	2,112.5 BTC
SunContract	$0.0400	$0.2560	1.64M	80.00%	$0.0361	8,089 ETH
Voise	$2.5300	$1.7700	1.36M	93.00%	—	—
Encrypfen	—	$0.0162	1.29M	80.00%	—	—
Neblio	$1.1300	$0.0957	1.24M	100.00%	$0.6079	289.49871959 BTC
Equibit	—	—	1.3M	—	—	397.615313 BTC; 136,234 USD
Ethbits	$3.3500	$1.1600	1.20M	80.00%	$1.2400	13,644.99 ETH
FundYourselfNow	$1.4000	$0.1535	1.15M	60.00%	$1.1100	5,666.47 ETH
Incent	$0.1800	$0.0478	1.1M	50.00%	$0.0954	1,094 BTC; 1,148,558 WAVES
Starcredits	—	$0.2700	1.08M	20.00%	—	750.57 BTC
BitBay	$0.0200	$0.0011	1.08M	100.00%	$0.0005	3,000 BTC
Databits	$0.5100	$0.0672	1.07M	70.00%	$0.1026	895 BTC
Adelphoi	$0.0900	$0.0317	1.05M	33.33%	$0.2248	430.9 BTC

(Continued)

(Continued)

Name	Current price[10]	ICO price[11]	USD raised	Token percentage for investors	First day trading price (USD)	Tokens raised
Monster Byte Inc	$0.0500	$0.1018	1.02M	25.00%	$0.0501	—
Pluton	$8.7200	$1.2600	1.01M	4.25%	$3.0900	1,122.847 BTC; 20,471.2718400 ETH
ARK	$3.0400	$0.0107	998K	75.00%	$0.0327	177 BTC; 4,691,413 Lisk
ZiftrCoin	$0.2100	—	875K	11.00%	$0.2100	—
Particl	$7.2800	$0.5429	750K	16.50%	$6.8000	590 BTC; 5,150,210 SDC
DigiPulse	—	—	711.66K	98.00%	—	1,862.981 ETH
Paquarium	$0.0900	$0.0005	619.81K	100.00%	$0.2200	182.41 BTC
Stratis	$4.4800	$0.0071	590K	85.70%	$0.0138	915 BTC
Royal Kingdom Coin	$0.2300	$0.2140	577.76K	18.00%	$0.0600	1,925.85 ETH

References and Further Readings

Allison, I. (2016). Ethereum reinvents companies with launch of The DAO. Retrieved from http://www.ibtimes.co.uk/Ethereum-reinvents-companies-launch-dao-1557576

Breber, D. (August 20, 2016). On tokens and crowdsales: How startups are using blockchain to raise capital. Coindesk. Retrieved from https://www.coindesk.com/tokens-crowdsales-startups/

Chwierut, M. (2017a). Token Rights: Key considerations in designing a token economy. Smith + Crown. Retrieved from https://www.smithandcrown.com/token-rights/

Chwierut, M. (2017b). Token sale market performance. Smith + Crown. Retrieved from https://www.smithandcrown.com/token-sale-market-performance/

Coindesk. https://www.coindesk.com/ico-tracker/

CoinSchedule. https://www.coinschedule.com/

El-isa, M. (2017). The difference between protocol tokens and traditional asset tokens. Retrieved from https://medium.com/melonport-blog/the-difference-between-protocol-tokens-and-traditional-asset-tokens-89e0a9dcf4d1

Goodman, L. M. (2014). Tezos — A self-amending crypto-ledger. White paper. Retrieved from https://www.tezos.com/static/papers/white_paper.pdf

Hajdarbegovic, N. (2013). Mastercoin Foundation lets virtual currencies use Bitcoin protocol. Retrieved from https://www.coindesk.com/mastercoin-foundation-virtual-currencies-bitcoin-protocol/

Kastelein, R. (2017). What Initial Coin Offerings are, and why VC firms care. Retrieved from https://hbr.org/2017/03/what-initial-coin-offerings-are-and-why-vc-firms-care

Keane, J. (2017). The state of ICO regulation? New report outlines legal status in 6 nations. Retrieved from https://www.coindesk.com/state-ico-regulation-new-report-outlines-legal-status-6-nations/

Lea, T. (2016). An introduction to Initial Coin Offerings (ICO's) — The venture capital disrupters. Retrieved from https://www.linkedin.com/pulse/introduction-initial-coin-offerings-icos-venture-capital-tim-r-lea

Lee, K. C. D., Guo, L., & Wang, Y. (2017). Cryptocurrency: A New Investment Opportunity? Working paper. Retrieved from https://ssrn.com/abstract=2994097

Lewis, A. (2017). A gentle introduction to Initial Coin Offerings (ICOs). Retrieved from https://bitsonblocks.net/2017/04/25/a-gentle-introduction-to-initial-coin-offerings-icos/

Lex, S. (2017). Token mania. Autonomous NEXT. Retrieved from https://autonomous.app.box.com/v/tokenmania

Reuben, B. (2017). The perfect token sale structure. Retrieved from https://blog.gdax.com/the-perfect-token-sale-structure-63c169789491.

RIALTO.AI. (2017). Understanding RIALTO.AI Crowdsale. Retrieved from https://medium.com/ico-brief/understanding-rialto-ai-crowdsale-ce10616e3033

Skinner, C. (2017). The crazy world of crypto currencies and ICOs. Retrieved from https://thefinanser.com/2017/06/crazy-world-crypto-currencies-icos.html/

Smith + Crown. https://www.smithandcrown.com/wp-content/uploads/2017/05/Token-Sale-Market-Overview.png

Tomaino, N. (2017). On token value. Retrieved from https://thecontrol.co/on-token-value-e61b10b6175e

Vincent, J. (2017). China bans all ICOs and digital currency launches as "illegal public financing". Retrieved from https://www.theverge.com/2017/9/4/16251624/china-bans-ico-initial-coin-offering-regulation

Voshmgir, S. & Kalinov, V. (2017). What is an ICO? Initial Coin Offering — Blockchain tokens. Retrieved from https://blockchainhub.net/ico-initial-coin-offerings/

Xie, L. (2017). A beginner's guide to Tezos. Retrieved from https://medium.com/@linda.xie/a-beginners-guide-to-tezos-c9618240183f

Zysman, L. (September 30, 2016). DAOs and securities regulation. Smith + Crown. Retrieved from https://www.smithandcrown.com/daos-securities-regulation/

Chapter 4

The Characteristics of Token Investors

Written Jointly and Mainly Contributed by Matt CHWIERUT,
Weston ANDERSON, Brian LIO and Brant DOWNES

4.1 Introduction

Initial coin offerings or token sales have become a popular way for
companies (projects) to raise money (tokens or cryptocurrencies)
over the blockchain. In this event, a company issues a digital
token that it sells to people around the world; money or tokens
(cryptocurrencies) raised is used to build products and services that
can cause the newly created project token or coins to increase in
value. Token sales are becoming more popular but are still markedly
understudied. This Chapter provides an overview of the token sale
market and investments, and characterises token sale investors. Our
analysis makes use of two primary datasets — transaction histories
for six token sales, and a public survey implemented by CoinFund, a
blockchain fund. Overall, we find that token sale investors contribute
to sales at a wide range of participation levels, ranging from
$1 to $100,000, with a typical participation of less than $500.
Token sale investors themselves come primarily from the technology
industry, and most have some experience with traditional investment
decision-making. Many have over half of their investment holdings
in blockchain-based assets. Their participation and engagement in

125

learning about the industry vary greatly, and those with more exposure to the industry tend to spend more time learning about it. Token sale participants approach opportunities from a variety of perspectives — as investors interested in profit, as enthusiasts looking to support the emerging industry, and as future users. This Chapter concludes with takeaways for entrepreneurs, investors, and policy makers, and provides questions for further research.

Blockchain start-ups can raise development funds in several ways, including loans, donations, traditional venture capital, and token sales, also commonly known as initial coin offerings (ICOs). ICOs have become an important method for raising funds and building community in the blockchain industry. The earliest blockchains, such as Bitcoin in 2008, were launched without formal investment rounds by simply uploading open source code to the Internet (Nakamoto, 2008; Smith + Crown, 2017a). Over time, communities developed around Bitcoin and other blockchains to provide the hardware infrastructure needed to validate transactions and support the exchange of crypto-assets (Chwierut, 2016a). As the blockchain industry and the cryptocurrency economy evolved, blockchain start-ups began offering their tokens in crowdsales prior to a formal launch of their network. In addition to helping raise development funds, these token sales facilitated the organisation of networks of users and contributors required for a successful launch of a blockchain protocol (Kalla, 2016). They are an example of what Professor David Lee calls the "4Ds" of the new digital economy: digitalisation, disinter-mediation, democratisation, and decentralisation (Lee, 2017). Token sales digitise the capital raising process for early-stage companies by collecting digital blockchain-secured currency; disintermediate it by excluding brokers and investment banks that traditionally mediate capital raises; democratise it by removing restrictions on who can participate; and decentralise it by raising funds in a crowdsale-like process from anyone around the world.

Despite the growing importance of token sales, little is known about token sale investments. This lack of data is largely due to the opaque and informal nature of the cryptocurrency community. In traditional investment markets, laws around investment contracts and capital markets in most countries proscribe degrees of transparency and investor protection. In contrast, for token sales, there are no existing requirements for transparency and little information about investors. Token sales are not registered with any government or private agencies, lack advertising requirements or limitations, and allow anonymous contributions over the Internet. This means that virtually anyone with an Internet connection and access to cryptocurrency could be a potential token sale investor. This presents challenges to entrepreneurs, investors, policy makers and regulators.

Entrepreneurs need information on who the potential investors are and how to communicate with them most effectively. This is important because token sales not only raise capital but also build a community, and it can be challenging to know which audiences to target. It can also be difficult to plan future fundraising scenarios without a broader understanding of token sale investors. Investors could benefit from investor profiles indicating who is typically investing in these opportunities. In venture capital fundraising, investors can usually see the cap table showing who has previously invested, and the equity they hold. In token sales, investment amounts are publicly displayed on public blockchains, but who makes those investments is generally only known by the investors themselves and (if the sale in question follows know your customer (KYC) standards) the token sale operators. Finally, as policy makers and regulators develop and enforce regulations over this industry, they too would benefit from a deeper understanding on token sale investors.

This Chapter considers two questions about token sale investments: first, what is the investment pattern (if any) for individual token sales? Second, who are token sale investors? To explore investment patterns, we analyse transaction histories related to six token sales spread across three years. As to the question of who invests in token sales, because token sale contributions are anonymous, it is virtually impossible to know exactly who invests, or even how many people invest, in a given sale. Even public conversations about token sales are limited to several social media channels in which people use pseudonyms to share information and opinions. In order to characterise token sale investors and answer our second research question, we analyse the results of a survey conducted by CoinFund, a blockchain fund. We use the survey to describe token sale investors along with several dimensions, including demographic information, professional and investment background, participation size, and exposure to crypto-tokens.

Overall, our analysis shows that anyone can be a token sale investor, regardless of prior investment experience and age. In addition, investors participate in token sales at levels ranging from $1 to over $50,000 with the typical investment below $500. Those who contribute large sums make up a small portion of overall investors but usually contribute a majority of total capital raised. A strong predictor for how much an investor will contribute is his or her overall exposure to blockchain-based assets; token sale investors include both aspiring future users and investors. Before we discuss the data and present our analysis, we first define token sales and offer a brief history and description of the token sale market.

4.2   Token Sales: Definition and Classification

A token sale is a method of raising funds, generally for early-stage start-ups in the emerging blockchain industry (Investopedia, 2017; Kalla, 2016). Hull et al [n.d.] define a token sale as "a public offering of a new cryptocurrency related to a venture, typically for the purpose of starting that venture" or funding future growth. Product tokenisation, the practice of integrating cryptocurrency into some aspects of a venture's business model, is a requisite of raising funds through a token sale and the primary factor that differentiates token sales from crowdsales, venture capital, and other sales of equity. Crowdsales sell off completed products at discounted prices and are open to the general public, while venture capital agreements involve the sale of equity shares to a small cohort of stakeholders. Neither crowdfunding nor venture capital results in liquid secondary markets. Like crowdsales, token sales are often (but not always) open to the public, but do not involve the sale of a final product. Instead, token sales involve the distribution of crypto-tokens that represent value in a final product and lead to the establishment of liquid secondary markets (Kalla, 2016). While token markets may resemble traditional markets for stocks and bonds because they are as liquid as stocks and are typically viewed as a good indicator of a project's value, they do not represent ownership of the company or provide their holders with any legal rights (Kalla, 2016).

Entrepreneurs can integrate crypto-tokens into their business model by offering several distinct classes of tokenised products. Tokenisation involves linking a cryptographic token to a product's value. This is generally achieved by creating a token that grants its holder certain rights on the network. We suggest classifying token rights into seven distinct categories based on a review of tokens offered in public sales since 2013. These categories are: access rights, payment rights, profit sharing rights, voting rights, block creation rights, contribution rights, and asset ownership rights (Chwierut, 2017a). We describe each category in Table 4.1.

4.3   Token Sale History

A brief review of the history of token sales shows that interest and activity in this area have grown rapidly since 2013. The first token sale was held in 2013; from there, the token sale market grew slowly until 2016 when it rapidly expanded (Kalla, 2016; Chwierut, 2017b).

As Table 4.2 shows, in 2016, there were 69 token sales that raised more than \$25,000, almost seven times as many as in 2015 (11), and four times as many as in 2014 (16).[1] The total amount of capital earned through token sales in 2016 was over \$101.3 million, more than double what was raised in the previous three years combined (\$41.8 million). In 2017, the token sale market continued to surpass previous benchmarks. In the first four and a half months of 2017, 59 token sales were successfully completed, raising a total exceeding \$340 million, more than three times the amount raised in all of 2016. The trends of both the number of token sales and the amounts raised increasing strongly were clearly very powerful in early 2017.

---

[1]Unless otherwise stated, all dollar values are reported as USD.

Table 4.1.   Token Rights.

Token category	Description	Example
Access rights	Required to access a platform, transact across the platform, or prove membership	*Ethereum*: Small amounts of fractional Ether called Gas are required to execute smart code/make transactions
		Legends Room Token: Required to access the VIP lounge of a Las Vegas club
Payment rights	Only accepted form of payment for goods and services offered by the company	*Golem*: Native token used to pay for services rendered on the network of the distributed supercomputing project Golem
Profit rights	These most resemble traditional stocks in that they represent partial ownership of the profits generated by the company	*DigixDAO Tokens*: Give holders a portion of fees generated through the sale of Digix precious metals tokens
Voting rights	Allow holders to participate in network governance. Most often, voting rights tokens are used in a liquid democracy where every token is worth a single vote	*Aragon Network*: Aragon tokens provide their holders with a vote in the Aragon DAO. Token holders are entitled to weigh in on blockchain protocol changes as well as many business decisions
Block creation rights	Allow users to participate in a block creation consensus process — The means by which the nodes of a blockchain network maintain consensus about the state of the ledger	Typically, any project that utilises a Proof-of-Stake-based consensus process will issue a token that has block creation rights. STEEM.it, a decentralised social network, is one example

(Continued)

Table 4.1. *(Continued)*

Token category	Description	Example
Contribution rights	Grant holders the right to contribute to or perform certain functions on the network	*First Blood*: An e-Sports tournament platform on which users with enough 1ST tokens can run "witness" nodes to validate game outcomes. These users receive a portion of fees collected over the network
Asset ownership rights	Asset ownership tokens are backed by a defined quantity of a good or product	*Tether*: A currency pegged to the value of USD and backed 1 to 1 by USD reserves
		Zrcoin: Each token is redeemable for 1kg of zirconium oxide, an industrial product used in kilns and refineries

Source: By authors.

Table 4.2. Token Sale Market Overview.

Year	Number	Amount raised	Average	Median
2013	1	$682,000	NA	NA
2014	16	$29,550,000	$1,846,000	$555,000
2015	11	$11,325,000	$1,029,000	$557,000
2016	69	$101,381,000	$1,469,000	$367,000
2017	59	$340,470,000	$5,770,000	$1,274,000

Total Token Sales: 156
Source: Smith + Crown data.

2017 was a record-breaking year for token sales. In March 2017, Qtum, a China-based blockchain infrastructure platform, became the most lucrative token sale in history with a raise of $15.8 million. This broke Ethereum's record of $15.2 million, which it held for roughly 18 months. However, Qtum held that record for less than a month.

In April 2017, the Cosmos Network raised $16.8 million in their token sale. Aragon broke that record again in May 2017 when it raised $24.5 million. This trend of increasing raise amounts was clearly just getting underway; three sales concluded at the end of May 2017 after raising more than $25 million each. Equally significant, these record-breaking token sales were not the only noteworthy aspect of early 2017's sales: the breadth of sales in terms of both the range of projects and the substantial number of sales raising amounts greater than $5 million was strong evidence of a transformative period of significant growth for the industry. A further indication of strength of the token sale markets in early 2017, was that through March 2017, the median raise for token sales year-to-date was around $1.65 million, more than triple 2016's median of $367,000.

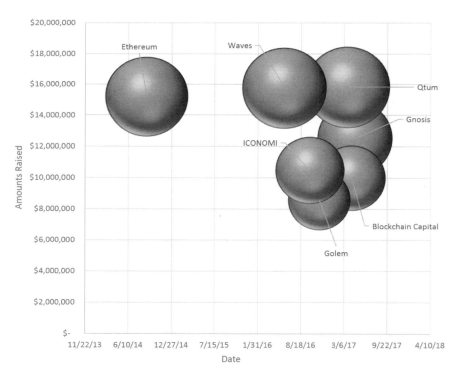

Figure 4.1.   Largest ICOs through 30 April 2017.

Source: Smith + Crown data.

While the opening four months of 2017 represented an unprecedented period for the ICO market, the next four months from May to August were even stronger, developing into yet another record-setting period strongly suggesting that even greater momentum was shifting towards the industry as both interest in and capital available for ICOs grew dramatically. Bolstered by significant price increases in bitcoin and Ethereum, the two most well-known cryptocurrencies, the entire ICO industry appeared to undergo a step-change as it moved to a new and previously unknown level, by virtually any metric one cared to consider.

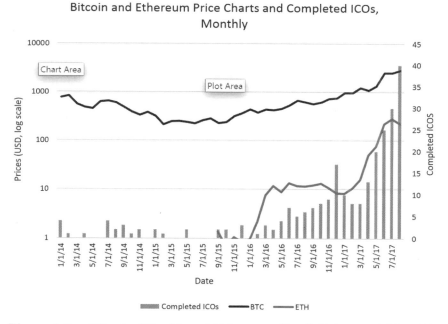

Figure 4.2.   Bitcoin (Black) and Ethereum (Red) Prices and Monthly Token Sales.

Source: Smith + Crown data.

The sheer number of sales was one striking indication of the enthusiasm of the market for new token sales. In 2017, May–August saw 115 sales being completed, sizeable growth over the preceding period and dwarfing the 22 sales completed during the same period in 2016. Equally impressive was the amount of capital these sales generated, with nearly $1.7 billion raised. If two large sales completed during the first half of September were added, the amount for the period rose to nearly $2 billion. Also noteworthy is that while 2016 represented a record-breaking year in the ICO markets when more than $101 million was raised from investors, this middle third of 2017 saw four individual sales exceed $100 million, with two of them raising more than $225 million! Figure 4.3 shows the growth of ICO activity from 2014 to mid-2017. In particular, the steady rise in the number of token sales suggests the activity is gaining momentum, while the sharp rise and fall of the monthly amount raised shows the influence in the second quarter of sales that raised over $100 million. Amidst this period that saw a record number of sales, record amount raised, and largest individual sales, the average amount raised unsurprisingly rose as well, to $13.6 million, leaping past earlier averages and raising the 2017 YTD average amount raised to $10.9 million.

In terms of individual record-breaking sales, Qtum's record of a $24.7 million token sale established in mid-May was surpassed three more times even before May had ended, by Storj ($30 million), MobileGo ($53.9 million) and Basic Attention Token ($35.9 million). Those sales were themselves quickly exceeded by both Status ($101 million) and Bancor ($148 million) in June, in addition to an additional five sales exceeding Qtum's previous record during June. The trend continued in July, with both Polybius Bank and PressOne exceeding $30 million, with Tezos also establishing a new record during this period when it raised $233 million in one sale. August 2017 then saw six sales exceeding $25 million (Stox, Tierion, 0x, Decentraland, Montha, and Everex). Finally, early September saw Tezos' previous all-time record broken when Filecoin raised $262 million from investors for its decentralised storage project. Figure 4.4 shows how quickly the projects in the industry broke previous records for total amount raised in a token sale.

Historically, venture capital has dwarfed token sales as a form of funding. As seen in Table 4.3, in 2014 blockchain start-ups raised a total of $302 million in venture capital but only $30 million through

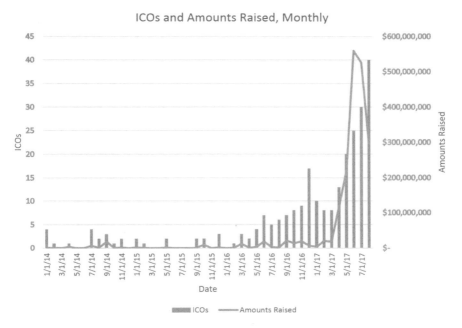

Figure 4.3. Token Sales and Total Amounts Raised (USD).

Source: Smith + Crown data.

token sales (CoinDesk, 2017). In 2015, venture capital raised 24 times as much seed and Series A investments in the blockchain industry as token sales did. In 2016, however, the number of successful token sale projects increased, and we argue that this signals venture capital's declining dominance in the blockchain industry. In early 2017, blockchain start-ups raised more early investment capital through token sales than traditional venture capital. During the second quarter of 2017, the amount of early-stage investment in blockchain projects via token sales had surpassed the amount raised in venture capital for any quarter on record. If this trend continues, token sales will be recognised as the funding route of choice for early-stage blockchain projects.

As the volume of sales has risen, investor interest has also increased. High profile periodicals including Wired, Bloomberg, Harvard Business Review, and The Economist published articles

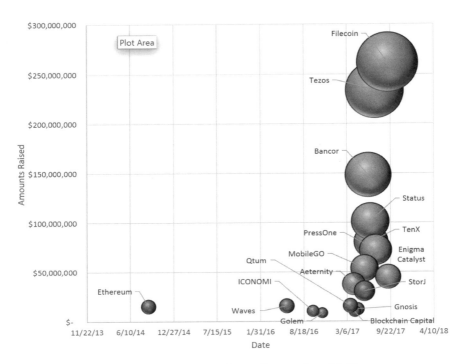

Figure 4.4. Largest ICOs through 15 September 2017.

Source: Smith + Crown data.

Table 4.3. Token Sales vs Venture Capital (VC) Fundraising.

Year	Raised in token sales	Raised in early VC
2013	$682,000	$64,490,000
2014	$29,550,000	$301,980,000
2015	$11,325,000	$271,930,000
2016	$101,381,000	$277,810,000
Q1 2017	$38,504,000	$34,800,000
Q2 2017	$302,966,000	$193,200,000

Total Respondents: 173
Source: CoinDesk.

about token sales in the first several months of 2017 (Kastelein, 2017; Laurent, 2017; Metz, 2017; The Economist, 2017). We attribute the attention received by token sales to the perception that they are a high-reward, high-risk investment opportunity open to anyone, irrespective of his or her income or experience. Unlike traditional equity, which often has a high barrier to entry, virtually anyone can become a token sale investor and reap the rewards of the speculative market for crypto-tokens. This perception is at least partially based on fact. Since mid-2016, the price of bitcoin has nearly tripled (Smith + Crown Markets; CoinDesk BTC Price). However, bitcoin is not the only cryptocurrency to provide large returns on investment. Ethereum enjoys little of bitcoin's notoriety in mainstream media, but since its launch in 2015, Ethereum's price has increased almost 400 fold (Coinmarketcap). These rates of return are higher than for most other investment opportunities on the market.

Ethereum has also contributed to the rising rate of activity in the token sale market by making it easier for projects to launch their own crypto-tokens and raise funds through a token sale. Ethereum is a platform that supports the issuance of meta tokens, which are tokens that have their own independent functions, governance, and token economies, but exist on a host blockchain. Although it was not the first meta-token platform, Ethereum was the first blockchain platform to support the execution of arbitrarily complex programs, making it an attractive option for developers who want to launch tokens that have more complex functions than can be supported by the Bitcoin protocol. Since the Ethereum network launched in mid-2015, the number of projects hosted there has increased steadily. In the second quarter of 2017, Ethereum meta-tokens accounted for more than 65% of token sale projects. The rise of Ethereum has not stopped projects from launching new blockchains; other meta-token platforms have also recently gained popularity, most notably WAVES, which has become host to many of the tokens launched by projects based in Eastern Europe and Russia.

One of the major impacts of the growth in token sale activity is how the expanding number of sales has both required and shaped an evolving set of practices and procedures surrounding token sales. The earliest token sales represented both a novel form of fundraising, as discussed, and projects targeting relatively modest amounts raised. In many cases, the earliest ICOs had a limited public presence and hardly a mention in the popular press or mainstream investment commentaries, and thus were primarily engaging with investors and supporters already interested in and familiar with the emerging technologies allowing these innovations. In important ways, all of the above combined to create a situation where the earliest ICOs were completed on the backs of white papers that focused much more on the technical innovations and ambitions of the projects, and much less on questions such as corporate strategies, what rights or revenue streams token holders had a claim on, whether the company would publish investor updates or financial statements, and in some cases even the identity of founders and team members. Thus, contributions were usually accepted anonymously as that was generally seen as embodying the spirit of the new decentralised entities being established on and around the new blockchain technology. Given the modest scale of these early operations, whether in total amounts raised or in amounts contributed by individuals or single entities, and the largely unknown state of the industry, these practices were largely considered satisfactory at the time.

Just as comparing the quantity of funds raised from token sales in 2017 to amounts raised in 2013 suggests an almost entirely different industry in terms of scale and scope, so too have many of the practices and customs around token sales evolved over time. These evolutions have been in response to three themes that have emerged as significant aspects of the industry. One is continuing investor demand for information such as increased disclosure around token sales and the companies holding them. Two is regulatory interest in the sector that has emerged in part as increasingly large sums are raised from investors. Three is unfortunate series of hacks and thefts that have led companies to improve their procedures surrounding events like token sales. Innovations such as fuller disclosures in white papers have increased the ability of analysts and investors to better understand and more fully analyse these companies. Newer practices such as KYC and anti-money laundering (AML) procedures have also become increasingly common as companies seek to ensure they do not fall afoul of regulators within a broader legal and regulatory climate that remains highly opaque. Finally, while ICO's have been largely conducted by honest entrepreneurs sincerely focused upon advancing their projects, and as such have not suffered major thefts or scams obviously attributable to management or insiders, a number of hacks have resulted in investors losing substantial amounts, in some cases millions of dollars. Although these losses have been painful for those involved, they have also been instrumental in propelling the industry forward towards an emerging consensus on the nature of best practices for different situations and events within the industry, and have helped to reduce the size and frequency of thefts. These efforts have also played a part in improving the image of the sector, and in allowing increasingly wider pools of investors and institutions to feel comfortable investing in the space. We anticipate this trend to continue as practices within the industry come to resemble, at least in terms of clarity of reporting and both initial and ongoing disclosure, the standards to which investors in other industries are accustomed to.

The preceding review of token sales shows a field that is growing rapidly. Development and sales of diverse types of crypto-tokens have expanded dramatically over the past four years, and now represent an important source of start-up funds. However, it is not clear whether investment patterns in this new market follow existing trends, for example, similar to those of venture capital investment, or whether they represent new behaviour on the part of investors. Similarly, the nature of investor decisions regarding investment in token sales has not yet been studied but has clear implications for the continued growth of the market and the success of token offerings.

To address the lack of knowledge on token sale investments and investors, we analyse data on recent token sales and present the results of a survey of token investors. First, we describe data on token sales and investments that we use to characterise the token sale market. Second, we discuss a recent survey of token sale investors.

4.4   Token Sales and Investments

Smith + Crown maintains a database of select token sales that have raised money over the public blockchain ledger. For this analysis, we downloaded transaction-level data from the Ethereum blockchain (accessed through etherscan.io), the Bitcoin blockchain (accessed through blockexplorer.com), and the Omni protocol (accessed through omnichest.info). The sample includes token sale data for several new funding events including:

- **DECENT Software:** DECENT Software will be a digital content-distribution network, with an initial soft focus on video content. Its white paper lays out several challenges in existing content-distribution that DECENT aims to solve, including censorship, poor relationships between consumers and content-producers, and existing distribution channels taking a large portion of payments. DECENT uses its own blockchain, which stores file metadata, proof of custody/authorship, proof of payments, and feedback from consumers about the content itself. The token sold is called decent content token (DCT), which represents the fuel and payment mechanism for the network. It can be used to buy content on the network and to pay storage fees for Publisher nodes (Chwierut, 2016b).

- **DAC Play:** Decentralised Autonomous Corporations (DACs) represent one of the most interesting and potentially disruptive applications of blockchain technology. DACs contain the power to automate and organise complex processes, systems and organ-isations (e.g., corporations) that previously would have been impossible to move outside of a human control structure. At their simplest level DACs allow for much the same concept as the blockchain itself — the ability for individuals to collaborate, trade or otherwise transfer information via a system that provides a set of rules that are known and inflexible. While the blockchain itself is a way to store information (what addresses hold which units of currency), DACs allow for a more complex set of rules to be implemented amongst a group, especially around the control of financial resources (Lio, 2016).

- **Ethereum:** Ethereum was the first cryptocurrency to feature a Turing-complete programming language to execute smart contracts on a blockchain. It is one of the most ambitious "Bitcoin 2.0" technologies. The Ethereum team introduced several new technologies to blockchain tech. Most significantly, the programming language Solidity allows developers to write code for complex transactions that are not supported by the Bitcoin protocol. Ethereum also uses a custom hashing algorithm called Ethash that is ASIC resistant. Due in a large part to their smart contract technology, Ethereum has become a popular platform to build decentralised applications, Decentralised Autonomous Organisations, and launch meta-tokens. On 2 September 2014, Ethereum's 42-day public crowdsale ended. They raised 31,591 bitcoin, worth over $18 million at that time of the sale's close. However, the Ethereum foundation ended up with a lower dollar value because of a subsequent drop in the price of bitcoin before the foundation decided to sell their bitcoin (Smith + Crown, 2017b).
- **First Blood:** First Blood is a platform that lets e-Sports players challenge each other to competitive games and win rewards. Players put up a stake of in-platform tokens, similar to a wager on who will win the game. The system is made possible by smart contracts and decentralised Oracles on the Ethereum blockchain, and it utilises 1ST tokens, which were sold in the sale. Initially, they will stake in 1ST tokens through smart contracts that serve as escrow, but in the future, First Blood plans to include other cryptocurrencies. First Blood's crowdsale ended within minutes of launching: $5.5 million raised in what must be the quickest major cryptocurrency crowdsale to date. First Blood partnered with Chinese exchange Yunbi to host the sale to a Chinese-speaking audience. Yunbi purchased a large share of tokens and resold them on their platform. Our analysis counts as investments the resale of tokens from Yunbi to their customers (Chwierut, 2016c).
- **Matchpool:** Matchpool is a platform intended to facilitate matchmaking economies in dating communities. The platform is built around exclusive dating communities called pools. Individuals will be able to create their own matchmaking pools via the Matchpool

mobile app, curated according to demographics, geography, and interests. Like Tinder, Facebook profiles will be used to verify user identities. Users who fit a pool's curation parameters are able to join as subscribers using GUP, the native token of Matchpool. The team has described a pool as "a slack group with payment rules". Users can join multiple pools. Although the first implementation will be dating, the team is interested in exploring social networking solutions for other industries including education, health, and recruitment (Weiler, 2017).

- **Project Decorum:** Project Decorum is intended as a decentralised social communication platform built on the SAFE network. The platform's Clike tokens can be used as a special endorsement type for content. The sale lasted from April 2016 to May 2016 and raised approximately \$422,000 in Bitcoin and MAID.

Our analysis examines investment-level data for the aforementioned token sales. We look at the average and median investment, the total number of investors, and the percentage of the amount raised was attributable to a smaller number of investors.

4.5   CoinFund Survey Data

In early 2016, CoinFund, a private investment fund and research group focused on blockchain technology, conducted a survey about token sales across multiple channels. CoinFund manages a \$1 million portfolio spread across a variety of blockchain-based assets, as well as a community on Slack focused on tracking new projects and companies in the blockchain industry. It advertised its survey on its Slack channel, several Reddit posts, Twitter, and private direct outreach. The survey was only available in English. It has made its data and initial findings public.[2]

The survey asked about the following topics:

- Demographic information, including age and region;
- Professional background;

---

[2]https://www.reddit.com/r/ethereum/comments/62q1ah/thank_you_for_particip ating_in_the_coinfund/

- Prior investment experience;
- Participation in token sales and exposure to blockchain-based assets;
- Thoughts on the future of the blockchain industry;
- Hypothetical participation in a potential token sale.

The total sample comprised 224 responses. Our analysis focuses on the subsample of respondents who indicated they typically participated in token sales at a level of \$1 or more ($N = 173$), although the survey also captured people who held blockchain-based assets but did not participate in token sales. We first describe the subsample and comment on its limitations as a representative sample of token sale investors. Then we explore several key variables in the survey to glean insights into token sale investors. Finally, we look at correlations among key variables using a series of chi-square tests. The first series looks at the strength of association between typical participation levels in token sales and several other key variables. The second series looks at the strength of association between total investment exposure to blockchain-based assets (as a percentage of one's total investments) and other key variables. For the chi-square tests, we omitted two respondents who gave uninterpretable responses to the question of how much of their total investments were held in blockchain-based assets.[3]

4.6 Blockchain Investments Analysis

In this section, we examine descriptive data from DECENT, Ethereum, DAC Play, First Blood, Matchpool and Decorum token sales between 2013–2017. The number of transactions involved in each token sale varied dramatically. In this analysis, we treat each investment as a different investor. This will likely overestimate participation, because investors can send funds from multiple addresses. Table 4.4 summarises the distribution of investments made in each token sale we examine.

---

[3]https://www.reddit.com/r/ethereum/comments/62q1ah/thank_you_for_particip ating_in_the_coinfund/. Enough to resist recoding into an existing category. Their exclusion did not significantly alter the results of the chi-square test.

Table 4.4.   Token Sale Investment Distribution.

	DECENT	DAC Play	Ethereum	First Blood	Matchpool	Decorum	Averages
Mean	$6,189	$2,325	$2,031	$777	$2,545	$1,023	$2,482
Median	$1,164	$512	$483	$150	$254	$345	$485
Amount invested by top 10%	66%	14%	24%	70%	82%	58%	52%
Share of total invested							
$1 – $1,000	5%	2%	11%	1%	6%	21%	8%
$1,001 – $5,000	15%	25%	18%	10%	14%	42%	21%
$5,001 – $10,000	6%	11%	13%	13%	11%	18%	11%
$10,001 – $50,000	22%	38%	25%	25%	23%	19%	27%
$50,001 or more	52%	25%	33%	33%	46%	0%	34%
Share of investments							
$1 – $1,000	45%	65%	75%	33%	73%	77%	61%
$1,001 – $5,000	42%	25%	18%	42%	18%	19%	27%
$5,001 – $10,000	6%	5%	4%	6%	5%	3%	5%
$10,001 – $50,000	5%	6%	2%	5%	3%	1%	4%
$50,001 or more	2%	>1%	>1%	2%	1%	>1%	1%
Total Invested	$3,658,000	$628,000	$18,291,000	$5,514,000	$6,253,00	$434,000	$5,796,000
Total Investments	589	269	8,948	590	2,456	415	2,211
Dates	Nov. 2016	Feb. 2015	Sep. 2014	Sep. 2016	Apr. 2017	May 2016	

Source: CoinFund Survey.

DAC Play had the least number of investments, at 269. Ethereum had by far the most at 8,948. The next highest was Matchpool at 2,456. First Blood had 590, including the sales that occurred on Yunbi, and DECENT had 589. Finally, Decorum had 415. The average number of participants was 2,211, though the range is quite broad. In general, sales with more investors raised more money. While unsurprising, this finding should reinforce the importance of investor education and develop a following within the community.

The average amount invested in individual transactions ranged quite significantly from \$700 (First Blood) to over \$6,000 (DECENT), though the other four sales were more tightly clustered. Matchpool had an average investment of \$2,545. DAC Play's average investment was \$2,325. Ethereum's was \$2,031.10. Finally, Project Decorum's was \$1,023. For all token sales examined, the average mean investment amount was \$2,482. This is far more than the \$80 average pledged on Kickstarter, a finding which reinforces the distinction between Kickstarter-style crowdfunding and token sales.[4] The projects that were closest to this average varied widely in how much they raised: Ethereum raised just over \$18 million, Matchpool raised just over \$6 million, and DAC Play raised just over \$600,000.

In all sales, the median amount invested was lower than the average, implying a long tail of large investments and a cluster of many smaller ones. First Blood had the lowest median at \$150. Matchpool had the next lowest at \$254. Project Decorum had \$345. Ethereum had \$482.51. DAC Play had \$512. Finally, DECENT had \$1,164, the highest median. DECENT also had the highest average. This suggests that over half of many token sale investments were fairly small — less than \$500.

While the majority of token sale investments are less than \$1,000 — and in many sales, less than \$500 — the total amount invested was highly influenced by larger investments, so-called "whales".

In DECENT, over half of the total amount of funds raised came from investments valued at \$50,001 or more. First Blood and

---

[4] As of 25 May 2017, 3,060,155,733 had been given in 38,277,059 pledges. Numbers taken from https://www.kickstarter.com/help/stats, accessed on May 25, 2017.

Matchpool also had almost all of their funding from investments of this magnitude. Project Decorum had no investments of this size and most of its funding came from smaller investments, valued at $1,000–5,000. This suggests that there are projects that fail to gain the outsized support of larger investors and are instead more strongly supported by a grassroots community. Ethereum is the sale in which total funds raised came from the broadest distribution of investment levels: even small investments of $1–1,000 made up over 10% of the funds raised. Ethereum has emerged as having one of the strongest with more widespread developments and user communities. Many factors contributed to this, but the broad base of people who invested to enable Ethereum's creation has helped.

Some sales had most of their funds come from larger investments, on the order one would typically find in a seed stage start-up investment round: $10,000 or more. Four of the sales had around two-thirds of the funding come from large investments. The concentration of investment and, by extension, token ownership is concerning for projects that want to distribute their tokens widely. Individuals with large holdings can influence both the token price, through market manipulation, and in some cases, features on the platform, if token balance gives users special benefits such as voting. Nonetheless, large investments seem important for large raises.

Some of the key takeaways from this analysis are that typical token sales involve investments of varying sizes, ranging from $1 to over $50,000 and likely represent a variety of people, motivations, and investment approaches. The typical (median) investment is less than $500, but the class of investments who invest over $10,000 is critical to having a successful sale.

4.7 CoinFund Survey Analysis

Readers who are not interested in the technical details can skip Sections 4.7 to 4.9. Here, we outline some original work that we have done. In particular, we investigate the following questions:

(1) Who are token sale investors?
(2) How active are they in the token sale market and the blockchain industry?

(3) What features of their backgrounds are associated with their participation in the token sale market?
(4) What features of their backgrounds are associated with their activity in the blockchain industry?
(5) What is their philosophy for investing in token sales?

4.7.1 *Survey sample*

Little is known about the broader crypto-investment and cryptocurrency communities, making it difficult to assess how representative this particular sample is of all cryptocurrency investors. This survey has several limitations worth acknowledging before considering the data. First, self-response introduces bias, and responses were limited to those who encountered the survey through Twitter, Reddit, or the CoinFund slack. However, we can compare this sample to what is known about token sale investments from raises that happened over a blockchain. One question in the survey asked how much the respondent typically invests in a token sale: $0, $1 − $1,000, $1,000 − $5,000, $5,000 − $10,000, $10,000 − $50,000, $50,001+. We can compare the distribution of responses to the distribution of investments across all the sales we examined to see whether the sample captures representative investors.

In fact, the survey heavily over-represents larger investors. As Table 4.5 shows, only 38% of the respondents who said they invested any money in sales invested between $1 and $1,000, compared with an average 61% across all sales. Even First Blood, which had the smallest number of small-scale investors, had just 33% of its investments come in amounts less than $1,000. There should be some gap between an investment-level numbers and investor-level numbers (including the portion attributable to investments between $1 and $1,000), because the investment data look at investments and the survey queries investors. It is likely that people will invest through multiple addresses and multiple wallets, so three investments of $400 could actually represent one investor who invested $1,200. Accordingly, we might expect the survey data to have a smaller share of those who invest at $1 − $1,000 and $1,000 − $5,000, but it seems unlikely to explain the observed gaps, particularly the gap between

Table 4.5.   Token Sale Investment Level.

Amount	Number	Percentage
$1 - $1,000	65	38%
$1,001 - $5,000	64	37%
$5,001 - $10,000	18	10%
$10,001 - $50,000	19	11%
$50,001 or more	7	7%

Total Respondents: 173
Source: CoinFund Survey.

the 25% of the sample that invested over $5,000 and the 10% shown on blockchain investments.

The gap also matches expectations: the industry likely has many small-scale crowd investors who do not follow CoinFund. Participating in the CoinFund community is itself an act of self-selection. It also indicates a level of engagement and effort that small-scale investors might not spare: they are too busy looking for the next sale rather than participating in an investment community.

The survey was also not offered in languages other than English, so it likely does not capture the token sale investor community not following English blockchain media. Not enough is known about the non-English-speaking blockchain communities to assess how this would bias findings.

In sum, the sample likely underrepresents investors who make small investments and over-represents those who make larger ones. It also likely over-represents English-speaking token sale investors.

4.7.2   *Sample demographics*

The survey characterised participants by gender, age, background, and knowledge level. We summarise the findings here in order to describe trends in the general characteristics of token sale investors.

Gender: The survey asked one question about gender. Table 4.6 shows that 92% of respondents indicated that they identified as a man, while 8% indicated they identified as a woman. This matches

Table 4.6.   Gender.

Gender	Number	Percentage
Man	160	92%
Woman	13	8%

Total Respondents: 173
Source: CoinFund Survey.

Table 4.7.   Age of Survey Respondents.

Age	Number	Percentage
18 years old or younger	2	1%
19–24	22	13%
25–30	42	24%
30–40	66	38%
40–50	26	15%
50+	15	9%

Total Respondents: 173
Source: CoinFund Survey.

the general perception of the industry as male-dominated. CoinFund made specific public appeals for increased women's participation.[5]

Age: The survey asked about respondents' age. Not all age brackets were of equal length in years. Table 4.7 shows that the most common age bracket selected was 30–40, at 38%. The table also reveals 24% selected 25–30, and 13% selected 19–24. Only 1% were under 18, while 15% were 40–50 and 9% were 50+. Although the industry has had a reputation of being dominated by young males in their 20s, this distribution suggests this is changing, as older experienced professionals become more active in the industry.

Residence: Table 4.8 summarises the survey respondents' location of residence. The most common residence among the respondents was the United States at 39%. Another 39% indicated various countries in Europe. Only 7% of respondents indicated East Asian countries

---

[5]https://twitter.com/coinfund_io/status/840372406749450240

Table 4.8.   Location of Residence.

Country	Number	Percentage
USA	67	39%
Europe	67	39%
Canada	10	6%
East Asia	12	7%
Middle East	3	2%
Australia or New Zealand	3	2%
Russia	3	2%
India	2	1%
Central America	1	>1%
South America	2	1%
Other	3	2%

Total Respondents: 173
Source: CoinFund Survey.

and only 2% indicated Russia. While the US dollar and the Euro are large trading markets, trading between crypto and Chinese Yuan has long been a significant source of trading volume. Recently, large markets have opened between cryptocurrencies and Japanese Yen and Korean Won. This either suggests that the crypto-investor community is predominately North American and European — that is, a geographic subset of the entire market — or that the survey failed to adequately capture investors outside of those regions, possibly because it was in English.

Professional Background: The survey asked about respondents' work background and occupation. Respondents could select one of several categories or fill in their own. Unfortunately, the categories were not very granular; as Table 4.9 shows, 60% of both the entire sample and the token sale investors indicated their background was in Technology, Engineering, or Sciences. Another 18% of token sale investors indicated their background was in or related to finance. Many of the fill-in responses could be reasonably recoded into other categories, but there was no significant grouping beyond technology and finance.

Investment Background: The survey asked about respondents' prior investing and trading experience in the following categories: Stocks,

Table 4.9.   Professional Background.

Industry	Number	Percentage
Technology	103	60%
Finance	31	18%
Other	39	23%

Total Respondents: 173
Source: CoinFund Survey.

Table 4.10.   Investment Background.

Investment experience	Number	Percentage
Cryptocurrency (after launch)	167	97%
Token sale, ICO or crowdsale	160	92%
Stocks, bonds or foreign exchange	116	67%
Private start-up or equity fundraising	48	38%
Equity crowdfunding	30	17%
Precious metals	1	>1%

Total Respondents: 173
Source: CoinFund Survey.

bonds, or foreign exchange; Cryptocurrency (like bitcoin, Ether, etc.); Token sale, ICO, crowdsale, or "token launch"; Private, start-up or equity fundraising; Equity crowdfunding campaigns (like AngelList or Crowdfunder); and Gold/Silver. Respondents could select multiple choices. Table 4.10 summarises the results from this question.

From the results, 67% of respondents had experience with stocks, bonds, or foreign exchange, which suggests an expert professional crypto-investor community. The wording of the question does not clarify whether it is limited to the respondent's personal investment or includes the services of an investment professional. As a benchmark, according to Gallup, in 2016, only 55% of working adults had invested in the stock market.[6] This number includes anyone who has

---

[6]http://www.gallup.com/poll/182816/little-change-percentage-americans-invested-market.aspx

any assets tied up in the stock market, including passively managed funds like Exchange Traded Funds (ETFs), 401(k), and Individual Retirement Accounts (IRAs). This is different from actively trading stocks, bonds, or foreign exchange. We would suspect that many respondents interpreted the question as asking whether they had experience actively trading rather than simply having funds in the stock market, though the ambiguity should make us cautious in our interpretation of the findings.

Unsurprisingly, 97% had experience investing in cryptocurrencies like bitcoin and Ether. It is also shown that 28% had experience with private, start-up, or equity fundraising. This group likely includes people who work in the venture capital and private equity industry (invest on behalf of others) and individuals who have invested their own money, likely accredited investors.

Moreover, 17% had experience with equity crowdfunding campaigns (like AngelList or Crowdfunder). To participate in an equity crowdfunding campaign in the United States, one must be an accredited investor.[7] Estimates suggest that only 8.25% of American working adults are accredited investors, and it is unlikely all have participated in an equity crowdfunding campaign.[8] Therefore, the survey sample percentage is much higher than one might expect. Angel funding is more often done with one's own money rather than through a managed fund, and it is less likely respondents meant that they had funds involved in equity crowdfunding that others performed on their behalf. Rather, this is more likely to indicate active investment experience,

Only one respondent had experience investing in Gold or Silver. This is a surprising finding, given the popular association between

---

[7]The US Securities and Exchange Commission defines the term "accredited investor". The current definition can be found at https://www.sec.gov/fast-answers/answers-accredhtm.html. An accredited investor must meet any of the following conditions: Individuals with an individual annual income over $200,000 or $300,000 with a spouse over the last two years and an expectation of the same this year; individuals with net assets over $1 million, excluding one's primary residence, unless that asset is a liability.

[8]https://dqydj.com/how-many-accredited-investors-are-there-in-america/

bitcoin and gold as alternatives to fiat currencies. Given the low response rate, we do not include experience investing in gold in subsequent analysis.

Participation Level: The survey asked about how much respondents typically invest in a token sale. As noted before, we omitted respondents that indicated they invested $0 — that is, they did not invest in token sales. Based on the survey, 38% indicated they typically invested between $1 and $1,000, while another 37% indicated they typically invested between $1,001 and $5,000. As highlighted earlier, this differs from the distributions observed in publicly auditable token sales.

Exposure to Crypto-Tokens: The survey also asked the total share of one's investments that are invested in blockchain-based assets. Table 4.11 shows that 31% had 75–100% of their investments in blockchain-based assets: almost all their investments were wrapped up in token sales. The table also reveals that 24% had only 0–25% of their investments in blockchain-based assets, indicating these assets were a smaller part of their overall investment portfolio. Furthermore, 21% had 25–50% of their investments, and only 13% had 50–75%. The two most popular categories are the highest and the lowest amount of investments in blockchain-based assets, indicating it is popular to focus on blockchain-based assets entirely or have them as a small part of a larger portfolio, likely to hedge against the risk that comes with the industry.

Table 4.11. Investment Exposure to the Blockchain Industry.

Exposure	Number	Percentage
No blockchain exposure	1	>1%
Less than 25%	11	6%
25–50%	33	19%
50–75%	29	17%
75–100%	53	31%

Total Respondents: 173
Source: CoinFund Survey.

It is possible respondents interpreted "investments" as either investment activity, total financial savings, or total savings *and* assets (including a house). There is no way to verify, but it is worth noting for future uses of the survey data and future surveys.

Research and Reading: The survey asked respondents how many hours per week they spend reading about and researching the blockchain industry. Table 4.12 summarises the results from this question. One option was that the respondent worked in the blockchain industry: 27% of token sale investors indicated they do. On top of that, a full 30% of token sale investors indicated they spent more than 10 hours each week researching or reading about the blockchain industry — almost as much as a part-time occupation or a very serious hobby. In addition, 17% spent 5–10 hours, while 19% spent 2–5 hours and 6% spend 0–2 hours. This is a somewhat surprising finding: one might have expected that time was the only limiting factor in spending time reading about the industry and that the 5–10 hour category would be the next largest, rather than the 2–5 hour category. The actual distribution suggests that either respondents worked full-time in the industry, had a lifestyle that allowed them to spend a significant amount of time reading and researching, or fit as much as they could in on the side.

Investment Motivation: The survey asked respondents why they might invest in a potential token sale for a social media platform that rewards content creators with tokens. Responses included a range of

Table 4.12.   Hours per Week Spent Researching the Blockchain Industry.

Time spent	Number	Percentage
0–2 hours	11	6%
2–5 hours	33	19%
5–10 hours	29	17%
10+ hours	53	31%
I work in the blockchain space	47	27%

Total Respondents: 173
Source: CoinFund Survey.

Table 4.13. Investment Motivation.

Question: What is the number one reason you would invest in a social media platform that used a token to reward content creators and readers?

Response	Motivation	Number	Percentage
I want to capture the value of the user base as an investor in the platform	Investor	45	26%
I want to participate in a digital economy using tokens	Enthusiast	39	23%
I speculate on the value of tokens and I believe this one would do well	Investor	37	20%
I want to be compensated in tokens as a content creator or other user of the platform	User	20	12%
I speculate on the value of tokens and I don't care what the product is	Investor	3	2%
I would not invest	Uninterested	32	18%

Total Respondents: 173

Summary of motivation: Excluding respondents who would not invest

Motivation	Number	Percentage
Investor	82	58%
Enthusiast	39	28%
User	20	14%

Total Respondents: 141

Source: CoinFund Survey.

motivations that spanned wanting to be a future content creator to wanting to speculate on the token value, regardless of the product. We recoded the responses to fall into one of four categories: a User who intends to use the platform, an Investor who is primarily interested in profits, an Enthusiast who wants to participate in the emerging token ecosystem, and those who are uninterested. Table 4.13 shows the distribution of investment motivations among respondents.

For purposes of this commentary, we focus on those token sale investors who would participate in this hypothetical token sale.

The majority would approach the project as an Investor, while almost one-third would approach as an Enthusiast and 14% would approach as a User. One would expect over time that the share of Enthusiast investors would fall as the novelty of the token digital economy wear off, while the share of Users might rise as more people become aware of these platforms. Even though they were a smaller portion of participants, Enthusiasts and Users comprised a significant share of potential investors. This shows that token sale campaigns are a means of raising funds, as well as building a community and acquiring initial users. We should be cautious in our conclusions, because respondents were reacting to a particular token sale and might have a different philosophy for other products or services.

4.8   Token Sale Participation Analysis

In this section, we examine variables closely associated with the level of participation in token sales. We performed a chi-square test to evaluate the strength of association between typical investment size and the following variables: investor age; investor background; whether they had experience investing in stocks, bonds, or foreign exchange; whether they had experience investing in private, start-up, and equity funding opportunities; whether they had experience with equity crowdfunding campaigns (like Angellist or Crowdfunder); their overall investment exposure to blockchain-based assets; how much research and reading they do per week; and their investment philosophy in investing in the hypothetical token sale.

Overall, we hypothesise that token sale investors will reflect intuitions about traditional investors. While investors come from a range of diverse age groups and backgrounds, factors that might influence investment patterns in traditional investment markets will still hold. In particular, we hypothesise the following:

- Age will be significantly associated with the level of participation in token sales. Someone who is older is more likely to have wealth to invest in the blockchain industry.

- The background will not be associated with the level of participation in token sales. People with a background in technology or finance seem equally likely to participate in token sales at similar investment levels.

- Investing in stocks, bonds, or foreign exchange will be associated with the level of participation in token sales; in particular, those with such experience are more likely to participate at a smaller level. Actively trading stocks, bonds, and foreign exchange often involves a shorter-term perspective than token sales and usually requires technical analysis on existing market activity that is not applicable to token sales. In addition, stocks, bonds, and foreign exchange markets offer greater legal protection than token sales, meaning the individual might see token sales as much riskier and be less likely to participate at higher levels.

- Investing in private, start-up, and equity funding opportunities will be associated with the size of token sale participation; in particular, those with such experience will participate at greater levels of investment. Private start-up and equity funding bear a resemblance to token sale funding, and the typical private, start-up, and equity funding investment is large, often $100,000 or more.

- Investing in equity crowdfunding campaigns will not be associated with the size of token sale participation. In many ways, these investment activities are similar.

- Overall investment exposure to blockchain-based assets will be associated with the size of token sale participation. We expect that those with greater exposure to blockchain-based assets will be more likely to invest more money in token sales. Both are indicators of either confidence in the blockchain industry, a greater appetite for risk, or both. In addition, those with a smaller portion of their holdings will be more likely to invest in token sales at smaller amounts. These individuals would be less comfortable with blockchain-based assets and would more likely to spread investments across a wide array or be investing simply to experiment and learn rather than see outsized investment returns.

- Research and reading about the blockchain industry will be associated with the size of token sale participation; in particular, those who read and research more will be more likely to invest more in token sales. These individuals would be more confident they have spotted a valuable investment opportunity.

- Token sale philosophy will not be associated with the size of token sale participation.

Age did not appear to be significantly associated with the size of token sale participation: X^2 (20, N = 173) = 16.95, p = 0.66, suggesting no statistical relationship. This is somewhat surprising: one might have thought older investors would be willing to invest more money, simply because they are more likely to have funds available for investment, but this appears not to be the case. It is possible that older investors are also more diversified in their investments and are more comfortable participating at lower levels. It is also possible many younger token sale investors accumulated wealth by being in the industry early and now feel comfortable participating in token sales at higher levels with their wealth.

Background also did not appear significantly associated with typical participation levels: X^2 (8, N = 173) = 4.86, p = 0.77, suggesting no statistical relationship. Given some of the drawbacks of the background variable — responses can be meaningfully divided only between technology, finance, and then a handful of other industries — this relationship is not surprising.

Experience in investing stocks, bonds, and foreign exchange did not appear significantly associated with typical participation levels: X^2 (4, N = 173) = 4.16, p = 0.38, suggesting no statistical relationship. This fails to support our original hypothesis.

Experience investing in private, start-up, or equity fundraising did not appear significantly associated with typical participation levels: X^2 (4, N = 173) = 6.7, p = 0.15, suggesting no significant relationship. This ran counter to our hypothesis and suggests that experience investing large amounts in early-stage companies does not lead to investing larger amounts in early-stage tokens. The average seed-stage investment in 2016 was $1.1 million, and early-stage venture capital deals are typically five to seven figures.[9]

---

[9]https://techcrunch.com/2016/09/07/crunchbase-sees-rise-in-average-seed-round-in-2016/

Experience investing in crowdfunding campaigns did not appear significantly associated with typical token sale participation levels: X^2 (4, N = 173) = 1.99, p = 0.74, suggesting no significant relationship.

Total investment exposure did appear significantly associated with typical participation levels: X^2 (16, N = 173) = 25.92, p = 0.06, suggesting a weakly significant relationship. In particular, those who had 75–100% of their investments in blockchain-based assets were more likely to have a typical participation level of \$50,000+ and less likely to have a typical participation level of \$1 − \$1,000: 8% versus 4%. This was a surprising finding, though it describes only six respondents. This could possibly be attributed to the "blockchain-wealthy" — people who made almost all of their current wealth in blockchain-based assets and who make a majority of their investments using cryptocurrencies.

In addition, those who had less than 25% of their investments in blockchain-based assets were more likely to have a typical investment level of \$1 − \$1,000: 60% versus 37% overall. This possibly reflects a less aggressive investment philosophy: people who hold only a smaller portion of their investments in blockchain-based assets are less hesitant to participate at high levels. This group was also less likely to participate at the \$1,000 − \$5,000 level: 21% versus 37%.

Those who had 25–50% of their investments in blockchain-based assets were more likely to have a typical investment level of \$1,000 − \$5,000: 59% versus 37%. This could indicate a greater comfort with blockchain-based assets — the more you expose your investment portfolio to blockchain technology, the more you are comfortable investing greater amounts in activities like token sales.

The survey did not ask about income, wealth, or overall investment activity. It is impossible to infer how many token sales in which a respondent has participated, nor is there any way to infer how much of his or her investment activity is in token sales versus trading already live blockchain-based assets. Therefore, it is impossible to calculate the size of the total investment portfolio and whether the value of total holdings influences these responses.

Time spent reading and researching the blockchain industry did not appear significantly associated with typical participation levels: X^2 (16, N = 173) = 20.64, p = 0.19, suggesting no relationship. That is, spending more time researching the industry did not influence or was influenced by the amount of money typically invested in a token sale. This is surprising: one would expect that an investor to spend more research on larger investments he or she would on smaller investments. This suggests some investors may be approaching this as a speculative and highly risky market, hoping they will get lucky. The survey did not ask how many sales the respondent typically participates in, so it could also be the case that one investor evaluated many sales and chose only one to invest in at a high amount while another evaluated the same sales and invested in all at varying but lower levels.

Token sale investment philosophy was significantly associated with typical participation levels: X^2 (12, N = 173) = 20.47, p = 0.06, indicating a moderately strong relationship. Enthusiast participants were more likely to have an investment level of $5,000 − $10,000. This could reflect people who made significant profits within the blockchain industry and want to reinvest it to see the entire industry grow. Users were more likely to support at smaller levels, typically $1 − $1,000. This could temper enthusiasm for attracting future Users sale participants, since they are more likely to contribute smaller amounts but these investors also could bring marketing and product development benefits, since they are excited to use the platform once it has launched. Finally, those who were Uninterested were more likely to be large investors, at the $10,000 − $50,000 level. This could reflect this group simply seeing less of an opportunity for returns in a social media platform.

Our hypotheses were based on assumptions that token sales investors would typically be older, wealthier, more experienced investors with knowledge of finance and technology fields broadly, and the blockchain industry more specifically. However, our analysis showed that this profile is likely too narrow, as age, background, investment experience, and research on the blockchain industry were not associated with participation levels. These findings support the characterisation that nearly anyone could be a token sale investor, regardless of his or her background, experience, or level of involvement in the blockchain industry. Investment exposure was most associated with participation levels, suggesting that individuals who invest in the token sale at higher levels are also more likely to have a greater portion of their assets tied up in crypto-token markets.

4.9 Investment Exposure Analysis

In this section, we will examine other variables closely associated with one's exposure to blockchain-based assets. We define exposure as how much of one's investment activity is involved in blockchain-based assets. Exposure was strongly correlated with participation levels, and both represent some level of comfort with the industry and/or appetite for investment risk. Relative to many other types of investment, holding blockchain-based assets is risky due to regulator ambiguity, lack of recourse in case of technical failure, and overall infancy of the industry. Exposing one's holdings to blockchain-based assets is as much a vote of confidence as investing large amounts of funds in token sales.

We performed a chi-square test to evaluate the strength of association between how typical investment level in a token sale and the following variables: age; background; whether they had experience investing in stocks, bonds, or foreign exchange; whether they had experience investing in private, start-up, and equity funding opportunities; whether they had experience with equity crowd-funding campaigns (like Angellist or Crowdfunder); their typical investment level in token sales; and how much research and reading they do per week.

We hypothesise the following:

- Age will be associated with total investment exposure to blockchain-based assets, in particular; those who are younger are more likely to have a larger portion of their investment portfolio held by blockchain-based assets. We think younger individuals are less likely to have any investment portfolio, and if most of their wealth so far has been made in cryptocurrency markets, it has likely stayed in cryptocurrency markets. Similarly, we think older individuals are more likely to have a smaller portion of their investments in blockchain-based assets, largely because they have a larger portfolio to begin with.

- The background will be associated with total exposure; in particular, those with a technical background will be more likely to expose a greater amount of their investments in token sales.
- Experience investing in stocks, bonds, and foreign exchange will be associated with total exposure. In particular, those with experience will be more likely to expose a smaller portion of their investments in blockchain-based assets. This represents more conservative investors who have funds in traditional global markets, which are more stable and protected than blockchain-based assets.
- Experience investing in private, start-up, and equity funding opportunities will not be associated with total exposure. While these investment opportunities are riskier than many stock market investments, they are also more protected legally than token sales. The greater comfort with risk may offset the comfort with traditional investment opportunities but not make one more likely to expose a greater portion of their investments to the blockchain industry.
- Experience investing in equity crowdfunding campaigns will not be associated with total exposure.
- Time spent in research will be associated with total investment exposure to blockchain-based assets; in particular, the more one is familiar with the industry, the more likely one is to have a greater portion of his or her investment portfolio held in blockchain-based assets.
- Investment philosophy will not be associated with total investment exposure to blockchain-based assets.

We find that age was not associated with total investment exposure to blockchain-based assets: X^2 (20, N = 173) = 27.78, p = 0.11, suggesting no significant relationship, although the value is close to a weak level of significance. We can reject our hypothesis that younger investors are more likely to have blockchain exposure.

Background was associated with total investment exposure to blockchain-based assets: X^2 (8, N = 173) = 14.41, p = 0.07,

· indicating a weak statistically significant relationship. In particular, those with a background in finance were more likely to have 25–50% of their investments in blockchain-based assets and less likely to have 75–100% of their investments in blockchain-based assets. This could indicate that professionals are unwilling to jettison existing investments in traditional markets or simply a more conservative investment philosophy.

Experience in trading stocks, bonds, or foreign exchange was strongly associated with total exposure to blockchain-based assets: X^2 (4, N = 173) = 31.64, p = 0, indicating a strongly significant relationship. In particular, those without such experience were much more likely to have 75–100% of their investments held in blockchain-based assets: 70% versus 41% overall. They were also less likely to have 0–25% and 25–50% of their holdings: 12% versus 24% overall and 7% versus 21% overall, respectively. Those with experience trading stocks, bonds, or foreign exchange were less likely to have 75–100% of their investments in blockchain-based assets: 27% versus 41%. This broadly supports our hypothesis: those who have experience are less comfortable exposing a larger portion of their investment portfolio to an industry that currently experiences regulatory ambiguity and has few investor protections. It is also possible that those without experience trading bonds, stocks, and foreign exchange are less likely to have other investment holdings at all, making them de facto more exposed to blockchain-based assets.

Experience with private, start-up, or equity fundraising was slightly associated with total exposure to blockchain-based assets: X^2 (4, N = 173) = 7.702, p = .10, suggesting a weakly significant relationship. In particular, those with such experience were less likely to have 75–100% of their holdings in crypto: 25% versus 41%. This disproves our initial hypothesis, though the strength of association between these two variables was on the threshold for statistical insignificance.

Experience with equity crowdfunding campaigns was not associated with total investment exposure to blockchain-based assets: X^2 (4, N = 173) = 2.643, p = .62, suggesting no significant relationship.

Time spent researching and reading about the blockchain industry was associated with total investment exposure to blockchain-based assets: X^2 (16, N = 173) = 30.65, p = 0.01, indicating a moderately significant relationship. In particular, those who spent 10+ hours per week reading or researching were less likely to have 0–25% of their investments in blockchain-based assets: 8% versus 24%. This supports our hypothesis: those who spend time following the industry are likely more confident in its future, and so investments in the industry would represent a larger portion of their total investments. This works the other way as well: those with a greater portion of their investments in blockchain-based assets have more incentive to read and research. Those who spent 0–2 hours per week and 2–5 hours per week are much more likely to have just 0–25% of their investments in blockchain-based assets. This relationship is also intuitive — if one does not understand the industry or have time to follow it closely, he or she would be less comfortable being so exposed to assets that are complex and lightly regulated.

Interestingly, those who actively worked in the industry were not significantly more or less likely to have more of their holdings in blockchain-based assets than the overall sample. One might have thought that work in the industry would make one more comfortable exposing more of their investments in blockchain-based assets. This difference could be attributable to several factors. It is possible that those in the industry already are more established professionals with already diverse investment portfolios. Any bump their industry affiliation might give would counterbalance the already more diverse portfolio they have. It could also be that while many people see the promise in the technology overall, they are focused on private implementations or potentially see company equity as their way of investing in the overall industry.

Investor philosophy was not associated with investment exposure to blockchain-based assets: X^2 (12, N = 173) = 12.48, p = 0.41, suggesting no relationship.

Overall, the analysis did not support some of our hypotheses regarding the profile of highly exposed investors. However, it did show a stronger association between exposure and level of research, which makes intuitive sense, and between exposure and participation in investment markets in general. Importantly, the association was negative, suggesting that investors with greater exposure are less experienced and less involved in traditional investment markets. In the next section, we discuss the implications of these findings.

4.10 Discussion and Conclusion

Overall, this Chapter gives us a much deeper understanding of the existing token sale market investment community. The survey indicated that people participated in token sales for a variety of reasons. Most participants approached as Investors seeking a return on their investment. A significant portion invested as Enthusiasts, to participate in the emerging digital economy, while a smaller portion invested as future Users. We find that, unsurprisingly, the community skews heavily male, has primarily a technology or finance background, and has more than average experience with traditional investment opportunities like stock market trading, venture capital, and equity crowdfunding. The community is primarily based in the United States and Europe, although as noted earlier, it is likely the survey failed to capture token sale investors in Central and Southeast Asia.

Token sale investors participate in token sales at varying amounts, ranging from the amount one might spend on a smartphone app to the amount an accredited investor might give as an angel investment. Token sales rarely have minimum investments levels, so participants are free to participate at any level they like. Over two-thirds of investors typically invested between $1 - $5,000 in a token sale, equally split between $1 - $1,000 and $1,001 - $5,000. A smaller portion invested at much larger amounts, over $50,000, though these larger investments can make up a significant portion of overall funds raised, as we found in the analysis of token sale investment transactions.

Many blockchain investors are confident about the market and are knowledgeable about the industry. Many have large amounts of their investment holdings in blockchain-based assets, and many follow the industry closely. Over half either worked in the industry or spent more than 10 hours per week reading and researching about it. Given the complexity of the technology and the investment opportunities, this is not surprising.

Overall, people who have a greater proportion of their investments held in blockchain-based assets are more likely to participate in token sales at greater amounts. Those that invest smaller amounts of money in token sales are more likely to have a smaller portion of their holdings in blockchain-based assets. This proportional relationship between investment levels and levels of exposure to the blockchain industry could represent two basic investment strategies. The latter strategy represents a more cautious investor who diversifies his or her portfolio by spreading his or her holdings across both traditional investment and blockchain investment opportunities or is just beginning to experiment with token sale investments. The first strategy represents someone who is "all in" when it comes to blockchain technology. Such individual holds most of his or her investments in token sales and is more likely to participate in token sales at very high amounts, $50,000 or more. These could be investors with little exposure to traditional investment opportunities, the so-called "crypto-rich", or early blockchain adopters and converts who believe strongly in the transformational power of these new technologies. These individuals' investments were made almost entirely in blockchain-based assets.

This characterisation is supported by the fact that total investment exposure to blockchain-based assets was associated with people who had less traditional investment experience and who did more research into the industry. Those who held less of their investments in blockchain-based assets were less likely to do substantial research into the industry or work in it. They were also more likely to have a traditional investment experience in stocks, bonds, or foreign exchange. Finally, those with a background in finance were more likely to have only moderate exposure to blockchain-based assets.

The preceding discussion shows that token sale investors are a diverse community within the blockchain industry in terms of age, prior investment experience, and engagement with the blockchain industry. People who are more financially exposed to the blockchain industry tend to spend more time reading about and researching it. At the same time, time spent in research does not appear correlated with the amount of money typically invested in a token sale. This is concerning for those worried about too much uninformed investment speculation in the industry and believe that investors should understand the complexity of the tokens they are buying.

People who are more financially exposed to the blockchain industry tend to invest more money in token sales, but have less of their assets in other more traditional investments. This suggests a class of investors whose wealth is almost entirely held in blockchain tokens and whose investments in some cases would comprise over one-third of the total funds raised in the sale. It also suggests those who are only marginally exposed are more likely to invest smaller amounts — a less risky investment approach.

Finally, the survey seems to support the characterisation that virtually anyone could be a token sale investor, this combined with the media buzz around Bitcoin and token sales could explain, at least in part, the rapid growth of the token sale market in recent months. The survey results around age suggest that perhaps new money (young money) is entering the crypto-investment market. This is a demographic that might not have previously been involved in investment markets. Additionally, the fact that time spent researching the blockchain industry is correlated with increased investment participation could suggest that increasingly available information about token sales is driving increased investment in token sales, at least in part.

4.11 Implications

These insights complement one of the few previous studies on this topic. In a forthcoming paper, Hull et al [n.d.] examine factors that help predict the amount of money that tokens will raise. The paper studied several features of the blockchain projects and their marketing campaigns. Overall, they found that longer marketing periods — a proxy for awareness building — were associated with larger raises; tokens that had access rights tended to raise less money; and broader market conditions, particularly the price of Ethereum, predicted larger raises. Entrepreneurs were advised to design or market their token as if initial investors were planning to resell it rather than use it. They were also advised to launch when Ethereum was doing well.

Entrepreneurs can integrate these insights into their marketing and budget planning. In particular, they should understand that most sales depend on large-scale investments, at the level of $10,000 or more. The median investment likely less than $500, and they should plan on recruiting a large base of supporters. The investor community is diverse in terms of age, background, and prior investment experience, and they do not conform to the expected background of venture capital investors, i.e., an investment professional with a background in equity investing. That said, because larger investors are more likely to have all their holdings in blockchain-based assets, entrepreneurs can emphasise how their project might benefit other tokens. This could also help appeal to Enthusiast investors, who are more likely to invest at moderate levels. Larger investors are more likely to have an Investment approach to token sales, so emphasising the merits of the sale as an investment could help in attracting them. While User investors might be more likely to participate at lower levels, they can still have other benefits, such as community building.

The results in this Chapter are useful to investors and policy makers as well. It may benefit token sale investors to know that many fellow investors are not like them because investors come in so many different forms. It is likely that the investor group includes a couple "whales" who invest at high amounts and get a large portion of tokens, but there should also be a broad base of smaller token holders. Policy makers benefit from knowing that token sale investors are a diverse group and should be wary of regulating them as if they were a homogenous group resembling venture capital investors. Given that some are quite young and many hail from a technology rather than a finance background, many might be ignorant of existing laws that govern early-stage company capital raising. It is concerning that research into the industry is not associated with how much people typically invest, suggesting there might be uninformed speculation in the existing industry.

4.12   Areas for Future Research

In order to better understand token sale investments and investors, we recommend a follow-up survey that clarifies some of the ambiguities noted with the CoinFund survey analysed here. Expert interviews would generate additional qualitative data regarding investor experience with and approach to token sales. We have identified several issues for further analysis. Our analysis shows that token sales may appeal to a new demographic that is not already active in other investment markets, a finding that suggests a worthwhile starting point for future research. We also show that different investor profiles are active in different ways, and that it may be beneficial to target a broad spectrum of users, not only large investors but also users who may be active in community building. Future research should focus attention on the different investor profiles and their experience on token sale platforms. In general, further analysis on token sale philosophy and investment approach will help characterise this dynamic and novel marketplace and the investors who choose to be involved. As well, the question of the distinction between projects garnering the support of large-scale investors through sizeable contributions and those that complete their token sales with the broad support of numerous small-scale investments is a particularly intriguing one that merits further consideration. Are the differences attributable to project focus or development stage, the strength or experience of project teams, market conditions, approaches to developing community awareness, some other factors or even combination of the above? Insight into this question would be useful both for project teams and for investors looking to exploit underappreciated opportunities, or avoid those that have acquired excessively enthusiastic support.

References and Further Readings

Anderson, W. (2017a). The Legends Room Token Sale: Tokenized Membership to a Private Las Vegas Lounge. Working paper, Smith + Crown. Retrieved from https://www.smithandcrown.com/legends-room/

Anderson, W. (2017b). Zrcoin: Crypto-Tokens Backed by a Zirconium Oxide Factory. Working paper, Smith + Crown. Retrieved from https://www.smithandcrown.com/sale/zrcoin/

Chwierut, M. (2016a). A History of Bitcoin. Working paper, Smith + Crown. Retrieved from https://www.smithandcrown.com/a-history-of-bitcoin/

Chwierut, M. (2016b). DECENT "Software Sale". Working paper, Smith + Crown. Retrieved from https://www.smithandcrown.com/sale/decent/

Chwierut, M. (2016c). First Blood Token Sale. Working paper, Smith + Crown. Retrieved from https://www.smithandcrown.com/sale/first-blood/

Chwierut, M. (2017a). Token rights: Key Considerations in Designing a Token Economy. Working paper, Smith + Crown.

Chwierut, M. (2017b). Token Sales Market Performance. Working paper, Smith + Crown. Retrieved from https://www.smithandcrown.com/token-sale-market-performance/

CoinDesk. Bitcoin venture capital. Retrieved from http://www.coindesk.com/bitcoin-venture-capital/

The Economist. (2017, April 27). The market in the Initial Coin Offerings risk becoming a bubble. Retrieved from http://www.economist.com/news/finance-and-economics/21721425-it-may-also-spawn-valuable-innovations-market-initial-coin-offerings. Accessed on June 9, 2017.

Glaser, F. & Bezzenberger, L. (2015). Beyond Cryptocurrencies — A Taxonomy of Decentralized Consensus Systems. 23rd European Conference on Information Systems (ECIS), Münster, Germany. Retrieved from https://ssrn.com/abstract=2605803

Hull, C., Chwierut, M., Lio, B. & Anderson, W. (2017). Cryptocurrency, Digital Innovation, and the Digital Entrepreneur: How Blockchain Technology and ICOs (Initial Coin Offerings) Facilitate Digital Entrepreneurship and Innovation. (Forthcoming).

Investopedia. (2017). http://www.investopedia.com/terms/i/initial-coin-offering-ico.asp. Accessed on March 30, 2017.

Kalla, S. (2016). What Is an ICO?. Working paper, Smith + Crown. Retrieved from https://www.smithandcrown.com/what-is-anico. Accessed on March 6, 2017.

Kastelein, R. (2017). What Initial Coin Offerings are, and why VC firms care. Harvard Business Review. Retrieved from https://hbr.org/2017/03/what-initial-coin-offerings-are-and-why-vc-firms-care. Accessed on June 9, 2017.

Laurent, L. (2017, April 18). Want to be a VC just flip a Bitcoin. Bloomberg. Retrieved from https://www.bloomberg.com/gadfly/articles/2017-04-18/beating-vc-funds-is-as-easy-as-flipping-a-bitcoin. Accessed on June 9, 2017.

Lee, D. K. C. (2017). The Deep Skill of Business Blockchain. Retrieved from April 25, 2017. Presentation.

Lio, B. (2016). Introduction to Decentralized Autonomous Corporations (DACs). Working paper, Smith + Crown. Retrieved from https://www.smithand crown.com/introduction-decentralized-autonomous-corporations-dacs/

Metz, C. (2017). The Initial Coin Offering, the Bitcoin-y stock that's not stock — But definitely a big deal. Wired. Retrieved from https://www.wired.com/ 2017/03/initial-coin-offering-stock-thats-not-stock/. Accessed on June 9, 2017.

Nakamoto, S. (2008). Bitcoin: A Peer-to-Peer Electronic Cash System. Working paper. Retrieved from http://www.cryptovest.co.uk/resources/Bitcoin% 20paper%20Original.pdf. Accessed on March 30, 2017.

Smith + Crown. (2016). Daos Securities Regulation. Retrieved from https://www. smithandcrown.com/daos-securities-regulation/

Smith + Crown. (2017a). Bitcoin. Retrieved from https://www.smithandcrown. com/currency/bitcoin/. Accessed on March 30, 2017.

Smith + Crown. (2017b). Ethereum. Retrieved from https://www.smithand crown.com/currency/ethereum/

Weiler, A. (2017). Matchpool Token Sale (ICO): Curated Dating Communities with the Security of a Blockchain. Working paper, Smith + Crown. Retrieved from https://www.smithandcrown.com/matchpool-token-sale-ico-curated-dating-communities-security-blockchain/

Chapter 5

Blockchain: An Introduction

5.1 Advancement beyond Cloud Computing

In 1946, ENIAC (the first generation computer) was first introduced. In 1977, it was the beginning of Apple II and in 1981 the IBM (Intel 8088) personal computer (PC) was introduced. In 1991, the start of the first website (Internet) began. In 2006, the cloud computing framework was taking over of the client/server framework. Cloud computing is a form of Internet-based computing that provides shared computer processing resources and data to computers and other devices on demand with central administration or authority. But some have argued that it is facing its demise, however defined. While some claim that decentralised computing network will dominate, others think that cloud computing is here to stay. The truth is possible somewhere in between and may be a combination of both existing side by side, handing different data and providing different computing power.

Hinted since the development of the modern computers in 1946 (and Internet in 1991) and proven in industrialisation is that manual labour is increasingly replaced by machine-based production. The essence of cloud computing for centralisation of authority is to provide a single platform to consolidate the hardware and software resources administered by different groups in different regions. Cloud computing has indeed lowered the cost of operation and improved efficiency. However, centralisation has its shortcomings too.

Issues include data security, disconnection between cloud computing and server and challenges to data accountability and trust mechanism. The Fourth Industrial Revolution[1] discussed in the World Economic Forum in Davos in 2016 mulled over the economic effects of artificial intelligence, wondering if fast-changing technology will end up creating more new jobs than it displaces, especially of millions of middle-income jobs (see https://www.wsj.com/articl es/mulling-the-economic-effect-of-artificial-intelligence-1484766372). Concerns include if even democracy will survive (see https://www. theguardian.com/sustainable-business/2017/jan/11/can-democracy-survive-the-fourth-industrial-revolution-should-it). One such disruptive technology is by FinTech companies.

5.2   Introduction to Blockchain

The response to these challenges of cloud computing begs the question, is there a technology that can overcome these shortcomings? The answer as will be explored in this Chapter is blockchain which has been evolving quietly and steadily since 2008.

In October 2015, the First Global Blockchain Summit was held in Shanghai.[2] Geeks, entrepreneurs, academic experts, investors, corporate executives, and regulatory policy makers gathered and discussed the business applications and opportunities of blockchain technology in the industry. These include areas such as payment, Internet of Things (IoT), securities trading, digital asset management and many others. Over 200 guests from the financial industry, including banking, payments, securities and commodities, attended the summit.

The first question is who invented the term "blockchain"? The word blockchain was not mentioned in the 2008 white paper by the creator of Bitcoin (Satoshi, 2008). The term "Chain of Blocks" was

---

[1]The Fourth Industrial Revolution is the fourth major industrial era since the initial Industrial Revolution of the 18th century as a range of new technologies that are fusing the physical, digital and biological worlds, and impacting all disciplines, economies and industries.

[2]http://www.8btc.com/wanxiang-blockchain-labs-20151015

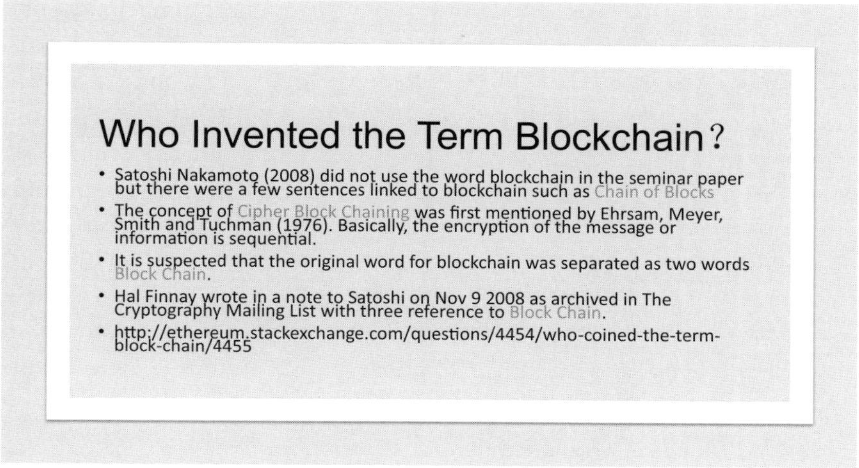

Who Invented the Term Blockchain?

- Satoshi Nakamoto (2008) did not use the word blockchain in the seminar paper but there were a few sentences linked to blockchain such as Chain of Blocks
- The concept of Cipher Block Chaining was first mentioned by Ehrsam, Meyer, Smith and Tuchman (1976). Basically, the encryption of the message or information is sequential.
- It is suspected that the original word for blockchain was separated as two words Block Chain.
- Hal Finnay wrote in a note to Satoshi on Nov 9 2008 as archived in The Cryptography Mailing List with three reference to Block Chain.
- http://ethereum.stackexchange.com/questions/4454/who-coined-the-term-block-chain/4455

Figure 5.1. Inventor of Blockchain.

Source: By authors.

mentioned but not blockchain. It turned out that the term slowly evolves over a period of time via private correspondence among those pioneers in the Bitcoin community. In particular, Hal Finney used the phrase "block chain" several times in his correspondence with Satoshi. The two words were later combined to form the word blockchain (see illustrations in Figures 5.1, 5.2 and 5.3).

The response from blockchain by financial technology is applied to trade financing, payroll and insurance payments, banks, brokerages, exchanges, investments, merchants, compliance trading platforms, capital markets, money services and more. These applications will be amplified in Section 5.4.

In its most simplified form, blockchain enables a centralised platform to be decentralised, leading to distribution. Figure 5.4 depicts the process of the centralised platform to decentralised and distributed to various nodes. Figure 5.5 shows the first distributed payments ledger from bitcoin in six steps. These involve first, the encrypted transactions being formed into a block from the online transactions. The block is distributed to all the participants with validation done by cryptography contest or by consensus algorithms.

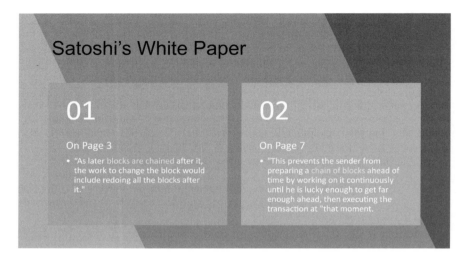

Figure 5.2.   Satoshi Nakamoto and Chain of Blocks.

Source: By authors.

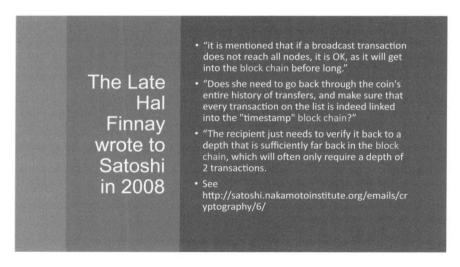

Figure 5.3.   Block Chain or Blockchain?

Source: By authors.

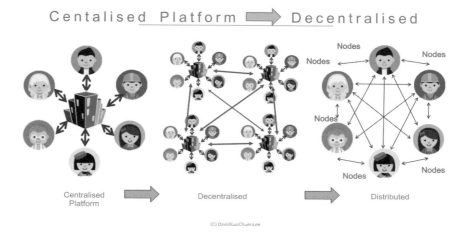

Figure 5.4.   Centralised, Decentralised and Distributed.

Source: By authors.

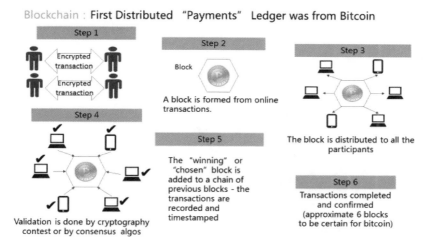

Figure 5.5.   Forming a Blockchain.

Source: By authors.

The winning or chosen block is added to a chain of previous blocks and the transactions are recorded and timestamped. Transactions are completed and confirmed (approximate six blocks to be certain for bitcoin).

5.3   Features of Blockchain

Types of blockchain can categorise as public (ungated) chains as in bitcoins or private (gated) chains. Some would classify public blockchain as open blockchain and private blockchain as permissioned blockchain. The latter may be further classified as fully private chains or consortium chains such as R3 CEV (see Figure 5.6). There will be other permutations and combinations. Data in Public Chain can be encrypted or transparent (see http://www.8btc.com/what-is-blockch ain; http://community.qingcloud.com; https://blog.ethereum.org).

There is another commonly used term called distributed ledger system that includes blockchain network as a subset. A distributed ledger (also called shared ledger) is a consensus of replicated, shared, and synchronised digital data geographically spread across multiple

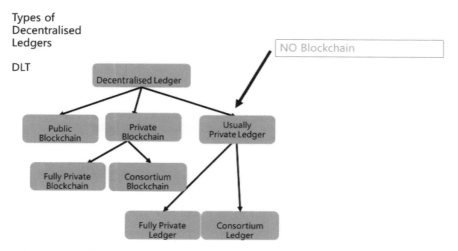

Figure 5.6.   Decentralised Ledger and Distributed Ledger Technology.
Source: By authors.

sites, countries, or institutions with no central administrator or centralised data storage.

Drilling down to the features of the blockchain, there are six, beginning with distributed/decentralised. Data are replicated on all the nodes in a distributed Peer-to-Peer (P2P) network, and each copy of the ledger is identical to others. It can also be decentralised with some lighter nodes not having full data storage with limited connection.

Second is a consensus mechanism whereby all users in the network can come to a pre-determined programmable agreement on the method of validation and can be by consensus. Third is built-in irreversibility and cryptosecurity. One would need to command at least 51% of the computing power (or nodes or stake) to take control of the blockchain (in the case of bitcoin). Fourth, openness is an important feature as the platform and data can be open and transparent to those who participate. However, openness is also accompanied by the fifth feature of anonymity. This allows individual parties who can be anonymous. Security keys (public and private key pairs) are required to gain access to transaction output. Finally, multiplatform means every blockchain node has the same calculation and data structure.

5.4 Applications of Blockchain to Different Domains

Applications of blockchain in different domains can include stock and securities exchange depicted in Figure 5.7. Both Bitshares system (left-hand side) and Blockchain equity exchange system (right-hand side) are quite self-explanatory.

In banking as in cash transfer, banks traditionally play the intermediary role to transfer money from one customer's account to the payee's account. The banks will be disintermediated by FinTech. By this direct transfer process, the development of blockchain technology will change how central banks operate, let alone the commercial banks as an intermediary to morph incommensurate to leverage on the benefits of blockchain (see http://www.businessinsider.sg/11-banks-in-r3-consortium-use-blockchain-technology-to-trade-2016-1/?r=UK&IR=T). It includes security as irreversible, immutable and

Stock/Securities Exchange

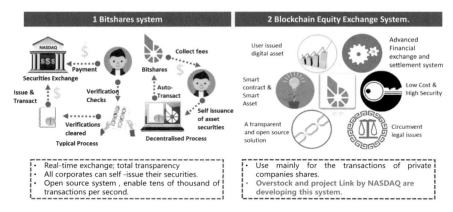

Figure 5.7.　Bitshares and Blockchain Equity Exchange System.

Source: By authors.

traceable transactions. There is also the benefit of ease of governance in utilising the name base of blockchain and every node will be identified, e.g., alliances, issuers, general users. Also, the low operating cost will reduce the cost of transactions. The benefit of shortening the settlement time of financial transactions is demonstrated by a UBS white paper which found that business process time can be reduced to 15 seconds. For Santander Bank, its benefit in using blockchain technology means it will help the banking sector to reduce expenses by USD20 million. Finally, lower counterparty risks is a benefit for all concerned.

In particular, Figure 5.8 shows that R3 is a consortium of many parties involved in building the consortium chain. According to the R3 website, it is building the new operating system for financial markets with a distributed ledger platform called Corda. R3 CEV investors included Bank of America Corp, SBI Holdings Inc, HSBC Holdings Plc, Intel Corp, and Temasek Holdings have invested USD107 million.

Over 40 institutions from more than 15 countries participated in the first two tranches of the New York company's fundraising round

Blockchain applications for banking :
From vision to realisation

•R3 (R3CEV LLC) leads a consortium of 40+ financial companies in research and
development of blockchain usage in the financial system.
•11 banks conducted trials on transactions through distributed ledger using
Ethereum and Microsoft Azure.

Figure 5.8.   Blockchain Application in Banking.

Source: By authors.

in 2016.[3] R3 has the backing of nine of the world's largest investment banks and its membership has rapidly grown to about 80 financial institutions.

In insurance, the traditional coverage system involving an insurance company providing centralised services to its individual clients will be replaced by a decentralised coverage system serving the same pool of clients. The new model features all data that are recorded into the blockchain with any user being able to start and end individual insurance coverage anytime. The advantages include the decentralised system as irreversible, immutable and impartial to ensure self-authentication and fairness. The decentralised system also removes the need for the middleman (agents and insurance company) which ensures efficient utilisation of the fund.

In telecommunication, the design flow of traditional communication devices can be improved by having all nodes to connect through the shortest or the most efficient route. In particular, Bitmessage is a

---

[3]https://www.reuters.com/article/us-r3-cev-blockchain-fundraising/bofa-hsbc-intel-others-invest-107-million-in-blockchain-startup-r3-idUSKBN18J1T6

central link for message delivery for a message is sent to users of the network and users can only access using their private key. It avoids being tracked and ensures data security and data transfer security. Another is GetGems as a decentralised hub with its communication function being similar to that of Bitmessage. It is equipped with Bitwallet and transacts and earns cryptocurrency "gems". Users can click on advertisements for monetary rewards.

In voting, followmyvote.com[4] is open source, secure, inexpensive and convenient. For instance, any annual general meeting (AGM) will be transformed by voters using the app which downloads and installs the voting booth. With securely submitting identity information for verification plus voters register for elections they are qualified to vote in, the results are each voter has been authorised to cast a ballot by both the verifier and registrar as doubly secure. The voters then vote and submit their ballots to a secure blockchain-based ballot box while retaining anonymity and ballot secrecy.

If voters change their minds, they can change their votes in the days leading to the election. Election officials can decide to turn off or on this capability depending the laws and election rules. There is no more need for paint on the fingers of those who have voted as in multiple voting by "paid" voters; no more cheating at the ballot box. Using their accounts, voters can go to the polls and verify for themselves that their votes were cast as intended. The voters can even audit each ballot box to confirm the election results are accurate, all while retaining privacy and top-level security.

For notorisation, irreversibility and incorruptibility allow blockchain to be widely utilised as in seven cases.[5] One is Blockai which aims to develop a new tool that enables the artist to prove and state the copyright to his or her artworks. Two is Stampery which uses blockchain to replace notarisers and to provide authentication for the legality of sensitive information. Three is Chronicled which utilises blockchain technology to authenticate collectables sports

---

[4]https://followmyvote.com/
[5]http://www.8btc.com/blockchain-item?tagname=%E5%85%AC%E8%AF%81%E9%98%B2%E4%BC%AA

shoes. Four is Uproov which uses blockchain for time stamp ability. Five is Bitproof which has set up a one-stop service to notarise education certificates. Six has BitSE in developing Vechain — the first blockchain-based anti-counterfeiting technology. Finally, Factom utilises blockchain to help businesses and government to simplify records management, record business processes, and address security as well as compliance issues.

More common to the public is medical healthcare, with applications for population health, electronic medical records (EMRs), patient data among others. The strengths include one, to increase the transparency of healthcare services and two, to protect patient privacy (involving insurance, credit providers and patients who can utilise blockchain solutions to manage claims and payments). Other strengths include averting major data leak (e.g., Anthem has 80 million patient and employee records; UCLA Health 4.5 million patient records). In all, the increase in the efficiency of bills payments process is evident. Two cases involve a collaboration between Estonia government and guardtime as a blockchain as well as another, Healthbank which also utilises blockchain technology to manage and share personal medical data with medical professionals.

For Visa/DocuSign,[6] the project is in the Proof-of-Concept stage. It brings DocuSign's Digital Transaction Management (DTM) platform and eSignature solution together with Visa's secure payment technology (via Bitcoin blockchain). Alipay will have a similar project. Consumers can hop into a car in a showroom, configure the lease, insurance and other expenses such as parking and tolls, notarise it, pay via Visa, and drive off.

The blockchain comprises a contract (which utilises DocuSign to verify lease and insurance), a report (to check driving records), in-car payment (via Visa card) and service (connections through apps). In essence, users, through their cars, will be able to pay for toll fees, buy pizzas or subscribe for satellite broadcast programmes.

---

[6]https://www.docusign.com/blog/the-future-of-car-leasing-is-as-easy-as-click-sign-drive/

For government administration, Ukraine will be the first to employ blockchain technology in its government administration system. Bitnation is collaborating with Estonia to utilise blockchain to administer government affairs.[7] A new political party in Australia is advocating for the use of blockchain as a mechanism for voting.

5.5   Internet of Things

For IoT, today's supply chain has buyers, sellers and their banks are linked with one another while tomorrow's supply chain maintains the same direct connections, plus complete trustable visibility into the flow of goods and the movement of transactions.[8]

Companies such as IBM and Samsung Electronics have jointly developed the Autonomous Decentralised Peer-to-Peer Telemetry (ADEPT). ADEPT has several capabilities that are fundamental to building a decentralised IoT. It operates on three open source protocols: Telehash for messaging, BitTorrent for file sharing and Ethereum, a blockchain protocol for autonomous device coordination functions. Once a product is assembled, the manufacturer will register on the production system blockchain. When a consumer purchases the product, he or she can register the product on the manufacturer's regional blockchain for authentication purpose.

5.6   Blockchain in China

Figure 5.9 shows blockchain in China with more to come as China is particularly agile in FinTech. This section shows a glimpse of some selected blockchain.

Wanxiang Blockchain Labs is a frontier research lab focusing on blockchain technology.[9] The lab will gather experts in this field to work on technological development, business applications, industrial strategy and other aspects. The lab will also guide

---

[7]http://www.wanbizu.com/fazhan/201512015809.html; http://www.wanbizu.com/news/201602186602.htm   and   http://www.wanbizu.com/news/201602186602.html

[8]http://www.skuchain.com/; http://www.8btc.com/ibm-ethereum

[9]http://www.blockchainlabs.org/

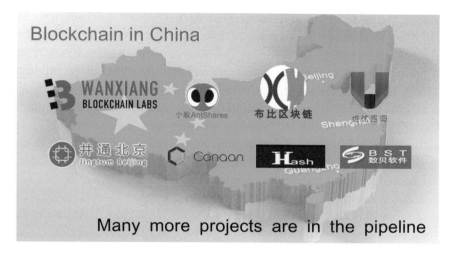

Figure 5.9.   Blockchain in China in 2016.

Source: By authors.

entrepreneurs, and provide a reference for the development of the industry and policy making. Its overall aim is to benefit the society and economy with blockchain technology. Its products include (a) Bitcoin blockchain-based development platform; (b) Ethereum blockchain-based development platform; (c) Bitshares blockchain-based development platform; and (d) Factom blockchain-based development platform.

AntShares, rebranded as NEO in 2017, utilises blockchain technology to digitise real-world physical assets and ownership rights.[10] Through the node-to-node connection in the network, AntShares decentralises financial service processes, such as registrations, security issuances, asset transfers, and settlements administrations. In particular, areas for applications include equity crowdfunding, P2P online lending, employee shares issuance and authorisation of e-contract.

Another is blockchain collaboration by Jingtum Beijing and HNA,[11] featuring three applications. One is the Corporate Wallet

---

[10] https://www.antshares.com

[11] http://www.8btc.com/jingtong-hna

with procurement details leading to cash transfer and settlement, utilising blockchain to develop a low-cost settlement system. This blockchain increases the efficiency of information dissemination. Two is supply chain financing which utilises the encryption technology that is based on Jingtum blockchain. It aims to solve the difficulties in cashflow and financing and in high loan interest faced by suppliers. Three is awarding welfare bonuses whereby HNA awards employees with product discounts, rewards, and bonuses through the blockchain application developed by Jingtum. This blockchain ensures confidential information of employees are secured, and allows the employees to enjoy more discounts and rewards.

Figure 5.9 also shows BuBi blockchain(布比区块链).[12] Its applications are one, in equity to secure private equity transactions; two in reward points as management of customer reward points; and three, in the supply chain as immutable data management and supply chain management. The value propositions of BuBi blockchain include having efficient verification of transactions, efficient access to accounts ledger, multiple assets, issuance, multiple signatories authorisation, smart contract and blockchain exchanges as a whole package deal.

Another blockchain is by ViewFin[13] offering customised blockchain solutions and accreditation of digital assets and risks management. Four product snapshots show what ViewFin does. One is Project Prometheus in equity management with solutions as private or permissioned blockchain for equity management used in equity registration, transfer, or over the counter (OTC) trades. Its clients included those involved in crowd-funding, equity exchanges, P2P leading, private equities and OTC trades. Two is Project Hermes for royalty/reward points management offering solutions to manage customers reward points through permissioned blockchain. Its uses include managing multiple reward points programmes with clients as all Business-to-Consumer (B2C) businesses and services. Three is Project Gaea in land registration with solutions

---

[12]http://www.bubi.cn/#page4
[13]http://viewfin.com/

in private or permissioned blockchain for land registration. Its uses include providing trustless proofs for cross-regional land rights-transfer, real-time information validation, decentralised immutable data storage and instant settlement for digital transactions. Four is Project Themis as RegTech Chain, in private chain solution for its clients to implement effective regulatory governance. Its uses include immutable and timestamped record management. This improves integrity of information and increases transparency with clients being governments, regulatory bodies and non-government organisations (NGOs).

Digital Wallet (数贝荷包)[14] is another blockchain developed by Yi Cheng Interactive Technologies and it has Sunshine Insurance Group as the first corporate user of the digital wallet. It allows Sunshine insurance clients to manage, transfer and transact customer reward points. Its decentralised reward points system enables users to self-negotiate, transfer and transact reward points, which increases the liquidity of reward points. It thus enhances B2C and Consumer-to-Consumer (C2C) interactions.

Another blockchain is developed by Yangtze Delta Region Institute based in Tsinghua University together with Canaan, 1Hash and BST which collectively established China's blockchain applications research centre with the aim to develop the use of blockchain technology.[15] Founded in 2012, Canaan Creative is the worldwide leader in producing blockchain servers and solutions for repetition Application-Specific Integrated Circuit (ASIC). Its products are sold to over 150 countries around the world. 1Hash provides a professional and reliable service platform for efficient bitcoin management and development platform for blockchain research. BST provides cloud computing service (Paas) and software management service (Saas) for the Beijing government to manage information resources. The main product/service is Digital DXS-Cloud (Paas) and iTaxonomy.

---

[14]http://m.caijing.com.cn/api/show?contentid=4090411
[15]www.btc798.com/article-8759-1.html; http://canaan.io/zh/%E7%BD%91%E7
%AB%99%E9%A6%96%E9%A1%B5/; http://www.synball.com/synball/home/;
and http://www.1hash.com/index.html

In line with China's One Belt, One Road[16] (OBOR and now Belt and Road Initiative, BRI), blockchain applications cover three aspects.[17] One is to improve financial cooperation and communication. As the countries along the BRI project transact using US dollar, the China government wishes to utilise blockchain technology to develop a cryptocurrency system which these countries can transact on (see Figures 5.10, 5.11 and 5.12 for more information). Through the Asia Financial Cooperation Association (to be established), country members can work and decide on the rules and protocols to ensure the security and the legality of the cryptocurrency system. Two is to help China corporates to internationalise. This involves aiding China corporates to minimise foreign investment pitfalls by digitising investment/trade information of the investments in countries along the BRI project. This BRI blockchain will ensure data security, transparency and allow co-verification and authorisation of information. It will also protect intellectual property rights. Three is to solve China's problem of overproduction capacity or excess capacity, especially with China's slowdown or "new normal" since the global financial crisis in 2007–2008. Through the digitisation of production capacity and blockchain network, China corporates

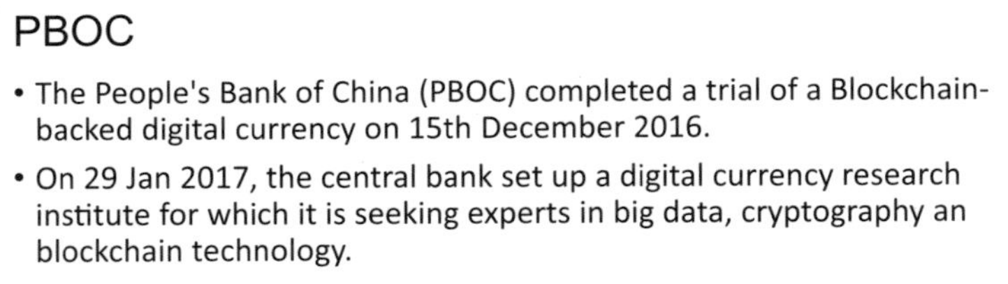

PBOC

- The People's Bank of China (PBOC) completed a trial of a Blockchain-backed digital currency on 15th December 2016.
- On 29 Jan 2017, the central bank set up a digital currency research institute for which it is seeking experts in big data, cryptography an blockchain technology.

Figure 5.10.   PBOC and Blockchain.

Source: By authors.

---

[16]The OBOR is China's plan to invest almost USD1 trillion in infrastructure in some of the world's poorest countries, stretching all the way from China, Association of Southeast Asian Nations (ASEAN) to India, Central Asia, Middle East, Africa all the way to Europe. It represents President Xi Jinping's signature foreign policy initiative as he envisions a new wave of global growth spurred by roads and rail links. Renamed as Belt and Road Initiative (BRI).
[17]http://www.ftchinese.com/story/001065381?full=y

Blockchain in China

- Central Government's 13th 5-Year Plan
  - BlockChain" is the key in building "modern information technology and Industrial ecological system
- Ministry of Industry and Information
  - Issued China's Blockchain Technology and Application Development Whitepaper in Oct 2016.
  - 1. Create a good environment for blockchain development
  - 2. Accelerate the development of blockchain applications
  - 3. Set Standards for Industrialisation

Figure 5.11.   China Government and Blockchain.
Source: By authors.

Local Government and PPP

- Local Government: Shanghai, Beijing, GuiZhou, HangZhou, Shenzhen, Hong Kong
- Pulbic Private Partnership:
  - WanXiang USD20 billion Smart Blockchain City on 10 Sqkm
  - Largest project ever known supported by Fenbushi Capital with 50 companies and USD200-300m Portfolio including USD500k Ether that grew to USD125m in 18 months
  - Partners include most of the Fintech Giants like Tencent, Alibaba etc

Figure 5.12.   Chinese Local Government and Blockchain.
Source: By authors.

can attract investors in countries under the BRI project, carry out crowdfunding in these countries or internationally. One can also conduct initial public offer (IPO) on the blockchain network.

China has more than 50% bitcoin mining power, the largest mining farm, fastest machines and its exchanges account for more than 50% of bitcoin trades. AntRouter is a wireless networking device containing a bitcoin mining chip. AntMiner S7 with 4.73th/s uses less energy and is more efficient.[18]

---

[18]https://www.bitmaintech.com/product.htm

Another blockchain from China is Blockchain 2.0 Core Ethereum,[19] supported by Microsoft, R3, Samsung, Deloitte, RWE and IBM. Ethereum is a decentralised platform that runs smart contracts with applications that operate exactly as programmed without any possibility of downtime, censorship, fraud or third party interference. Its objective is to develop apps which run on a custom-built blockchain that enables shared global infrastructure and that represents the ownership of property. Its value proposition is to enable developers to create markets, store registries of debts or promises, move funds in accordance with instructions or a future contract among many other potential developments, all without a middleman or counterparty risk. In essence, Blockchain 2.0 Core Ethereum featuring smart contract and smart asset is a decentralised smart application. It rents, sells or shares anything without middlemen. Slock.it utilises the Ethereum computer to turn personal assets into income by securely rent access to any space or compatible smart object, without intermediaries. Underused assets such as temporarily vacant apartment form an opportunity to make a profit. It also develops applications for smart contract and smart asset to find, locate, rent and control any object managed by an Ethereum computer.

5.7   Enterprise Perspective of Blockchain

The potential of decentralised ledgers and blockchain is limitless, starting from Factom as based out of Austin, Texas with its world famous BBQ and music festivals expanding the FinTech scene.[20] It has expanded into Shanghai, Beijing, Honduras, London, and Sunnyvale, California. This blockchain has the aim of making the world's systems honest as its Chief Architect Paul Snow is quoted as "honesty is subversive". Factom views the global economy where trust is in rare supply. Incidents such as the 2010 United States foreclosure crisis demonstrate that the current processes are terribly inaccurate, inefficient and prone to failure. This lack of trust requires the devotion of a tremendous amount of resources to audit and verify

---

[19]https://slock.it/ethereum_computer.html
[20]http://factom.org/

records. The result in reducing global efficiency, return on investment and prosperity is where Factom steps in to remove the need for blind trust by providing a precise, verifiable and immutable audit trail.

Factom's blockchain technology can be adapted to almost any organisation. Its application usages include one, for businesses and governments to simplify records management, record business processes, and address security and compliance issues. Two is Factom powers a remarkable range of applications, e.g., audit systems, medical records, supply chain management, voting systems, property titles, legal applications and financial systems. Its network value is being Factom Proof as Factom maintains a permanent, timestamped record of data in the blockchain. This reduces the cost and complexity of conducting audits, managing records, and complying with government regulations. Specifically, it offers proof of existence that a document existed in this form at a certain time. Its proof of process is having the document linked to this newly updated document. Its proof of audit lies in verifying the changes in the updated document.

Three cases illustrate the usefulness of Factom. In Case 1, Factom is saving Bank of America (BoA) USD17 billion. The background was multiple mortgage companies were fined billions of dollars due to a mishandling of mortgage records. One of these companies was BoA which fell victim to a USD17 billion fine, also known as the largest fine in history. As a solution, Factom utilises the bitcoin blockchain to keep BoA records permanently engrained in the distributed public ledger. The entries are then "filed" into directory blocks and secured to the bitcoin blockchain every 10 minutes. They can then be audited in real time and verified instantly, allowing everyone to double check the work completed and detect any mistakes that can become a problem.

Factom Use in Case 2 is protecting Sony Pictures with blockchain technology. On November 24, 2014, a hacker group leaked confidential data from the film studio Sony Pictures Entertainment. The data included personal information about employees and their families, e-mails, salaries, copies of then-unreleased Sony films. The solution is by Factom storing the data for its clients using encryptions that are called hashes in blockchain in a decentralised system. Because the data are encoded, no one except the user who created the encryption can decipher it. Blockchain technologies thus prevented the disastrous Sony hack and shifted big companies away from central databases.

Factom Use in Case 3 is Factom unlocking USD9 trillion in land value. The problem in many developing countries is landowners do not have proof of rights to land ownership. As noted by Hernando De Soto, the main problem of development is not that the poor lack capital, but that many have no assets. There are also those that lack legal title to assets they already hold. Giving them a legal title will unleash this "dead capital" so that it can be used as collateral for loans to fund businesses or expand homes. The solution lies in Factom's ability to digitise landownership documents and store them in a decentralised blockchain. Any land transactions and transfers can be tracked. Furthermore, unauthorised or illegal changes can be detected and corrected.

Another global player in blockchain is Zcash. One feature is Zcash payments as a decentralised and open source cryptocurrency that offers privacy and selective transparency of transactions using advanced cryptography. Zcash payments are published on a public blockchain, but the sender, recipient, and amount of a transaction remain private. A second feature is transaction metadata. Bitcoin transactions work using triple-entry accounting, as transactions combine the "outputs" of previous transactions and split into new outputs of arbitrary value. The spend-authority of the "inputs" of a transaction, as well as the balance of the transaction, are checked manually by all nodes. This means that all fully verifying nodes must keep all unspent outputs, but also, that all nodes are aware of all values and parties involved in transactions. The third feature is zero-knowledge proofs with its zero-knowledge proving scheme making it possible to hide values and other identifying information from the public. Using advanced cryptographic techniques, users simply prove that the values balance and that they are authorised to spend such value (noting that they have not spent it before). Zcash evolves from Zerocoin to Zerocash. Zerocash improves on an earlier protocol, Zerocoin, developed by some of the same authors, both in functionality (Zerocoin only hides a payment's origin, but not its destination or amount) and in efficiency (Zerocash transactions are less than one kilobyte and take less than 6 milliseconds to verify). The scientists, advisors and engineers of ZECC Zerocoin Electric Coin Company developed and launched the Zcash protocol. In 2017, J.P. Morgan announced that it is partnering with Zcash on blockchain security by integrating ZSL with its Ethereum-based Quorum project. ZSL is a zero-knowledge security layer designed to securely and anonymously settle transactions on the blockchain.

5.7.1 *The multinationals and major players*

Airbnb Co-founder and Chief Technology Officer (CTO), Nathan Blecharczyk has his eyes on blockchain tech for user reputation and trust, noting on 13 March 2016, that Airbnb would be looking into blockchain integration in 2017 or a similar distributed ledger system, to authenticate a user's reputation and establish trust on the platform.

Similarly, Microsoft and IBM declare that blockchain is open for business. On 17 February 2016, IBM has announced the official launch of its digital ledger deliverance to bring blockchain services to a cloud-based system. The platform will allow users to create, deploy and run blockchain-based applications. The London Stock Exchange Group is also engaged in the development of open blockchain technologies with IBM to create solutions that will help manage risk and bring additional transparency to global financial markets.

With the environment shifting fast, the Hyperledger project formed in early 2016 is to advance blockchain technology. Major players are involved, not just banks and FinTech companies, but more traditional companies such as Hitachi and Fujitsu are also participating. It is a collaborative effort to advance blockchain technology by identifying and addressing critical features for a cross-industry open standard for distribution ledgers that can transform the way business transactions are being conducted globally.

5.7.2 *PwC Vulcan digital asset services: NETKI, Libra and Bloq*

"Big Four" audit firm PwC's Australia division together with a trio of start-ups are making a play aimed squarely at altering this narrative by convincing financial institutions that bitcoin (and the open network of digital currencies that has sprung up around it) could help them launch new services and better serve existing customers. The platform Vulcan is a joint effort by Bloq, Libra, NETKI and PwC started in 2016. It aims to enable the professional services firm's clients to launch digital assets that would be interoperable with and trade alongside bitcoin and its many alternatives.

NETKI is a company that focuses on risk and compliance with an open permissionless network built on open source and open standards. Its name system like the Domain Name System provides the standard and infrastructure for the Internet to map easily to remember domain names like google.com to a numeric Internet Protocol (IP) address. Its World Network Service (WNS) is designed to allow service providers, using any blockchain to replace the cumbersome public addresses provided to users (e.g., 1CpLXM15vjULK3ZPGUTDMUcGATGR9xGitv) with easy to remember, domain-style wallet names. Next, its identification, the BIP 0070 payment protocol is another useful (yet underutilised) extension, which allows a sender to ensure that he or she is paying the correct/desired recipient, before he or she permanently signs away his or her funds.

For NETKI, its verification is in addition to a green lock or check that appears next to a correctly inputted recipient. BIP 0070 can be used to provide transacting parties with a more detailed record surrounding the specific aspects of a particular transfer (eg., what was purchased, the reason for the transfer, etc.) before the sender "presses send" (initiating an irreversible transaction). These details can be recorded in the "memo field" of a payment request, which is transmitted directly between the sender and receiver, without having to record them on the blockchain permanently. By its timestamping, these payment requests, when

Travel Rule Compliance Solution

- Validated digital identity certificates
- Work across private and public blockchains
- Aid companies with US Travel Rule [31 CFR 103.33(g)], Department of Treasury compliance for Money Service Business (MSB)
- Contain validated identity information
- Work in conjunction with blockchain Payment Protocol (BIP70/75)
- Can be used for non-repudiation

Figure 5.13. NETKI.

Source: By authors.

combined with transaction details timestamped on the blockchain, provide companies and individuals with a more complete digital "paper trail". This trail can be used as an effective substitute for traditional receipts, while never inputting sensitive information onto the blockchain, or exposing any of the extended transaction details to anyone not a party to the transaction. Moreover, the utilisation of these payment requests can help companies/services remain compliant with existing AML/KYC/CTF regulations, which generally require financial institutions and DNFBP (Designated Non-Financial Businesses and Professionals) to maintain more detailed records of the transaction (see Figure 5.13).

Finally, NETKI has offered validated digital identity certificates which work across private and public blockchains. It helps companies complied with US Travel Rule [31 CFR 103.33(g)], Department of Treasury for Money Service Business (MSB). It works in conjunction with blockchain Payment Protocol (BIP70/75) and can be used for non-repudiation.

Figure 5.14 shows another blockchain company Libra. Libra Tech is a universal control, compliance, and reporting solution for distributed ledger technology with Libra's digital assets (video,

LIBRA **As An Interface**

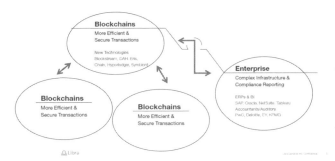

LibraTax:

Harnessing Data
And Drawing Data
From Different Sources
For Tax Reporting.

China will have Global
Taxation from next year.

Figure 5.14.   Libra Tech.

Source: By authors.

audio, picture, bitcoin, DAC, DAH etc.) (see Figure 5.15). It is the next asset class to monitor, manage, custodise and monetise. Its consulting services comprise auditing, accounting and advisory, with applications as wallets, smart contracts and identity in conjunction with other blockchains such as Eris, Consensys and NETKI. Its protocol (blockchain) features open system (Ethereum, Hyperledger, bitcoin) and permissioned system (Chain, DAH, Ripple). Libra is thus strategically placed (see Figure 5.15).

Bloq, an enterprise grade blockchain company, provides services with the philosophy of open source, decentralised, enterprise class and interoperable. BloqEnterprise has five key offerings that enable users to create, test, update, customise and analyse their own public, private and permissioned blockchains. BloqThink complements BloqEnterprise with strategic architecting, design, development and education. Blocklabs is a blockchain technology research and testing centre formed to work with and foster innovation between global businesses and the open source community.

Bloq, together with PricewaterhouseCoopers (PwC) Australia, Libra and NETKI, have launched a new FinTech business platform

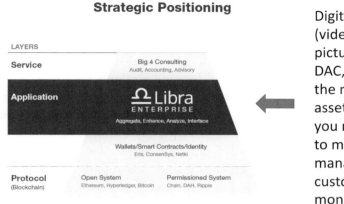

Digital Asset (video, audio, picture, bitcoin, DAC, DAH etc) is the next asset class and you need to monitor, manage, custodise and monetise.

Figure 5.15.   Strategic Positioning of Libra Tech.

Source: By authors.

called Vulcan Digital Asset Services to enable digital assets to be used for everyday banking, commerce and other personal currency and asset related services. Vulcan will provide digital currency wallets, international payment processing, and investment and trading services, and will soon offer Point of Sales and merchant services and the ability to create and support native digital currencies and rewards-based systems. Vulcan is exploring projects with an international banking group, a central bank, a regional airline and six other banks.

5.8   Developments in Blockchain

Since 2016, there are a lot of developments in blockchain that are collaborations of governments with industry to explore the strategic potential of blockchains. Three factors drive implementation of blockchains. First, is the ability of blockchain to provide a basis for cryptographic trust in a similar way to public key infrastructure (PKI). A PKI is a set of rules, policies, and procedures needed to create, manage, distribute, use, store, and revoke digital certificates and manage public-key encryption. Public-key cryptography, or asymmetrical cryptography, is any cryptographic system that uses pairs of keys: public keys which may be disseminated widely, and private keys which are known only to the owner. Blockchains could leverage PKI's deployed scale and governance. PKIs could also leverage blockchain's payment and ledger functions.

Second, permissioned ledgers or blockchains can contain a data field of unlimited size. There is information about a transaction, including the contract, licence or copyright, could be included, providing a strong additional factor for trust. Third, it enables "smart contracts", offering efficiency and non-repudiation. Smartphones are becoming the de facto trusted user device. The latest smartphones include new security features such as: Trusted Platform Module which secures digital certificates and cryptographic keys for authentication, encryption and signing. Moreover, consumers can sign transactions (e.g., using a blockchain) and payments (e.g., using a "trusted Bitcoin") using smartphones.

5.9   Shortcomings of Blockchain

Four issues and concerns can be noted (see Figure 5.16). First is application suitability. Is blockchain superior to current solutions? What are the benchmarks? Can blockchain reduce cost, improve service quality or enhance user experience? All these questions are relevant. The immutable public ledger, standardised contracts, accounting, and transactions may seem too idealistic. The different nature of businesses and changing needs of the organisation will impede the establishment of a single standard. To succeed, blockchain applications need to create true value for the users.

Second is consolidation and allocation of research resources. With issues on the consolidation and allocation of resources, how should research resources be allocated? Can related or similar resources be consolidated to create synergies? What solutions and which industry domains should receive the most funding? These are only some questions.

Three is the likelihood of reducing costs. In reality, by contrast, ensuring security and immutability of data may drive up the cost.

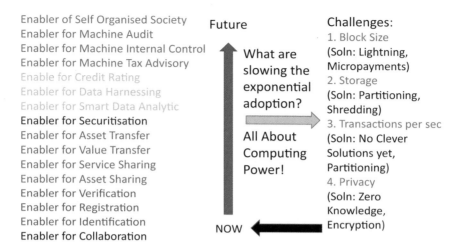

Enabler of Self Organised Society
Enabler for Machine Audit
Enabler for Machine Internal Control
Enabler for Machine Tax Advisory
Enable for Credit Rating
Enabler for Data Harnessing
Enabler for Smart Data Analytic
Enabler for Securitisation
Enabler for Asset Transfer
Enabler for Value Transfer
Enabler for Service Sharing
Enabler for Asset Sharing
Enabler for Verification
Enabler for Registration
Enabler for Identification
Enabler for Collaboration

Future

What are slowing the exponential adoption?

All About Computing Power!

NOW

Challenges:
1. Block Size
(Soln: Lightning, Micropayments)
2. Storage
(Soln: Partitioning, Shredding)
3. Transactions per sec
(Soln: No Clever Solutions yet, Partitioning)
4. Privacy
(Soln: Zero Knowledge, Encryption)

Figure 5.16. The Present, the Future and the Challenges for Blockchain Technology.

Source: By authors.

To ensure immutability of data implies incurring huge storage and electricity cost. Low storage efficiency is due to one, huge amount of copies and two, blockchain size cannot be reduced (expired and useless data will also be stored). Moreover, rebooting of data is time-consuming. New content times the number of copies, coupled with distance and bandwidth, will all be time-consuming. These issues affect user experience, e.g., high-volume trading, processing huge database.

Finally, over-regulation is the fourth concern. Concerns include illegal activities, e.g., money laundering, financing terrorism, fraud and impersonation. A decentralised framework may not meet regulatory requirements. Early intervention and overregulation by regulators may impede blockchain developments, and the potential benefits of blockchain may not realise. There are also other challenges such as the block size, storage, transactions per second, privacy, legality and Oracle issues.

Blocksize/Gas Limit: Transaction data are permanently recorded in files called blocks. Blocks are limited to one megabyte in size in bitcoin. Miners can mine blocks up to the one megabyte fixed limit, but any block larger than one megabyte is invalid. This limit cannot be modified without a hard fork.[21] Ethereum has a gas limit rather than a block size. The gas limit is a cap on both processing and storage/bandwidth because the cost of a transaction/function is fixed in units of gas for each type of instruction. The gas limit is voted up or down by each miner and each miner determines what gas price it is willing to accept which is like bitcoin transaction fees but on a per gas basis rather than a per transaction basis. The Lightning Network is dependent upon the underlying technology of the blockchain. By using real bitcoin/blockchain transactions and using its native smart-contract scripting language, it is possible to create a secure network of participants which are able to transact at high volume and high speed. The Raiden Network is an off-chain scaling solution, enabling near-instant, low-fee and scalable payments. Other concepts such as sidechains, drivechains, and two-way pegging are other solutions that we will not discuss in this Chapter but done in Chapter 2.

Storage: Maidsafe, BigChainDB, Swarm, Storj and IPFS are examples of distributed object storage/distributed file system. They use various strategies for smearing out copies and shards across participating nodes, but they are not putting all things in all places at all times. New systems are being created and it is an area of great interest.

The other challenges are transaction per seconds which is too low for scaling; privacy issues as computing power is still inadequate for meaningful mass adoption other than using hashes; legality and Oracle that are issues with the execution of smart contracts. We shall not dwell further on these technical ideas in this Chapter.

Banks are only the beginning of the FinTech evolution. What is happening and what will happen? Clearly noted is unbundling

---

[21] "Hard Fork" relates to blockchain technology. A hard fork (or sometimes hardfork) is a radical change to the protocol that makes previously invalid blocks/transactions valid (or vice-versa), and as such requires all nodes or users to upgrade to the latest version of the protocol software. See http://www.invest opedia.com/terms/h/hard-fork.asp

and decentralisation of financial services as happening now with the same data, same page, but fewer errors. Everybody has the same data ledger. This means fewer mistakes and less mismatch of data. Transactions are done within seconds because middlemen are cut out. A flatter structure and fewer errors mean less redundant services. The result is a real-time settlement without a need for financial intermediaries, which also helps in shaving off duplicative and redundant services. All of these mean a boost for security compared to SWIFT as error prone with a time lag and can be exploited by criminals. This can easily be avoided through the use of permissioned ledgers by registered banks using blockchain.

Challenges and responses to them are limited only by human imagination. From the perspective of capital markets, smart contracts post-trade settlement as automated, efficient and no need for trusted third parties. Financial markets can simplify current siloed post-trade systems, automated by using smart contracts. Australian Securities Exchange, or ASX, commissioned Digital Assets, a US firm, to develop Distributed Ledger Technology, or DLT, for the Australian market. Interdealer broker, ICAP, also has private P2P DLT network using smart contracts. Other areas that DLT can be used include personal insurance and digital identities. DLT with hospitals will allow seamless processing, authentication of persons and boost claims efficiency. In personal insurance plus digital identities, these can be as distributed ledgers with hospitals, seamless processing, Keyless Signatures Infrastructure (KSI) authentication and boost claims efficiency. KSI is a globally distributed system for providing timestamping and server-supported digital signature services.

Keyless signatures are an alternative solution to traditional PKI signatures. Keyless does not mean that no cryptographic keys for signature. Keys are still necessary for authentication, but the signatures can be reliably verified without having continued secrecy of the keys. Keyless signatures are not vulnerable to key compromise. For those not so technically savvy, KSI provides a solution to the problem of the long-term validity of digital signatures.

To sum up for trade and real-time accounting, Figure 5.17 shows immediate data flow, programmable accounting entries, one master

Figure 5.17.   Real-time GDP Using Blockchain.
Source: By authors.

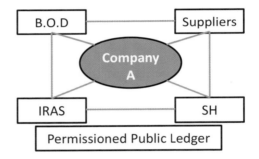

Figure 5.18.   Real-time Accounting.
Source: By authors.

prime ledger to serve management, bank lending, regulatory purposes and fewer errors as also free of manipulation (see Figure 5.18).

Figure 5.17 for government budgets enables programmable smart contracts for budget allocation, real-time gross domestic product (GDP) and key data reporting, and use of blockchain as verifiable and trusted.

5.10   Keeping up with Blockchain

The regulatory challenge remains to be resolved. With more elaboration in a later chapter highlighting Singapore, suffice to note is

Monetary Authority of Singapore's (MAS) managing director Ravi Menon noting: "If you start regulating every one of those, you stifle a lot of innovation, and they don't get a chance to grow." Thus this implies that MAS will regulate FinTech firms only when they pose risks.

Regulators should aim to promote greater interoperability across data systems as a top priority. For example, an "all-in-one" addressing system will enable e-payments using the payee's mobile number, email address, social network account or other proxies without the need to know the payee's bank account number. The MAS will therefore introduce a "regulatory sandbox" approach that aims to give financial institutions (FIs) more confidence to experiment and launch their innovative products or services within controlled boundaries.

Blockchain and FinTech are about financial inclusion as reaching out to all, not just in developing countries. Blockchain and DLT are more than just technology as it is going to be a strategy and it is going to transform the way business is conducted in the future. The underserved in the world turn to non-traditional forms of alternative financial services such as those provided by cheque cashers, loan sharks and pawnbrokers. As a reminder, even the 7.7% of US households are unbanked and 20% are underbanked. For example, illegal workers in the US who cash cheques via agents such as cheque cashing depots or convenience stores. Any new technology is by nature disruptive, but progress is about transformation and that includes making disruption technology an acceptable threshold to greater stability with widespread usage with infinite imagination.

Finally, we should end this Chapter by looking at two charts: (1) the Gartner's hype cycle (see Figure 5.19) and have a sense of where blockchain is; (2) the cryptocurrency, usually a form of open blockchain, as a comparison to other investable class of assets (see Figure 5.20). Blockchain is still nearing the peak of inflated expectations and it will be interesting to see where all these experiments are leading to.

GARTNER'S HYPE CYCLE FOR DIGITAL BANKING

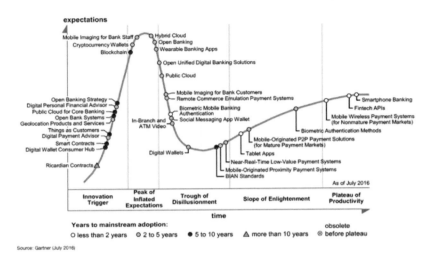

Figure 5.19.   Blockchain in a Hype.

Source: Newton (2017).

Bitcoin Risk-Adjusted ROI vs Other Asset Classes

Figure 5.20.   Bitcoin as an Investment Class.

Source: Woobull, http://charts.woobull-com/bitcoin-risk-adjusted-return/

5.11 Final Note

This Chapter was written between 2014 and 2016. Readers may wish to access the latest materials through sussblockchain.com, slideshares, or the social media account of the first author at http://www.linkedin.com/in/david-lee-kuo-chuen-%E6%9D%8E%E5%9B%BD%E6%9D%83-07750baa/@DavidkChuenLee.

References and Further Readings

Bloq. (2017a). Retrieved from http://bloq.com/#team

Bloq. (2017b). Retrieved from http://bloq.com/bloq-and-pwc-australia-launch-vulcan-to-accelerate-global-adoption-of-digital-money.html

Buldas, A., Kroonmaa, A., & Laanoja, R. (2013). Keyless Singatures' Infrastructure: How to build global distributed has-tress. Retrieved from https://eprint.iacr.org/2013/834.pdf

Factom. (2017). Retrieved from https://www.factom.com/about/team

Fink, B. (2017, June 22). Antshares rebrands, introduces NEO and the new smart economy. Retrieved from https://bitcoinmagazine.com/articles/antshares-rebrands-introduces-neo-and-new-smart-economy1/

Handler, J. (2015, July 28). Addressimo: Making BIP 0032 & BIP 0070 easy for developers. Retrieved from https://blog.Netki.com/2015/07/

Irrera, A. (2017, May 23). BofA, HSBC, Intel, others invest $107 mln in blockchain startup R3. Retrieved from https://finance.yahoo.com/news/bofa-hsbc-intel-others-invest-123000543.html

Lee, D. K. C. (2016a). Blockchain as an enabler. Retrieved from https://www.slideshare.net/DavidLee215/blockchain-as-an-enabler16-july-2016david-leefinal

Lee, D. K. C. (2016b). The future of FinTech and blockchain. Retrieved from https://www.slideshare.net/WanfengChen/the-future-of-FinTech-and-blockchain-63339789

Libra. (2017). Retrieved from http://www.libra.tech/

Medium. (2016). Blockchain applications beyond the financial services industry. Retrieved from https://medium.com/@LetsTalkPayments/blockchain-applications-beyond-the-financial-services-industry-ef7fcce216d6

Moh-Rokib. (2016). Zcash — All coins are created equally. Retrieved from https://steemit.com/zcash/@moh-rokib/zcash-all-coins-are-created-equal

Nakamoto, S. (2008). Bitcoin: A peer-to-peer electronic cash system. Retrieved from https://bitcoin.org/bitcoin.pdf

Newton, A. (2017). Hype cycle for digital banking transformation. Retrieved from https://static1.squarespace.com/static/581ca875f5e2313c7cbad236/t/59c423157131a59f8b16b10a/1506026265604/hype_cycle_for_digital_banki_328960.pdf

PwC. (2017). PwC's digital asset services: Powering the future of financial services. Retrieved from https://www.pwc.com.au/financial-services/FinTech/digital-asset-services.html

Reddit. (2016, March 12). What is Ethereum block size? https://www.reddit.com/r/ethereum/comments/4a3kqo/what_is_ethereums_block_size/

Samman, G. (2017). Sammantics. Retrieved from http://sammantics.com/

Scardovi, C. (2016). Restructuring and Innovation in Banking. Springer International Publishing.

UK Government. (2016). Distributed Ledger Technology: Beyond blockchain. UK Government, Office for Science. Retrieved from http://www.the-blockchain.com/docs/UK%20government%2088%20page%20Blockchain%20Report.pdf

Woobull. http://charts.woobull.com/bitcoin-risk-adjusted-return/

Zerocash. (2017). Retrieved from http://zerocash-project.org/

Chapter 6

Blockchain: A Technical Introduction

Written Jointly with Swee Won LO

6.1 Introduction

The concept of blockchain was first introduced in the Bitcoin protocol published in Nakamoto (2008). The Bitcoin blockchain is the first sound design of an open, transparent and secure distributed ledger technology (DLT) that solves the double-spending problem of digital currency without the need of a trusted authority. It records bitcoin transactions in an immutable and trusted manner through collaboration between a distributed group of users using cryptographic techniques and distributed consensus algorithm. Since then, there are numerous efforts that extend Bitcoin's public and permissionless blockchain to provide additional functionality and feature that is more well-suited for commercial and enterprise-level application. This eventually led to the emergence of private and permissioned blockchain.

A public blockchain is where anyone in the world can send transactions and participate in the consensus process to validate transactions. To achieve the purpose of decentralisation, a public blockchain commonly has its own intrinsic token with the main objective being an incentive to reward honest users who participate in the consensus process and help to maintain the integrity of the blockchain state. In addition, by imposing a cost (in the form of the built-in token) for the user to perform a transaction, spamming can be effectively inhibited. On the other hand, a private blockchain is commonly used by enterprises as a shared database to record information (such as business processes or documents) in an immutable manner. Users of a private blockchain — commonly the employees — are therefore legally obligated to upkeep the integrity of the blockchain. Thus, private blockchain can be implemented without an intrinsic token to provide economic incentives. However, some enterprises may opt to periodically anchor their blockchain state to a public blockchain to provide public accountability.

In this Chapter, we survey several prominent token-based and tokenless blockchain systems. We examine how the distributed consensus algorithm is designed in these systems to ensure that the blockchain is secure against attacks. In addition, we study the security features provided by these systems in terms of data confidentiality, user privacy and access control. Next, we discuss the cryptographic techniques that are employed in existing blockchain systems, including their security properties and features, and point out possible improvement or security considerations that should be taken into account in a blockchain design. Two sources (Lai and Lee, 2017; Lee and Deng, 2017;) provide good references.

6.2 Characteristics of a Blockchain

Blockchain is commonly considered as an immutable and ordered record of transactions. It leverages the salient features of cryptographic techniques and distributed consensus algorithm to provide a transparent, accountable and synchronised "ledger" that is maintained by a group of mutually distrusting users across a geographically distributed network. Blockchain effectively eliminates the need to have a centralised party as the single source of truth while significantly lowers the cost and complexity of financial transaction and data sharing.

6.2.1 *Distributed ledger technology*

Blockchain is a form of distributed ledger with the main enabling technology being the Peer-to-Peer (P2P) network (Schoder, Fischbach and Schmitt, 2005). Instead of relying on a centralised party to relay information, every node in a blockchain system communicates with each other directly. A transaction that occurs in the system is broadcasted in a P2P manner, validated by all nodes using identical validation rules, and added to the copy of "ledger" maintained by each node. At this point in time, each node will have an updated state of the blockchain. However, it is possible that due to network delay or congestion, nodes in a blockchain system do not have the same version of the blockchain state at all times. To mitigate this, each node keeps a higher scoring version of the state (the scoring system is dependent on the blockchain specification) to the best of its knowledge. Whenever it receives a higher scoring version, it will overwrite its own version and broadcast the information to its peers (Morabito, 2017). To verify a particular transaction on the blockchain, a node simply queries its nearby (peer) nodes for their copies, and confirms the transaction after it obtains sufficient identical copies from its peers.

6.2.2 *Single version of truth*

A blockchain system provides a single version of truth in a distributed manner. This is achieved by leveraging cryptographic techniques and distributed consensus algorithm. To this end, note that a blockchain provides an immutable and ordered record of transactions in a chain of blocks that are bounded cryptographically. More specifically, in each time epoch, a new block containing the cryptographic hash values of an ordered list of validated transactions and the cryptographic hash value of the previous block in the chain is added to the blockchain, after it is digitally signed by one or more validating nodes. This effectively creates a secure *chain* of immutable records as the properties of cryptographic hash function and digital signature ensure that the attempt to remove or alter the records is computationally infeasible. Consensus algorithm, on the other hand, is a mean for all mutually distrusting nodes to reach an eventual agreement on the state of the blockchain, provided that at least 50% of nodes in a blockchain system are honest. With a well-designed consensus algorithm in place, an attacker must corrupt at least 51% of the nodes (in order to be in control of the total amount of computing power) or possess at least 51% of the total built-in tokens powering the blockchain to be able to influence the outcome on the blockchain state. This effectively makes the cost of cheating extremely high and de-incentivises attacks.

6.2.3 *Cryptography*

Cryptography is one of the key techniques to realise a secure blockchain. Data such as the transactions, digital assets, state of accounts or financial agreements must be *authenticated* and *integrity-protected* before they can be executed and trigger a change in the blockchain state. It is also essential to have a *non-repudiation* service in place to hold user accountable for all data sent in a blockchain, whether it is a transaction that triggers a state change or a validation proof sent by a notary or a validating node. Private blockchains deployed by enterprises may also desire additional functionalities such as data *confidentiality* as well as an *access control* mechanism to be in place to specify the type of resources that a particular user can access, depending on its role in the organisation. Finally, privacy can be defined in three aspects, namely user *anonymity* (the ability for a user to transact without revealing its identity), *unlinkability* (the ability to prevent two transactions from being identified as belonging to the same user) and *untraceability* (the ability to hide the flow path of a financial asset).

6.2.4 *Consensus algorithm*

Consensus algorithm is a method that allows a majority of mutually distrusting nodes to come to an agreement on a common state of the blockchain. It essentially specifies a set of rules and procedures that should be abide by all nodes to validate transactions. A well-designed consensus algorithm gives incentives to honest nodes that work to maintain consistency of the blockchain state while imposing a penalty to dishonest nodes.

Synchrony: A consensus algorithm depends heavily on the blockchain system's ability to keep time. The FLP Impossibility Proof (Fischer, Lynch and Patterson, 1985) has shown that if nodes in a distributed system have no bound on the time it takes for a message to be sent to another node or on the relative time difference in processing speed between two nodes, then there is always a chance that the system cannot converge in consensus. The Proof-of-Work (PoW) consensus algorithm achieves a weak form of synchrony by controlling the block production frequency and timestamp. For example, in the Bitcoin blockchain, the PoW difficulty target is adaptively adjusted such that a block is produced, on average, every 10 minutes and the block timestamp is considered valid, if its value lies between the median timestamp of the last 11 blocks on the chain and two hours after the network adjusted time. It was also shown that the PoW algorithm can provide strong consistency guarantee in an asynchronous network under known conditions (Pass, Seeman and Shelat, 2017). The Proof-of-Stake (PoS) and Practical Byzantine Fault Tolerance (PBFT) consensus algorithms ensure synchrony by either imposing a timeout period for a node to respond to a message, after which it would be replaced by another active node to run the consensus process, or imposing a timeout for a transaction in which the transaction will be discarded if consensus is not achieved within the timeout period.

Liveness and Safety: All consensus algorithms are designed to guarantee either one or both of the liveness and safety property. Safety means that nothing bad will happen during execution, i.e., the result of the consensus algorithm will be valid and identical at all honest nodes whereas liveness means that something good will eventually happen, i.e., nodes that do not fail will always produce a result, thereby guaranteeing termination of the algorithm.

6.2.5   *Public and private blockchain*

A public blockchain does not require nodes be accounted to a real-world and legally binding identity. Therefore, a public blockchain is often token-based as it needs a native token to drive incentives for the nodes to validate transactions. Consensus in a public blockchain is commonly achieved by PoW or PoS. PoW provides incentives to nodes who contribute electricity and power to validate transactions and penalises nodes that try to subvert the network because the cost of real-world electricity investment to perform the PoW will outweigh any gains that can be derived out of it. PoS delegates power to nodes holding higher stakes (therefore having more vested interest in securing the blockchain) to secure and validate transactions. Dishonest nodes will risk losing all stakes in the event of a misconduct. Private blockchain, on the other hand, is a blockchain network where all nodes are known and trusted (e.g., employees, customers or organisations), therefore they are subjected to human rules and regulations as well as liabilities and obligations that are legally enforceable in the real world. Since the environment is controlled, the PBFT algorithm is more commonly employed to achieve a much faster consensus compared to PoW.

6.2.6   *Unspent transaction output and smart contract*

The Unspent Transaction Output (UTXO) model is mostly described in reference to the Bitcoin blockchain (Nakamoto, 2008). In this model, the sender formulates a transaction specifying the input bitcoins, the receiver, the amount of bitcoins to be transferred, and the change (also called the "unspent output"). The unspent output will be returned to the sender to be the input for subsequent transaction. The main advantage of the UTXO model is that transactions can be verified with minimal effort but the drawback is that the model cannot handle more complex payment conditions, i.e., it is not Turing complete. A smart contract, on the other hand, is mostly described in reference to the Ethereum blockchain (Ethereum Foundation, 2017), where developers can formulate complex transactions in a smart contract using Ethereum's Turing complete language called Solidity.

A smart contract specifies business logics in a structured way, and a transaction will be executed automatically when the condition in which the transaction can take place is satisfied (Wood, 2017).

6.2.7 *Oracle*

Blockchain systems utilising smart contract may rely heavily on off-chain data to support the execution of business logic. It is thus imperative to maintain a consistent state of the blockchain as all nodes must converge at the same result eventually (the safety property). Hence, there is a need to deploy a smart contract oracle as a gateway to provide a single and consistent source of data. Doing so on a public blockchain may seem to be in conflict with the original zero-trust intent, but in a private blockchain, the security aspect is more manageable because the oracle is authenticated and permissioned.

6.3 Work Flow in a Blockchain

In a blockchain system, a transaction is first formulated by a user and broadcasted to the network for validation. When all nodes converge in an agreement that the transaction is valid, it will be executed and an update to the blockchain state will be applied by all nodes in the network. In the following, we detail the flow of a transaction in a blockchain system.

6.3.1 *Formulating a transaction*

A "transaction" in a blockchain may refer to a statement of buying, selling or transferring of digital assets, or it can carry a payload containing metadata that triggers certain state transition on the blockchain. Therefore, it is vital that all transactions are accompanied by a digital signature of the sender for the purpose of authentication and non-repudiation protection. Authenticated transactions are broadcasted to other nodes in the network. Depending on the underlying blockchain technology, the blockchain can be a record of the transaction itself, or a record of change in the state of the blockchain which is triggered by the transaction. For ease of illustration, unless stated otherwise, we assume what goes onto a blockchain are transactions formulated as statements of transferring digital assets between two nodes.

6.3.2   *Consensus algorithm*

Once a transaction is broadcasted, each validating node in the network will compile a list of transactions in their sequential order and verify their respective digital signature. Upon verification, the nodes will proceed to validate all transaction input and output (e.g., ensure no double-spending occurs), the correctness of transaction payload (if the transaction contains smart contract code) and so on. Once a transaction is validated, nodes will run the underlying consensus algorithm.

Proof-of-Work: In a PoW consensus, the set of validating nodes are also referred to as "miners". Miners would race each other in the effort to find (or rather, mine) a valid block hash for the new block containing the set of validated transactions. This effort typically involves finding a particular nonce that can produce a block hash satisfying a certain difficulty target. When the nonce is found, the successful miner would broadcast its result and then be rewarded with the digital currency powering the blockchain. A PoW consensus algorithm rewards miners who contribute their computing power to keep the blockchain secure and makes the effort of attacking the blockchain extremely costly as an attacker needs to possess more than half of the computing power of the entire blockchain community in order to make the network subvert to its version of the blockchain state.

Proof-of-Stake: A PoS consensus algorithm works by identifying a set of validating nodes with the most stakes that will be responsible for validating transactions and generating new blocks. Validation is performed by appending the node's digital signature on the new block containing the validated transactions, and new blocks are usually forged, or minted, instead of being mined. Thus, a validating node is also called a "forger" or "minter". A variant of PoS consensus algorithm called the Delegated PoS (DPoS) algorithm is where nodes with the most stakes can select their own "delegate" to work as forger; the rest of the DPoS working principles are the same as in a PoS algorithm, and consensus is achieved when majority of the forgers agree with the validity of a new block. As a result, PoS (and DPoS) achieves consensus in a much faster way compared to PoW algorithm. The rationale behind a PoS (or DPoS) consensus is that the more stakes a node owns, the more vested interest it will have in securing the network. To launch an attack, an attacker would need to acquire enough stakes, which would result in price hike, making the attack economically unsustainable. Even if the attack were to succeed, the damage from the attack will create a devaluation of the tokens, resulting in a substantial economic loss to the attacker.

Practical Byzantine Fault Tolerance: Another type of consensus algorithm is the PBFT algorithm. In PBFT consensus, a validating node maintains a list of trusted peers that it can count on to reach an agreement on the validity of a new block. There are typically several rounds of consensus in a PBFT algorithm, where in each round, a block of transactions is accepted if and only if a quorum of trusted peers agrees on its validity. Depending on the type of blockchain, the list of trusted peers can be fixed by the system during setup (e.g., Ripple, 2013), defined by the node itself (e.g., Hyperledger Fabric (The Linux Foundation, 2017), Stellar (Stellar Development Foundation, 2014)), or even formulated based on the amount of stakes a node holds (e.g., Tendermint (All In Bits, Inc., 2017)). A PBFT consensus is normally deployed in private and permissioned blockchain systems, where all nodes in the network belong to a controlled membership and therefore subject to human rules and regulations as well as liabilities and obligations that are legally enforceable in the real world. For this reason, a PBFT consensus algorithm does not require the use of cryptocurrency to create intrinsic incentive.

6.3.3 *Record proving*

When nodes arrive at eventual consensus, the new block will be added to the blockchain. Each block contains a list of validated transaction (with or without the payload), the previous block's hash value, the public key of the miner (in PoW) or the signature of the forger/minter (PoS/PBFT), the signature of an oracle or notary (if applicable) and a nonce (PoW). There are several approaches for a user to prove a record of his or her transaction on a blockchain. In blockchains that allows simple payment verification (e.g., Bitcoin), a user simply queries sufficient nodes to obtain the list of block hashes of the longest blockchain, and requests for a proof of inclusion (in the form of Merkle branches if the transactions are organised in a Merkle hash tree (Merkle, 1988) structure). Another approach requires the user to download the entire blockchain (e.g., Ethereum) to trace the state transitions triggered by transactions. Some blockchain allows record proving by SQL queries (e.g., Corda (R3 Limited, 2016), Stellar) since the blockchain is stored in a relational database.

6.4   Token-based Blockchain Systems

We study a few prominent token-based blockchain systems by discussing the type of data that is recorded on the blockchain, the consensus algorithm used and the security properties of the blockchain system.

6.4.1   *Bitcoin*

Bitcoin was created by Satoshi Nakamoto in 2008 and it is commonly regarded as the "original" blockchain and the most widely used case of public and permissionless blockchain. Bitcoin Core is released with its own underlying digital currency called the Bitcoin (BTC) and the blockchain is a record of BTC transactions occurring in the network. When a transaction is broadcasted to the network, all nodes verify the digital signature and validate the transaction to ensure that no double-spending occurs. Upon validation, the transaction will be added to a block containing a list of other validated transactions. Nodes (miners) will then run an instance of PoW consensus, where they race each other to find a nonce that produces a block hash that satisfies a difficulty target, and the successful miner is rewarded with newly created bitcoins or bitcoins offered in terms of transaction fees.

A transaction is confirmed after at least six more blocks are appended to the blockchain (Rosenfeld, 2014); this amounts to a total waiting time of one hour as the difficulty target is set such that a new block can only be produced every 10 minutes.

Bitcoin's PoW achieves a weak form of synchrony by controlling the block frequency and timestamp. The difficulty target will be adjusted if a new block hash cannot be found within the stipulated time frame and block with an out-of-range timestamp will also be rejected. The Bitcoin blockchain is based on the UTXO model with scripting language that is not Turing complete. As such, it does not support smart contract nor deploy the use of oracles. The network is pseudonymous in the sense that although its users transact using public keys that are not associated with real-world identities and can be newly generated in every single transaction (i.e., anonymously), the flow of BTCs in and out of a wallet associated with a public key could be traceable and linkable (Ron and Shamir, 2013).

6.4.2 *Ethereum*

Ethereum is a decentralised platform featuring smart contract functionality. The cryptocurrency in Ethereum is called an Ether (ETH) and the basic unit is "account". Each user owns a private key-controlled externally owned account (EOA) and a contract account (CA). The EOA can send transactions or message that triggers the CA, which contains contract code that would execute when its condition is satisfied by an incoming message. The Ethereum blockchain records the states of account and state transitions are triggered by contract code residing in CA, which is in turn triggered by transaction messages sent from either EOA or another CA. The contract code in a CA is Turing-complete and is commonly referred to as "smart contract" by the blockchain community, and it queries an oracle to access other on-chain data.

The consensus algorithm in Ethereum is also PoW, but instead of using a cryptographic hash function like Bitcoin does, Ethereum designs its own hash-like algorithm, called the Ethash (Wood, 2017). Ethash uses a large, transient and randomly generated dataset which forms a directed acyclic graph (DAG) that is generated for each epoch (every 125 hours). It works as follows:

(1) The pre-processed header (derived from the latest block) and the current nonce are combined using a SHA-3-like algorithm to produce a 128-byte Mix_0.
(2) Each Mix_i is used to find out which of the 128-byte page from the DAG to retrieve. Each Mix_i is then combined with the retrieved DAG page using an Ethereum-specific mixing function to generate the next mix, Mix_{i+1}.
(3) The previous step is repeated 64 times to get Mix_{64}, which is then post-processed, yielding a 32-byte *Mix Digest*.

If the *Mix Digest* is less than or equal to a difficulty target, then the current nonce is successful and an update on the blockchain state is applied; otherwise, a miner will increment the nonce and repeat the earlier steps. Ethereum's PoW is memory hard in the sense that a miner needs to fetch random data using large amount of memory before getting Mix_{64}, thereby creating an ASIC (application specific integrated circuits)-resistant PoW that is a "fairer" lottery system. A new block is generated in Ethereum every 15 seconds, allowing it to handle much more transactions compared to Bitcoin.

Ethereum is a public blockchain with almost the same security properties as the Bitcoin blockchain. However, contrary to Bitcoin's UTXO model, the Ethereum blockchain records only the state of an account before and after transaction. This makes the tracking of a transaction a tedious effort as it requires a user to download the entire blockchain and study the state transitions of the account.

6.4.3   *Ethereum Classic*

Ethereum and its blockchain were "hard-forked" in the aftermath of the June 2016 hack on "The DAO" (Atzei, Bartoletti and Cimoli, 2017). Several miners and members of the community opposed to hard forking Ethereum to transfer and recover the funds stolen due to an exploit in the contract code. As a result, the Ethereum Classic blockchain (DaxClassix, 2016) was quickly formed to support and mine an alternative version of the Ethereum blockchain that did not include the DAO-related hard fork (Hertig and Rizzo, 2016). Ethereum Classic has its underlying cryptocurrency called ETC and the blockchain essentially works in a similar manner as the Ethereum blockchain. Although Ethereum is now migrating towards a PoS consensus algorithm called Casper (Ladha, Pandit and Ralhan, 2016), Ethereum Classic is set to continue using the PoW consensus algorithm originally used in Ethereum. On April 2017, Ethereum Classic Trust is created by the Digital Currency Group to provide a platform for investors to invest in Ethereum Classic through a regulated channel — an event that significantly boosted the demand and price of the ETC token (Higgins, 2017).

6.4.4 *Dash*

Dash (The Dash Network, 2017) is a fork of the Bitcoin protocol. It is built upon Bitcoin's core code with additional features such as privacy and with negligible transaction fees. Dash is a public blockchain that records transactions of its native currency DASH. The blockchain is a two-tier network that is powered by miners (tier-1) and masternodes (tier-2). In the first tier, miners run the PoW consensus algorithm using the X11 hash function (Duffield and Diaz, 2017). X11 is a chained hashing that uses 11 rounds of different hash functions (all of which are SHA-3 (Dworkin, 2015) contestants), with an average mining rate of 2.5 minutes. The main advantage of PoW using X11 over SHA-2 is the effectiveness, i.e., it is power-saving and fast to compute, and the ASIC hardware is more complicated to be implemented. The second tier is powered by a set of masternodes. A node in the network can become a masternode with a collateral of 1,000 DASH and masternodes are selected from a list of masternodes (the MN list) in a deterministic order, i.e., the masternode that obtains mining reward the longest time ago and is in the list for a long enough time will be selected.

The purpose of the masternodes in the second tier is to provide additional functionalities such as PrivateSend (Kiraly, 2017b) and InstantSend (Kiraly, 2017a). PrivateSend is a process to provide untraceability of transactions, where a masternode uses the CoinJoin detailed in Maxwell (2013) protocol to mix unspent outputs of the same denomination from multiple nodes (who chose to invoke the PrivateSend function) in a pool and randomly selects an input for the next transaction. This occurs after the tier-1 mining, where the miner and masternode obtain 45% of the mining rewards each and the remaining 10% goes to the treasury system. InstantSend bypasses the mining process and a set of masternodes come together to validate a transaction by requiring a quorum of masternodes to agree on the transaction. Therefore, in addition to anonymity, transactions in the Dash blockchain aim to be untraceable.

6.4.5   *DigixDAO*

DigixDAO (DigixGlobal, 2016) is built on Ethereum and it tokenises physical assets onto the Ethereum blockchain. There are three different types of players on a DigixDAO system, namely the asset vendor, i.e., ValueMax Singapore, that supplies London Bullion Market Association (LBMA) certified gold bullion bars through Digix Marketplace; the independent auditor, i.e., the Bureau Veritas Inspectorate that checks the quality and quantity at a custodian vault; and the participating custodian vault, i.e., Malca-Amit. Transactions at each stage of the gold purchase are validated by the relevant and well-established party using a Proof-of-Asset (PoA) protocol, and audit documents resulted in each stage are stored on a distributed P2P file storage system (the Interplanetary File System (IPFS) by Benet (2014)). The final "proof" of ownership in the form of an asset card (containing information such as the timestamp of creation of the card, the Stock Keeping Unit (SKU) of gold bar, serial number and all relevant chain of custody's digital signatures and receipts) is kept in an Ethereum wallet and recorded onto the Ethereum blockchain. DigixDAO has an underlying token called the Digix Gold Token (DGX). Smart contract can be created to exchange DGX with PoA asset cards; each DGX represents one gram of gold and it is divisible to 0.001 grams. In addition, DigixDAO rewards its users with Digix Dao Token (DGD) that can be claimed based on the DGX collected through transaction fees. DGD can act as a share and it can be used to pledge for proposals on DigixDAO.

6.4.6 *Factom*

Factom allows the use of different chains for different applications, where each chain can apply its own rules, languages or platforms (Factom, 2017). Users can publish data to the chain and have the data recorded immutably on Bitcoin's blockchain. The Factom blockchain has its native token called Factoid (FCT). Factoid is used to purchase Entry Credit, which in turn is used to purchase for Entry. Each Entry, upon validation, will be assembled into an Entry Block and a set of Entry Blocks will be assembled into a Directory Block. The Directory Block will be attached to the Bitcoin blockchain every 10 minutes. Therefore, the native currency in the Factom blockchain is used for incentivisation as well as spam prevention.

Players in a Factom blockchain are the users, a set of Audit Servers (AS, standby servers in case Federated Servers fail) and a set of Federated Servers (FS). Nodes in the Factom blockchain do not validate Entries. Instead, they validate transactions involving Factoid trading, whereas Entries to chains in different applications are validated client-side by the users and the applications using any set of rules and any convention to communicate their rules. Thus, the Factom blockchain does not have a specific consensus algorithm. Each Entry specifies the business process and a ChainID, and is confirmed by FS after it is added to the Entry Block, which would subsequently be immutable after the Directory Block is anchored onto the Bitcoin blockchain. Each FS is responsible for a set of chains and they are rotated every minute. Every four hours, FS are re-ranked by means of voting by users with a profile in Factom, and the weight of a vote is determined by the user's amount of Entry Credits purchased and the number of Entries used. To avoid censorship by FS, Factom uses a commitment scheme (it is unsure which commitment scheme is used) for its users to hide the Entry content, and the user will only reveal the Entry after it is confirmed by the FS. Data confidentiality is achieved as only the hash value of Entry is published in the Entry Block.

6.4.7 *Lisk*

Lisk (Dell et al, 2017) is a public blockchain with its own underlying cryptocurrency called LSK. It attempts to solve the congestion problems on the blockchain using sidechains that can either use LSK tokens from the main chain or an entirely new custom token. The Lisk blockchain records different types of transaction including transfer of funds using LSK, registering a delegate, or submitting a vote for delegates. The consensus algorithm is a DPoS algorithm, where the top 101 delegates are chosen by stakeholders through voting, and the weight of vote depends on the amount of LSKs the stakeholder possesses.

In each round of the consensus protocol, a delegate signs one randomly assigned block in a round robin manner. If a delegate does not respond, then it will be automatically down-voted and removed from the list. A block is produced every 10 seconds and is confirmed only when more than 51% of the delegates agree with a *BroadHash* value, which is an aggregated rolling hash of the past five blocks. A delegate is rewarded for forging a block. Additionally, transaction fees in each round are aggregated and the round fees are split between all active participants in the round.

6.4.8 *Litecoin*

Litecoin is an open source, global payment network created by forking the Bitcoin client for a decreased average block time, increased supply and modified consensus mechanism structure (Litecoin Project, 2011). The Litecoin is a public blockchain that records the transactions of the native currency (LTC). It uses a PoW consensus algorithm that employs Scrypt designed by Percival and Josefsson (2016), instead of SHA-2 hash function as in Bitcoin, producing a block on an average of 2.5 minutes. Similar to other ASIC-resistant algorithms, Scrypt requires large memory to pseudo-randomly access a large vector of pseudorandom bit strings. Each time, a miner is rewarded with 25 LTC, which will be halved every four years. Litecoin uses the UTXO model and it inherits the security properties of the Bitcoin blockchain. However, it is recently reported that ASIC hardware for Scrypt mining has been manufactured by Zeusminer (Chen, 2014), which would considerably speed up the mining process.

6.4.9 *Monero*

Monero is an open source cryptocurrency with a strong emphasis on privacy (The Monero Project, 2014). Transactions involving the underlying currency XMR are recorded onto the blockchain after consensus is reached using a PoW algorithm. The PoW algorithm used in Monero is based on the CryptoNote protocol by van Saberhagen (2013) that relies on random access to a slow memory and emphasises latency dependence. The CryptoNote PoW algorithm is a combined use of the Keccak (Dworkin, 2015) hash function with the Advanced Encryption Standard (AES) (NIST, 2011), and ended with a selection of either the BLAKE2 (Saarinen and Aumasson, 2015), Groestl (Gauravaram et al, 2009) or Skein (Ferguson et al, 2010) hash functions. As long as the output of the selected function (as determined by a random number) is less than a difficulty target, then the miner is considered successful in mining the new block.

An important feature in Monero is that it is private by default. The privacy that Monero offers includes unlinkability using the notion of one-time random addresses. Using a recipient's long-term public key and a random number, the sender computes a one-time random address to send the transaction to such that only recipient with the correct long-term private key can spend the transaction. Thus, as long as a new random number is used every time a transaction is to occur, it is not possible to link accounts belonging to the same user. Another feature that Monero offers is untraceability. This is achieved using ring signature (Yuen et al, 2012), where an unspent transaction output is grouped with a pool of unspent outputs of the same amount belonging to other users in the network, and each of them is signed using ring signature algorithm by their respective owner. The property of ring signature is such that a verifier can successfully verify the signature given the public keys of all users in the "ring", and there is no way to revoke the anonymity. However, the work of Kumar et al (2017) shows that Monero is still vulnerable to traceability attacks by passive analysis and temporal analysis.

6.4.10   *NEM*

NEM is a cryptocurrency built on blockchain technology. It is one of the top 10 blockchains (by market cap) worldwide and has been recognised by the Chinese government as one of the most secure blockchains examined (Li, 2017). The underlying cryptocurrency of the NEM network is called XEM. Each account's XEM balance is split into "vested" and "unvested" parts at which all incoming XEM are added to the unvested balance while outgoing XEM are taken from both the vested and unvested balances.

The NEM blockchain records changes in an account state, which are triggered by transactions. A transaction can be a transfer of XEM or operations such as converting a normal account to a multisignature account. NEM uses what they call a Proof-of-Importance (PoI) consensus algorithm. In a PoI algorithm, only eligible accounts can "harvest" new blocks. More specifically, a difficulty level for a new block is calculated based on the last 60 blocks — if there are less than 60 blocks available, only those available will be taken into account. An account is eligible to harvest if it has a vested balance of at least 10,000 XEM *and* if its "hit" value (calculated using its public key and the generation hash of the previous block) is less than a target value (calculated using variables such as the time since the last block, importance of the account and difficulty of the new block). The account that successfully harvests a new block will be rewarded with transaction fees.

NEM also supports a node type called the supernodes. Supernodes provide access to the NEM blockchain, especially for lite wallet users, without having to sync to a blockchain locally. Account with 3 million XEM gets paid 140,000 XEM divided by the total number of supernodes every day for running a supernode that meets minimum technological requirements. The NEM blockchain provides privacy protection by encrypting transactions using AES block cipher (NIST, 2001).

6.4.11   *Ripple*

Ripple is developed to power the fastest and cheapest payment platform for global value transfer (Ripple, 2013). Ripple is a private and permissioned blockchain system that may handle transactions involving its native asset — the XRP — or another form of digital currencies, and it records state information of accounts in the network. The XRP provides additional liquidity and transactional options as a bridge between different assets to reduce cross-border payment and foreign exchange market inefficiencies using its Ripple Payment Protocol (Schwartz, Youngs and Britto, 2014).

The blockchain employs a PBFT-like consensus algorithm, where each transaction that changes the state information would first go to a node that puts them into a candidate set that is made public every two seconds. Every node maintains a Unique Node List (UNL) that is initialised by the system, and nodes on the UNL will vote on the veracity of the transaction by signing the transaction with their own private keys. As a node would have to trust that at least 50% of the nodes in its UNL would not collude, it is imperative that a node's identity is known and verified before it could be added to the UNL.

Depending on the design of the consensus algorithm, a transaction may undergo several rounds of voting, each round requiring a specific ratio of nodes to validate the transaction. In the final round, the transaction must obtain at least 80% of a node's UNL to agree. Once this is achieved, all nodes would come to an agreement on a new version of the ledger.

6.4.12 *Steem*

Steem is designed with a similar concept as blogging or social news websites with the social content saved on a blockchain (Larimer et al, 2016). The public blockchain aims at supporting social media and online communities by incentivising contribution through the underlying token called "STEEM". Images can be uploaded and hosted on Steemit while other multimedia content must be embedded from other web hosts.

In a Steem blockchain, a user can be an author, curator or witness, and he or she can be anonymous. Authors whose content gets up-voted can receive a monetary reward in STEEM or US dollar-pegged tokens called Steem Dollars. Curators are also rewarded for curating popular content, including voting for comments and post submissions; the vote strength and curation are influenced by the amount of STEEM Power held by the voter.

Steem blockchain utilises a DPoS consensus algorithm. In each round, 21 witnesses are selected to be the current set of active nodes and they are shuffled and scheduled to produce a new block every three seconds; thus, each round takes around 63 seconds if every witness produces a block. Among the 21 witnesses, 19 are elected by Steem stakeholders (who have committed to a multi-year vesting schedule) through voting, One witness is timeshared by all other unselected candidates and one is selected by PoW mining. The PoW mining involves finding a nonce that solves a digital signature verification problem and the successful node would broadcast a transaction with the result of the PoW and will be added as the witness for the next round of consensus.

6.4.13 *Zcash*

Zcash (ZECC, 2017) is the first public blockchain that implements a full privacy protection on transactions. The blockchain records encrypted transactions involving its underlying digital currency ZEC, where information on the sender, receiver and the amount involved is kept private. It bridges the existing Bitcoin blockchain with a shielded payment scheme using zero-knowledge succinct non-interactive arguments of knowledge (zk-SNARKs). The zk-SNARKs algorithm proposed by Ben-Sasson et al (2014) allows users to verify the validity of a transaction in encrypted form such that no information about the transaction is leaked to any other parties.

The Zcash blockchain uses a PoW consensus algorithm with mining rewards. The PoW consensus is realised using the Equihash algorithm (Hopwood et al, 2017) that runs on the BLAKE2 hash function. In the Zcash PoW consensus, miners are required to find a solution that encodes to a valid Equihash solution. More specifically, miners must find 2^k distinct bit-strings X_i, where each X_i is derived from the block header and a nonce, such that the exclusive-OR of the 2^k bit-strings resulted in a bit-string of all zero bits. The Equihash imposes additional requirement on the process of finding the 2^k bit-strings such that in each round, the number of possible solutions that conform to the requirement is only two on average. The second stage of the PoW requires miners to encode their solution (specifying the 2^k bit-strings) onto the block header, and compute the hash value of the block header. The miner succeeds if the resulting hash satisfies a difficulty threshold, which can be adjusted to control the block production frequency at around 2.5 minutes per new block.

Zcash provides data confidentiality of encrypting all transaction data, and it protects user privacy by using the zk-SNARKs algorithm to provide anonymity, transaction untraceability and unlinkability.

6.4.14 *Summary and remarks*

Token-based blockchain systems such as Bitcoin, Lisk and Litecoin are used to record transactions involving the blockchain's intrinsic token. These blockchain systems are public in the sense that they allow any party to transact and participate in the consensus process. Therefore, the underlying token is also used as a mean to incentivise users who help to maintain the integrity of the blockchain state. On the other hand, the Factom blockchain is an instance where the underlying token FCT is used to buy credits needed to initiate a transaction, effectively demonstrating the purpose of a native token for spam prevention. In the Ripple blockchain, the underlying native token XRP is used as a bridge to exchange assets in different chains (each belonging to a different enterprise) in the Ripple network, whereas the Steem blockchain uses its native token STEEM to encourage users to post and curate quality contents on social network.

Apart from carrying out simple transactions of transferring assets from one party to another, the Ethereum blockchain introduces the notion of smart contract to realise the possibility of incorporating simple but reliable execution of business logic in the blockchain system. DigixDAO, building upon the Ethereum blockchain, is an instance where blockchain is used to regulate and record the ownership of hard assets.

Tables 6.1 and 6.2 show a comparison of the token-based blockchain systems. As can be seen, most token-based blockchain systems are public, except DigixDAO and Ripple. Due to the nature of

Table 6.1. List of Token-Based Blockchain Systems.

	Bitcoin	Ethereum	Ripple	Litecoin	Steem	Ethereum Classic
Symbol	BTC	ETH	XRP	LTC	STEEM	ETC
Market Cap	$34 billion	$12 billion	$14 billion	$1.4 billion	$283 million	$689 million
Obtainable from	— Mining — Transaction fees — Buy from exchanges	— Mining — Transaction fees — Buy from exchanges	— Buy from exchanges using fiat or digital currencies	— Mining — Buy from Litecoin — Buy from exchanges using other currencies	— Posting, curating rewards — Buy from exchanges using BTC	— Mining — Transaction fees — Buy from exchanges
Current market value	$2,082.83	$131.11	$0.36	$26.90	$1.21	$7.50
Security properties (*Authentication, integrity protection and non-repudiation are assumed by default*)	Anonymity	Anonymity	—	Anonymity	Anonymity	Anonymity
Consensus algorithm	PoW — SHA-2	PoW — Ethash	PBFT with Unique Node List	PoW — Scrypt	PoS	PoW — Ethash

Support for smart contract	No	Yes	No	No	No	Yes
Organisation	—	Ethereum Foundation	Ripple	Litecoin Foundation	Steemit Inc.	—
Token usage example (*not exhaustive*)	Accepted by Paypal, Microsoft Xbox and Windows apps etc.	Traded on OCTAGON Strategy's OTC trading desk	Fidor, Accenture, SBI Holdings etc. have adopted Ripple Payment Protocol	Benz and Beamer, eGifter, Ellenet	Convert to Steem Power (SP) that gives a share in Steem	Ethereum Classic Investment Trust investment channel by Grayscale Investments LLC
Public or Private	Public	Public	Private	Public	Public	Public

Note that the *market cap* and *market value* are obtained from http://coinmarketcap.com and are accurate as at 21 May 2017, and the table states *security properties* that are explicitly mentioned by the blockchain system.

Table 6.2.   List of Token-Based Blockchain Systems.

	Dash	Monero	NEM	Lisk	Factom	DigixDAO	Zcash
Symbol	DASH	XMR	XEM	LSK	FCT	DGD	ZEC
Market Cap	$733 million	$512 million	$2.1 billion	$88 million	$89 million	$148 million	$146 million
Obtainable from	— Mining — Buy from exchanges with fiat or digital currency	— Mining — Buy from exchanges with fiat or digital currency	— Transaction fees — Supernode rewards — Buy from exchanges	— Forging rewards — Round rewards — Buy from exchanges	— Forging incentive — Buy from exchanges	— Obtained from gold purchases — Crowdsale — Selling of asset cards	— Mining — Buy from exchanges with fiat or digital currency
Current market value	$100.25	$35.29	$0.23	$0.82	$10.20	$73.84	$108.55
Security properties (*Authentication, integrity protection and non-repudiation are assumed by default*)	Anonymity Untraceable	Anonymity Unlinkable Untraceable	Anonymity Confidentiality	Anonymity	Anonymity	—	Anonymity Unlinkable Untraceable Confidentiality

	PoW — X11	PoW — CryptoNote	Proof-of-Importance	DPoS	Occurs between two parties; anchored to Bitcoin blockchain	Based on Ethereum	PoW — Equihash
Consensus algorithm							
Support for smart contract	No	No	No	No	No	Not applicable	No
Organisation	The Dash Network	Monero	NEM.IO Foundation Ltd.	Lisk Foundation	Factom Foundation	DIGIXGLOBAL Pte Ltd	Zerocoin Electric Coin Company
Token usage example (*not exhaustive*)	Has own Dash debit card, accepted by VPNs, email providers etc.	Tradeable at Bittrex, Kraken, ShapeShift, Bitfinex etc.	Recognised by Xhai Studios, SBI Sumishin Net Bank	Tradeable at Poloniex, Bittrex, BitMEX etc.	Purchase Entry Credits to submit data to the blockchain	DGD can be used to pledge for proposals at DigixDAO	Tradeable at HitBTC, Poloniex, Yun Bi, Bittrex, Kraken etc.
Public or Private	Public	Public	Public	Public	Public	Private	Public

Note that the *market cap* and *market value* are obtained from http://coinmarketcap.com and are accurate as at 21 May 2017, and the table states *security properties* that are explicitly mentioned by the blockchain system.

public blockchain, it is vital that the consensus algorithm is designed such that no particular node (or group of nodes) can dominate and influence the result of the consensus. The PoW consensus algorithm in Bitcoin blockchain is essentially a lottery system leveraging on the properties of a cryptographic hash function. However, the Bitcoin's PoW algorithm takes an average of 10 minutes for a block to be verified and requires the user to wait a minimum of an hour before the block is considered immutable, and the PoW algorithm is not ASIC-resistant. The PoW consensus in Ethereum, Dash, Lisk, Litecoin and Monero are designed to address the shortcoming of Bitcoin's PoW consensus algorithm using a variety of cryptographic algorithms that are ASIC-resistant. It is worth noting that the PoI consensus in NEM is essentially also a lottery system that is similar to PoW without the ASIC problem and with a shorter waiting time.

Privacy is a security issue addressed explicitly by the Dash, Monero and Zcash blockchain systems and it will be discussed in a later section of this Chapter.

6.5   Tokenless Blockchain Systems and Others

Tokenless blockchain systems are commonly designed for enterprises to manage and record business flow. It is, however, still possible for enterprises to create their own personalised token in these systems to facilitate business flow. We survey several other blockchain systems in terms of each primary functionality, the underlying consensus algorithm and the properties that the blockchain system possesses.

6.5.1   *Chain Core*

Chain Core (Chain Inc., 2017) is a blockchain platform that enables institutions to issue and transfer financial assets on private and permissioned blockchain networks. It enables different institutions to launch and connect to blockchain networks operating on the Chain protocol. Each network maintains a multi-asset shared ledger, with the digital assets sharing a common, interoperable format and can represent any units of value that are guaranteed by a trusted issuer. Blocks in the Chain Core blockchain record the hash of all transactions and the hash of the current state, i.e., the set of current unspent outputs; this snapshot facilitates the joining of new nodes without having to replay the entire history of the blockchain. A transaction may involve asset issuance, payment or asset retirement, and it may contain many different types of assets from multiple sources to multiple destinations.

The Chain Core network consists of a set of blockchain operators, one of which is designated as the block generator and the others are block signers, and a network of user nodes. Consensus is achieved using a PBFT-like algorithm, termed as a "Federated Consensus" (Chain Inc., 2016). In this process, the block generator receives transactions from the network, removes invalid transactions, aggregates them into a block and sends it to nodes acting as block signers. Each block signer will verify and sign the block when all validity checks passed. Once the block generator receives signatures from a quorum of block signers (as determined by the consensus algorithm specified in the block header), it broadcasts the block to the network and all nodes and updates their copy of the blockchain state. While the block generator is deemed to have a privileged role, it is argued that its role is similar to current business use cases, where in a permissioned network, there exists a single company or market utility that is responsible for continued operation of the network. Safety is guaranteed as long as no more than ($2M$-N-1) block signers violate the protocol, where M is the quorum of required signers and N is the total number of block signers in the network.

While Chain Core allows the coexistence of multiple core networks that can interact with each other, every client who wishes to connect to a particular core network must obtain access token with cross-core authorisation grant, which can be given by an administrator through the Chain Core Dashboard. It is worth noting that any addition or removal of members in the set of blockchain operators must incur a change in the consensus program and a quorum of existing block signers must agree to the change, but the tools for this procedure are still under development. It is also unclear whether block generators are elected in a round robin manner to avoid any form of "centralisation" that could result in domination or a single point of failure.

6.5.2 *Corda*

The Corda blockchain (Brown et al, 2016) is developed by R3 and is originally intended to solve financial sector issues, although there are signs that it is moving outside the financial sectors towards Internet of Things and that the codes for Corda blockchain platform will be handed over to the Hyperledger project (The Linux Foundation, 2017). Corda is a private and permissioned blockchain, where nodes in the Corda blockchain communicate on a point-to-point manner and transactions are communicated in a lazy manner, i.e., there is no global broadcast of transactions. The Corda blockchain records "state objects", which are referred as digital documents that record the existence, content and state of an agreement between two or more parties. Each transaction in Corda specifies the input and output states, contains contract code that enforces business logic, and each state points to a particular notary. Each transaction's input states have to be validated and verified as unique before the blockchain state can be updated.

Determining the validity and uniqueness of a transaction involves reaching two types of consensus — validity consensus and uniqueness consensus. The transacting parties perform validation by executing contract code to ensure their correctness, whereas uniqueness check is performed by notary to verify that the input/output states are unconsumed. Data confidentiality is preserved as validation is performed by the transacting parties where as in most cases, the notary assumes that transactions are valid by default and verifies only the uniqueness of the input/output states. Having said that, the Corda blockchain is not tied to any particular consensus algorithm and it is known to be a database sharing on a need-to-know basis and trades are agreed bilaterally rather than on consensus.

6.5.3 *Hyperledger fabric*

The Hyperledger Fabric is one of the Hyperledger projects hosted by The Linux Foundation. It is a private and permissioned blockchain designed with a modular architecture, allowing components such as consensus and membership services to be plug-and-play. The blockchain provides a verifiable history of all successful and unsuccessful state changes, which are the results of chaincode (the smart contract in Hyperledger) execution that is invoked by transactions sent by clients (nodes). A chaincode comprises the application logic of the system and an endorsement policy that specifies one or more endorsing peers (endorsers). Each time a node formulates a transaction, the transaction is sent to endorsing peers who will validate and commit to the transaction by returning an endorsement signature. The node forwards the transaction and the endorsement signature to an ordering service (orderer) to sort transactions in an ordered manner before they are added to a block and appended immutably to the blockchain.

Hyperledger Fabric provides enrolment certificates to assign identity to its users, giving them permission to join and issue transactions. Alternatively, it also provides transaction certificate (unlinkable to enrolment certificates) to give the capability to issue one or more transactions anonymously. Confidentiality is enforced by allowing part of the chaincode to be encrypted (in part or in total) using AES and access control is implemented outside of the blockchain using the access control list (ACL) technique (Sandhu and Samarati, 1994).

6.5.4 *MultiChain*

MultiChain (Coin Sciences Ltd., 2017) is a blockchain that is used for building and developing private and permissioned blockchains. Each time a new blockchain is created on MultiChain, an administrator (the creator) is granted the highest access rights, including the rights to assign a second administrator, the rights to issue/transfer assets and the rights to read/write to the blockchain stream (Greenspan, 2015). To create a new blockchain on MultiChain, the administrator first chooses a name for the chain and obtains a configuration file generated by MultiChain. The configuration file can be modified by the administrator, specifying information such as the target time for a block, permission types, level of consensus required and so on. The genesis block is then mined by MultiChain, granting the administrator, i.e., its creator, all user privileges.

The consensus algorithm in MultiChain is close in spirit to PBFT. The first user (administrator) with the highest privilege can grant administrator privileges to another node (address), and subsequently assign different nodes with different privileges. Depending on the consensus level, each higher-level node shall grant their permission prior to a new permission grant. To validate a block, the set of all permitted nodes, or forgers (after applying the instructions specified by transactions in the block), is chosen by defining a mining diversity (md), where $0 \leq md \leq 1$. The mining diversity is multiplied by the number of forgers and rounded up to get *spacing*, and the forger of this block should not have forged any of the previous $(spacing - 1)$ blocks. The aim of defining a mining diversity is to avoid the event of a forger monopolising the consensus process.

Due to the nature of MultiChain, at least one administrator will have information of the identity of all nodes. MultiChain is distinguished from other blockchain applications in that access control rights are granted by consensus and recorded immutably on the blockchain itself before the network is deployed. Data confidentiality is also provided using RSA–AES hybrid encryption.

6.5.5　*Openchain*

Openchain is an open source distributed ledger technology for large financial institutions (Coinprism, 2015). It is a public blockchain but it can also be configured as a "closed-loop" ledger (i.e., private blockchain) with an administrator granting access rights to the nodes. The Openchain blockchain is a record of transactions involving the issuance and management of digital assets which may include digital currency, securities, commodities and titles of ownership. It consists of a set of validator nodes and a set of observer nodes. A validator node accepts and validates transaction based on the validation rules, whereas an observer node holds a copy of the state of the ledger.

It is worth noting that Openchain does not use the concept of "blocks", i.e., transactions are verified on a transaction basis instead of on a block basis, and each transaction is validated by a single validator node based on a set of rules defined by the administrator (termed as Partitioned Consensus). It is, however, unclear how a validator node is chosen to validate a particular transaction.

Openchain achieves immutability of the blockchain state by anchoring onto the Bitcoin blockchain, where a cumulative hash (i.e., hash of the entire ledger) will be sent to the Bitcoin blockchain once in every 10 minutes. Users of the Openchain can either be anonymous or they must have their identity approved by an administrator depending on whether the blockchain is configured to be public or private, and access control is provided by means of an ACL.

6.5.6 *QTUM*

QTUM (pronounced "Quantum") is a UTXO-based smart contract blockchain system (Dai et al, 2017). It creates an account abstraction layer (AAL) that translates the Bitcoin's UTXO model to the account-based interface for Ethereum. Whenever a UTXO-based transaction comes in, the AAL uses opcodes to check if a transaction is spendable, and it uses a consensus-critical coin picking algorithm to ensure all miners pick the same coins from an account to be spent, effectively preventing any possibility of a fork. The UTXO-based transaction then serves as a "message" that may trigger a smart contract execution. The input and output of the transaction are then recorded onto QTUM blockchain using a PoS consensus algorithm.

The PoS algorithm works by letting users with the most stakes become forgers. More specifically, a node can only become a forger when its *Proofhash* value satisfies

$$Proofhash \leq coins \times difficulty\ target.$$

QTUM rewards its forger by awarding 1–8% of rewards per year for staying online (and therefore increases the population of forgers and decreases the chance of a successful Sybil attack (Douceur, 2002)). The smart contract on QTUM is called a "master contract" as it uses an oracle to read and select data, both on-chain and off-chain. QTUM is also configurable as a private blockchain with the provision of an identity module that can be used to authenticate users in an enterprise setting. It uses a native token called QTUM.

6.5.7　*Stellar*

Stellar is an open-source protocol for value exchange where servers run a software implementation of the protocol and connect to other servers, forming a global value exchange network. The Stellar blockchain keeps a record of all account balances and transactions, and it uses a PBFT consensus algorithm with a UNL. The UNL consists of a set of peers that a node can trust to achieve consensus on the validity of a transaction. In contrast to Ripple, every node in the Stellar blockchain network can select a list of peers in their quorum, e.g., reputable banks and co-operators, thus allowing different nodes trusting different subsets of the system. The consensus algorithm is termed Stellar Consensus Protocol (Mazieres, 2016), and is a federated Byzantine Agreement protocol that produces a new block every 2–5 seconds. The Stellar blockchain allows simple smart contract execution, e.g., "sending from User A to User B if and only if User B sends to User C". A transaction as such requires the signatures of User A and User B, and will be executed once the condition is satisfied. The token used in the Stellar blockchain is called Lumens (XLM).

6.5.8　*Sawtooth Lake*

Sawtooth Lake is an enterprise distributed blockchain project by Intel's modular blockchain suite. It supports both permissioned and permissionless deployments, and it includes a novel consensus algorithm called the Proof of Elapsed Time (PoET) (Intel, 2015). The PoET algorithm achieves random distribution of node validator election, in each round of consensus, by building on trusted execution environments using secure central processing unit (CPU) instructions to ensure the safety and randomness of the node validator election process. Specifically, every validator node requests for a waiting time from an enclave. The validator with the shortest waiting time for a transaction block is elected as the leader, and the distribution of elected leaders across the entire population of validators is similar to what is provided by other lottery algorithms. Sawtooth Lake blockchain also provides a PBFT consensus algorithm similar to Ripple and Stellar for transactions that require immediate validation of finality.

6.5.9 *Tendermint*

Tendermint is a partitioned open source public blockchain. The partitioned blockchain can be written in any language and include Bitcoin, Ethereum and others, which is enabled by an application interface called the Application BlockChain Interface (All In Bits, Inc., 2017). Tendermint is made up of a set of validator nodes and a consensus engine called the Tendermint Core. It uses a PBFT consensus algorithm coupled with a stake concept. More specifically, the set of validating nodes run (at least) two rounds of consensus. In the first round, at least two-thirds must pre-vote for a block and in the second round, at least two-thirds must pre-commit before the block becomes immutable. However, each validating node has different voting power depending on their stakes in the network and a validator will be skipped if it does not respond to a block upon timeout. The blockchain consensus engine, Tendermint Core, is responsible for ensuring that the same transactions are recorded in the same sequence.

6.5.10 *Dragonchain*

Dragonchain is a mixture of open and closed blockchain developed by Disney (2017) for record keeping and trades. The blockchain records transactions with payload containing arbitrary structure and content. Each transaction is validated at different levels. Level 1 defines where transacting parties validate transaction using business logic, and the transaction payload will be stripped before passing on to the next level, guaranteeing data confidentiality. Subsequently, transactions passed onto Level 2 and go through validity check by checking the digital signatures and the output is a block containing a list of valid and invalid transactions. Level 3 validating nodes ensure network diversity by outputting record counts of validating nodes at Level 2 in terms of their location, key management authority information etc. External notaries are located at Level 4 and they sign the verification records from Level 3. The final level of Dragonchain provides a checkpointing to external blockchain (e.g., the Bitcoin blockchain).

It is worth noting that Dragonchain does not use a particular consensus algorithm in Levels 1 to 4. Furthermore, Dragonchain defines a two-dimensional blockchain. More specifically, each block at Level i is chained to the previous block at the same level and its corresponding block at Level $(i-1)$. In other words, a block j at level i, $B_{i,j}$, contains the list of transactions (valid or invalid), the hash of $B_{j-1,i}$, the hash of $B_{j,i-1}$, and auxiliary data of the validating node. The rationale behind the two-dimensional design stems from the fact that throughout the process of business logic approval (captured at Level 1 on a one-dimensional level), each business concern will have its own requirement of process flow (captured by Level 2 to Level 5 at the second dimension).

6.5.11   *Summary and remarks*

Tokenless blockchain systems are mostly private blockchain and eliminates the need to have a consensus algorithm that incentivises its users to upkeep the integrity of blockchain state. As can be seen in Table 6.3, most tokenless blockchain systems employ PBFT consensus algorithm with different configurations on the UNL, with the exception of the Corda blockchain, Dragonchain, QTUM, and Sawtooth Lake.

The Corda blockchain differs from the conventional definition of a blockchain system as communication occurs on a point-to-point basis and information is propagated in a lazy manner. Similarly,

Table 6.3. List of Other Blockchain Systems.

	Chain Core	Corda	Hyperledger	MultiChain	Openchain	QTUM	Sawtooth Lake	Stellar	Tendermint	Dragonchain
Public or Private	Private	Private	Private	Private	Configurable	Configurable	Configurable	Configurable	Private	Private
What is recorded on the ledger?	Financial assets; currencies, securities	Financial agreements between institutions	Assets — tangible or intangible	Digital currency transactions; user permissions	Financial assets; currencies, securities	Digital currency transactions	Assets — tangible or intangible	Account balances and digital currency transactions	Digital currency transactions	Digital documents
Consensus algorithm	PBFT-like, termed "Federated Consensus"	Not tied to particular algorithm; consensus is achieved between transacting parties only	PBFT	PBFT	"Partitioned Consensus"; achieved on transaction basis; anchored to Bitcoin blockchain	PoS	PoET	PBFT with configurable UNL	PBFT with "stake" concept	Not tied to particular consensus algorithm
Is smart contract supported?	Yes	Not Applicable	Yes	Yes	No	Yes	Yes	Yes	Yes	Not Applicable
Industrial application example (*not exhaustive*)	Visa B2B Connect	Collateral lending solution on liquidity; with CIBC, Commerzbank, Credit Suisse, ING, UBS and HQLA?	Introduced in March 2017, working with financial institutions, consortia of banks and start-ups	Integrated into the Wolfram Language; contract discovery and analytics platform (with Seal Software)	License compliance validation (with Nextcloud)	Open-source blockchain stack for legacy business use cases (with BlogLabs); Partners with PwC Asia	Prototype for bond transactions with R3 and its consortium members (on trial)	Micropayment, partnered with Deloitte	Powered the Cosmos (Internet of blockchains) Hub in the Cosmos Network	Possible use cases: Ticketing, identity systems, voting systems etc.
Company	Chain Inc.	R3	The Linux Foundation	Coin Sciences Ltd	Coinprism	Qtum	Intel	Stellar Development Foundation	All In Bits Inc.	Walt Disney

Dragonchain does not have a specific consensus algorithm as transactions are validated using business approval verification between two transacting parties. The QTUM blockchain, on the other hand, aims to bring the advantages of the Bitcoin and Ethereum blockchain together by creating an account abstraction layer that takes UTXO transactions as input messages to trigger smart contract execution and records the input and output using a PoS consensus algorithm. QTUM is thus not intended to be a private blockchain. The Sawtooth Lake, on the other hand, uses a lottery-like consensus algorithm called PoET, where nodes rely on secure hardware to decide whether they are able to validate a block in each round. However, Sawtooth Lake also employs PBFT consensus in the event that a transaction has to be validated urgently.

As private blockchains are commonly implemented by enterprises, there may be a requirement to impose access control to dictate the kind of information that employees with different roles can access. Hyperledger Fabric, for instance, implemented this outside of the blockchain system using an access control list whereas MultiChain integrates access control within the blockchain itself by specifying each user's access rights in the form of a transaction, and the access right will be granted once relevant parties in the system reach a consensus on the decision.

6.6   Cryptography

In existing blockchain systems, data integrity, authenticity and non-repudiation are inherently addressed through the use of hash function and digital signature. User anonymity is also inherent in most public blockchain as a user generates a new random public address that is not associated to its identity for every new transaction. It is, however, pointed out in several studies that while anonymity is provided, transactions remain traceable and linkable (Ron and Shamir, 2013), and the traceability allows an attacker to derive profile of users in a university setting (Androulaki et al, 2013). In this section, we review the cryptographic techniques used in existing blockchain systems and discuss how cryptographic algorithm is able to provide security functions such as integrity and authenticity protection, non-repudiation, data confidentiality, privacy protection and access control in a public/private blockchain system.

6.6.1 *Hash function*

Cryptographic hash function is essentially a compression function. It takes as input data of arbitrary length and outputs a fixed-length hash value that can uniquely identify the data. A hash function is deterministic and the computation of the hash value of an input string x can be done in time bounded by a small-degree polynomial in the size of x. A cryptographically secure hash function $Hash(.)$ is characterised by the following properties:

(1) Pre-image resistance (One-wayness): Given a hash value h, it is computationally infeasible to find an input string x, such that $h = Hash(x)$.
(2) Collision-resistance: It is computationally infeasible to find two distinct inputs x and y, where $x \neq y$, such that $Hash(x) = Hash(y)$.

The salient properties of the hash function allow it to be widely used in many applications, to name a few:

(1) Hash functions are used to accelerate database lookup by using hash value as the unique identifier for different files, and duplication can be detected quickly and efficiently. An example of an application is in the distributed file system called the InterPlanetary File System (IPFS) (Benet, 2014), where each file and all of the blocks in the file are given a unique hash value, and each node stores only the content (i.e., blocks) it is interested in. To lookup a file with a particular content, a node sends a query to find a peer node that stores the block identified by a unique hash value.
(2) A hash function with an additional input of a "secret information" is a Message Authentication Code (Bellare, Canetti and Krawczyk, 1996). A use case example is the security token provided by the bank to generate a one-time password (M'raihi

et al, 2005) for users to log in to online banking services. The token is embedded with a secret key that is shared with the bank and an accurate clock that is synchronised with the clock on the bank server. Each time a user logs in to online banking service, a one-time password is generated with the secret key and the current time epoch as input to a hash function. The main advantage of a one-time password is the resistance to replay attack (as it is valid only within a time frame) and the security token serves as the second level of authentication ("what the user has") in addition to the username and password authentication ("what the user knows").

(3) In cryptographic application, the hash function is used extensively with a digital signature algorithm. As mentioned earlier, the hash function is computationally efficient regardless of the input data size, whereas a digital signature algorithm, being a public-key cryptography, is extremely time-consuming to compute on large data. Thus, instead of signing on raw input data, a unique fingerprint (i.e., the hash value) of the data is computed and a digital signature is computed on the hash value. This guarantees message authentication (proof of origin), integrity protection and non-repudiation (as will be discussed in Section 6.6.2).

The current state-of-the-art standard for hash function is the SHA-256 and SHA-512, as described in FIPS PUB 180-4 (NIST, 2015). The SHA-256 and SHA-512 hash functions produce a hash value of 256 and 512 bits, respectively, with SHA-256 being the more commonly used algorithm and serving as the hash function that is used in Bitcoin's PoW consensus algorithm.

Other Hash Functions: The Bitcoin's PoW consensus using SHA-256 is not ASIC-resistant, i.e., it is possible to use ASIC to speed up mining, resulting in an unfair advantage (a skewed lottery system). Numerous alternatives have been proposed. For example, Ethereum and Zcash designed their own algorithm called the Ethash and Equihash, respectively, whereas Dash uses the X11 algorithm designed by its developer Evan Duffield as a sequential application of 11 SHA-3 candidate hash functions, and Monero uses the CryptoNote protocol which involves the use of SHA-3 candidates Keccak (the SHA-3 algorithm itself), BLAKE, Groestl, Skein and the AES encryption function.

To this end, note that the Litecoin blockchain employs a PoW consensus using the Scrypt algorithm (Percival and Josefsson, 2016). The Scrypt algorithm does not belong to the family of hash functions. Rather, it is a *password derivation function* which is intentionally designed to be computationally intensive, and it is published as RFC 7914. However, as of May 2014, ASIC mining hardware is already available for Scrypt-based cryptocurrencies (Chen, 2014).

6.6.2 *Digital signature*

A digital signature is a means for the signer to bind its identity to a piece of data. A digital signature is a public-key cryptography technique in which a user is equipped with a pair of private and public keys (sk, pk). The private key sk is kept secret and is used to generate the user's digital signature on a data m whereas the public key pk is bounded to the user's identity, and it is registered to a trusted authority and can be publicly distributed to any other user. A digital signature consists of two main algorithms $(\text{Sign}_{sk}(.), \text{Verify}_{pk}(.))$:

(1) Signature Generation, $\text{Sign}_{sk}(.)$: The signature generation algorithm $\text{Sign}_{sk}(.)$ takes as input a message m and a private key sk and outputs a digital signature on m as $Sig_m = \text{Sign}_{sk}(m)$.
(2) Signature Verification, $\text{Verify}_{pk}(.)$: Given a message-signature pair (m, Sig_m), a verifier will accept the signature as being valid if $\text{Verify}_{pk}(m, Sig_m)$ outputs "True".

A digital signature algorithm possesses the following properties. Firstly, it is unforgeable. This means that given Alice's signature where $\text{Verify}_{pk\_Alice}(m, Sig_m)$ outputs "True" can only be generated by Alice's corresponding private key sk_Alice. Secondly, it provides authentication and integrity protection for the signed message, i.e., a valid signature Sig_m with respect to a public key pk_Alice implies that m indeed originates from Alice and that the message m has not been tampered with, as this would invalidate the Sig_m. Thirdly, it provides non-repudiation service in the sense that the signer cannot deny having signed on the message m as a valid digital signature can only be generated with the signer's private key.

The RSA digital signature (Moriarty et al, 2016), Elliptic Curve Digital Signature Algorithm (ECDSA) (Johnson, Menezes and Vanstone, 2001) and the Edwards-Curve Digital Signature Algorithm (EdDSA) (Josefsson and Liusvaara, 2017) are the more prominent digital signature algorithms that are currently in used. More notably, the RSA digital signature is based on computationally hard discrete logarithm problem and it is the standard algorithm used in the SSL and TLS protocols (Rescorla, 2001) as a mean to verify the authenticity of digital certificates, which are in turn used to verify the authenticity of a webpage. The ECDSA is based on elliptic curve cryptography (Hankerson, Menezes and Vanstone, 2006), and it is the standard algorithm used in software including the Pretty Good Privacy (PGP) (Zimmermann, 1995) and its open source version Gnu Privacy Guard (GPG) (Callas et al, 2007). Compared to RSA, the ECDSA stood out in terms of its signature generation time and signature/key size at the same security level (at present, the recommended key size for RSA is 2,048 bits whereas for ECDSA is 256 bits) (Gura et al, 2004). The EdDSA (or its variant Ed25519) is also an elliptic curve-based digital signature, but with a much faster computation time compared to ECDSA. It is worth noting that ECDSA is the digital signature algorithm used in the Bitcoin and Ethereum blockchain systems whereas EdDSA is used in most of the other blockchain systems surveyed in this Chapter.

Ring Signature: Ring Signature is one of the most important variants of digital signature algorithms used in blockchain. In a typical application that provides authentication and non-repudiation, every user must register to a certificate authority (CA) its identity and associate the identity to its public key. This implies that a digital signature algorithm is not anonymous and that a digital signature that is verified as valid with respect to a public key is used to associate the user identity in order to be attestable. In a public blockchain, however, although a user does not need to register its identity to be associated with a particular public key, it is still possible to trace the transactions originated from the same public key (wallet address). The Monero blockchain mitigates such loss of privacy by employing ring signature. In the work of Bernstein et al (2012), the notion of ring signature is proposed to enable the possibility of specifying a set of possible signers without revealing which member actually produced the signature on a particular data.

A ring signature works as follows: Suppose there is a group of N users, each having its own private and public key pair (pk_1, sk_1), $(pk_2, sk_2), \ldots, (pk_N, sk_N)$. A user i with the key pair (pk_i, sk_i) can compute a ring signature Sig_m on a message m using the inputs $(m, sk_i, pk_1, pk_2, \ldots, pk_N)$. The message-signature pair (m, Sig_m) can be verified using any one of the public keys from the set $\{pk_1, pk_2, \ldots, pk_N\}$.

A ring signature algorithm inherits all security properties of a normal digital signature algorithm, in addition to the fact that it should be anonymous, i.e., it is computationally infeasible to determine which user in the group produces the signature on message m. In the work of Rivest, Shamir and Tauman (2001), ring signature is described as "a way to leak a secret" as it provides privacy protection to the user who generated the signature.

Comments on Multisignature: Most of the blockchain systems surveyed in this Chapter support multisignature. A multisignature request can be imposed on a wallet address to require a minimum quorum of signatures to be present in order for a transaction to be considered as valid. At present, a multisignature scheme requiring M-out-of-N signatures works by appending at least M signatures with a transaction in order for it to be considered valid. An alternative that can be considered to reduce the payload due to multisignature is threshold signature (Shoup, 2000). A threshold signature works by dividing the secret (signing) key into N portions that are shared among N different users. To generate a signature on a piece of data D, at least M (the "threshold") secret key portions, i.e., users, must be present. This approach effectively implements a multisignature with a significantly reduced payload size.

6.6.3   *Encryption algorithm*

Data confidentiality is achieved by means of encryption. The most commonly used encryption algorithm at present is the AES algorithm (NIST, 2001). The AES encryption algorithm is a block cipher, i.e., it takes as input data to be encrypted and partitions the data into blocks of equal sizes (128 bits), and performs a series of substitution and permutation on the blocks with respect to an input secret key. Therefore, AES is fast in terms of both software and hardware (regardless of the input data size) implementation and it is widely used to encrypt files on disk and emails.

The AES encryption algorithm is a symmetric encryption, which implies that the encryption and decryption must be performed using the same secret key. This, however, creates a scalability problem as it is almost impossible for two (or more) users to meet physically to agree upon a common secret key, or to agree upon a common secret without first establishing a secure channel with encrypted communication. To mitigate this problem, AES is used with asymmetric encryption to realise a hybrid encryption scheme.

Recall that in public-key cryptography, each user has its own private and public key pair. Public-key cryptography in the context of encryption (termed "asymmetric encryption") works as follows: Alice who wishes to send an encrypted message m to Bob would encrypt her message using an asymmetric encryption function $AE(.)$ with Bob's public key, pk_Bob, to produce a ciphertext c, i.e., $c = AE_{pk\_Bob}(m)$. The resulting ciphertext is then delivered to Bob, who will be able to decrypt using his secret key, sk_Bob, to recover $m = AD_{sk\_Bob}(c)$, where $AD(.)$ denotes an asymmetric decryption function. The most popular asymmetric encryption schemes are the RSA encryption scheme used in the Secure Sockets Layer (SSL) and Transport Layer Security (TLS) protocols, and the ElGamal encryption scheme (ElGamal, 1985) used in open source software such as the GNU Privacy Guard.

However, note that although asymmetric encryption eliminates the scalability problem in symmetric encryption by not requiring a pre-shared key beforehand, it is extremely time-consuming to be performed on large data. Therefore, the concept of hybrid encryption is applied as follows:

— Suppose Alice wishes to talk secretly to Bob. Alice would choose a random secret key k, and encrypt her message m to Bob using k as input to a symmetric encryption algorithm $SE(.)$, i.e., Alice computes $c_{se} = SE_k(m)$.
— Alice retrieves Bob's public encryption key pk_Bob, and uses asymmetric encryption $AE(.)$ to encrypt the secret key k and obtain the ciphertext $c_{ae} = AE_{pk\_Bob}(k)$.
— Alice transmits the ciphertext pair (c_{se}, c_{ae}) to Bob.
— Bob uses his private key sk_Bob to decrypt c_{ae} using the asymmetric decryption function $AD(.)$ and obtain $k = AD_{sk\_Bob}(c_{ae})$.
— Bob proceeds to use the secret key k to decrypt c_{se} using a symmetric decryption function $SD(.)$ and obtain Alice's message $m = SD_k(c_{se})$.

Hybrid encryption effectively eliminates the weaknesses of symmetric encryption (in terms of the need to establish a shared secret key) and of asymmetric encryption (in terms of computation cost on large data). This "envelope" technique is deployed in virtually all protocols that require secure communication.

Comments on Encryption for Data Confidentiality: Several blockchain systems involve the transfer of cryptocurrency and some support the process of "voting" for delegates to undertake the consensus algorithm. A possible implementation to protect data confidentiality in these processes is the use of homomorphic encryption (Gentry, 2009). Homomorphic encryption is a form of asymmetric encryption that allows computation (e.g., addition and/or multiplication) to be carried out on ciphertexts, generating an encrypted output with the same result as if the computation is applied on the plaintexts. More specifically, a homomorphic encryption scheme $H.Enc(.)$ is able to realise $H.Enc(m_1) \cdot H.Enc(m_2) = H.Enc(m_1 \cdot m_2)$, where the operator $\cdot$ can be either an addition or a multiplication operation.

6.6.4   *Zero-knowledge proof*

A zero-knowledge proof is a cryptographic protocol executed between a Prover and a Verifier in which the Prover proves to the Verifier that a given statement is true without leaking any information about the statement to the Verifier (Goldreich, Micali and Wigderson, 1991). The first design of a zero-knowledge proof scheme is an interactive protocol consisting of three phases, namely the Commit, Challenge, and Response phase. The Commit phase involves the Prover running a commitment scheme. A commitment scheme is a cryptographic primitive that allows a Prover to commit to a value while keeping it hidden to the Verifier and it possesses the following properties:

— Binding: Once the Prover commits to the chosen value, the Prover cannot change the value that he or she has committed to.
— Hiding: Given the commitment to a value, the Verifier cannot derive any information about the committed value.

We illustrate a simple example of an interactive zero-knowledge proof extracted from Mao (2003). In this protocol, let $f(.)$ be a one-way function with homomorphic property, i.e., $f(x+y) = f(x) \times f(y)$. Both the Prover and the Verifier agree on a value $X = f(z)$, where z is a secret held by the Prover. The aim is for the Prover to prove knowledge of z without revealing z to the Verifier.

(1) Commit: The Prover randomly picks a value k and commits to k by computing *Commitment* $= f(k)$ and the Prover sends *Commitment* to the Verifier.
(2) Challenge: The Verifier picks at random a challenge, either a bit 0 or 1, and sends the *Challenge Bit* to the Prover.
(3) Response: If *Challenge Bit* $= 0$, then the Prover sends *Response* $= k$ to the Verifier; otherwise, the Prover sends *Response* $= k + z$ to the Verifier.

If *Challenge Bit* $= 0$, the Verifier accepts if *Response* $=$ *Commitment*, else if *Challenge Bit* $= 1$, the Verifier accepts if *Response* $=$ *Commitment* $\times X$.

For the Verifier to be convinced that the Prover indeed knows the secret value z, the zero-knowledge proof protocol must be run in sufficient number of rounds with different k values in the Commit phase so that the probability of the Prover guessing the challenge bit correctly is minimised.

zk-SNARK: The Zcash cryptocurrency utilises a zero-knowledge succinct non-interactive argument knowledge (zk-SNARK) proof (Ben-Sasson et al, 2014). It eliminates the "interactive" part of existing zero-knowledge proof. Note that in the protocol illustrated earlier, the Prover can easily cheat if he or she knows the challenge bit before each round is executed. The zk-SNARK protocol achieves non-interactivity by publishing the challenges during initial setup and encrypting the challenges using a homomorphic encryption scheme to allow subsequent verifications.

6.6.5 *Access control*

Given a system that has authenticated and identified a user, an access control scheme further determines what resources that the user can access. This is particularly important in private blockchains where it is imperative to allow users to share resources while preventing activities that could lead to security breaches. In the Hyperledger Fabric and Openchain blockchain systems, access control list (Sandhu and Samarati, 1994) is used outside of the blockchain system to regulate user permissions. An access control list is mostly used in operating systems such as UNIX to restrict accesses to file objects. Each object is stored with the access rights specifying the subject (entity) and the associated privileges (e.g., read, write or delete). An interesting implementation of access control is in the MultiChain system, where the creator of the chain is granted an administrator privilege, and subsequent privilege assignments are recorded on the blockchain after consensus is achieved among the privileged users.

6.6.6 *Discussion*

In the Bitcoin blockchain, each time before a user sends a new transaction, a new public key will be used and the transaction will be

sent from a random wallet address. The public key is not associated
to user identity, thus guaranteeing an anonymous transaction. Most
public blockchain follows the same design convention in Bitcoin to
provide user anonymity. However, an unspent transaction output
remains traceable and two different unspent transactions can be
linked if they originate from the same wallet address. To solve these
issues, Dash implemented a PrivateSend feature, where a masternode
is deployed to mix unspent outputs of the same denomination in
a pool and randomly select one as input for the next transaction.
Monero uses ring signature by letting a group of nodes to come
together and a ring signature generated on a transaction can be
verifiable using public key belonging to any node within the group,
effectively hiding the real sender of the transaction. On another
note, Zcash solves the privacy problem by completely hiding the
sender, receiver, and transaction amount using a non-interactive
zero-knowledge proof.

Data confidentiality can be provided via the use of encryption
algorithm such as AES block cipher and RSA encryption. This is
demonstrated by blockchain systems such as Zcash, MultiChain,
NEM and Hyperledger. In retrospect, another form of data confidentiality can be achieved through a tweak in the consensus process.
For example, Corda and Dragonchain restrict transaction validation
among transacting parties and strip the transaction payload before
sending it for notarisation. The Factom blockchain that anchored
itself to the Bitcoin blockchain for public accountability publishes
only the block hash instead of the transaction data.

6.7   Concluding Remarks

Blockchain leverages the salient properties of cryptographic techniques and distributed consensus algorithm to provide a secure and
immutable ledger without the need of a trusted authority. When
a new transaction is broadcasted in the blockchain system, all
nodes will run the consensus algorithm to verify the validity of the
transaction. Once they converge in agreement, the transaction will
be added to a block, which would then be appended to the blockchain

in an immutable manner using cryptographic techniques. In this Chapter, we surveyed several prominent token-based and tokenless blockchain, as well as the underlying cryptographic algorithm that are used in these blockchain systems.

It is imperative to note that the design of the consensus algorithm should guarantee sufficient "diversity" in selecting the set of nodes involved in the consensus process to ensure no nodes are able to dominate the consensus process. A counter example would be the old PoS algorithm used in Peercoin (Vasin, 2014), where nodes are selected based on coin age, resulting in most nodes staying dormant and coming online only during the consensus process, consequently resulting in a form of domination. It is also vital to filter out inactive nodes in a timely manner to guarantee synchrony. Another issue to address is loss of private keys. In current blockchain implementation, the loss of private key implies that a user lost ownership of its wallet and the digital tokens held at the wallet address. However, due consideration should be exerted on the security of the consensus algorithm in the event of loss of private keys, especially for public blockchain that uses PoS consensus. In particular, the loss of private key of a stakeholder will pose significant risk as an attacker will be able to influence the result of the PoS consensus process. Such a risk is non-existent in PoW and PBFT consensus because the former is essentially a fair lottery system and the latter is commonly implemented in private blockchain, where node identities are known and regulated by an administrator.

References and Further Readings

All In Bits, Inc. (2017). Tendermint — Blockchain consensus. Retrieved from https://tendermint.com/

Androulaki, E., Karame G. O., Roeschlin M., Scherer T., & Capkun S. (2013). Evaluating user privacy in Bitcoin. In Sadeghi, A. R. (Ed.), Financial Cryptography and Data Security, Lecture Notes in Computer Science 7859 (pp. 34–51). Berlin, Heidelberg: Springer. Retrieved from https://link.springer.com/chapter/10.1007/978-3-642-39884-1_4

Atzei, N., Bartoletti M., & Cimoli T. (2017). A survey of attacks on Ethereum Smart Contracts (SoK). In Maffei, M., & Ryan, M. (Eds.), Principles of Security and Trust. In Proceedings of the 6th International Conference on

Principles of Security and Trust, POST 2017. Springer, 164–186. Retrieved from https://link.springer.com/chapter/10.1007%2F978-3-662-54455-6_8

Bellare, M., Canetti, R., & Krawczyk, H. (1996). Keying hash functions for message authentication. In Koblitz, N. (Ed.), Advances in Cryptology — CRYPTO' 96. In Proceedings of 16th Annual International Cryptology Conference, Santa Barbara, California, USA, August 18–22, 1996. Springer, 1–15. Retrieved from https://link.springer.com/chapter/10.1007%2F3-540-68697-5_1

Benet, J. (2014). IPFS — Content addressed, versioned, P2P file system. arXiv preprint arXiv:1407.3561. Retrieved from https://arxiv.org/pdf/1407.3561.pdf

Ben-Sasson, E., Chiesa, A., Tromer, E., & Virza, M. (2014). Succinct non-interactive zero knowledge for a von Neumann architecture. In Proceedings of the 23rd USENIX Conference on Security Symposium (SEC'14). USENIX Association, 781–796. Retrieved from https://www.usenix.org/system/files/conference/usenixsecurity14/sec14-paper-ben-sasson.pdf

Bernstein, D. J., Duif, N., Lange, T., Schwabe, P., & Yang, B.-Y. (2012). High-Speed High-Security Signatures. Journal of Cryptographic Engineering, 2(2), 77–89.

Brown, R. G., Carlyle, J., Grigg, I., & Hearn, M. (2016). Corda: An Introduction. White Paper.

Callas, J., Donnerhacke, L., Finney, H., Shaw, D., & Thayer, R. (2007). OpenPGP Message Format. Network Working Group RFC 4880, November 2007.

Chain Inc. (2016). Chain Protocol Whitepaper. White Paper.

Chain Inc. (2017). Chain | Enterprise blockchain infrastructure. Retrieved from https://chain.com/

Chen, C. (2014, May 21). Zeusminer delivers Lightning, Thunder and Cyclone Scrypt ASICs for Litecoin and Dogecoin mining. Retrieved from https://www.cryptocoinsnews.com/zeusminer-delivers-lightning-thunder-cyclone-scrypt-asics-litecoin-dogecoin-mining/

Coin Sciences Ltd. (2017). MultiChain|Open source private blockchain platform. Retrieved from https://www.multichain.com/

Coinprism. (2015). Openchain — Blockchain technology for the enterprise. Retrieved from https://www.openchain.org/

Dai, P., Mahi, N., Earls, J., & Norta, A. (2017). Smart-contract value-transfer protocols on a distributed mobile application platform. Retrieved from http://bit.ly/2vceYYW

DaxClassix. (2016). Ethereum Classic. Retrieved from https://ethereumclassic.github.io

Dell, I., Beddows, O., Meunier, L., & Kordek, M. (2017). The Lisk Protocol. Retrieved from https://docs.lisk.io/docs/the-lisk-protocol

DigixGlobal. (2016). Digix Global. Retrieved from https://www.dgx.io/

Disney. (2017). Dragonchain. Retrieved from https://dragonchain.github.io/

Douceur, J. R. (2002). The Sybil attack. In Druschel P., Kaashoek F., & Rowstron A. (Eds.), Peer-to-Peer Systems. In Proceedings of the 1st International

Workshop on Peer-to-Peer Systems (IPTPS). Springer, 251–260. Retrieved from https://link.springer.com/chapter/10.1007%2F3-540-45748-8_24

Duffield, E., & Diaz, D. (2017). Dash: A Privacy-Centric Crypto-Currency. White Paper.

Dworkin, M. J. (2015). SHA-3 Standard: Permutation-Based Hash and Extendable-Output Functions. NIST Federal Information Processing Standard 202, 2015.

ElGamal, T. (1985), A public key cryptosystem and a signature scheme based on discrete logarithms. IEEE Transactions on Information Theory, 31(4), 469–472.

Ethereum Foundation. (2017). Ethereum Project. Retrieved from https://www.ethereum.org/

Factom. (2017). Factom — Making the world's systems honest. Retrieved from https://www.factom.com/

Ferguson, N., Lucks, S., Schneier, B., Whiting, D., Bellare, M., Kohno, T., Callas, J., & Walker, J. (2010). The Skein Hash Function Family. Submission to NIST (round 3) 7, 2010.

Fisher, M. J., Lynch, N. A., & Paterson, M. S. (1985). Impossibility of distributed consensus with one faulty process. Journal of the Association for Computing Machinery, 32(2), 374–382.

Gauravaram, P., Knudsen, L. R., Matusiewicz, K., Mendel, F., Rechberger, C., Schläffer, M., & Thomsen, S. S. (2008). "Grøstl — A SHA-3 candidate. Retrieved from http://www.groestl.info

Gentry, C. (2009). A Fully Homomorphic Encryption Scheme. Working paper, Stanford University.

Goldreich, O., Micali, S., & Wigderson, A. (1991). Proofs that yield nothing but their validity or all languages in NP have zero-knowledge proof systems. Journal of the ACM (JACM), 38(3), 690–728.

Greenspan, G. (2015). MultiChain private blockchain — White paper. Retrieved from https://www.multichain.com/download/MultiChain-White-Paper.pdf

Gura, N., Patel, A., Wander, A., Eberle, H., & Shantz, S. C. (2004). Comparing Elliptic Curve Cryptography and RSA on 8-bit CPUs. In Joye, M., & Quisquater, J. J. (Eds.), Cryptographic Hardware and Embedded Systems — CHES, Lecture Notes in Computer Science 3156 (pp. 119–132). Berlin, Heidelberg: Springer.

Hankerson, D., Menezes, A. J., & Vanstone, S. (2006). Guide to Elliptic Curve Cryptography. NY: Springer Science & Business Media.

Hertig, A., & Rizzo. P. (2016, July 28). Ethereum's two Ethereums explained. Retrieved from http://www.coindesk.com/ethereum-classic-explained-blockchain/

Higgins, S. (2017, April 26). Grayscale opens Ethereum Classic vehicle to accredited investors. Retrieved from http://www.coindesk.com/grayscale-ethereum-classic-vehicle/

Hopwood, D., Bowe, S., Hornby, T., & Wilcox, N. (2017). Zcash Protocol Specification. White Paper.

Intel. (2015). Hyperledger Sawtooth documentation. Retrieved from https://intelledger.github.io/

Johnson, D., Menezes, A., & Vanstone, S. (2001). The Elliptic Curve Digital Signature Algorithm (ECDSA). International Journal of Information Security, 1(1), 36–63.

Josefsson, S., & Liusvaara, I. (2017). Edwards-Curve Digital Signature Algorithm (EdDSA). The Internet Engineering Task Force RFC 8032.

Kiraly, B. (2017a, February 21). InstantSend. Retrieved from https://dashpay.atlassian.net/wiki/display/DOC/InstantSend

Kiraly, B. (2017b, April 7). PrivateSend. Retrieved from https://dashpay.atlassian.net/wiki/display/DOC/PrivateSend

Kumar, A., Fischer, C., Tople, S., & Saxena, P. (2017). A Traceability Analysis of Monero's Blockchain. IACR Cryptology ePrint Archive 2017.

Ladha, A., Pandit, S., & Ralhan, S. (2016). The Ethereum scratch off puzzle. arXiv preprint arXiv:1612.04518, 2016.

Lai, R., & Lee, D. K. C. (2017). From public to private. In Lee & Deng. Handbook of Blockchain, Digital Finance and Inclusion. Elsevier.

Larimer, D., Scott, N., Zavgorodnev, V., Johnson, B., Calfee, J., & Vandeberg, M. (2016). Steem: An incentivised blockchain-based social media platform. Retrieved from https://steem.io/SteemWhitePaper.pdf

Lee, D. K. C. & Deng, R. (2017). Handbook of Blockchain, Digital Finance and Inclusion: Vol 1 and 2. Elsevier.

Li R. (2017, January 12). Blockchain software security report by China CERT, Ripple the worst. Retrieved from http://news.8btc.com/blockchain-software-security-report-by-china-cert-ripple-the-worst

Litecoin Project. (2011). Litecoin — Open source P2P digital currency. Retrieved from https://litecoin.org/

M'Raihi, D., Bellare, M., Hoornaert, F., Naccache, D., & Ranen, O. (2005). HOTP: An HMAC-Based One-Time Password Algorithm. The Internet Engineering Task Force RFC 4226.

Mao, W. (2013). Modern Cryptography: Theory and Practice. NJ: Prentice Hall Professional Technical Reference.

Maxwell, G. (2013). CoinJoin: Bitcoin privacy for the real world. Post on Bitcoin Forum.

Mazieres, D. (2016). The Stellar Consensus Protocol: A federated model for Internet-level consensus. Retrieved from https://www.stellar.org/papers/stellar-consensus-protocol.pdf

Merkle, R. C. (1988). A digital signature based on a conventional encryption function. In Pomerance, C. (Ed.), Advances in Cryptology — CRYPTO '87, Lecture Notes in Computer Science 293 (pp. 369–378). Berlin, Heidelberg: Springer.

Morabito, V. (2017). The security of blockchain systems. In Business Innovation through Blockchain. Cham: Springer International Publishing.

Moriarty, K., Ed., Kaliski, B., Jonsson, J., & Rusch, A. (2016). PKCS #1: RSA Cryptography Specifications Version 2.2. Internet Engineering Task Force RFC 8017.

Nakamoto, S. (2008). Bitcoin: A peer-to-peer electronic cash system. Retrieved from https://bitcoin.org/bitcoin.pdf

NIST. (2001). Federal Information Processing Standards Publication 197 — Announcing the Advanced Encryption Standard (AES). Retrieved from http://nvlpubs.nist.gov/nistpubs/FIPS/NIST.FIPS.197.pdf

NIST. (2015). Federal Information Processing Standards Publication 180-4 Secure Hash Standard (SHS). Retrieved from http://nvlpubs.nist.gov/nistpubs/FIPS/NIST.FIPS.180-4.pdf

Pass, R., Seeman, L., & Shelat, A. (2017). Analysis of the blockchain protocol in asynchronous networks. In Coron, J. S., & Nielsen, J. (Eds.), Advances in Cryptology — EUROCRYPT 2017, Lecture Notes in Computer Science 10211 (pp. 643–673). Cham: Springer International Publishing.

Percival, C., & Josefsson., S. (2016). The Scrypt Password-Based Key Derivation Function. The Internet Engineering Task Force RFC 7914.

R3 Limited. (2016). Corda: Frictionless commerce. Retrieved from https://www.corda.net/

Rescorla, E. (2001). SSL and TLS: Designing and Building Secure Systems, Boston: Addison-Wesley Longman Publishing Co., Inc.

Ripple. (2013). Ripple — One frictionless experience to send money globally | Ripple. Retrieved from https://ripple.com/

Rivest, R. L., Shamir, A., & Tauman, Y. 2001. How to leak a secret. In Boyd, C. (Ed.), Advances in Cryptology — ASIACRYPT 2001, Lecture Notes in Computer Science 2248 (pp. 552–565). Berlin, Heidelberg: Springer.

Ron, D., & Shamir, A. (2013). Quantitative analysis of the full Bitcoin transaction graph. In Sadeghi, A. R. (Ed.), Financial Cryptography and Data Security, Lecture Notes in Computer Science 7859 (pp. 6–24). Berlin, Heidelberg: Springer.

Rosenfeld, M. (2014). Analysis of hashrate-based double spending. arXiv preprint arXiv:1402.2009.

Saarinen, M. J., & Aumasson, J. P. (2015). The BLAKE2 Cryptographic Hash and Message Authentication Code (MAC). The Internet Engineering Task Force RFC 7693.

Sandhu, R. S., & Samarati, P. (1994). Access control: Principle and practice. IEEE Communication Magazine, 32(9), 40–48.

Schoder, D., Fischbach, K., & Schmitt, C. (2005). Core concepts in peer-to-peer networking. In Subramanian, R., & Goodman, B. (Eds.), P2P Computing: The Evolution of a Disruptive Technology. Hershey: Idea Group Inc.

Schwartz, D., Youngs, N., & Britto, A. (2014). The Ripple Protocol Consensus Algorithm. Ripple Labs Inc White Paper 5.

Shoup, V. (2000). Practical threshold signatures. In Preneel B. (Ed.), Advances in Cryptology — EUROCRYPT 2000, Lecture Notes in Computer Science 1807 (pp. 207–220). Berlin, Heidelberg: Springer.

Stellar Development Foundation. (2014). Stellar — Develop the world's new financial system. Retrieved from https://www.stellar.org/

The Dash Network. (2017). Dash official website | Dash crypto currency — Dash. Retrieved from https://www.dash.org

The Linux Foundation. (2017). Hyperledger Fabric — Hyperledger. Retrieved from https://www.hyperledger.org/projects/fabric

The Monero Project. (2014). Monero — Secure, private, untraceable. Retrieved from http://getmonero.org/

van Saberhagen, N. (2013). CryptoNote v 2.0. White Paper.

Vasin, P. (2014). BlackCoin's Proof-of-Stake Protocol v2. White Paper.

Wood, G. (2017). Ethereum: A Secure Decentralised Generalised Transaction ledger. Ethereum Project Yellow Paper.

Yuen, T. H., Liu, J. K., Au, M. H., Susilo, W., & Zhou, J. (2013). Efficient linkable and/or threshold ring signature without random oracles. The Computer Journal, 56(4), 407–421.

ZECC. (2017). Zcash — All coins are created equal. Retrieved from https://z.cash

Zimmermann, P. R. (1995). The Official PGP User's Guide, MA: MIT Press.

Chapter 7

Inclusive FinTech

Assisted by Ernie TEO and Several Research Assistants in an
Earlier Version of This Chapter

7.1 Introduction

There is an estimated 38% of the world population that has no formal
bank accounts and another 40% that is underserved by banks. The
2014 statistics by the World Bank estimated 2 billion adults were
without an account as compared to 2.5 billion in 2011 (Demirguc-
Kunt and Klapper, 2012). Sustainable and profitable enterprises use
financial technology to lower business costs to serve the underserved
and unbanked. Low-cost financial services via mobile technology
facilitate financial inclusion. Financial inclusion means that individuals and businesses have access to useful and affordable financial
products and services that meet their needs delivered in a responsible
and sustainable way. These financial products and services include
transactions, payments, savings, credit and insurance.

About 62% of the world's population do not use formal banks or
even semi-formal financial institutions to save or borrow money. Due
to high compliance and infrastructure costs, financial institutions
such as banks are unable or unwilling to serve this group. Providing
financial services to the unbanked and the underserved aids world
development. It increases equality among nations and brings about
financial integration.

There are three main barriers to financial inclusion. First, mainstream financial institutions such as banks and fund managers are constrained by domestic and international regulations that prevent them from servicing those at the bottom of the pyramid. Second, the business culture of financial institutions to pursue profits and to invest only in unsolvable problems perpetuates the focus on customers at the top of the pyramid. Lastly, most business units are organised in silos with Key Performance Indicators focusing on individual performance that is a single channel or single product focus. FinTech that enables information, technology, and capital sharing may provide a sustainable business model to serve the entire pyramid.

7.1.1   *Asset allocation and investment strategy*

The returns on equity (ROE) for most financial institutions, especially the major banks, is dropping. Fund managers, especially asset allocators, are struggling to find alternative asset classes that will protect the portfolio on the downside in a low growth, low yield and over-valued regime. The central banks balance sheets have grown at a rate not seen before. Since 2005, the balance sheet of the Bank of Japan (BoJ) had grown 100% to JPY300 trillion by 2014, the balance sheet of European Central Bank (ECB) had increased three times to EUR3 trillion by 2012 (and another two times by 2015), and the balance sheet of Federal Reserve Board (FED) had grown more than five times to USD4.5 trillion at end 2014. In terms of a percentage of gross domestic product (GDP), BoJ has reached 62%, ECB has reached 20% and the FED 26%. At the time of writing, these numbers have not improved nine years after the start of the Global Financial Crisis in 2008. FinTech has been a sought-after alternative class given its reach to the unbanked and underserved that have a higher marginal propensity to consume.

With quantitative easing (QEs), many managers and sovereign wealth funds (SWFs) have increased exposures to private equity and real estate. Besides buying "Trophy Estates", savvy investors such as Singapore Sovereign Wealth Fund GIC had made 33 direct investments with a total value of USD4.65 billion in the first six months of 2014 according to a Bloomberg report. GIC has found a niche in e-commerce and technology investments before other SWFs with a new investment framework that looks for idiosyncratic opportunities. GIC invested an undisclosed amount in India's biggest online retailer Flipkart.com. Moreover, GIC allocates 11–15% to private quality and another 9–13% on real estate as a target policy. With 20–28% allocation as a strategic policy and actual investment of 16% (7% and 9%) into these two alternative Investment classes, GIC is unique among SWFs.

Given the massive liquidity, it does make sense to increase allocation to asset classes that have negative correlation with the returns of existing portfolio. Delinking from short-term irrational price fluctuation caused by capital flow in an overly liquid environment is important for long-term investment and its sustainability. It is crucial that the portfolio is not left to the mercy of market prices that are influenced by rapid capital flow such as those stocks and bonds that are traded on exchanges. In the case of real estate and private equity, a third party valuation via professional valuer's report and audited accounts will reflect the net asset value better than valuations that are distorted by short-term capital flow or money contraction. GIC, buying into smooth valuation as well as eco-system of e-commerce, is ahead of its peers in terms of its innovative approach.

Singapore's SWF Temasek, another savvy institutional investor, has invested in the secondary market platform for primary capital raise (SecondMarket) in February 2010 and a multichannel payment company outsourcing payment services to an international merchant (Adyen) in December 2014 besides Alibaba and others. Its subsidiaries Fullerton Financial Holdings, as we shall describe later, has invested and operated a portfolio that not only has a positive impact on its returns but also has great social impact. Such investment strategy makes sense in a world where most businesses are serving the top 38% of the pyramid with high correlation among those businesses. Investing in the 62% underbanked may be a viable financial innovation strategy that reduce income inequality, promote growth, increase aggregate consumption and smooth out the business cycle in the process. This provides a missing link of the QE where bank lending is not filtering down to the micro, small and medium enterprises (MSMEs) despite the abundance of liquidity. The compliance cost, reserve/capital requirement, and other restrictive regulation have made such attempts for investing for financial inclusion impact commercially not viable. The larger institution funds are beginning to realise the potential of inclusive FinTech with increased mobile penetration.

As technology advances, major disruptions in financial services are looming. In the West, we saw advancements in an Internet protocol for money with cryptocurrencies; this allows for low transaction costs and cheap international transfers. Companies such as Apple and Google are also jumping on the mobile payment bandwagon with the introduction of Apple Pay and Google Pay. In the East, giants in the Internet industry such as Baidu, Alibaba, Tencent and JD (collectively known as the BATJ) are rising to become providers of banking and insurance services with branchless banks such as WeBank, microfinancial services such as Ant Financial, online insurance services such as ZhongAn, and supply chain financing services such as JD Finance. Financial institutions such as PingAn Insurance has the P2P/Wealth Management platform LuFax, and eICBC has its own e-commerce platform Rong-e-Gou.

These technologies not only enhance the financial sector but also complement the traditional banking and financial services. The unbanked and underbanked can be reached with financial technologies which are low margin, asset light, scalable, innovative and compliance easy (LASIC Principle). The 62% unbanked can now be served by the institutions and the institutions now realise the huge untapped market opportunities with technology that brings in valuable big data.

In the subsequent sections, we look at how financial technologies can bring about both financial disruption and financial inclusion.

7.1.2 *Financial technologies and disruption*

Financial technologies will play a major role in redefining finance. Business costs for mainstream financial institutions continue to rise as capital adequacy requirements become stricter, and compliance procedures become more complicated. Revenues are also being squeezed as firms compete for clients.

Financial institutions are lowering operating costs to increase profits. FinTech has been used to smooth out operation pain points to lower costs. At the same time, data technology provides opportunities to create new services for untapped customers: the unbanked and underserved. Lower margin businesses like micro-insurance and micro-loans will become viable with lower costs. Consumers will turn to these new FinTech businesses attracted by their low fees and better user experience. Institutions with heavy assets and large fixed costs will be unable to respond to such low-cost competitors. Institutions that use data and digital technology realise that there is a lower lending risk associated with the non-traditional source of real-time data. With these data provided by the borrowers, the new lending model is possible with a lower amount, lower risk, and higher aggregate volume.

7.1.3 The economics of financial inclusion — The unbanked and underbanked

The problem of financial exclusion does not just exist in undeveloped countries. The Federal Deposit Insurance Corporation 2013 National Survey found that 7.7% of US households are unbanked[1] and 20% are underbanked.[2] The underserved in the world turn to non-traditional forms of alternative financial services such as those provided by cheque cashers, loan sharks, and pawnbrokers. For example, illegal workers in the US (who are unable to cash the cheque in person due to a lack of personal identification) may cash cheques via agents such as cheque cashing depots or convenience stores which will charge a high commission. The agents then redeem these cheques from the issuing bank.

Many workers from developing countries seek work outside of their own countries. A large part of their income to be sent home is

---

[1]The unbanked refer to adults without an account in a financial institution.

[2]The underbanked refer to adults with poor access to mainstream financial services offered by retail banks.

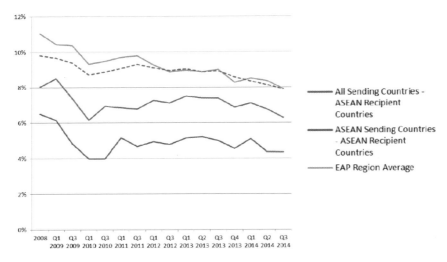

Figure 7.1.   Remittances Charges Are Falling but Remain High.
Source: World Bank.

diminished by the high remittance fees. Remittance charges remain
(at its lowest) 5% of the total remitted amount for Association
of Southeast Asian Nations (ASEAN) to ASEAN remittances (see
Figure 7.1).

Thus, high demand exists for cheap remittance services. In 2016,
there were remittance payments of more than USD575 billion around
the world according to the World Bank. The global average cost
of sending USD200 remained flat at a very high rate of 7.45% in
the first quarter of 2017. This number is significantly higher than
the United Nations' Sustainable Development Goal (SDG) target of
3%. By 2030, the target of the SDG 10c (reduce inequality within
and among countries) is to reduce to less than 3% the transaction
costs of migrant remittances and eliminate remittance corridors with
costs higher than 5%. Sub-Saharan Africa, with an average cost of
9.8%, remains the highest-cost region. Sub-Saharan Africa, including
Botswana, Lesotho and Swaziland, has the largest share of account
holders using remittances services. Much potential exists for the
provision of remittance services and many interesting technologies
such as cryptocurrencies have emerged to address the issue. This
will be explored in later sections of this Chapter.

NUMBER OF ACTIVE MOBILE-BROADBAND SUBSCRIPTIONS:
DEVELOPED VS. DEVELOPING COUNTRIES + WORLD TOTAL
2007-2014·

Source: ITU World Telecommunication/ICT Indicators Database

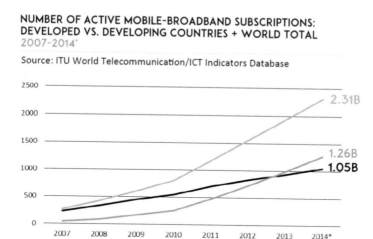

Figure 7.2.   Active Mobile Phone Subscriptions.
Source: ITU World Telecommunication/ICT Indicators Database.

The global emergence of mobile technology will play a large role in enabling financial inclusion. Through mobile and other smart devices, many under banked and underbanked segments of the world will be able to gain access to financial services. The following figures demonstrate the exponential increase in mobile adoption in the world over the past few years.

Innovative financial services need not require smart devices or even Internet connections. Telecommunication companies have successfully launched mobile money which operated via PIN-secured Short Message Service (SMS) messages such as M-PESA in Kenya and GCash in the Philippines. These services allow money transfers between users and are used as a store of account. In Kenya (where 79% of the population owns a mobile phone), 86% of mobile phone users are mobile money users, and 43% do not have a formal account. In Kenya, M-PESA's users are exempted from documentations usually required by the banks. In contrast, many other countries require mobile money schemes to be operated by banks or financial institutions, resulting in low penetration rates. India is one such

ACTIVE MOBILE-BROADBAND SUBSCRIPTIONS PER
100 INHABITANTS: DEVELOPED VS. DEVELOPING
COUNTRIES + WORLD AVG.
2007-2014'
Source: ITU World Telecommunication/ICT Indicators Database

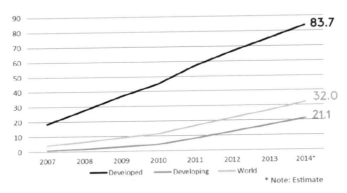

Figure 7.3. Active Mobile Phone Subscriptions per 100 Inhabitants.
Source: ITU World Telecommunication/ICT Indicators Database.

example with only 4% of the population reporting the use of remittances or bill payment services on their mobile phones.

Financial inclusion is key to leveling income inequality. Economic inclusion can be achieved much faster via financial inclusion. Four in five adults, earning less than USD2 a day, do not have a formal bank account. Only 41% of adults in developing economies have formal bank accounts compared to 89% in high-income economies. Increasing global income inequality has prompted Group of Twenty (G20) countries and other key stakeholders such as the World Bank to act on financial inclusion efforts. Efforts were concentrated in spurring broader and stronger economic growth via deepening financial intermediation and increasing efficiency. The access to payment, savings, insurance and credit services is important for economic development. Cost efficiency and increased transparency of remittances are key initiatives. Rapid development and extension of digital platforms and payments are essential to ensure speed, security, transparency and cost efficiency. The use of digital platforms makes such services scalable to extend their reach globally.

Anson et al (2013) have noted that widespread presence of post offices in rural and poor areas can play a leading role in advancing financial inclusion. Using data from 60 countries where postal accounts are offered, they have found that post offices are more likely than mainstream financial institutions to provide accounts to financially vulnerable groups such as the poor, less educated and the unemployed. They have also found that the network effect of post offices is significant and that post offices can boost account ownership by acting as cash-merchants for transactional financial services. In other words, if post offices can work with financial institutions or intermediaries (to act as an electronic government or remittance payment agent), this will result in a higher penetration rate for account ownership.

The post office can play an important role in advancing financial inclusion. Account maintenance costs need to be low, and there should be greater proximity to financial intermediaries or mobile devices. Allen et al (2012) have found that cost of an account is a major factor in determining the penetration of financial service providers. Overall, their results suggest that policies to reduce barriers to financial inclusion may increase the numbers of formal accounts and encourage existing account holders to use the accounts more frequently. Most interesting of all, reducing barriers to financial inclusion encourages saving. Indeed, this is a trend that we see in Internet Finance. Internet Finance has provided a way for cheaper remittance and payment transfers. It has also enabled a whole range of financial services to be made available to the 70% underserved.

7.1.4 *Plan of this Chapter*

In the next section, we first lay the foundation for our analysis with the LASIC principle which outlines five important attributes for successful FinTech businesses. Next, we examine three areas of business investment that fall under the heading of impact investment with financial inclusion using the LASIC principle. These areas may provide an answer to creating a sustainable business with the social objective of improving income and reducing wealth inequality. We point out that the performance of such business models will face the least resistance from the social media and be encouraged by governments, thus improving profitability with support from the masses and governments in both the financial and social aspects.

We will begin by studying the rise of a payment system in China called Alipay that was a by-product of its original parent Alibaba, an e-commerce platform. Alipay, an e-wallet application, has been downloaded more than 800 million times. We will describe the circumstances leading to its rise and the services it provides to the unbanked and underserved. We will devote substantial coverage to the environment in China and how the objective of servicing those ignored by the mainstream banks has led to a profitable business based on the LASIC principle.

The second company that we will be studying is M-PESA, a telecom-based payment system in Kenya. While telecom companies are saddled by huge depreciation in its balance sheet, the add-on payment system is what we described as a LASIC entity. We will describe how a capital-intensive industry can reinvent itself to serve the unbanked and underserved.

Finally, we will look at a traditional bank Fullerton Financial Holdings (FFH) that services the middle and the bottom of the pyramid. Microfinance, being defined as a source of financial services for entrepreneurs and small businesses lacking access to banking and related services and resembling the retail finance model prevalent in mainstream banking, has seen its mission drifted from financial inclusion to servicing the less needy. This has resulted in lending at an interest rate beyond the ability to service for borrowers who are supposed to be poor. FFH has its mission set on financial inclusion, and it has achieved a respectable ROE.

We conclude by arguing that the disrupting forces of the Internet, whether centralised or decentralised, will have a major role in redefining finance. The cost of doing business continues to escalate for the traditional financial firms because of capital adequacy requirements and compliance costs. The growth in revenue is also slowing with many firms serving the same customers at the top of the pyramid and providing similar services. In contrast, the unbanked and the underserved will pose exciting business opportunities for businesses that utilise FinTech to lower operating costs. FinTech can help consumers lower transaction costs of payment, remittance and credit transfers as well as aid merchandise businesses in reducing operating costs. With quick and instant approval of primarily small and short-term loans, the default rates will be low enough for a lending business to the bottom of the pyramid to be viable. Similarly, with innovation and scalability, low margin businesses like micro-insurance will become attractive. With improved user experience and lower cost, crowdfunding and portfolio management services to the underserved will be viable.

7.2 The LASIC Principles

The LASIC principle defines five important attributes of business models which can successfully harness financial technology to achieve the objective of creating a sustainable social business for financial inclusion and impact investment. The five attributes are as follows: (1) Low profit margin, (2) Asset light, (3) Scalability, (4) Innovative, and (5) Compliance easy.

7.2.1 *Low profit margin*

In a world of wide-spread Internet access where information and services are readily available for free, users have low willingness to pay for service providers of any kind (such as video streaming or Internet games). High network effects exhibited in such technologies require an initial phase of building up critical mass. This is a costly process which requires marketing efforts. Once a critical mass is built, monetisation becomes possible through channels such as advertising or subscription fees. Constant efforts need to be made to ensure lock-in of users through the reinforcement of network externalities and the increase of switching costs. Profit margins will remain low at the user level. The idea is to obtain a large mass of users and attain profitability through low margins and high demand. Low profit margin is a key characteristic of successful FinTech businesses.

In the technology and Internet space, most users will expect information to be provided free. Service providers are looking for a sustainable business model that may incur a high burn rate in the beginning, followed by a user acquisition period, and finally enter into a monetisation period with good revenue per user. This will entail a period of high burn rate with low or no revenue period, followed by exponential growth with multiple sources of revenue. Over a long period of time, the margin will appear low and will increase over time as different sources of revenue are captured. It will eventually achieve the target of having a large pool of sticky customers that pay for different services.

7.2.2 *Asset light*

Asset light businesses are innovative and scalable without incurring large fixed costs on assets. This will allow relatively low marginal costs which reinforces the first principle of "Low profit margin". One can add on to an existing system (such as a mobile phone) that depreciates quickly but offers an alternative revenue source (such as an Internet phone messaging service) at low marginal costs.

7.2.3 *Scalability*

FinTech businesses may start small but will have to scale to reap the full benefits of network externalities. Scalable business will be to scale without drastically increasing costs or compromising the efficiency of the technology.

7.2.4 *Innovative*

Successful FinTech businesses also need to be innovative both in their products and operations. With the increasingly wide-spread use of mobile phones and Internet services, much innovation can be made in mobile technologies (such as contactless technologies) in the FinTech space. Some examples of such innovations will be described in the following sections.

7.2.5 *Compliance easy*

The business model must be in alignment with the government's social, political and economic objectives or remain low profile. The business may be assisting the government to achieve its goals. It may also be in an area that the government is not in a hurry to regulate. In some cases, the business is simply not easy to regulate because of the decentralised nature.

7.3 Internet Finance in China and Alipay

The great trend that we see in China is the growth of Internet Finance. China's economic policy has been inclusive and emphasises the use of Internet Finance to reach out to the rural area via mobile devices. Financial Inclusion has always been on the agenda, and its regulation or the lack of it has driven businesses to operate in the grey area. This has accelerated a high penetration for financial inclusion resulting in China being the leader in the world. The following trends are observed in China:

(1) Third party payment is disrupting the traditional way of pay-ment. As it is, the young or digital natives will unlikely be issuing cheques. The number of transactions settled by cheques (−7.88%) and bank drafts (−11.75%) continued to trend down in China according to 2012 statistics (People's Bank of China, 2012). Meanwhile, bank cards (+19.84%) continued to rise. Back in 2012, the number of Internet payment increased by 22.76%, phone banking decreased by 18.41% and mobile phone increased by 116.46%. With 245 million users generating RMB2.31 trillion in volume, an increase of 132.39% from previous year. The payment itself may not be profitable, but it has become the low margin business that can be a door to economies of scope by adding on other profitable services. By 2017, Alipay had 520 million payments customers in China and 112 million outside China. It controls 51% of Internet payments in China and is 16 times larger than Paypal!

(2) P2P lending is disrupting the services that act as a middleman for borrowing and lending. Commercial banking thrives on trans-actions and lending. Its core activities involve taking deposits, granting loans and facilitating transactions. The scale of P2P lending business in China is more than 10 times larger than the

US and the UK. If the default rates are low, this will be an area
of huge value-added profitable business.

(3) Cloud Computing, big data and social network are new technologies that spur Internet Finance. Traditional finance activities
such as risk management and Personal Financial Management
are benefitting from big data analysis. Alipay had announced
that the default rate for its lending business was 0.89% in 2014
and it was noted to have benefitted from smart data analysis
from the e-wallet. Figure 7.4 outlines the client base of Alibaba.

(4) Access to Internet has increased business opportunities in micro-
insurance with a rise in the use of e-commerce. On Singles Day
(11 November 2016) alone, the premium from micro-insurance
of 657 million delivery orders had resulted in USD1.93 billion
premiums with a turnover of USD17.6 billion and 210 million
policies. This has demonstrated that e-wallet is a facilitator and
a sticky strategy for providing more value-added and profitable
business.

(5) Crowdfunding may replace the securities business. Alipay is offering additional services such as crowdfunding for movies and other
ventures using the mobile wallet. Given the oversubscription
with almost every movie being crowdfunded, it is clear that the
conduit via Alipay is an excellent channel for fundraising and
a good margin business that may replace the stock exchange
attempting to facilitate the trading of debt instruments for
digital media. The assets can also be pledged for borrowing
making cross-selling via the mobile wallet platform a new channel
for profits.

Figure 7.4 shows the client base of Alibaba Finance and Alipay.
Figure 7.5 shows the risk management process of Alipay. Both
are heavily reliant on the Internet, digital devices and big data
technology. There has never before been a technology with such an
impactful influence on financial services. This technology enables
banking services to be provided by non-bank institutions. It has
started to disrupt third part payments, Internet P2P lending, Internet insurance, mobile payments, fundraising and other alternative

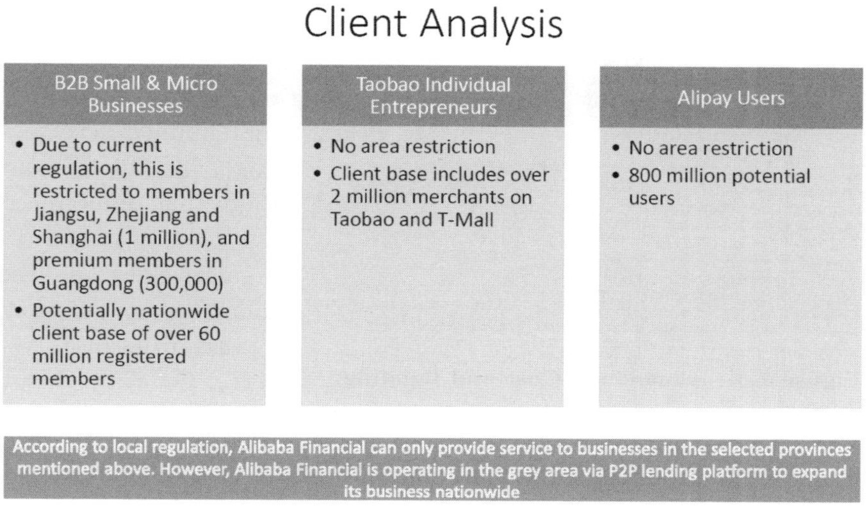

Client Analysis

B2B Small & Micro Businesses	Taobao Individual Entrepreneurs	Alipay Users
• Due to current regulation, this is restricted to members in Jiangsu, Zhejiang and Shanghai (1 million), and premium members in Guangdong (300,000) • Potentially nationwide client base of over 60 million registered members	• No area restriction • Client base includes over 2 million merchants on Taobao and T-Mall	• No area restriction • 800 million potential users

According to local regulation, Alibaba Financial can only provide service to businesses in the selected provinces mentioned above. However, Alibaba Financial is operating in the grey area via P2P lending platform to expand its business nationwide

Figure 7.4.   Alibaba's Client Base.

Source: By authors; Alibaba.

Big Data + Internet Technology

Before Loan Approval: Credit assessment through historical data and information, even psychological test	Loan Granted: Alibaba uses its system to monitor how the loan has been used	Loan Due: For default borrowers, Alibaba has various ways in penalising defaulters and getting the loan back

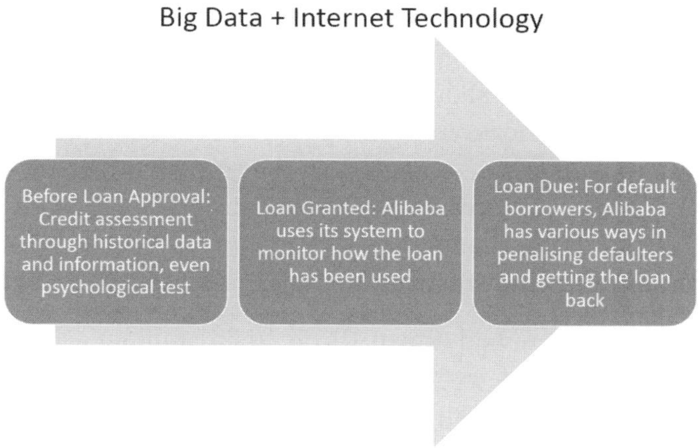

Figure 7.5.   Risk Management Process for Alipay Loans.

Source: By authors; Alibaba.

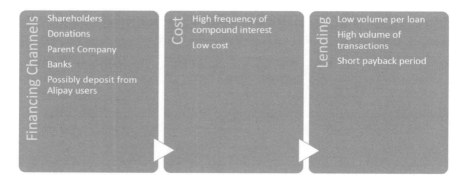

Figure 7.6.   Financing, Cost and Lending.

Source: By authors.

finance that mimic shadow banking. According to China Statistics (CNNIC, 2015), there were 649 million Internet users in China, with a penetration rate of 47.9% at the end of 2014. There were 557 million mobile users. In the rural areas, the penetration rate of the Internet was 27.5%. Access to the Internet via mobile phone was 85.8%. All these revolutions have been made possible because of the liberalisation of the economy in 1990 with Internet companies such as Alibaba formed 14 years later. Figure 7.7 shows the growth of e-commerce sector and Figure 7.8 shows the growth of Internet users. Mobile penetration is also shown in both figures. The e-commerce platforms grew with consumerism, stimulating the growth of finance on the Internet, which led to internet payments, Business-to-Business (B2B) payments, mobile payments, and other financial inclusion products. Some other interesting statistics about China as at end 2014 are:

(1) Online shoppers had grown 19.7% to 361 million accounting for 55.7% of Internet users;

(2) The largest increase was not the 20–29-year-old age group (23.7%) but the above 50-year-old age group which increased by 33.2%;

(3) Mobile phone shoppers increased 63.5% to 236 million, 3.2 times more growth than Internet shoppers;

(4) Mobile phone shoppers identified as Internet users increased from 28.9% to 42.5% of those who used the Internet;

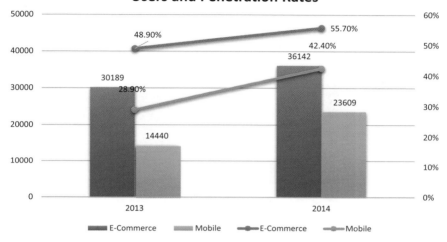

2013–2014 China E-Commerce and Mobile: Users and Penetration Rates

Source: China Internet Network Information Center

Figure 7.7. China E-Commerce and Mobile Users and Penetration Rates.

Source: China Internet Network Information Center.

(5) Internet payment users had increased by 17% to 304 million;
(6) Mobile payment users had increased by 73.2% to 217 million;
(7) Mobile payment was increasingly adopted by Internet users from 25.1% to 39%;
(8) Alipay remained the market leader with 88% penetration rate;
(9) Internet Finance had a usage rate of 12.1% with 78.49 million users;
(10) Mobile phone penetration was 71.9%;
(11) Mobile phone penetration overtook that of other devices in 2014.

7.3.1 *Alibaba*

On 19 September 2014, China-based Alibaba Group Holding Ltd. (Alibaba 阿里巴巴)'s initial public offering (IPO) became the first in history to raise an amount of USD25 billion. Two months later, it

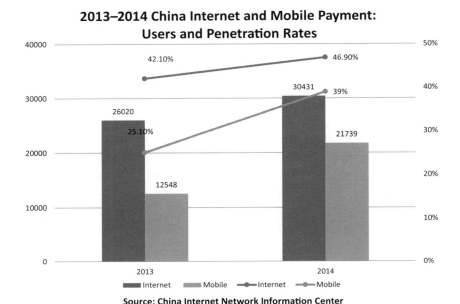

Figure 7.8.   China Internet Users and Penetration Rates.
Source: China Internet Network Information Center.

raised another USD8 billion from six tranches of bond issues with a coupon rate of 1.625%, 2.5%, 3.125% 3.6%, and 4.5% for three-year (USD1 billion and USD300 million floaters), five-year (USD2.25 billion), seven-year (USD1.5 billion), 10-year (USD2.25billion), and 20-year (USD700 million) senior unsecured notes respectively. These are issued primarily to refinance its existing credit facilities. The aforementioned bonds are rated "A+" by Standard & Poor's and "A1" by Moody's Investors Services, with ratings higher than that of other tech giants such as eBay, Baidu and Amazon, and on par with Oracle and Intel. With its original cash at hand of USD9.3 billion prior to its IPO, the company cash position was close to USD32.2 billion immediately after. Public fundraisings were achieved with group revenue as little as USD8.46 billion and Gross Merchandise Volume (GMV) of USD296 billion (Alibaba, 2014). The amount of cash in hand makes Alibaba a formidable force in the acquisition and a challenge to financial institutions.

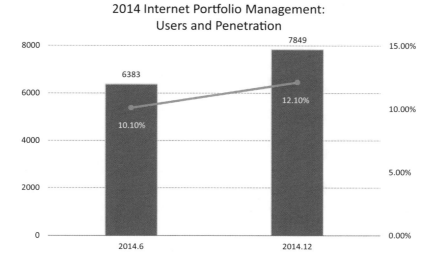

Figure 7.9. China Portfolio Management Users and Penetration Rates.

Source: China Internet Network Information Center.

Two of Alibaba's subsidiaries Taobao.com (淘宝网) and Tmall.com (天猫), ranked number one and two in e-commerce in China, have penetrated 87% and 69.7% of China Internet market respectively. For group discount store Juhuasuan (聚划算), another subsidiary, the penetration rate is 33.4% behind the market leader Meituan.com (美团网) with a rate as high as 56.6%. By investing in Alibaba, investors have not only bought into a US-listed company operating in China, but they also own an entire ecosystem with retail, wholesale, big data and financial operations that have the potential to go global. Alibaba provides not only an inroad into the consumer market but also the Internet Finance market. China has a large population base of 1.35 billion, 618 billion Internet users, and 500 million mobile Internet users. Despite the large base of 302 million Internet shoppers, online shopping accounted for a mere 8% of total consumption in China at the end of 2013. Alibaba has 14.5 billion annual orders, 279 million annual active buyers

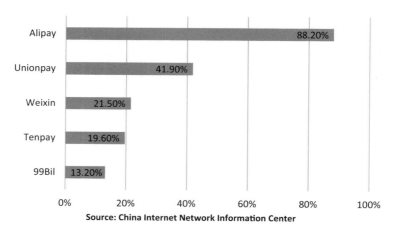

Figure 7.10.   China Internet Payment Penetration Rates.
Source: China Internet Network Information Center.

with 52 average annual orders per active buyer. These statistics are already humongous, but there is still much room for the group to grow not only in e-commerce but also Internet Finance.

7.3.2   *Alipay*

In 2004, an online payment system Alipay was established to address the issue of trust between Alibaba buyers and sellers. Alipay is not just a payment system, it also provides escrow services for all who transact within the Alibaba e-commerce business. This Internet financial system is likely to grow vertically and horizontally as the e-commerce business grows. Given Alibaba's ability to expand downstream to logistics and infrastructure, Alipay can ride on the expansion and expand horizontally into lending, insurance and other financial services. It is destined to become the cash cow for the group, but not as a subsidiary of Alibaba. Alibaba divested Alipay given the impending restrictions placed on foreign ownership about the payment system in China in 2011. Even though Alibaba does not own Zhejiang Ant Small and Micro Financial Services Group Co.

(commonly known as Ant Financial, parent of Alipay), it is entitled to a payment if Alipay or its parent holds an IPO according to a 2014 revision to an original agreement signed in 2011 (2014 SAPA).

As at June 2014, there were 600 million registered Alipay users, 188 million mobile monthly active users (MAUs), and USD71 billion mobile GMV, accounting for 87.2% of total mobile retail GMV in China according to Alibaba's IPO prospectus. Ant Financial, which owns Alipay, is estimated to fetch a valuation of USD50 billion with close to 190 million users and 45 million transactions a day at the end of 2014. Its subsidiary Sesame Credit Management Co. provides scoring service for consumers and small business owners. Data will be collected from more than 300 million real-name registered users and 37 million small businesses that buy and sell using Alibaba's e-commerce platforms. It provides similar services like those in entities such as Equifax, Experian and TransUnion in the US.

7.3.3 *The world of Internet and Alipay as an impact investment*

Reports have shown that the financial world has been focusing on a few companies such as Twitter, Facebook, Tencent, Apple, Amazon, and Google until the listing of Alibaba. Tencent, listed in Hong Kong Stock Exchange, was the darling of Internet stocks as its market capitalisation had risen 10 times from 2009 till the end of 2014. The growth of these stocks has been a phenomenon with Apple and Amazon growing 4.5 times, Google 2.7 times, Facebook growing 78% and Twitter 14% since their listing. Of course, Apple leads in almost every category from annual revenue, market capitalisation and cash on hand of USD159 billion. Its bond issue that raised USD17 billion in 2013 is double of that of Alibaba's issue. Alibaba is distant second in terms of cash on hand at USD34.2 billion after listing. While Tencent and Alibaba are Chinese companies, the rest are based in the US. There is no doubt that when it comes to the Internet, the US is leading the world with its developed nation status. However, in most areas of Internet Finance, China is the leader with Alipay leading the way. This has to do with the attention paid to serving the 70% underserved by banks in transition economies such as the market-driven socialist economy of China.

The reason why Alipay is allowed to grow at the fringes of a supposedly regulated financial space in China is that the country is in a transition from a communist regime to a socialist-based market economy. The banking sector in China is dominated by state-owned banks and reform at the bank is difficult top-down but more effective with privately-owned Internet Finance enterprises. Given the large population base, e-commerce which facilitates a lot of transactions and payments is a perfect candidate to service those that less efficient state-owned banks are not able to service. Financial inclusion is a national and communist slogan in China that happens to be consistent with many developed countries who have been struggling with the foreign aid programmes under the Washington Consensus regime. Instead of believing that aid programmes are the main approach to economic development, it is now believed that teaching the poor on how to fish via financial inclusion, may be a more appropriate way to develop underdeveloped countries. However, given the massive income inequality, it is not only the underdeveloped countries that need financial inclusion, but developed countries are also having a substantial number of people suffering from economic inclusion with access to financial institutions.

7.3.4 *Internet and mobile finance: Alibaba, Alipay to Ant Financial*

The rise of Ant Financial group originated from e-commerce. The major function of a commercial bank is to facilitate transactions, deposit and lending. Cheques, credit cards, Automatic Teller Machine (ATM), and Point of Sale (POS) systems are all part of the banking ecosystem. The firms that engage in e-commerce need facilities for transactions beyond banking services. This then led to the rise of non-bank third party payment systems such as Paypal and other services. Given the cost structures and the relatively low margin of such services, banks may not necessarily view the said services as profitable or one of their priorities.

Alibaba Financial Structure

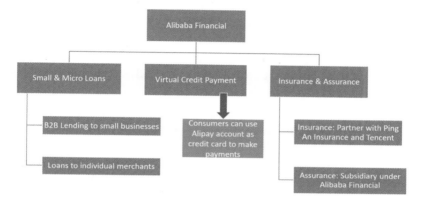

Alibaba Group Structure

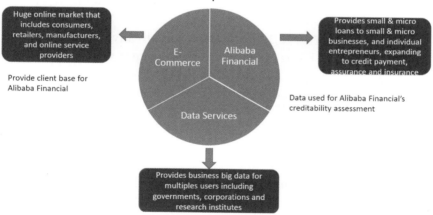

Figure 7.11. Alibaba Finance Structure.

Source: Alibaba.

When many people heard about the leading e-retailer Amazon's entrance into the lending market via Amazon Lending by Amazon Capital Services Inc. that was started in the last quarter of 2012, they were amazed that the company would provide loans to its online sellers. These sellers were mainly small businesses and the loans to purchase inventory enabled them to increase their sales to

Amazon. The strategy was to attract more small merchants from its competitor eBay Inc. to join its platform thus translating into an additional revenue source. The business model was that the merchant could apply for loans with monthly repayment from their account until the loan was paid off. It took only four days for the loan to be approved and the interest rate was around 13% compared to small-business credit-card interest rates of 13–19%. Amazon increased its sales from new sellers as well as existing heavy sellers that could increase their range of items. It was charging its merchants 99 cents for every sale and a small percentage of everything they sell if they list less than 40 items. Once they sold 40 items or more, Amazon was paid USD40 a month and a revenue share. So, it paid to grant loans to its merchants who would then expand their number of items via the access to quick loans. Online lender Kabbage ran a similar business model of lending to online merchants who sold through sites like eBay and Amazon.

Three years earlier in 1991, Alibaba had already adopted a similar strategy in China. Using big data analysis on small and medium-sized enterprises (SMEs) to assess their creditworthiness, Alibaba (later spin off as Ant Financial) grew their loan book to USD16 billion in three years and raised USD87 billion to be the largest fund manager in China via Tianhong, through offering 15 times higher than the standard saving rates. It captured 20% of new RMB deposit only nine months after its launch.

In April 2010, Alibaba Microfinance had already started lending to merchants dealing with Taobao and Tmall. Two micro-lending subsidiaries were subsequently set up, one in Zhejiang province in June 2010 and another in Chongqing in June 2011. Alibaba Microfinance grants loans to merchants dealing with Taobao by checking the borrower's credit rating and the state of their business. Both applications and approval of unsecured loan are done online for Taobao merchants throughout China. As for the Alibaba which deals in wholesale marketplaces, Alibaba Microfinance personnel may visit the borrower's place of business as part of the credit screening and due diligence process. The loans are available only in certain cities and provinces. As at end June 2013, it had extended a cumulative total of over RMB100 billion to more than 320,000 micro-enterprises and individuals. The default rate on its micro-loans, of which lending amount never exceeds RMB1 million, is 0.87%. The loan terms are usually short and ranging from a few days to several months.

Given that China Banking Regulatory Commission (CBRC) and People's Bank of China (PBOC) imposed lending limits based on capital adequacy, Alibaba Microfinance's securitisations will be an important way of increasing its lending capacity. Specifically, micro-loan companies are not allowed to have bank borrowings exceeding 50% of their capital. Zhejiang and Chongqing subsidiaries of Alibaba Microfinance each has capital of RMB600 million and RMB1 billion, respectively. SCRC's approval would rest heavily on risk management ability as well as the financial backing of the issuer, and Alibaba would have fared well on both. Other e-commerce firms such Jing Dong and Suning have also successfully launched micro-lending businesses.

Alibaba Microfinance has successfully capitalised on the advantages of Internet Finance via the use of big data from its e-commerce platform to provide small, fast and flexible loan services to small and micro-sized enterprises. It is therefore not surprising that Alibaba Microfinance has the blessing of the authority to launch its asset securitisation products on the Shenzhen Stock Exchange.

This is in contrast to LendingClub Corporation's lending profile. Lending Club is an online marketplace that facilitates P2P loans to consumers and businesses. It offers investors an opportunity to finance the loans. As at June 2014, it had facilitated approximately 379,060 loans totaling USD5 billion since inception with 628 employees and contractors. Using credit bureaus such as TransUnion, Experian or Equifax, the platform identifies and screens borrowers so as they can obtain unsecured loans with interest rates that they find attractive. The unsecured personal loans and corresponding notes have initial terms of three to five years.

7.3.5 *How did Alipay grow?*

Table 7.1 shows the growth of the number of users for Alipay compared to Paypal given the multi-channel approach of the entire Alibaba Group.

The Yu'e Bao platform was launched in 2013 by Tianhong Asset Management and Alipay, which provides electronic payment services for transactions on China's largest online shopping websites, Taobao Marketplace and Tmall.com. In addition to the automatic transfer functions, Yu'e Bao accounts can be used to shop, pay utility bills, buy lottery and train tickets, book holidays, and pay off credit cards, among other services. Account holders can handle all transactions online through personal computers and via Alipay Wallet-enabled smartphones.

It is also a money market fund and allows Alipay's account holders to invest their excess cash in the fund with the entry level at RMB1. Account holders are allowed to redeem the fund at any time to pay for their online purchase from Alibaba. The fund manager is Tianhong Asset Management, and the money is invested in Zenglibao Money Market Fund. Zhejiang Alibaba E-commerce Co., the parent company of Alipay, bought 51% of Tianhong Asset Management Company for RMB1.18 billion from Inner Mongolia

Table 7.1. Comparison of Alipay and Paypal.

	Registered Alipay users	Active PayPal users
2008	120	70
2009	210	8
2010	550	94.4
2011	625	106.3
2012	700	122.7
2013	850	142.6
2014	Unannounced	161.5

Registered Alipay Users are estimates of active and non-active number of accounts which may or may not be active.

Active Paypal Users are customers that have conducted at least one transaction in the past 12 months.
Sources: PayPal; Mercator Advisory Group; other sources.

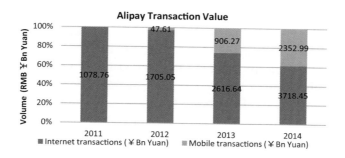

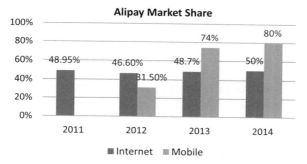

Figure 7.12. Alipay Transaction Value and Market Share.

Sources: By authors; Alipay.

Junzheng Energy & Chemical Industry Co., Ltd. in October 2013 increasing its registered capital from RMB180 million to RMB514.3 million (USD83.69 million).

- First 18 days: 2.5 million users and Net Asset Value (NAV) RMB6.6 billion;
- NAV March 2013: RMB1.9 billion;
- NAV March 2014: RMB500 billion (USD89.5 billion);
- NAV June 2014: RMB574.1 billion (USD92 billion);
- NAV Sep 2014: RMB534.89 billion (USD87.45 billion).

Zenglibao had a net inflow of RMB360 billion in the first three months of 2014 according to Wing, the dominant operator of China financial terminals. PBOC's statistics recorded a reduction of RMB940 billion in bank deposits for January 2014. The total size of money market funds increased to RMB1.44 trillion in the first quarter of 2014 from RMB696 billion at end 2013, a net gain of RMB700 billion according to China Merchants Securities.

China Asset Management Co., Ltd (China AMC) was the first to launch an online product in January 2013. It has started selling mutual funds through the WeChat social network, run by Alibaba's chief rival, Tencent Holdings. It increased assets by 38.1% to USD76.6 billion. ICBC Credit Suisse offered fund products through smartphone apps and grew 70% to USD37.3 billion. By offering yield above 5% and withdrawal at request, these online platforms have tapped savings formerly locked up in term deposits at Chinese banks that pay a maximum of 3.3%. However, Yu'e Bao's NAV has declined in part due to competition. China AMC, along with China Citic Bank, launched a fund with 4% interest on money that is also available for shopping with a bank card. China Universal Asset Management, ranked ninth, launched the Cash Pot money market fund that pays 4.56% through WeChat and its assets grew 44%. Online fund supermarket, Fund Eastmoney, offers online and mobile platform for subscriptions to funds and switching between funds.

Interest rates in China remain tightly regulated. Although there have been talks of interest rate liberalisation to allow rates to be driven by market forces as part of China's financial reform, the ceiling on interest rate was centrally set. In July 2013, the PBOC removed the floor on the discount that banks can offer on the centrally set interest rate, but the ceiling for interest rates remained capped until October 2015.

7.3.6 *P2P lending*

Wangdaizhiijia (网贷之家) estimated that by end 2014, there would be 1,500 P2P lender websites, with loans of RMB74 billion, transaction volume of RMB202 billion, interest rates stabilising at 17% in 3–6 months' duration, and borrowers reaching 200,000 and lenders 780,000. At the beginning of 2014, there were only 800 websites, RMB11.6 billion transactions, loans of RMB32 billion and interest at 19.45%. This reached a peak at 22.23% in 5.67 months, with 33,500 borrowers and 145,630 lenders.

It should be noted that since the Yu'e Bao boom, P2P lending has been a key market driver of interest rate liberalisation. Instead of serving as a platform to facilitate lending and borrowing, many P2P lenders are crowdfunding via the Internet and lending those funds to individuals and small businesses. These P2P businesses are competing with microfinance companies or forming alliances with microfinance companies to tap into the expertise of these partners while raising fund via the P2P platform.

This sector remained unregulated as a form of shadow banking, bypassing bank regulations. In 2013, the PBOC's tightening stance and restrictions on banking lending to finance local governments' projects had led to the rapid growth in this sector. P2P lenders are sometimes viewed as being loan sharks that raise funds via the Internet with some of the operators disappearing with third party funds or after failures to collect loans on expiration. There were also cases of fraud that saw P2P criminals absconding with investors' money the first day that they opened for business.

These P2P businesses were operating in the grey area as they had no licenses to raise fund, accept deposits or provide a guarantee of principals. The positive side of P2P businesses is that they are providing liquidity to SMEs with crowdfunding. This alleviates the problem of having specialised SME banks in providing funding and allowing market forces to work.

Alipay has been successful because of its extensive use of big data. The growth of P2P lending in an unregulated environment is due to low compliance cost given that it is not subject to the minimum capital requirements and other regulatory constraints such as qualified investor programme, mandatory reserves against loan losses and other risks. Once market entry standards are set and investors' protection measures are in place, the cost of setting up will be much higher. Higher operating costs will also deter new entrants and increase the cost of business.

There is also little infrastructure building in the lending industry to provide credit information and rating. There are credit information services such as PBOC's Credit Reference Centre (CRC). CRC subsidiary Shanghai Credit Information Services, which was established in July 1999 and became a CRC subsidiary in April 2009, has built a nationwide P2P credit information system known as the Net Financial Credit System in June 2013.

7.3.7 *The future of Alipay*

The future of Alipay is embedded in the future of hospitals, transportation systems, businesses and almost every facet of our life. Alipay is already working on establishing a medical service system providing services like registration, estimated waiting time, payment, and medical results via mobile phones. It has cooperation with over 10 hospitals in Beijing, Shanghai, Guangzhou, Hangzhou and others. For transportation, its taxi calling service and payment system are already well accepted. Online-to-Offline (O2O) and Location-Based Services (LBS) services for online and offline shopping are running in Hangzhou and Zhejiang provinces. With the agreement with Universal Air Travel Plan (UATP) at end 2013, Alipay users can now buy directly from US airlines, worldwide railway companies, hotels, travel agencies and even rent cars. With overseas trips (from China) hitting 100 million, the growth of Alipay is going to continue.

Launched on 2 February 2015, "2015 Let HongBao Fly Campaign" started jointly by Weibo and Alipay has reached new heights integrating online and offline marketing resources. The Hongbao or red packet tradition is not new, but it has evolved into a whole new game with many ways to give and collect Hongbao (China Internet Watch, 2015).

Zhao Cai Bao (招财宝) is a platform for P2P lending that allows for automatic subscription (预约抢购), secured lending with invested assets (变现), SMEs' P2P lending (中小企业贷), retail P2P lending (个人贷), and crowdfunding (直接融资项目). Products are rated and guaranteed by financial institutions such as insurance companies and banks. Yu'e Bao is the trustee guaranteed by the PingAn Insurance. With RMB1, an investor can subscribe and redeem on a daily basis with a Gold ETF Product (存金宝), which is managed by mutual fund company Bosera Funds (博时基金). Jifenbao (集分宝) is a loyalty programme with points accumulated in a variety of activities including answering questions after reading an advertisement. The points can be redeemed at a fixed rate of 100 points to RMB1 for payment.

7.3.8 *Banks and competitors fight back*

In a report on Information Communication Technology on the future of financial services, Ericsson (2014) argues that the level of competition between banks will intensify due to Internet banking. As Internet banking is an internally driven value chain improvement that reduces business costs for banks and its customers, it increases the ability of customers to adopt multichannel approaches to banking. In the case of Alipay, it is interesting that stickiness (or consumer lock-in) was created with the e-commerce.

Given the statistics mentioned earlier, the disruption of the payment system by Internet financial firms like Alipay presents a real and present danger for banks. Several attempts by the banking regulator to slow down the disruption have not been successful. With the backing of the e-commerce firms such as Alibaba, Baidu and Tencent, these payment companies have access to consumer loans, SME loans and small-scale fund management capabilities. During Chinese New Year in past years, the red packet and Internet Cab Calling services dominated the mobile payment market. Soon after, under the leadership of UnionPay, banks were aggressively promoting the NFC payment system to compete with other third party payment operators.

PBOC gave a stop order to Alipay and Tencent digital card services. In response, these operators pushed ahead with Baitiao (白条) and Ant Check Later (花呗). To address the central bank's concern about consumer protection, small payment was encouraged, and micro-insurance was used for guaranteeing the payment accounts for fraud and the loss of mobile equipment. Concurrently, cross-border attempts by third party payment operators such as Alipay were bearing fruits. In particular, Alipay with Global Blue has initiated tax refund services, penetrating the business of traditional banks in international tax rebates business.

In February 2016, there were calls for more regulations to clamp down on Yu'e Bao and similar platforms. One of the reasons is that the large size of Yu'e Bao has given more bargaining power for higher rates from banks with whom the Fund deals by matching the maturities based on data analysis. China banks are predominantly state-owned and lack incentives to innovate. Lending and sales of third party securities investment funds were the main revenue generator. Since the liberalisation for banks to engage in wealth management, banks have been slow in response to changes, especially in risk and fund management.

After the Yu'e Bao episode, some banks fought back by restricting transfers to Alipay. Industrial & Commercial Bank, Agriculture Bank of China, Bank of China, and China Construction Bank capped the amount of transfer to Alipay, to amounts such as RMB5,000 per transaction and a maximum of RMB50,000 per month. Banks would also renegotiate the terms of the loan agreements that had allowed money market funds to withdraw deposits early but still enjoy a pre-agreed interest rate. Treasury products of the similar offering were made available via the Internet platform. Bank of Communications, China Merchant Bank, Industrial & Commercial Bank, and Minsheng Bank all offered similar products to compete with Yu'e Bao, allowing automatic investment into their money market funds and automatic ATM withdrawal or on customer card spending.

Baidu, China's top search engine, launched an investment product Baifa in December 2013 with Harvest Fund Management. Tiantian Fund Sales also partnered with E Fund Management, Penghua Fund Management and Xincheng Fund Management to launch new wealth management products. Tencent Holdings launched wealth management products not only with ChinaAM but with Huitianfu Fund Management and Guangfa Fund Management for its WeChat messaging app.

7.3.9   *Summary*

With the online and mobile platforms beyond banks' outlets, the investors have now broadened to include the Y generation with a minimum sum of RM1, which is affordable to most. The investors now enjoy the benefit of a demand deposit that pays market interest rates. The Yu'e Bao episode has shown that the combination of Internet, mobile and finance has driven market-based financial innovation that the regulator failed to achieve. In particular, there were clear disruptions to the banking and insurance sectors with interest rate liberalisation, liberalisation of financial services, and liberalisation of cross-selling of products.

The story of China is significantly different from the model of financial inclusion in Africa. Large mobile network operators (MNOs) are the main driver of mobile usage and therefore contribute to an increase in mobile financial accounts. In China, on the other hand, financial inclusion is driven by the socialist political system assisted by the political will of the ruling party. The innate desire to serve the rural area and the underprivileged has seen the innovative Internet Finance companies backed by e-commerce giants or social networks, servicing the underserved and the poor, and providing them access to markets, services and information. On the other spectrum, the banks are mainly serving the upper pyramid and the state-owned enterprises. While many of the Y generation and banked people already use mobile banking in China, the absolute number of unbanked people remains high. The country has the potential to emerge as an important success story for branchless banking and financial inclusion. A new paradigm in China will likely unfold seeing a convergence of forces coming from banks and financial institutions which are forced to innovate.

7.4 Fullerton Financial Holdings Pte. Ltd.

Fullerton Financial Holdings (FFH), formally known as Asia Financial Holdings (AFH), is a fully owned subsidiary of Temasek Holdings Pte. Ltd. engaging in long-term strategic investment and operation of financial institutions globally. Its current operations involve mainly banks, credit unions and other financial institutions that provide banking services mainly in Asia. Incorporated in January 2013, it acquired a major stake in PT Bank Danamon Tbk (Indonesia), Bank Internasional Indonesia (Indonesia), 5% in ICIC Bank Limited (India) in 2003, a stake in Alliance Bank (Malaysia), 5% pre-IPO stake in China Construction Bank (China), 5% pre-IPO stake in

Bank of China (China), and NIB Bank (Pakistan) in 2005. In the same year, it started the greenfield project in India with Fullerton India. In 2007, it was renamed after Robert Fullerton, the first Governor of the Straits Settlements, reflecting the pioneering nature of the company. FFH is a very low-profile company with its first annual report published in 2014 for Financial Year 2012. It is interesting because it is a leading Asian institution that focuses on serving the consumers such as the self-employed, as well as the MSMEs in the emerging market.

7.4.1   *Acquisition versus greenfield projects*

The development of FFH is interesting as it started its foray into banking via acquisition from 2003 to 2005. Later, its business focus was on greenfield development in India via Fullerton India, China via BOC Fullerton Community Bank and Fullerton Credit, the United Arab Emirates via Dunia, Cambodia via Cambodia Post Bank Plc. and Myanmar via Fullerton Myanmar. Notably, the initial acquisition stakes were companies with total assets of over USD10 billion such as Danamon and Alliance Bank. In more recent times, the greenfield investments are into companies with much smaller asset base and in the region of USD45 million (Cambodia Post Bank Plc.) to USD1.4 billion (BOC Fullerton Community Bank).

FFI now has 10 operating financial institutions in nine countries.

7.4.2   *Fullerton India*

Fullerton India's Urban Business has over 219 branches across 20 states serving individuals and MSMEs. Core products suite includes Personal Loans, Loans Against Property, Commercial Vehicle Funding, as well as Life and General Insurance products. The main differentiation of Fullerton India is that it uses analytics to choose its customers by combining knowledge from the customer base and information from credit bureaus. By using technology, it can shorten the decision period and turnaround time on its products. Most important of all, it provides services and has gathered enough experience in customer segments that are not targeted by banks or

Table 7.2. Fullerton Financial Holdings' Financial Institutions.

Entity	Country	Greenfield/ Acquisition	Total assets (US$)	ROE	Shareholdings
Danamon	Indonesia	Acquisition (Jun 2003)	14.7b S$19.1b	14.3%	68%
Alliance Bank	Malaysia	Acquisition (Mar 2005)	14.3b S$18.5b	13.7%[#] 13.7%	14%
NIB Bank	Pakistan	Acquisition (Feb 2005)	1.6b S$2.12b	8.5%	88.6%
Mekong Development Bank	Vietnam	Acquisition (Dec 2010)	297m S$386m	1.6%	20%
Fullerton India	India	Greenfield (Dec 2005)	1.2b S$1.28b	15.8%	100%
BOC Fullerton Community Bank	China	Greenfield (Feb 2011)	1.4b S$1.8b	−2.9%	10%
Fullerton Credit	China	Greenfield (Oct 2008)	378m S$491m	5.6%	100%
Dunia Finance	UAE	Greenfield (Jun 2008)	286m S$373m	29.3%	40%
Cambodia Post Bank Plc.	Cambodia	Greenfield (Sep 2013)	129.7m S$99.2m	3.9%[#] −6.7%	45%
Fullerton Myanmar	Myanmar	Greenfield (May 2014)	NA	NA	100%

Data as at 31 December 2013. [#]2014 figures are stated for both Alliance Bank and Cambodia Post Bank Plc. 2013 ROE numbers are stated below 2014 figures.

are underserved by banks. The end use of the unsecured loans to low-income individuals are for home renovation, wedding, children's education and emergencies. For others, the unsecured loans are for business expansion or to fulfill working capital requirements. Using analytics and credit bureau information to select the right customers remains the driver for business growth with sustainable profits.

Technology plays a pivotal role in enabling growth at Fullerton India. In particular, there are transformation projects that embraced innovation by using mobile technology and cloud-based solution. Mobile operating system using Android has been deployed for rural business. These mobile technology solutions combine data availability on the field with controls like biometric fingerprint-based authentication on the field. Fullerton India GramShakti provides rural financial services, and its financial inclusion mission is to make financial services available to the doorstep of rural customers in seven states. This is an important financial inclusion service for those in the rural areas that account for 50% of India's GDP. It plans to cover the "last mile" between its branch where financial services are provided and the home or place of business of the customers. Within six years to end 2014, it had grown from eight branches in 2008 to over 200 branches serving 30,000 villages. Rural assets grew 80% as at 31 March 2014, with collection efficiency continued to be good at 99%, resulting in a profit growth of over 81% over the previous year. The use of mobile technology will further enhance the profitability.

7.4.3   *Fullerton Myanmar*

Fullerton Myanmar started operations on 7 November 2014 offering short-term and micro-loans to groups of five and individual loans of not more than 500,000 tenors. The loan tenure ranges from as short as three months to the longest of 18 months. Loans are mainly for productive assets or micro business working capital such as livestock, sewing machines, shop stock, agriculture seed, health or education needs. It is clear that the model is replicated from the success in India with the potential use of biometric technology to ensure secure and quick transactions with doorstep service.

7.4.4   *Summary*

FFH has come a long way from its initial strategy of acquiring strong brands to greenfield project of serving the unbanked and underbanked via the use of mobile technology and analytics. Learning costs were steep in the beginning, but it was inevitable to gain a foothold, attract the right talents and harness the big data in some of the countries. Given that more information can be collected

Table 7.3.   M-PESA Financials.

Year	M-PESA revenue (Kshs bil)	Percentage of Safaricom's revenue	Safaricom revenue (Kshs bil)	M-PESA users (mil)	Penetration rate for M-PESA	Safaricom users (mil)
FY08	0.37	0.60%	61.37	2.08	20.33%	10.23
FY09	2.93	4.16%	70.48	6.18	46.26%	13.36
FY10	7.56	9.00%	83.96	9.48	60.04%	15.79
FY11	11.78	12.42%	94.83	13.80	80.33%	17.18
FY12	16.87	15.77%	107.00	14.91	78.19%	19.07
FY13	21.84	17.57%	124.29	17.11	88.11%	19.42
FY14	26.56	18.36%	144.7	19.3	89.48%	21.57

Sources: By authors; M-PESA.

via movement and expenditure patterns of customers using mobile devices and wallets, the next stage of growth of the company will be exponential if the right low-cost FinTech can harness more big data for risk-return analysis and expand its reach in rural areas. The LASIC mobile financial inclusion strategy will be a natural progression.

7.5   Safaricom's M-PESA

Safaricom has a customer base of 21.5 million, and 34% of airtime top-ups were made directly through M-PESA. M-PESA (pesa means money in Swahili) is a mobile money transfer service launched in 2007, and it has the widest coverage in urban and rural areas in Kenya. It drives financial inclusion by providing money transfer services, local payments and international remittance services. The mission of Safaricom is to deepen financial inclusion and transform lives. M-PESA's has 81,025 agents, 122,000 merchants (24,137 active), and 19.3 million registered customers (12.2 million active). It has successfully penetrated 90% of its telecom customers. M-PESA accounts for 18% of Safaricom revenue and its agents employ more than 140,000 workers. The following figures and table provide more statistics of M-PESA.

M-Shwari (a paperless banking platform with loan services by M-PESA) has 3.6 million active customers with Kshs 4 billion in deposit and Kshs 1.2 billion worth of loans issued per

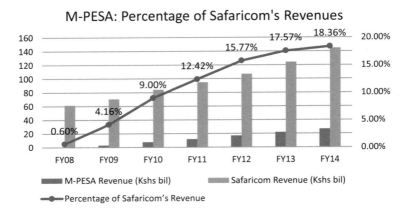

Figure 7.13.   M-PESA Percentage of Revenues.

Sources: By authors; Safaricom's annual reports.

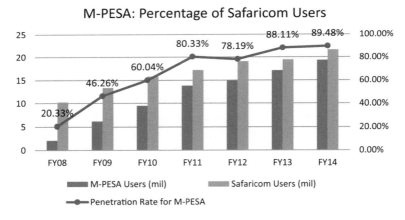

Figure 7.14.   M-PESA Users and Penetration Rates.

Sources: By authors; Safaricom's annual reports.

month with non-performing loans at only 2.7%. Cashless distrib-
utors have increased to 158 with 1,271 distribution points. The
growth is likely to be exponential given the system upgrade to
the API on a smartphone for near real-time processing of the
transaction.

Figure 7.15. M-Shwari Customers and Performance.

Sources: By authors; M-PESA.

Key services are Lipa Na M-PESA, Bank to M-PESA, Lipa Kodi, salary disbursements, utility payments, airtime purchase, M-Shawari and cashless distribution (described in the following table).

The growth of M-PESA by expanding to provide other services such as micro-insurance, lending and payment services is similar to Alipay. There are various reasons that M-PESA is an attractive option:

(1) Safety — eliminates the risks associated with handling cash for both customers and merchants;
(2) Reduce losses — eliminates losses associated with receiving fake currency;
(3) Enhanced record keeping — every transaction made is readily accessible;
(4) Short and flexible settlement cycles — allows timely collection;
(5) Acceptance of low-value transactions — as little as Kshs 10;
(6) Lower costs — avoids high POS and remittance fees.

7.6 Conclusion

The world of financial services is fast changing; consumers want more personalised services that increase convenience and yet retain security. The use of the Internet and mobile technology is possible only to the extent that regulation allows. Without net neutrality and decentralisation, the centralised authority can counter by disrupting

Table **7.4.**   **Services Provided by M-PESA.**

Service	Description	Launched FY	Information
Lipa Na M-PESA	Cash payments for goods and services	Revamped in June 2013	120,000 merchants to enable users and SMEs to collect and manage cashless payments.
Cashless FMCG distribution	Cash distribution	2014	It is used by 1,294 tills driving Kshs 2.8 billion in volume per month.
M-Shwari	Interest-bearing deposits and micro-loans	November 2012	It allows for deposit as low as Kshs 1 and borrowing at as low as Kshs 100 without having to visit a bank or complete account opening forms. The account is opened and operated from the phone. Free transfer takes place between M-PESA and M-Shwari account.
M-PESA IMT	International money transfer	Revamped in 2014	Eight partners and remittance to 100 countries at no fee.
Lipa Kodi	Rental payments to landlords	August 2013	88 housing agents with more than 60,000 housing units.
Linda Jamii	Health insurance premium payments	February 2014	It is an online micro-health insurance product developed by Safaricom, Britam and Changamka. Medical premium of Kshs 12,000 paid via M-PESA with Kshs 200,000 in patient benefits and Kshs 50,000 outpatient benefits as well as dental, optical, maternity care and funeral benefits.
Cloud SaaS	Software as a service for SMEs	2014	It encompasses accounting, payroll, domain and web hosting services to be part of the M-PESA ecosystem.

Sources: By authors; M-PESA.

the services of these Internet companies. The LASIC principle describes the attributes needed for such technologies to be successful in a sharing economy where services are shared. However, sharing of services will lead a concentration of wealth and power. It is likely that they will be a victim of their own success with incumbents exerting pressure on the regulator. The reaction of the regulators will depend on their belief in the Gig or Bounty economy. There are signs in China and UK that tolerance may have been reached with the disruption that has transpired. While new business models and jobs have been created in these countries, there are fears that these disruptions are just beyond business and alter how society is organised. We will be discussing decentralised technologies and the possibility of wealth sharing economy. The 5Ds (digitalisation, disintermediation, democratisation, decentralisation and disappearance) are some interesting concepts that we will introduce in a later chapter.

Many governments and institutions are exploring mobile and Internet finance. It is interesting to note that the HM Treasury and Cabinet Office of the UK commissioned Open Data Institute have engaged Fingleton Associates (2014) to explore how competition and consumer outcomes will be affected by allowing third parties to use external application programming interfaces (APIs) to access transaction data with the permission of the customers. It is not surprising that the main conclusion of the report is that there are benefits for consumers, banks and third party customers of data to having an open standard for banks' APIs that can be applied across the industry. In particular, the SME lending market will be priced more accurately for lending decisions. MAS has published the Open API Standard to encourage financial institutions especially banks to be more open. It is through openness that global talent can be sourced in the tight talent market. The traditional way of attracting these young developers may be a suboptimal way to get global talent to work for established incumbents as the mindset may not be aligned.

Google has moved into the payment business and has begun to work closely with Verizon, AT&T and T-Mobile to have the Google Wallet payments app pre-installed on Android phones sold by these carriers. Similar to other payment companies, it is also acquiring technology and intellectual property from the carriers' joint-venture, Softcard (formerly Isis Mobile Wallet) payments as announced on 23 February 2015. Neither Google nor the telcos were able to take off without co-operating with each other, and they have come to realise the advantages of working together. Apple Pay has launched the NFC-capable terminals and chip-and-PIN payment systems that improve the user experience.

Digital payment solutions that allow for more personalisation, convenience and yet retain security have become a priority. Constant communication and interaction between the financial institution and the application are also important. Companies like Gemalto and C-SAM (Commerce for Secure Active Mobile) are providing platforms for both mobile wallet and mobile commerce to reach out to users. MasterCard, C-SAM and Dai Nippon Printing (DNP) launched a white-label near field communication (NFC) mobile wallet service in 2012 and 2013 in Singapore and Japan, respectively. A joint mobile wallet service integrating C-SAM's Mobile Transaction Platform (MTP) and MasterCard's contactless technology was launched in Singapore in August 2012. The platform also includes Starhub, DBS Bank, and EZ-link. Mastercard's MasterPass also eliminates the need for consumers to enter detailed shipping and card information to complete their online shopping at MasterPass merchant sites. The consumer can store Mastercard and other credit, debit and prepaid card information, address book and more on MasterPass. It simplifies the process of completing a transaction from any connected device. However, these efforts have not been well rewarded; the adoption rates of these innovations are low.

What is more interesting is the development in the cryptocurrency space. Decentralised payment methods may be the only way to ensure frictionless international transfer. Low transaction per second of bitcoin (7 per second) and ether (14 per second) with a requirement of high storage size are problems. However, new techniques such as lightning, plasma, and sharding help to alleviate those issues. When there is cryptocurrency browser API on Microsoft, Google, Facebook, Apple and Mozilla, it would be much easier to buy goods online with cryptocurrency. This work was first started by World Wide Web Consortium (W3C) for a currency-agnostic payment standard. When the API is activated in Google's Chrome, Microsoft's Edge, Apple's Webkit, Mozilla's Firefox, the Samsung Internet Browser and Facebook's in-app browser, new payment information for cryptocurrency and other more traditional online payment methods can be stored directly in the browser. The W3C is working on getting the third party apps to integrate both distributed ledger solutions and non-credit card forms of payment into the API. TenX, which raised over USD80 million via an initial token sales or ICO, has started a debit card with cryptocurrencies as consumer's payment to the merchants via credit card companies' POS system. However, at the merchants' end, they can elect to receive payments of their choice.

It is important to recognise that there is a first-mover advantage; regulators should allow such technology to proceed without hindrance. They should ensure "development led regulation" rather than "development lagged regulation". However, regulation is only part of the equation; low marginal costs and having social/cultural appeal are both important factors. Initial conditions are also important. Some innovators succeeded because they started out as a monopoly, such as Kenya's M-PESA. Similarly, Alipay seems to be untouchable because of its dominant role in serving the underserved. But there are already signs that the expansion of Alipay and other Internet Finance business are being curtailed as these businesses have become too big to be left alone. The Chinese government plans to have all payment companies settling through a centralised system. The amount that each customer is allowed to transact and invest has also been kept at an amount suitable for financial inclusion rather than larger customers.

When mobile money is viewed as a banking service (not telco or e-commerce enabled money transfer) and regulated as such, there will be an emphasis on consumer protection and compliance. For long-term development to a much larger scale and other more complex financial services, regulation is essential and may prove to be a hindrance. India is a good example where telcos or start-ups offering financial services have to partner a bank due to regulation. As a result, only 4% of the population reports using remittance or bill payment services on their mobile phones. Know your customer (KYC), counter-terrorism financing (CTF) and other compliance requirements and the resulting costs (to consumers and companies) may have made the business less viable.

If identification continues to be an issue, scalability remains unattainable. We suggest registration solutions that lie somewhere between SIM (subscriber identity module) registration and due diligence done by the financial institutions. Once KYC requirements are easy to achieve or that an exempt status is given to small operators, the business can achieve scale with mass adoption. For example, Alipay can be easily downloaded into a mobile device by anyone but to use more complex functions, further compliance such as linking with a bank account, credit card or with further identification is required.

It is known that SIMs allow for end-to-end encryption and SIMs are controlled by MNOs. MNO-led solutions may offer full security, but these technology companies lack the experience in the finance industry. Telcos may have to trade control of the SIM in exchange for more participation in the financial sector. In some countries, governments have given a push by using mobile money to pay salary and thus weeding out fraud such as ghost or dead workers. Others like Xiaomi have virtual SIM cards that may revolutionalise how the telecom sector functions. The Virtual SIM feature is a paid service that allows for access to the Internet while roaming internationally, without the need to pay the expensive bills of roaming as well as the need to switch out SIM cards.

Pioneered by KnowRoaming, this SIM operates fully in software, easily implemented with drop-in integration, and can be deployed on any mobile device. It has global connectivity that operates a full mobile network that covers over 200 countries and the roaming rates are 85% cheaper than traditional carriers. KnowRoaming is a Canadian mobile virtual network operator (MVNO) which now owns a full American mobile network operator (MNO) located out of Nevada and licensed out of Missouri for spectrum.

> "KnowRoaming is excited to partner with TCL on Smart Roaming, a solution that integrates this Soft SIM Platform directly into TCL handsets. End users can seamlessly access low-cost roaming when traveling with TCL smartphones. For global travelers this means no more chasing Wi-Fi networks, buying expensive carrier packages, or swapping SIM cards. They manage usage transparently in the KnowRoaming app and take control of their roaming experience. KnowRoaming and TCL will launch the Smart Roaming solution in select phones, first in China, then in the USA and other markets. The collaboration is a result of the Alcatel OneTouch Accelerator program and launched at Mobile World Congress 2016 in Barcelona." — Announcement by KnowRoaming[3]

Financial technology can also bring about financial inclusion with its lower costs and large networks. Financial inclusion is not just a worthy cause but also opens a large pool of untapped demand for potential financial institutions. Although only 32% of the world has access to full banking service, much more own a smart mobile phone. The exponential growth of smartphone adoption has created an opportunity to offer financial services on this platform. Companies attempting to work in this area should work within networks with large existing critical mass such as telecommunication services and e-commerce platforms. The success of such companies would increase the amount of economic inclusion in the world and decrease wealth inequality.

Eventually, P2P financial services may prove to be the cheapest way for financial inclusion to globalise with no border, storage, compliance or access issues. The balance between identity and financial services is important. It will be interesting to see how the regulators can balance innovation with regulation where everyone is

---

[3]http://www.knowroaming.com/wp-content/uploads/2017/05/80-unlimited-data-packages-knowroaming.pdf

exchanging value and digital assets with everyone else globally with no friction.

Final Note

This chapter was written in 2015 using statistics prior to 2014. Given the rapid development in Chinese regulation, most of these discussions may not apply today since there has been a tightening of regulation in the Internet Finance sector in 2016. Nevertheless, we have left this Chapter unchanged and have not revised the work up-to-date so that we can sense the sentiments as well as the views at that point of time.

References and Further Readings

Alibaba, (2014). Alibaba Group Holding Limited IPO Prospectus, Form F-I Registration Statement Under the Securities Act of 1933, Securities and Exchange Commission. Retrieved from http://www.sec.gov/Archives/edgar/data/1577552/000119312514184994/d709111df1.htm

Allen, F., Demirguc-Kunt, A., Klapper, L., & Martinez Peria, M. S. (2012). The Foundations of Financial Inclusion: Understanding Ownership and Use of Formal Accounts. Development Research Group, World Bank.

Anson, J, Berthaud, A., Klappar, L., & Singer, D. (2013). Financial Inclusion and the Role of the Post Office. Development Research Group, World Bank.

Castillo, M. D. (2017). Bitcoin in the browser: Google, Apple and more adopting crypto-ready API. Coindesk. Retrieved from https://www.coindesk.com/bitcoin-browser-google-apple-move-adopt-crypto-compatible-api/

China Internet Watch. (2015). Weibo and Alipay's Hongbao Campaign Ggone viral. Retrieved from http://www.chinainternetwatch.com/12182/weibo-alipay-hongbao-2015/

CNNIC. (2015). China Internet Development Statistics (中国互联网络发展状况统计报告). Working paper in Chinese, CNNIC.

Demirguc-Kunt, A., & Klapper, L. (2012). Measuring Financial Inclusion: The Global Findex Database. Development Research Group, World Bank.

Ericsson. (2014). ICT & The Future of Financial Services. Networked Society Lab, Ericsson.

Federal Deposit Insurance Corporation. (2014). 2013 FDIC National Survey of Unbanked and Underbanked Households. Retrieved from https://www.fdic.gov/householdsurvey/

Federal Deposit Insurance Corporation. (October 29, 2014). FDIC releases National Survey of Unbanked and Underbanked. Retrieved from https://www.fdic.gov/news/news/press/2014/pr14091.html

Fingleton Associates. (2014). Data Sharing and Open Data for Banks. A Report for HM Treasury and Cabinet Office.

Herring, M. (2017). China's digital-payments giant keeps bank chiefs up at night: Ants in your pants The Economist. Retrieved from https://www.economist.com/news/business/21726713-ant-financial-500m-customers-home-plans-expand-chinas-digital-payments-giant-keeps

Jingu, T. (2014). Risks and Opportunities in China's Growing P2P Lending Market. Nomura Research Institute.

LendingClub. (2014). LendingClub Corporation IPO Prospectus. Form S-1 Registration Statement Under the Securities Act 1933, Securities and Exchange Commission. Retrieved from http://www.sec.gov/Archives/edgar/data/1409970/000119312514428454/d766811ds1a.htm

People's Bank of China. (2012). China Payment System Development Report. Payment and Settlement Department of the People's Bank of China, China Financial Publishing House.

Safaricom Limited. (2014). Annual Report. Retrieved from http://www.safaricom.co.ke/annualreport_2014/public/downloads/Full%20Report.pdf

Chapter 8

FinTech in Singapore

8.1 Introduction

Singapore is one of the financial hubs in the Asia-Pacific region. It has been ranked first in The World Bank's Ease of Doing Business study for the last 10 years. Also, it is regarded as one of the foremost examples of a smart nation with a wealth of initiatives to grow its FinTech start-up ecosystem.

With one-third of its citizens aged between 25 and 34 years old, Singapore has a rather high mobile penetration rate of 152%, standing as the country with the highest penetration of mobile broadband subscriptions per capita in the world. In addition, Singapore has an Internet penetration rate of 80%, which is the highest in Southeast Asia.[1] All of the aforementioned conditions have provided a strong foundation for the emergence and growth of FinTech enterprises in Singapore.

Much is attributed to a visionary government policy to drive Singapore and all have been working hard towards its positioning as the centre in Association of Southeast Asian Nations (ASEAN) if not the Asia-Pacific region for start-ups playing their roles in the FinTech industry. The Singapore government has initiated numerous schemes and grants to help develop this potential sector.

---

[1] http://fintechnews.sg/1312/fintech/infographic-fintech-singapore-ecosystem/

Figure 8.1. Singapore FinTech Landscape.

Source: The FinTech Consortium.[2]

8.2 Regulation

Singapore introduced the Personal Data Protection Act 2012 on a phased basis over 2013 and 2014.[3] The Act prohibits illegal data access and processing to manage the real risk faced by the whole FinTech sector in Singapore.

In July 2015, the Monetary Authority of Singapore (MAS) announced to set up a new FinTech & Innovation Group (FTIG), which would be responsible for "regulatory policies and development strategies to facilitate the use of technology and innovation to better

---

[2]The FinTech Consortium (FC) is FinTech Incubator and acts as FinTech Ecosystem Builder that aims to further the development, interaction and acceleration of the FinTech ecosystem in Southeast Asia. FC fosters synergies among market players, including government bodies, financial institutions, corporates, investors and innovators, who believe that technology can bring added value to the financial industry.

[3]http://www.hoganlovells.com/files/Uploads/Documents/HKGLIB01_1507772_v1_Fintech_in_South_East_Asia.pdf

manage risks, enhance efficiency, and strengthen competitiveness in the financial sector."[4]

FTIG comprises three divisions as follows:

- Payments & Technology Solutions Office, which will formulate regulatory policies and develop strategies for simple, swift and secure payments and other technology solutions for financial services.
- Technology Infrastructure Office, which will be responsible for regulatory policies and strategies for developing safe and efficient technology-enabled infrastructures for the financial sector, in areas such as cloud computing, big data, and distributed ledgers.
- Technology Innovation Lab, which will scan the horizon for cutting-edge technologies with potential application to the financial industry and work with the industry and relevant parties to test-bed innovative new solutions.

Entrepreneurs, who want to set up a new company in Singapore, just need a few days to complete the registration process. The intellectual property rights and private property are strongly protected by full-fledged law and a reliable judicial system in Singapore. The transparency of financial relations is guaranteed by the local financial regulator and some of the tax rates are the lowest in the world.

Back in 2005, the Inland Revenue Authority of Singapore (IRAS) introduced the start-up tax exemption scheme to spur entrepreneurship and help its local young companies grow and prosper. Under this scheme, newly-incorporated companies will obtain specific exemption on their taxable profits in their first three years.[5]

Furthermore, some government agencies, such as Economic Development Board (EDB), Infocomm Development Authority of Singapore (IDA) and SPRING,[6] have also taken a set of measures

---

[4]http://www.mas.gov.sg/news-and-publications/media-releases/2015/mas-sets-up-new-fintech-and-innovation-group.aspx

[5]https://www.iras.gov.sg/irashome/Businesses/Companies/Learning-the-basics-of-Corporate-Income-Tax/Common-Tax-Reliefs-That-Help-Reduce-The-Tax-Bills/

[6]Standard, Productivity and Innovation Board (SPRING) and International Enterprise Singapore (IES) have merged to form Enterprise Singapore in April 2018.

to build a favourable setting for technology start-ups. Such measures include grants, tax incentives, co-investment, conferences, etc.[7]

To give a more in-depth and policy-oriented appraisal, this Chapter on Singapore is fortunate to tap on three policy speeches (Appendices 8.1, 8.2 and 8.3):

(1) Speech by Dr Vivian Balakrishnan, Minister for the Environment and Water Resources, and Minister-In-Charge of the Smart Nation Initiative for SMU's Sim Kee Boon Institute for Financial Economics (SKBI) Annual Conference Dinner on Wednesday, 6 May 2015, 7.00pm at Fairmont Hotel;

(2) Keynote speech by Mr S Iswaran, Minister for Trade and Industry (Industry), at the SMU SKBI Fintech Conference, Thursday, 18 August 2016, 9.00am; and

(3) "Singapore's FinTech Journey — Where We Are, What Is Next" speech by Mr Ravi Menon, Managing Director, Monetary Authority of Singapore, at Singapore FinTech Festival — FinTech Conference, Wednesday, 16 November 2016.

8.3   Capital

Besides providing a conducive regulatory environment, MAS also launched the Financial Sector Technology & Innovation (FSTI) scheme to provide financial support. Under the FSTI scheme, MAS would invest SGD225 million over the next five years to the potential FinTech sector, according to their announcement in June 2015.[8] To be specific, the FSTI funds will be used for three main purposes as follows:

- Innovation centres: to attract and to sponsor financial institutions to set up their R&D and innovation labs in Singapore;
- Institution-level projects: to support and to catalyse the innovation-related projects launched by financial institutions;

---

[7]https://www.techinasia.com/talk/lifesreda-emigrussia-inspirasia
[8]http://www.mas.gov.sg/news-and-publications/speeches-and-monetary-policy-statements/speeches/2015/a-smart-financial-centre.aspx

- Industry-wide projects: to build and to upgrade technology infrastructure that is required for the growth of FinTech start-ups and the delivery of new, integrated services.

Up to now, several financial institutions have already set up their innovation centres or labs in Singapore. Some of them are exactly under the FSTI scheme: DBS, Citibank, Credit Suisse, MetLife and UBS. There are a couple of others still in the pipeline.

The MAS also disclosed some ongoing institution-level projects supported by the FSTI scheme:

- A decentralised record-keeping system based on blockchain technology to prevent duplicate invoicing in trade finance;
- A shared infrastructure for a know-your-client (KYC) utility;
- A cyber risk test-bed;
- A natural catastrophe data analytics exchange.

As a new initiative, the government also plans to set up a separate office for FinTech firms to promote Singapore as a FinTech hub. Singapore's central bank and the National Research Foundation (NRF) will lead in this proposal and set up the one-stop virtual office to review sector-related funding schemes across government agencies.[9]

Several FinTech-specific accelerators and incubators exist in Singapore, whilst banks have launched their own. Such institutions like Startupbootcamp, InspirAsia, PACT Incubator, and FinLab provide funding, office space, mentorship and even the access to a global network of investors and venture capitalists to the potential start-ups.[10] The latest being the LongHash and the non-profit NPower ecosystem builder, co-founded by Genesis Financials (one of the authors is a co-founder with Bo Shen and a multi-national group based in Shanghai) and located in Science Park and specifically for Blockchain and ICO projects.

Payment solution has become the mainstream of Singapore FinTech sector. New technology innovations are accelerating the changes

---

[9]http://business.asiaone.com/news/singapore-set-dedicated-office-attract-fintech-firms

[10]http://fintechnews.sg/747/fintech/fintech-singapore-accelerators-incubators/

in the payments scene in Singapore. Some of the notable start-ups in this field include Codapay, Fastacash and 2C2P. The retail banks have also launched their mobile wallets or mobile payment applications: DBS (PayLah!), UOB (Mobile Cash), OCBC (Pay Anyone), Standard Chartered (Dash), Maybank (Mobile Money).

8.4   Infrastructure

In accordance with the effort to grow a Smart Financial Centre in Singapore, the government established a platform for collaborations with the industry to produce innovative solutions for defined problems and needs. JTC LaunchPad @ one-north, located at Ayer Rajah Industrial Estate, has been growing into a pretty vibrant FinTech start-up community that generates ample opportunities for knowledge sharing and collaboration.[11] It acts as an incubator to help accelerate the growth of FinTech start-ups and facilitate their success in the Singapore marketplace.

8.5   Two Policy Speeches on FinTech in Singapore

Given Singapore's lack of resources, the government first tapped on industrialisation in the 1960s, including services as further diversification, notably financial services to make Singapore into a knowledge-based and liveable city. The government recognised FinTech's growing importance globally as in particular to Singapore in the context of ASEAN as its immediate neighbours, and Asia-Pacific in a wider dimension.

FinTech is transformative, revitalising as well as being disruptive. The Committee on the Future Economy (CFE) released in February 2017 has financial services as one of the three modern services (including advanced manufacturing and healthcare) to focus on building strong digital capabilities as digitalisation translates to Singapore as a Smart Nation.[12] Classifying financial services as

---

[11] http://www.jtc.gov.sg/industrial-land-and-space/pages/jtc-launchpad-one-north.aspx

[12] There are six broad sectors in the CFE report, with modern services as one, comprising professional services, infocomm technology and media and financial services; see Appendix 8.4

horizontal means many other sectors are affected. Financial services also as a key enabler in enhancing capacity, reflects the promise and potential of FinTech. In 2016, global investment in FinTech grew by more than 70% from 2015 to USD22 billion.[13] Cumulative global investment is projected to exceed USD150 billion over the next three to five years.[14]

Singapore as a leading financial hub in the region cannot miss FinTech as a new means of conducting financial transactions, as alternative payment solutions to Peer-to-Peer (P2P) lending, incorporating innovation and inclusive financial systems in ASEAN and Asia. This is as duly noted by the MTI, MAS, CPF and all related policy making bodies, including the universities and institutions of higher learning. As noted, Singapore has to be one step ahead as a thought leader on FinTech regulation and development.

The whole-of-government approach is among Singapore's strength as noted in Appendix 8.2 in the statutory boards involved. The number of FinTech start-ups in Singapore had more than doubled, from around 140 in 2015 to more than 290 in 2017. Going to the ground level, small and medium-sized enterprises (SMEs) need support to digitise their existing business processes; it is more than being paperless. Investment and training for workers and the general public are as supportive under various agencies and schemes.

Terminologies like e-payments, P2P, Business-to-Business (B2B), Business-to-Consumer (B2C) and all other forms of e-commerce are already in vogue. With China's Alipay and WeChat among others, there is a need to enable e-NETS as the first overseas debit payment mechanism for e-commerce as tourism grows. Tapping the wider market of the unbanked in ASEAN is as logical. A holistic, integrated and systemic FinTech ecosystem is being groomed.

Developing FinTech talent and capabilities is more than by institutions and participating partners. A mindset change is as imperative with assurances of safety and privacy as upheld. In short, Singapore is not unfamiliar to charting new territories, but FinTech may be more disruptive than most journeys taken by the

---

[13] Accenture Report
[14] PWC FinTech Report

country in the last half-century. This challenge needs a response by all.

Equally provocative and forward-looking is the policy speech from MAS, Singapore's central bank. Again, innovation and technologies are the keys in FinTech, just that the scale and disruptive nature is relatively newer. Equally stressed is unprecedented mobility with the ubiquitous smartphone and unprecedented connectivity via the 24/7 Internet. Digital is preferred to virtual in this context as the latter may have a negative connotation as in money laundering. Speed as convenience needs to be balanced by safety and security.

Interestingly, increasing computing power is contrasted with more inventive toy-like Pokémon as pocket-sized monsters for adult use. More than cloud-computing as centralised, FinTech devices as decentralised is the new advantageous feature. This also applies to blockchains or distributed ledgers. All are protected by equally innovative devices and regulations as in dealing with Big Data.

In 2015, the MAS laid out a vision for a Smart Financial Centre, with innovation as pervasive as it is FinTech. In a more collaborative world, the MAS and all authorities have to work with partners in the form of private, non-government organisations (NGOs) from civil society in and outside of Singapore. Businesses have to change as noted in earlier chapters of this book, in particular to physical and spatial ways of doing business. The journey is as exciting as the need to set the right pace and structure.

That the MAS has committed SGD225 million (or USD160 million) over five years to support the development of a vibrant FinTech ecosystem, speaks volumes. Together with the NRF, a FinTech Office was set up, but mind over matter is as important to bring awareness to users, and facilitate constant communication between service providers and regulators.

With all the new acronyms and new packages launched, such as LATTICE80 (the location has since been rebranded as 80RR) in 2017 as Singapore's first FinTech innovation village. A National KYC Utility is another acronym. Together with other Infrastructure for Electronic Payments as Unified Point-of-Sale (UPOS) and Central Addressing Scheme (CAS), Singapore remains world-class in infrastructure for electronic payments. With 24/7 functionality, a real-time inter-bank fund transfer system, called Fast And Secure Transfers or FAST in short (with Application Programming Interfaces, APIs), will be one of the most important building blocks for innovation in the future economy.

8.6 Singapore Leads in Blockchain and Initial Coin Offerings (ICOs)

SGInnovate was established in 2016 to help ambitious and capable people to build "technology-intensive" products borne out of science research. It believes Singapore has the resources and capabilities to "tackle hard problems" that matter to people around the world. It is to use the full power of the Singapore ecosystem to achieve this mission. We have seen many start-ups relevant to FinTech setting up their offices along Carpenter Street with frequent meetups conducted. Blockchain companies are particularly fond of having a desk office on the second floor with Ethereum founder Vitalik Buterin working on location.

The MAS opened its FinTech Innovation Lab in August 2016. The purpose-built facility, known as Looking Glass @ MAS1, is located within the MAS Building. Looking Glass @ MAS1 will serve the following purposes: (1) allow MAS to experiment FinTech solutions with financial institutions, start-ups, and technology vendors; (2) facilitate consultations for start-ups by industry experts on areas of interest such as legal, regulation, and business-related matters; and (3) provide a venue for relevant training sessions and networking activities for the FinTech community.

80RR is a FinTech hub that has many start-ups locating their office there right in the middle of Robinson Road. Meetings are regularly conducted, and it is founded by Marvelstone. The Singapore FinTech Association is located in the same building. Singapore FinTech Association is a cross-industry non-profit initiative, intended to be a platform designed to facilitate collaboration between all market participants and stakeholders in the FinTech ecosystem. It is designed to be an effective platform for members to engage with multiple stakeholders to find solutions to issues. It was set up with the following objectives:

(1) To be a platform designed to facilitate collaboration between all market participants and stakeholders in the FinTech ecosystem. It is designed to be an effective platform for members to engage with multiple stakeholders to find solutions to issues and to promote best FinTech practices in a collaborative, open, and transparent manner;

(2) To represent the FinTech industry, uphold the integrity of its members, and support the building of relationships within the FinTech community, and collaborate with regional and as well as international FinTech organisations;

(3) To educate, inform and communicate by developing a connected FinTech ecosystem, channelling effective and relevant information among members and externally; foster innovation among Association members and the Singapore FinTech ecosystem; accelerate development of FinTech companies operating in or entering into Singapore, and their subsequent integration and acceleration into the Singapore FinTech ecosystem; and represent, align and support common interests by coordinating and catalysing otherwise individual actions so that the Association can represent the FinTech community.

The educational landscape is fascinating in Singapore and organisations such as National Trades Union Congress (NTUC), Info-communications Media Development Authority (IMDA), The Institute of Banking and Finance (IBF), National University of Singapore (NUS), SMU, Singapore University of Social Sciences (SUSS) and Ngee Ann Polytechnic are all at the forefront of teaching and research in FinTech. SMU's Sim Kee Boon Institute for Financial Economics was the first in the world to conduct a conference on Cryptocurrency on campus in 2014. This was followed by a Smart Nation and Inclusion conference in conjunction with Stanford in 2015 with emphasis on FinTech, and then another joint conference with International Monetary Fund (IMF) on Digital Banking and Inclusion in 2016. Poly FinTech 100 aims to nurture a pool of skilled workforce to further develop Singapore as a Smart Financial Centre.

Polytech 100 by Ngee Ann Polytechnic seeks to work with the FinTech community globally to provide internships and mentoring opportunities to polytechnic students who are keen to pursue careers in FinTech, helping them understand markets, technologies, skills, ecosystem actors and regulatory environments. They have more than 100 FinTech Mentors.

SUSS has a list of close to 100 FinTech and Blockchain Fellows that constantly engage professors and students in universities. SUSS reaches out to the industry by organizing FinTech meetings regularly and broadcasting globally. Its undergraduate degree in finance has an emphasis on FinTech and Blockchain including programming, cybersecurity, cryptography, big data and asset allocation of digital assets. SUSS has appointed individuals who are experts in their field as Fellows. These SUSS Fellows provide support, give advice and perform the role of resource persons in FinTech education and research activities. It is the privilege of SUSS to invite these Fellows to share their areas of expertise at workshops, seminars and conferences. Fellows include Vitalik Buterin, Zooko Wilcox, Patrick Dai, Sopnendu Mohanty, Roy Teo, Roy Lai, and many others listed on the SUSS website (see Figure 8.2).[15]

SUSS has since held two Global Inclusive Blockchain Conferences and the latest bilingual conference attracted more than 1,000 attendees and 210,000 watching live streaming.

Publications on Cryptocurrency and Blockchain evolved from many of these conferences, and notable are *Handbook of Digital Currency, Handbook of Blockchain, Digital Finance and Inclusion* and others that originated from Singapore and in particular the Sim Kee Boon Institute for Financial Economics and the research team. The institute has produced researchers that now work for various universities and commercial organisations such as IBM and blockchain start-ups. Recent articles on ICO have urged a good balance between regulation and innovation.[16]

---

[15]http://www.suss.edu.sg/Collaborations/Pages/fellows.aspx
[16]http://www.straitstimes.com/business/companies-markets/the-good-the-bad-and-the-ugly-side-of-initial-coin-offerings

Figure 8.2.   SUSS Blockchain and FinTech Fellows and Courses.[17]

Source: SUSSBlockchain.com.

The following appendices give a clearer understanding of the MAS position on Cryptocurrency and ICO.

(1) Appendix 8.5: MAS clarifies regulatory position on the offer of digital tokens in Singapore;
(2) Appendix 8.6: Consumer Advisory on Investment Schemes Involving Digital Tokens (Including Virtual Currencies);
(3) Appendix 8.7: Reply to Parliamentary Question on the prevalence use of cryptocurrency in Singapore and measures to regulate cryptocurrency and Initial Coin Offerings.

The following quote by MAS Managing Director Ravi Menon sums it up:

Guarding against Gresham's Law

I have spoken about the good, bad, and ugly of crypto tokens. To be more exact, it is the uses of crypto tokens that assume these qualities.

Like Money, crypto tokens can a force for good or bad.

---

[17]Note that Tim Swanson is no longer a SUSS Fellow.

Lest we forget, money is not the root of all evil; it is the love of money that is so.

The same applies to crypto tokens — it is the enchantment with these tokens as a way to make a quick buck and their abuse for illicit activities that are at the root of our concerns.

There is an old axiom in economics called Gresham's Law, which is loosely interpreted as "bad money drives out good".

We must work together — regulators and the crypto industry — to make sure that bad money does not take hold.

And that a new generation of crypto tokens emerges, that harnesses the potential of blockchain technology for social good while mitigating the risks today's tokens pose.

This is a future worth securing and I hope that some of the talents gathered in this hall will help to make it happen. Thank you.[18]

8.7 The Singapore Pioneers

Singapore is pioneering in FinTech and Blockchain worldwide. The policy approach is innovative as few countries can demonstrate clarity and at the same time consistency in their regulatory efforts. Furthermore, the pro-stability, pro-business and pro-innovation do not seem to appear too contradictory. Financial institutions and ecosystem builders based in Singapore such as OCBC (see Figure 8.7), LongHash, NPower and BlockAsset (co-founded by one of the authors), have been leading the charge in blockchain applications. Evidently, the most innovative and global blockchain projects are seen happening in this country as it favours technology and financial innovation. Talents from China, Europe, ASEAN and the US are now gathering at few hot spots for innovation in Singapore.

8.7.1 *Project Ubin*

Project Ubin is a blockchain project by Singapore's central bank MAS, and it is into its first of two stages. The report by MAS is

---

[18] http://www.mas.gov.sg/News-and-Publications/Speeches-and-Monetary-Policy-Statements/Speeches/2018/Crypto-Tokens-The-Good-The-Bad-and-The-Ugly.aspx

The Pioneers!

- Government Initiatives
  - Singapore
  - China
  - Japan
- Financial Institutions
  - OCBC: NXT
- The Pioneers Converged in Singapore
  - China: Quantum Singapore HQ
  - European: TenX at Oxley Road
  - Thailand: OmiseGo at SGInnivate
  - Singapore: Inforcorp at Botanical Garden

Figure 8.3.   The Singapore Pioneers in FinTech and Blockchain.

Source: By authors.

comprehensive, and we summarise the key points as follows[19]:

(1) On 16 November 2016, MAS announced that it was partnering with R3 — a blockchain inspired technology company and consortium of the world's largest financial institutions — on the production of a Proof-of-Concept (PoC) to conduct inter-bank payments facilitated by DLT. This endeavour, known as Project Ubin, is a digital cash-on-ledger project run in partnership between MAS and R3, with the participation of Bank of America Merrill Lynch, Credit Suisse, DBS Bank, The Hongkong and Shanghai Banking Corporation Limited, J.P. Morgan, Mitsubishi UFJ Financial Group, OCBC Bank, Singapore Exchange, United Overseas Bank, as well as BCS Information Systems as a technology provider.

(2) The aim of Project Ubin is to evaluate the implications of having a tokenised form of the SGD on a DL, and its potential benefits to Singapore's financial ecosystem. MAS is Singapore's central bank and financial regulatory authority. MAS acts as a settlement

---

[19]Monetary Authority of Singapore.

agent, operator and overseer of payment, clearing and settlement systems in Singapore that focus on safety and efficiency.

(3) As part of its role, it operates an electronic payments and book-entry system, the New MAS Electronic Payment System (MEPS+). MEPS+ is a real-time gross settlement (RTGS) system that supports large-value local currency inter-bank funds transfers and the settlement of scriptless Singapore Government Securities (SGS) between MEPS+ participants, subject to the availability of funds and securities.

(4) MAS undertakes this role as a trusted third party and actively engages banks in the Singapore market, as well as with public and private sector bodies such as the Singapore Clearing House Association (SCHA) and The Association of Banks in Singapore (ABS).

(5) MEPS+ is a system that enables real-time and irrevocable transfer of funds and SGS. Key features include:

   (a) Use of SWIFT message formats to increase interoperability;
   (b) Parameterised queue management, which provides participants with better liquidity and settlement management;
   (c) Automated collateralised intraday liquidity facilities, that enable participants (particularly banks with low liquidity) to settle more payments quicker;
   (d) Automated gridlock resolution, which detects and resolves multi-party payment gridlocks to prevent or reduce payment queues and to increase overall efficiency of payments flow.

(6) All participating banks are contractually bound to operate in compliance with the MEPS+ operating rules and regulations. This presents an excellent opportunity for MAS to collaborate with the banks and assess the value that blockchain could bring to this existing relationship.

(7) Project Ubin is a multi-phase project (see Figures 8.4, 8.5 and 8.6). Phase 1, which ran for six weeks from 14 November 2016 to 23 December 2016, served as the foundation to assess the

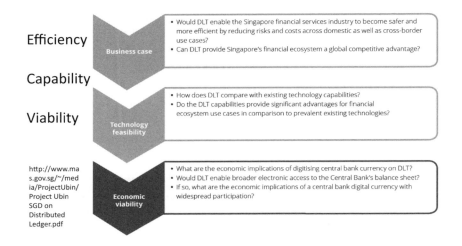

Figure 8.4.   The Three Key Variables for Project Ubin.

Source: Monetary Authority of Singapore.

http://www.mas.gov.sg/~/media/ProjectUbin/Project Ubin SGD on Distributed Ledger.pdf

The future is here
Project Ubin: SGD on Distributed Ledger

A report developed with the contributions of Bank of America Merrill Lynch, BCS Information Systems, Credit Suisse, DBS Bank, HSBC, J.P. Morgan, Mitsubishi UFJ Financial Group, OCBC Bank, R3, Singapore Exchange and UOB Bank

Project Ubin demonstrated the commitment of MAS and the industry to co-create concrete use-cases for technologies such as DLT. We believe that central banks like MAS can play a bigger role beyond just providing research funding: collaborative projects such as Project Ubin support the creation of open Intellectual Property and foster collaboration between industry players, creating a vibrant, collaborative, and innovative ecosystem of financial institutions and FinTech companies.

Figure 8.5.   What Is Project Ubin?

Source: Monetary Authority of Singapore.

feasibility and implications of DLT, and to identify the elements required for future enhancements.

The philosophy of the central bank is transparent, and the project poses few questions that focus on efficiency, capability and viability.

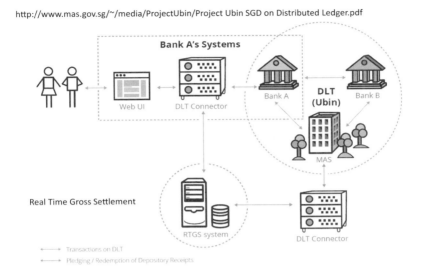

Figure 8.6.   The Project Ubin Distributed Ledger.

Source: Monetary Authority of Singapore.

Figure 8.7.   OCBC Blockchain Project.

Source: FinTech News.

Cross-border and local funds transfers using payment blockchain solution

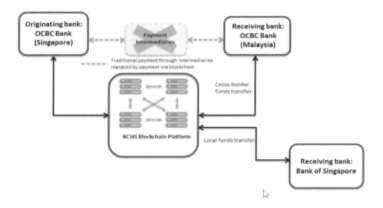

Figure 8.8. OCBC Project.
Source: OCBC.

The key figure in MAS has been Sopnendu Mohanty, an ex-banker with vast experience in various areas of banking. His vision and relentless pursuit of innovation have not only inspired many start-ups, but the entire team at FTIG has also made a mark worldwide of their professionalism and understanding of the challenges of transforming the financial sector.

8.7.2 *OCBC Blockchain Project*

Many banks are working on FinTech and blockchain in Singapore. OCBC has been one of the most innovative advocators of blockchain among the banks in Singapore. The team at OCBC demonstrate their ability to use blockchain technology for cross-border transactions and remittances (see Figure 8.8).

8.7.3 *Qtum Blockchain*

Given the enormous base of professionals in Singapore in the legal, audit and corporate secretarial services, and the ease of setting up companies and foundations, Singapore has been the favourite base for FinTech innovators. Almost all the successful ICOs are

Quantum = Best of Bitcoin and Ethereum

The Rise of Left Coast Thinking

Crowdsourced

Inclusive

Global

Figure 8.9.   Quantum and Left Coast Philosophy.
Source: Quantum.

China's Own Open Blockchain In Singapore

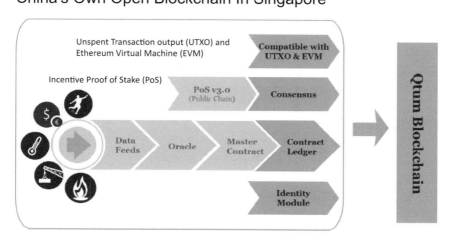

Figure 8.10.   Quantum Foundation Is Located in Singapore.
Source: Quantum.

PWC helped with Governance Design

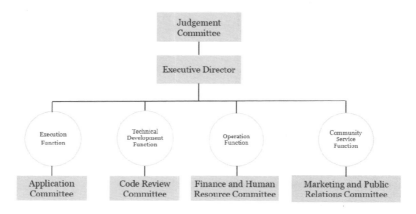

Figure 8.11.   Initial Corporate Governance by PwC.

Source: Quantum.

Control Objective	Control Activities	Control Owner		
Source Code Management				
Source code management	The underlying architecture of open source code is stored on Github; only the core development members are authorized to modify and approve the code.	Source Code Review Committee		
Source code modification	The requester can modify the source code only after the approval and authorization from the core development team.	Source Code Review Committee		
Code development and modification	After authorization from the Source Code Review Committee, the developers can develop and modify the source code.	Source Code Review Committee		
Code testing	The source code needs to be tested and documented in the testing report to ensure bugs are removed.	Source Code Review Committee		
Code review	The source code needs to be reviewed by software tools and manual checks before deployment to the community.	Source Code Review Committee		
Code deployment	Before deployment, the source code needs to be reviewed by the core developers.	Source Code Review Committee		
Vulnerability fix	When vulnerabilities are identified, developers remediate and test the source code. The Source Code Review Committee reviews the code before deployment.	Source Code Review Committee		
Drill testing	The Source Code Review Committee is responsible for performing drill tests periodically for the development and production environment.	Source Code Review Committee		
Code modification permissions	For non-public product code, code modifications need to be approved and authorized by the Source Code Review Committee.	Source Code Review Committee		

Source Code is Key!

Understanding the Risk and Compleity of Technology is Key!

Figure 8.12.   Source Code Management of Qtum.

Source: Quantum.

CIG: Technology, Funding, Wisdom, Talents
It is all about the community 80% of it!

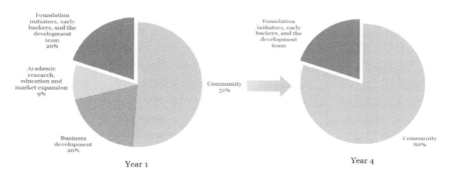

Figure 8.13. Community Project with 80% Entitlement after Four Years.

Source: Quantum.

headquartered in Singapore with a foundation or business entity as contracting party for their projects and experiments. Quantum or Qtum is one of them that embraces the "Crowdsourced, Inclusive and Global" thinking of the Left Coast. Known as the Chinese blockchain, Qtum was one of the earliest ICOs in the world. PwC assisted in the beginning with the governance structure. While this has been one of the most successful so far, the verdict is still out on whether these blockchain projects will be sustainable (see Figures 8.9 to 8.13).

What is most interesting about the project is that it is the first project with 51%, 20%, 20%, 9% structure. The 51% of token sales to the public is a declaration that this is a community experiment. Its intention to have 80% market owning the token after four years is a commitment to search for the best from the community to run the project. The thinking behind is that no one is indispensable and like Satoshi, once the project is completed, the community should take charge. Talented people should move on to a more interesting project.

8.7.4 *TenX*

TenX is one of the most interesting projects as it raised more than USD80 million in a record time of a few days. We have described the project in previous chapters, but the larger project behind TenX is Comit. The value of the Comit or any blockchain companies lies in its inclusiveness. The design standard and the clever use of smart contracts is what determines whether a blockchain can take advantage of the network effect to the fullest. One of the authors has been an advisor and angel investor in most of the ICO and blockchain projects discussed in this book. Many of these projects adopt the LASIC and the 5Ds philosophy described in earlier chapters.

The following figures (see Figures 8.14 to 8.20) show how Comit and TenX work to take advantage of network effect using smart contract as well as the role of the liquidity provider.

TENX – A Singapore Company

The TenX Wallet

The TenX wallet is the major game changer as it enables a user to spend their blockchain assets through their smartphone or a physical debit card at over 36 million points of acceptance online and offline. The TenX app is downloadable for free both on Android and iOS (iOS available from July 2017 onwards).

https://www.tenx.tech/whitepaper/tenx_whitepaper_draft_v04.pdf

Figure 8.14.   TenX: A Singapore Company.

Source: TenX Whitepaper, https://www.tenx.tech/whitepaper/tenx_whitepaper_draft_v04.pdf

TenX works with Mastercard

	TenX	WireX & Xapo	TokenCard
Physical card issuing fee (Incl. shipping & tracking)	$15	$20+	No working product
Virtual card issuing fee	$1.5	$3	No working product
Physical card annual fee	FREE ($10 if spend less than $1000/year)	$12	No working product
Virtual card annual fee	FREE ($10 if spend less than $1000/year)	N/A	$12
Domestic exchange fee	0%	0%	1.5%
Foreign exchange fee	0%	3%	4.5%

LIMITED EDITION: TenX Special

Startups @ **PayPal**

DBS
BLOCKCHAIN
HACK

Figure 8.15.   TenX Partners Mastercard.
Source: TenX.

Product Comparison Table

	TenX	WireX & Xapo	Monaco	TokenCard
Blockchain Support	Bitcoin, Ethereum, Dash and more	Bitcoin	Bitcoin, Ethereum	Ethereum
Fund Security	Hosted Wallet and Smart Contract (with planned integration with the COMIT network by Q2 2018)	Hosted Wallet	Hosted Wallet	Smart Contract
Double Spend Risk	Safe	Safe	Safe	Risky
Issuer(s)	Mastercard, and Visa	Visa	Visa	Visa
Status	Live	Live	Not applicable	Not applicable
User's Fund Security Control	Full Control	No Control	Little Control	Partial Control
Open Platform	Yes	No	No	No
Card Holder Incentives	0.1% On Every Purchase	None	None	None
Card Holder Transaction Fees	Free	Free Domestic Only	1%	1.5%

Figure 8.16.   TenX Comparison with Other Crypto Card Projects.
Source: TenX.

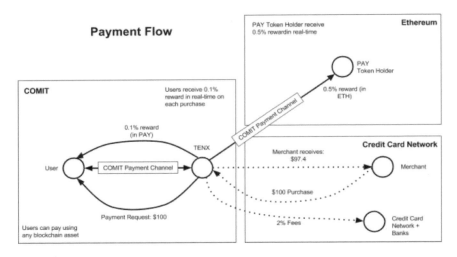

Figure 8.17.   TenX: Payment Flow.

Source: TenX.

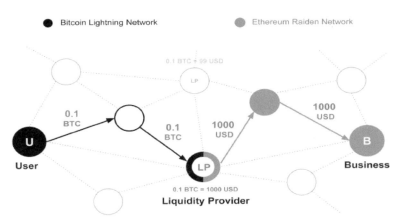

Figure 8.18.   TenX and Comit Network Routing.

Source: TenX.

This is how the features of the COMIT network compares to those of other transaction solutions:

	Traditional Banks	Online Banks	Blockchains	COMIT
Fees	High	Medium	Low	Near Zero
Speed	Slow	Fast	Fast	Instant
Security	Trust-based	Trust-based	Cryptographic	Cryptographic
Control	Centralized	Centralized	Decentralized	Decentralized
Accessibility	Low	Low	Medium	High
Interoperability	Low	Low	Medium	High
Flexibility	Low	Low	Medium	High
Business Profitability	Low	Low	Medium	High
Spurring Growth	Low	Low	Medium	High
Scalability	Low	Medium	Low	High

Figure 8.19.   Comit Network.

Source: TenX.

Singapore startup raises $80m in cryptocurrency sale; another follows suit

Jack Ellis (https://www.techinasia.com/profile/jack-ellis-2)
12:51 PM at Jun 29, 2017 | 3 min read

Just one year ago, Toby was spotted and did a presentaion at SKBI.

One year later, he raised USD 80m!

"
Around 4,000 people directly participated in the token sale – which lasted for less than seven minutes
"

Figure 8.20.   TenX from Zero to USD80 Million.

Source: TenX.

The Magic of SGInnovate

Meeting Vitalik Buterim and Thomsa Greco
at SGInnovate

OmiseGo ICO Finished before it even started!

While we're still getting our heads around ICOs that finish in 30 seconds, the
OmiseGo ICO managed to finish before the token sale even started.

Launched by an established Asia based payments provider, Omise – which
boasts of being the first to back the Ethereum Foundation's Devgrants program
– the ICO started with a token pre-sale on Bitcoin Suisse, a token investors pool
of sorts that requires AML/KYC.

Figure 8.21.   OmiseGo ICO.
Source: OmiseGo.

8.7.5   *OmiseGo*

OmiseGo is another interesting project that specialises in financial
inclusion through payments (see Figures 8.21 and 8.22). With Vitalik
Buterin and Thomas Greco from the Ethereum Foundation acting
as advisors and team members, the project was a popular ICO with
investors. One of the authors acts as a financial inclusion advisor and
is an investor in the company.

8.7.6   *Infocorp*

Infocorp is another interesting example founded by Singaporeans
focusing on financial inclusion (see Figures 8.23 to 8.32). The aim
is to use technology to serve the underserved and ideas include e-
wallet for migrants, Livestock Identification Certificate tokens or cow
tokens. The idea of cow tokens was originated in earlier lectures of
one of the authors, and some ideas are outlined in this interview.[20,21]

---

[20]Alternative Investment and Burmese Cow, http://www.digitalfinancemedia.
com/?s=David+Lee
[21]IMDA   Interview,   https://www.imda.gov.sg/infocomm-and-media-news/in-
conversation-with/2017/8/david-lee-serve-the-underserved

Apparently, 450 people pledged $60 million for a capped sale of $19 million, so "we will not be able to accept contributions from any participants in the second round," Omise says.

The OmiseGo (OMG) pre-sale opened on June the 7th, with some complaining why it ended so fast, while the ICO was meant to begin on June the 27th, but as the cap was already reached, the ICO didn't happen.

Figure 8.22.   OmiseGo: Unbank the Banked with Ethereum.
Source: OmiseGo.

Financial Inclusion Blockchain Solution Platform

- **2 billion** adults worldwide live without a bank account and depends on cash for survival.

- **73%** of SE Asia is "Unbanked" [1]

- **Low adoption** of card payments.

- **High mobile** penetration

- **Low access** to financial services.

Developed countries payment solutions are not designed for developing countries' unbanked use.

[1] https://home.kpmg.com/xx/en/home/insights/2016/04/fintech-opening-the-door-to-the-unbanked-and-underbanked-in-southeast-asia.html

Figure 8.23.   Financial Inclusion Solution according to InfoCorp.
Source: InfoCorp; Sentinel Chain Whitepaper.

Major Unbanked Developing Countries in ASEAN

Source: https://www.slideshare.net/SGFinTech/fin-tech-intro-to-financial-inclusionslideshare

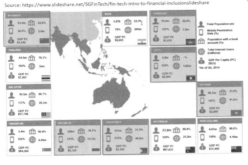

- 6 Countries with right potentials:
  - Myanmar
  - Cambodia
  - Laos
  - Vietnam
  - Indonesia
  - Philippines

- **Banked Populations** between 22.2% to 36.1% only

- **Mobile penetration** rate > 100%.

- **Myanmar** reported [2] 80% mobile penetration in 2017.

[1] http://www.ictworks.org/2015/09/30/wow-myanmar-is-going-straight-to-smartphones/

Figure 8.24.   Unbanked in Developing Countries in ASEAN.

Source: InfoCorp.

Local Currency for Financial Inclusion

BaliPay Community

- **Success story** in using local currency for financial inclusion.
- Pilot trial with a Bali community (BaliPay) with **500+** users.
- Facilitate **direct trading** between farmers and hotels.
- Making bank transfer = **65 cents**
- Using SMS payments = **0.065 cents**
- Problem: **Cannot scale**

Figure 8.25.   InfoCorp and BaliPay.

Source: InfoCorp.

Untapped potentials of Inclusive Financing

- Only **less than 0.1%** of all loans originated through Southeast Asia P2P lenders (compared to 10% in China and 2-3% in UK, USA)

- Unbanked Market Potentials
  - **4-5 million** enter "consuming class" each year.
  - **60%-70%** of the most populous economies in ASEAN is in working age.

- Problems with Traditional P2P Lending in Asia
  - Under-penetrated representing large untapped potential.
  - Restricted by in-country regulations on fiat currencies.
  - Cannot scale

Figure 8.26.   The Market for InfoCorp.

Source: InfoCorp.

How does it work?

Sentinel Tokens (SCTs) represents conversion tokens for exchange between Local Currency Tokens (LCTs) on different local blockchains. SCTs have Fixed Supply but Tradeable on public cryptoexchanges.

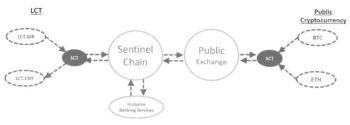

Figure 8.27.   Sentinel and Currency Tokens.

Source: InfoCorp.

What is the Value?

SCT Value is driven by **communities** and **inclusive financing** demands and facilitated by **crypto-economy liquidity**.

Figure 8.28.   The SCT Value Proposition.

Source: InfoCorp.

Local Blockchains

- Local Currency Tokens (LCTs)
    - Local fiat virtual currency.
    - Like a wallet account.
    - Not fixed. Can be issued and destroyed.

- Examples of unbanked communities
    - A durian plantation in Malaysia (Plantation Owner).
    - A village in Indonesia (Village Head).
    - A worker's dormitory in Singapore (Dormitory Operator).
    - Unbanked ecosystem
    - Community Owners, Local agents, etc.

- Use Cases
    - Payroll
    - Micro-lending
    - Micro-Payments / Remittances

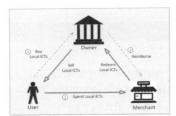

Local Blockchain describes a **private blockchain** used for local cryptocurrencies and assets.

Figure 8.29.   The InfoCorp Local Blockchains.

Source: InfoCorp.

CrossPay Mobile App

- **Truly designed for unbanked** - No accounts or login for peer-to-peer payments.

- **Zero Transaction Fees** – Free peer-to-peer payments.

- **Escrow + Geolocation** – Replace cash payments.

- **Not just a wallet!** – deliver inclusive banking services to unbanked.

Figure 8.30.   InfoCorp CrossPay Mobile App.

Source: InfoCorp.

Cow Token –Application Use Case

- Cow is a valuable asset for many unbanked villagers.
- Tokenisation of Cow transforms a store of value into a medium of exchange.
- A local community can not only issue local cryptocurrency but issues local assets as well.
- Cow Token is an asset backed token that is issued by the community owner (eg. village head) and sold on Sentinel Blockchain. Cow owner receives funding to support farming operations.
- Token holder receives dividends from cow produce and compensation when cow is sold.

Figure 8.31.   Cow Token.

Source: InfoCorp.

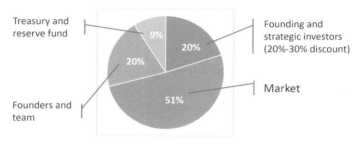

Figure 8.32.   The 51:20:20:9 Structure of ICO and InfoCorp.
Source: InfoCorp.

The aforementioned figures show the logic and how the Sentinel Coin is structured, the use case of cow tokens, and the same structure of ICO as Qtum and TenX.

Infocorp has recently signed an MOU with Maybank and a few other micro-insurance, as well as microfinancing companies for financial inclusion initiatives.[22] The project has been rebranded as Sentinel Chain and the ICO raised USD14 million worth of cryptocurrencies. The Appendix on Interviews, Podcasts and Videos gives an idea of how this idea was originally conceived by one of the authors. This is one of the projects that embraces both inclusive finance and inclusive technology using private, consortium and open blockchains.

8.8   Conclusion and Singapore Ahead

Besides hard and soft infrastructure as well as visionary policies and regulations, Singapore's status as the financial hub in the ASEAN region makes it susceptible to money laundering. This is

---

[22]http://sbr.com.sg/financial-services/more-news/maybank-infocorp-ink-deal-fin ancial-inclusion-projects http://www.businesstimes.com.sg/banking-finance/ma ybank-singapore-fintech-infocorp-launches-mobile-payment-app-for-migrant-workers

as unavoidable as the policy to attract high-net-worth individuals (HNWIs). Banks have been tasked to be more alert in all forms of surveillance and detection. Singapore may have a financial action task force to improve its pursuit of more complex transnational transactions. Terrorist financing is one worrisome development, but it is all part and parcel of globalisation in general, financial globalisation in particular, which also spells episodes of financial crises.

Singapore may be a good house, but the neighbourhood is beyond its charge. Thus, ASEAN cooperation, especially in banking and finance, comes back to the fore. Singapore is a member of The Financial Action Task Force (FATF) which is an international body that sets global standards on combating money laundering and terrorist financing.

Based on the FATF's inspection in December 2016, Singapore was commended for significant improvements since the last FATF visit in 2008. Its strong regulatory framework and record of international cooperation have been noted. Nonetheless, some criticisms are inevitable such as welcoming HNWIs, hence putting in place stringer checks-and-balances in a sensitive ASEAN and Islamic region, including alleged misappropriation of billions of dollars from Malaysian state-investment fund, 1Malaysia Development Berhad (1MDB).

The presence of many large Western banks, including Credit Suisse AG, Citigroup Inc., Deutsche Bank, and J.P. Morgan Chase & Co. in wealth management and other financial and Fintech activities is as inevitable. Assets under management (AUM) grew 30% to nearly USD1.8 trillion in 2014, with Singapore as the world's third most competitive financial centre by the think tank Z/Yen Group Ltd.[23] Since 2008, when the FATF placed Singapore in a review process, expressing concern over its implementation of measures to combat money laundering, particularly for cases originating from abroad, the 2011 follow-up report gave a more positive assessment. Singapore has largely addressed the criticisms highlighted in 2008.

Singapore's reputation as a clean and trusted financial centre among much larger ASEAN neighbours needs to be balanced, as

---

[23]Wall Street Journal, 27 September 2016 in https://www.wsj.com/articles/singapore-needs-to-do-more-on-money-laundering-report-says-1474961403

watched from ASEAN sources as by FATF. Singapore has too much at stake, with investment in time and money as well as manpower resources. FinTech offers as much in new business as the old one of money laundering from the region and the world as a whole. Singapore remaining fully committed and sensitive is the way all round.

On another constructive note, young Singaporean millennials may work well with their counterparts in ASEAN to begin with, as much and as well as more matured and older Singaporeans with values and mindsets with those of their contemporaries in other parts of ASEAN. With the future as digital as clearly identified by the Report of the Committee on the Future Economy of Singapore released in February 2017,[24] Singapore cannot forget the diversity of information and communications technology (ICT) and digital infrastructure and skills in ASEAN. A balance of exploiting regional and global opportunities will also create the needed balance and harmony of an ageing population in Singapore among its millennial youths.

Finally, the future of FinTech may just lie in inclusive tech, such as blockchain, to serve the underserved, such as those in ASEAN. In particular, the clarity in regulation is certainly a positive development for Singapore. The future is bright for Singapore as we have seen how this small country has been able to outshine many countries in its ability to attract the right talent, business and technology to Singapore.

Appendix 8.1

Speech by Dr Vivian Balakrishnan, Minister for the Environment and Water Resources, and Minister-In-Charge of the Smart Nation Initiative for SMU's Sim Kee Boon Institute for Financial Economics (SKBI) Annual Conference Dinner on Wednesday, 6 May 2015, 7.00pm at Fairmont Hotel

Mr. Lim Chee Onn, the Chairman of the Advisory Board SKBI
The family of Mr Sim Kee Boon: Ms Jeanette Sim, Mr Peter Sim

---

[24]Report of the Committee on the Future Economy: Pioneers of the Next Generation in https://www.gov.sg/.../about-the-committee-on-the-future-economy

The family of Prof Winston Koh,
Prof Arnoud De Meyer, our host,
Friends, Ladies and Gentlemen

1. It's always a challenge for an ophthalmologist, an eye surgeon, to address an audience like this, who knows far more than me about financial services and financial institutions.

2. Mr Stephen Aguilar-Milan is a futurist with the World Futures Society, and he has a hypothesis that every 50 years or so, there is a major technological wave. My hypothesis is that every time there is major technological wave, you have a period of intense disruption, a period of increased opportunities, a period of great inequality and robber barons, and it takes some time before the middle class adopts the same technologies and creates more wide spread prosperity. My thesis tonight is that we are in the midst of such a wave.

3. So let's start with Stephen's hypothesis. If you go back to 1770 in England, the time of mills and canals — the canals that you can still see in London and England — that was the start of cottage industries, of early industrialisation in England. The fact that it happened in England gave it a head-start in the Industrial Revolution.

4. You move forward another 40 or 50 years from there, you get to the early 1800s. The pivotal invention then was the steam engine, and with the steam engine came railways and railroads, and many fortunes were made by the successive rollout of railways in England, Europe and America.

5. Fast forward another 50 years to about 1870 — that was the age of steel, electricity and heavy engineering. That was also the age of large ocean-going ships, warfare, refrigeration and trade opened up on an industrial scale.

6. The 4th wave began sometime around 1910. That was really about oil, and oil opened up the possibility of the automobile, and especially in America, the age of the car, interstate highways, and the long American love affair with the car and all that it represents in popular culture.

7. If you stop to think about these waves, and think about some names associated with these waves — if you go back to 1910 and think about oil, what names come to mind? For instance, Rockefeller — that was how huge fortunes were made. If you go further back to the age of steel, the American name that comes to mind is Carnegie, and related to that, Mellon, the bank. And if you go back to the age of the steam engine and railways, there are pantheons of tycoons, technologists and early-adopters who made huge fortunes because suddenly, everything changed, and there was a period of big disruption — old industries were gutted, and new industries were made. The people who got in first made huge fortunes.

8. Now let's move forward to the 5th wave. You can roughly date the 5th wave to the late 1940s, after the Second World War, in particular the invention of the transistor, which replaced the old vacuum tubes. By accident or design, this started off in Silicon Valley. I think it was William Shockley who moved back to Palo Alto from New York, because he had an ageing mother in Palo Alto. At the same time, Stanford University was also trying to find and define an opportunity for commercialising its academic pursuits, and finding daily relevance for the discoveries in the labs and the work that its professors did. The transistor in turn led to an explosion of electronics, and in a later wave, electronics in turn led to computers and much of what we know of modern electronics today. So starting from the transistor in 1947, we move all the way to today.

9. If you believe this theory of 50 years, we are clearly past 50 years. This is where I will take a risk, and posit that there is a 6th wave. The difference in technological waves is that they don't come and go; each wave builds successively on preceding waves, and this 6th wave is actually about connectivity — meaning that the transistor led to the CPU, which led to the computer and now it is about the Internet, the World Wide Web, big data analytics, the Internet of Things, and telecommunications. We are moving beyond hardware to bits and ideas, and we are now living in a world which is far more densely connected than ever before.

10. Today, a lot of the political polemic is about inequality. My favourite theory is that inequality is not the result of a covert right wing conspiracy, but really just another episode of the fact that there is a major tectonic technological wave sweeping through our society, and the people who get it, the few people who understand and are first able to capitalise, will make fortunes as large, in historical terms, as the Rockefellers, the Carnegies and the rest. So it's no accident today that the names you hear about, whether it's Bill Gates, Mark Zuckerberg, Carlos Slim in Mexico, Jack Ma of Alibaba, are all people who are early riders of this emerging wave. The point I want to make, therefore, is that this is only just beginning. It will take some time for these tools and technologies to be democratised, commoditised and to be in the hands of ordinary people, and for the middle class to regain its wage-earning capacity, its productive capacity and its fair share of national wealth. So that is my hypothesis for what is currently happening in society and economics, and in the political arena as well.

11. Now let me cite a few examples. Many of these examples you will be familiar with, but they help make the point.

12. In the mobile banking space, many of you would have heard of Safaricom's M-Pesa. Since Kenya's M-Pesa brought banking-by-phone to Africa, this has grown from a novelty to a bona fide payment network. Even at a few dollars a transaction, mobile payments in sub-Saharan Africa will generate about US$1.5 bn in fees for mobile money providers by 2019, according to a report by the Boston Consulting Group. It was also reported that in sub-Saharan Africa, more people will have a mobile money account than Facebook account. Mobile phones are clearly spreading faster than bank branches, and especially in emerging markets like India, Bangladesh, Africa and other parts of Asia. It is no wonder therefore that many banks and telcos (such as Safaricom), and even Technology Giants (such as Google and Apple) are now focused on creating innovative financial services via the mobile channels.

13. If you move into the retail space, you've heard of the names: eBay, Amazon and Alibaba. Alibaba has come to dominate Internet Retailing in China, and frankly anyone who dominates any sector in China is going to be huge. Just to give you some idea of scale, Alibaba has moved beyond its remit of just connecting businesses to each other, which is how it started. It has moved far beyond that. It now allows companies to sell directly to the public, and for the members of the public to transact with each other. We've heard of Tmall, we've heard of Taobao. Taobao and Tmall processed 1.1 trillion yuan — which I think is about US$170 billion — in transactions in 2012, and in September 2014, Alibaba's market value was measured at US$231 bn. I am sure the numbers have changed since then, but these are numbers with many zeros.

14. In the crowdsourcing space, you have heard of Kickstarter and Indiegogo, and nowadays artists, entrepreneurs, communities, even people in trouble with the government can raise funds from crowdsourcing sites — to raise funds from the "4F Bank". You know what the 4Fs are? Fans, Family, Friends and Fools. We laugh about it. But the point is that it allows everyone to mobilise funds and it goes far beyond this 4Fs, because in this world currently awash with liquidity and low interest rates, people are looking for ideas and services to take a bet on. According to the Crowdfunding Industry Report by Massolution, in 2012, US$2.7 bn was raised online through crowdfunding, and this number can only grow.

15. In the virtual currencies space, Rajendra mentioned Bitcoin, and I think you had a convention or a seminar on it. Frankly, I am not sure about the future of cryptocurrency, although clearly if you think about the way governments are managing paper currency, it doesn't give you great confidence either. But actually what intrigues me more is the technology behind Bitcoin. I am not sure how many of you are familiar with the Blockchain Technology. Blockchain technology is a computational algorithm that enables distributed verification of the integrity of ledger items. Whether that item is a transfer of money, or cryptocurrency, or contracts,

or services, it is in fact a generic platform technology which I believe has not yet found the most appropriate use case. But nevertheless, further breakthroughs in this area will open up the world and will disrupt services in a major way.

16. And for those of you who are involved in banking and finance, you know that some key competitive advantages which banks have had are (i) funds (ii) reputation (iii) some kind of protection by government regulations and (iv) knowing your customers' businesses because you were lending them money — in other words you had access to information. But if you were to stop and think about it, what this technological wave has done is that it potentially disintermediates all those competitive advantages which banks and traditional financial institutions have had. You want access to funds, you can go to crowdfunding portals. As for having information on what businesses are doing, it is not just banks, and it is not just the consultants like Accenture, it is the people who have accurate pulse on the flow of bits, data, and transactions who know what is going on. I think David Lee was telling me just now that Alibaba employs hundreds of PhDs to do data mining. Is Alibaba really a retailer or is it actually in the information business? Are telcos really just selling you voice or are they preludes to the mobile banking business? Even Amazon or take any logistics company, are they really just delivering pizzas and electronics or are they really in the fulfilment business? So the point I am making is that if you can find the centre of gravity between money, information, fulfilment, and then the elusive quality called trust, that is where a huge focal point of opportunity is.

17. So I hope I have given you enough food for thought. I just want to appeal for you to do three things.

18. First, please for the sake of Singapore and Singaporean institutions, find new ways to deliver new services to our people and the people beyond Singapore. If our banks, financial institutions and businesses are doing exactly the same thing next year as they were doing last year, we are going to be swamped, because the

pace of change is not slowing down. So please find new ways to deliver new services.

19. Second, please focus on this field of data science and data analytics. Whether you are a bank, financial institution, consultancy firm or university, we now live in the age of big data. And I used to joke with my medical colleagues that you almost do not need to do a clinical trial now, when you can measure the universe. Why settle for a sample and then engage in fancy statistical gymnastics to prove your conclusions, when you can measure everything in real time. So pay attention to data analytics and data science.

20. Third, we need more rational, careful, and technologically-based conversations on the issues of cybersecurity, protection of privacy, and especially protection of identity. Because you cannot have a world that is fully able to take advantage of financial innovations, information revolution, even electronic medical records, if a decent level of security, protection from identity theft, and protection from a loss of privacy and confidentiality is not guaranteed. In other words, security is the essential flip side of the coin of utility; and if we can get that done right here, then we have a head start.

21. So my final point is why Smart Nation. The answer is: we do so because we have no choice. Like many things we have done in Singapore for the last 50 years, all the way back to the time when Mr Sim Kee Boon was a pioneer senior civil servant working for Mr Lee Kuan Yew, we had to break new grounds, we had to be adventurous, we had to be innovative because we have no choice. Jobs were going to disappear in the early 1970s as the British forces pulled out of all ports east of the Suez, and that's why we industrialised. Similarly, what I have described now is potentially another occasion when 20 to 30 percent of previously stable, good, middle class, white collar jobs are at risk because you cannot out-compete a robot, a machine, or a computer for routine, white collar work.

22. So we need to do all these things, and we believe we have an edge because we are small, and we have a single layer of

government. Half of our cabinet ministers are engineers. Our PM is a mathematician who can still code. If you do not believe me, you can check his Facebook account and so far after five days, people have only found a little boundary error in his algorithm. But it is a very elegant program.

23. So the point is that we get it, we understand technology, we are not afraid of Science and Technology, but we need to have not just the PM coding, we need an entire society that is capable of understanding and exploiting the opportunities that this wave provides for us. So I wish you all the very best and I hope SMU, and especially the Sim Kee Boon Institute, continues to break new ground, not just because it is fun, but because it is essential for our continued prosperity and progress as a nation. Thank you all very much.

Appendix 8.2

Keynote Speech by Mr S Iswaran, Minister for Trade and Industry (Industry), at the SMU SKBI Fintech Conference, Thursday, 18 August 2016, 9.00am

Professor Arnoud De Meyer, President, SMU
Mr. Piyush Gupta, Chairman, SKBI Advisory Board
Mr. Changyong Rhee, Director, Asia and Pacific Department, IMF
Distinguished Guests,
Ladies and Gentlemen,

1. Good morning. I am very happy to join you this morning at the SMU SKBI FinTech Conference. I want to start by congratulating SMU on hosting the 6th edition of this annual conference that brings together industry professionals, investors, financial innovators, regulators and academia to better understand the opportunities brought about by FinTech.

FinTech's growing importance globally and to Singapore

2. FinTech has been a transformative and revitalising force for the global financial services industry. From the Committee on the Future Economy (CFE)'s perspective, we see this as an

important horizontal. A horizontal, in the vertical sense, that's going to have a profound impact on the financial services industry. But because financial services is a horizontal that affects many other sectors, we see this also as a key enabler in terms of what we call as "capacity enhancement". This year, global investment in FinTech grew by more than 70 percent from 2015 to US\$22 billion.[25] Over the next 3–5 years, cumulative global investment in FinTech is expected to exceed US\$150 billion.[26] This is unsurprising given the promise and potential of FinTech. FinTech has enabled new means of conducting financial transactions, and it has fundamentally changed the ways in which we save, borrow, invest and spend money. From alternative payment solutions to peer-to-peer lending, FinTech has helped shape a more innovative and inclusive financial system. And I think in the context of Asia, it has particular relevance and significance because when you consider the increasing dimension of FinTech, and the fact that it will make financial services more accessible, I think we can truly appreciate the potential.

3. FinTech is also a critical differentiator for Singapore to remain a leading financial hub in the region. Our finance and insurance sector has been a key growth contributor in recent years, and the future outlook for this sector will be driven in part by the growth of FinTech. Hence, we want Singapore to be a leading global FinTech hub and, to this end, the Monetary Authority of Singapore (MAS) has been exploring ways in which Singapore can establish positions of leadership in this space.

Singapore strives to be a thought leader on FinTech regulation and development

4. The right regulatory environment is central to making sure that FinTech innovations can thrive. Here, we need to find the balance. The balance between ensuring the stability and security of the financial system, and being able to provide an environment that is conducive for FinTech innovation. And that is a tension,

---

[25] Accenture Report.
[26] PWC FinTech Report.

but an important tension that we must navigate to ensure that the benefits of FinTech innovation accrue the entire system. We have therefore sought to strike an optimal regulatory balance between ensuring the financial system's safety and stability, and providing an environment conducive for FinTech innovation. This is one of the main reasons why Singapore's FinTech scene has been so vibrant, with the number of FinTech start-ups in Singapore more than doubling, from around 140 in 2015 to more than 290 today.

5. Singapore has sought to be at the forefront of regulatory thinking on FinTech, even before the term was coined as such. Take the example of mobile payments. With the recent introduction of Samsung Pay and Apple Pay, mobile payments are now a feature of everyday life for consumers. Yet, as early as 2002, MAS had already issued a consultation paper on security guidelines for mobile banking and payments. In subsequent years, this was followed by guidelines and regulations to ensure that the widespread benefits of mobile payments would not be overwhelmed by risks such as terrorist financing and money laundering.

6. Regulation has to be calibrated to be in proportion to the risk posed to the financial system. In line with this approach, MAS recently announced a regulatory sandbox to provide companies with a safe testbed to experiment with innovative FinTech solutions. This is an example of the kind of balance that we seek, and also an example of the living laboratory that Singapore can serve as. This will allow firms to provide actual products or services to customers within a well-defined space and duration. While such a sandbox would not prevent product failures, it would contain the consequential impact on customers and allow us to learn, experiment and iterate our solutions. In doing so, the sandbox will reduce regulatory friction and give innovations a better chance to take root in Singapore and beyond.

7. Besides a sound regulatory environment, the Government will also support Singapore companies in the adoption of FinTech, particularly e-payments. E-payments confer on our SMEs — whether digital or traditional in their business model —

significant productivity gains through the digitisation of business processes and greater efficiency of e-payments. Indeed, the digital economy in its broader sense is going to be a key feature of the way Singapore economy evolves and beyond that, the way we integrate across the region. We want to facilitate the entry of our businesses into the space because that means they can scale up and access broad markets almost instantaneously. In other words, companies can in fact be born global, and it means that if we have the supporting fulfilment services and payment systems, then the process of that transformation can take place much more quickly.

8. We are helping our SMEs digitise their existing business processes like paper invoice reconciliation, so that they can fully benefit from e-payments. Such digitisation requires certain levels of investment that may not yield immediate dividends. So, one of the ways in which we are helping our SMEs is through SPRING Singapore's Capability Development Grant (CDG). This grant allows our SMEs to take on large scale upgrading projects in, among other things, digitising their business processes. Moreover, the inter-agency Electronic Payments Committee has set up a taskforce to work closely with SMEs to better understand the hurdles to the digitisation of their business processes and integration with e-payments.

9. Adopting e-Payments will also help our businesses participate more actively in e-commerce, which has become pervasive in B-to-B and B-to-C transactions. The Singapore Government also hopes to be able to take the lead in developing a regional e-Payments strategy, so that companies can tap on the region's growing middle class and large consumer base through e-commerce. This will empower individuals and small businesses across the entire region who seek to serve the broad population base in ASEAN and beyond.

10. First, we will help our Singapore merchants establish strategic partnerships with major payments players with the potential to reach out to a wide network of ASEAN cities. For example, IE Singapore has been helping NETS facilitate the link-up to Alipay

to enable e-NETS as the first overseas debit payment mechanism for e-commerce giant Alibaba. Second, we will support the development of payment solutions for the unbanked in the region. This is a very important objective. Given the size and need of this segment of the population, we believe this will have both economic and social ramifications. Riding on the high levels of Internet and mobile penetration in ASEAN, we aim to enable e-commerce with those who continue to be unbanked. These initiatives will help enable e-payments in the region and create new opportunities by driving the growth of e-commerce.

11. On top of such initiatives, we recently established a dedicated FinTech Office to serve as a one-stop virtual entity for all FinTech matters as well as to promote Singapore as a FinTech hub. Besides aligning and enhancing FinTech-related funding schemes across various government ministries, the FinTech Office will propose policies to deepen industry infrastructure, talent development and manpower to meet the needs of our growing FinTech sector. Doing so will also help maintain our attractiveness as a FinTech hub to investors and entrepreneurs.

12. Such moves have given firms like local start-up FundedHere, a crowdfunding platform, the support needed to grow. We must continue to innovate and adapt our regulatory environment and overall ecosystem, so as to ensure that Singapore remains a trusted and attractive financial hub. The Government continues to keep its eye on the future, and I understand that MAS will share further details tomorrow on its plans for the next phase of development in Singapore's payment landscape.

Singapore's FinTech ecosystem

13. While the government ensures that the regulatory environment and ecosystem is conducive for FinTech innovation, industry participants also play a key role in building our ecosystem by collaborating with each other. This is a nascent space, a space that is diverse and has its challenges but also opportunities. The ability to come together to collaborate across dimensions

is key. Our FinTech industry will be enhanced by the cross-fertilisation of ideas, co-ordinated implementation and testing, and a smooth route-to-market by bringing together the strengths of an entire ecosystem of industry participants, including: technology providers, finance players, start-ups, investors, and researchers.

14. One key way in which industry participants can collaborate is in sharing their latest research, insights and ideas. Indeed, in the course of our work in the CFE, what has become apparent is we are in an area where innovation will drive growth across every sector. And yet, when you look at the innovation models, open innovation is one that is only now beginning to take hold. The reason is because innovation is inherently risky, the nature of the challenge is complex, and yet the pay-offs can be significant if it's done right. So a collaborative approach, even among competitors, makes a difference. Open innovation and collaboration even among competitors has become a defining feature of many sectors today. Even more so, in an industry as wide-ranging and multi-disciplinary as FinTech — one that spans technology, banking, insurance and many other sectors — the bringing together of fresh perspectives can catalyse cross-sector collaboration and strengthen the overall ecosystem.

15. It was with this in mind that MAS launched the inaugural Singapore FinTech Festival, which will take place from the 14th to 18th of November this year. The festival will comprise a series of back-to-back events to facilitate knowledge-sharing, networking, the making of pitches, and the sharing of ideas. This collaborative dimension and fostering of environment to bring together, even unorthodox partners in order to seek out unorthodox solutions, is a key driver in the FinTech space and in many other verticals we are looking at.

16. I would therefore encourage FinTech and financial services companies here to continue to deepen and broaden their collaborations. This applies not just to knowledge sharing, but also to other industry-strengthening moves like setting common standards and enabling the seamless sharing of data. We need

our companies to consider not just the value to their individual businesses, but also to keep in mind the broader system-wide benefits that can result from industry collaboration. In doing so, we will raise the value proposition for the entire sector.

Developing FinTech talent and capabilities

17. Another focus of our work in this sector has been to develop talent and capabilities relevant to FinTech. We must nurture a strong pool of such talent to meet the new and constantly evolving needs of the FinTech industry. In particular, it calls for individuals with cross-disciplinary expertise who can catalyse innovation in the FinTech space.

18. We are therefore looking into creating schemes to promote the development of multi-disciplinary skills through the school curriculum, work placement programmes and mid-career retraining opportunities. To this end, we must foster close collaboration between industry and our institutes of higher learning to help ensure that our graduates acquire the skills and knowledge that are relevant to FinTech. In this regard, MAS has been actively engaging our universities and polytechnics to sharpen their academic curriculum and achieve greater alignment with industry needs. For example, in 2013, the National University of Singapore and IBM launched the NUS Centre for Business Analytics, which offers a one-year Master of Science degree programme that marries business strategy and data analytics.

19. To boost the FinTech proficiency of our workforce in the financial sector, MAS is partnering IDA, the Institute of Banking and Finance (IBF) and the Financial IT Academy (FITA) to equip financial professionals with greater digital skillsets. For example, FITA is delivering a digital transformation series that touches on various topics like artificial intelligence. In addition, MAS is working with IDA to engender good placement outcomes for IT professionals in the financial sector through the Finance Committee of Technology Skills Accelerator (TeSA) programme.

20. We have also worked to equip professionals with the right sets of infocomm skills to thrive, especially in the important cybersecurity sector. Cybersecurity is already a critical issue in FinTech, with the cost of cyber-crime expected to exceed US$2 trillion by 2019. Cybersecurity capabilities are therefore critical to our FinTech players. In collaboration with the Infocomm Development Authority of Singapore (IDA) and the Cyber Security Agency of Singapore (CSA), Singtel participated in the Cyber Security Associates and Technologists (CSAT) Programme to train infocomm professionals in cyber security. Under this programme, Singtel will train fresh infocomm technology professionals and equip them with basic cyber security skills. It will also provide experienced cyber security professionals with the opportunity to enhance their skills by training with leading cyber security experts. This is part of trying to meet a need in this space because there is a global shortage, and Singapore is no exception. All these efforts will help ensure that Singapore's FinTech ecosystem gets the talent it needs to flourish.

Closing remarks

21. So let me conclude by saying that our efforts in Singapore have a few key dimensions — certainly, in the space of developing the ecosystem and fostering the collaborations; in the area of regulatory environment and other initiatives, where we create an enabling and conducive environment for Fintech innovation; and in the area of manpower development — ensuring that we have the people with the appropriate skillsets. It is a role that Government can play, but for success that is sustained and lasting in this space, we will need the private sector and industry participants to be actively engaged. We have to complement the close collaboration that we already have with tighter coordination between the public and private sector, and also the involvement of international partners. I think this is an area where there is rich promise, but considerable work needs to be done. As we've already heard, we really can't be sure which are going to be the winning technology or winning pathway, but

we do know that there is a focus to it, in terms of inclusivity and the ability to reach out to much wider unserved customer bases, and also the enhancing of competitiveness of financial services systems.

22. I urge all of you to engage fully during this forum to forge new collaborations that can take us further in the FinTech space. Government will be a strong partner in that regard, and I urge you to take full advantage of what you see here in Singapore and to give us your ideas on how we can do more in collaboration with the private sector. I wish all of you a fruitful conference, and once again congratulate SMU on a successful event. Thank you.

Appendix 8.3

"Singapore's FinTech Journey — Where We Are, What Is Next" Speech by Mr Ravi Menon, Managing Director, Monetary Authority of Singapore, at Singapore FinTech Festival — FinTech Conference, Wednesday, 16 November 2016

Ladies and gentlemen, good morning and welcome to the inaugural Singapore FinTech Festival.

- We have more than 11,000 participants from more than 50 countries, attending one or more of the many events lined up over these five days.

Technologies transforming finance

Financial technology or FinTech is transforming financial services, in a way not seen before.

- We have unprecedented *mobility*. The smartphone is becoming our bank. People can consume financial services on the go.
- We have unprecedented *connectivity*. The Internet has compressed time and space. Interaction is real-time and unconstrained by physical boundaries.
- We have unprecedented *computing power*. The devices in our hands or on our wrists are literally *pokemons* — pocket-sized

monsters that pack more data and more processing power than super computers just a couple of decades ago.

Digital payments are becoming more widespread, propelled by advances in near-field communications, identity authentication, digital IDs, and biometrics.

Blockchains or distributed ledgers are being tested for a wide variety of financial operations, to make them faster, more robust, more efficient:

- to settle interbank payments;
- to verify and reconcile trade finance invoices;
- to execute, enforce, and verify the performance of contracts;
- to keep an audit trail and deter money laundering.

Perhaps the biggest potential is in what is called Big Data. We are beginning to aggregate and analyse large data sets to:

- gain richer insights into customer behaviour and needs;
- detect fraud or anomalies in financial transactions;
- sharpen surveillance of market trends and emerging risks.

Big data is in turn being driven by advances in:

- sensor networks and natural language processing to gather information from a wide universe of sources;
- cloud technologies to store and retrieve large volumes of information at low cost and on-demand;
- learning machines and smart algorithms that can continuously adapt and improve on their decision making with every iteration.

Smart Financial Centre vision

Be it countries, businesses, or people — those who are alert to technology trends, understand their implications, and harness their potential will gain a competitive edge.

- To be sure, many of these technologies are disruptive to existing jobs and existing business models.
- But if we do not disrupt ourselves — in a manner we choose — somebody else will — in a manner we will not like.

Last year, MAS laid out a vision for a *Smart Financial Centre*, where innovation is pervasive and technology is used widely.

Since then, MAS has been working closely with the financial industry, FinTech start-ups, the institutes of higher learning and other stakeholders towards this shared vision. MAS' role in supporting this FinTech journey is two-fold:

- provide **regulation** conducive to innovation while fostering safety and security; and
- facilitate **infrastructure** for an innovation ecosystem and adoption of new technologies.

REGULATION conducive to innovation

Let me start with a couple of general principles underlying our approach to FinTech regulation.

First, we believe regulation must not front-run innovation.

- Introducing regulation prematurely may stifle innovation and potentially derail the adoption of useful technology.
- But the regulator must run alongside innovation.
- It is important to keep pace with what is going on, assess what the risks might be, and continually evaluate whether it is necessary to regulate or leave things to evolve further.

Second, we apply a materiality and proportionality test.

- This means regulation comes in only when the risk posed by the new technology becomes material or crosses a threshold.
- And the weight of regulation must be proportionate to the risk posed.

Third, we focus on the balance of risks posed by new technologies or solutions.

- Many technologies mitigate existing risks but may create new ones.
- The regulatory approach must seek to incentivise the risk mitigation aspects while restraining the new risks.

Let me illustrate our approach to the regulation of FinTech with a few concrete initiatives:

- Activity-based regulation to keep pace with payments innovations.
- Specific guidelines to promote secure cloud computing.
- Enabling digital financial advice and insurance.
- A regulatory sandbox to test innovative ideas.
- Strengthening cyber security.

Activity-based regulation for payments

Some of the most visible FinTech innovations are taking place in the payments space.

- They are making payments cheaper, faster, better — delighting consumers and giving the banks a run for their money.
- But many of these e-wallet solutions are currently caught under two separate pieces of regulation in Singapore.

MAS will streamline the licensing of payments services under a single, activity-based modular framework. This means:

- holding just one licence to conduct different kinds of payment activities;
- meeting only those regulations pertinent to the specific payments activities they undertake, rather than the full gamut of payments regulations;
- adhering to common standards for consumer protection and cyber security.

Guidelines to promote secure cloud computing

There used to be a view within some quarters that *"MAS does not like the cloud"*. Lest there be any lingering doubt, let me reiterate: MAS has no objections to FIs using the cloud.

- Cloud computing provides economies of scale, enhances operational efficiencies, and delivers potential cost savings.
- In fact, a secure cloud infrastructure is an enabler for a variety of FinTech innovations, including banking-as-a-service (BaaS) platforms.

To put its money where its mouth is, MAS set out earlier this year specific guidelines on the use of cloud services by FIs.

- FIs are free to adopt private clouds, public clouds, or a combination of these to create hybrid clouds.
- But some of the distinguishing features of clouds — such as multi-tenancy, data commingling, and processing in multiple locations — can potentially pose issues for data confidentiality and recoverability.
- And so we expect FIs to conduct the necessary due diligence and apply sound governance and risk management practices to address potential vulnerabilities.

Enabling digital financial advice and insurance

The digital offering of financial advice and insurance is becoming more popular, catering to the needs of a growing segment of technology-savvy, self-directed consumers.

- MAS' regulatory framework for financial advice is technology-agnostic.
- But we need to update it to make it easier for consumers to benefit from the lower cost and greater choice that digital advice and insurance can potentially provide.
- While at the same time ensuring adequate safeguards for these consumers.

Automated, algorithm-based digital advice on financial or investment services by robo-advisers has taken off in the United States and will soon reach our shores.

- MAS will soon set out proposals on the governance, supervision, and management of algorithms for robo-advisers to ensure integrity and robustness in the delivery of financial advice.
- We will consult the industry before finalising the guidance.

In insurance, MAS already allows insurers to offer online without advice simple term life and direct purchase policies with broadly standardised features.

- MAS will now allow insurers to offer the full suite of life insurance products online without advice.
- MAS will be issuing guidance on the safeguards to be put in place for online distribution of life insurance products.

Regulatory sandbox to test innovative ideas

In June this year, MAS launched a *regulatory sandbox* for financial institutions as well as new FinTech players to test their innovations. The sandbox serves two purposes:

- First, it allows experiments to take place, even where it is not possible at the outset to anticipate every risk or meet every regulatory requirement.
- Second, it provides an environment where if an experiment fails, it fails safely and cheaply within controlled boundaries, without widespread adverse consequences.

How will the sandbox work?

- MAS and the applicant will jointly define the boundaries within which the experiment will take place.
- MAS will then determine the specific legal and regulatory requirements which it is prepared to relax for the duration of the experiment within these boundaries.

We have received several sandbox applications since June, from FIs and FinTech players.

- The proposals leverage a range of technologies including distributed ledgers, machine learning, and big data analytics.
- MAS is reviewing the applications and looks forward to having some of these proposals launched in the sandbox soon.

Meanwhile, we will be issuing today our finalised regulatory sandbox guidelines, incorporating feedback from the industry and road-tested against the actual sandbox applications we have received.

Strengthening cyber security

A smart financial centre must be a safe financial centre.

- As more financial services are delivered over the Internet, there will be growing security and privacy concerns from cyber threats.
- Users will have confidence in new technologies and innovative services only to the extent they have confidence in cyber security.

Strengthening cyber security is therefore an important part of Singapore's FinTech agenda. MAS works closely with other government agencies and the industry to help ensure cyber-defences are robust.

- Given the interconnectedness of financial activities and systems, an effective cyber defence strategy requires close co-operation and sharing of cyber intelligence.
- A good model for such co-operation among banks in the US is the Financial Services — Information Sharing and Analysis Centre, or FS-ISAC.
- It is the global financial industry's go-to resource for cyber threat intelligence analysis and sharing.

I am pleased to announce that FS-ISAC will set up in Singapore the industry body's only cyber intelligence centre in the Asia-Pacific region.

- This centre will help our financial industry better monitor cyber threats and provide better intelligence support.
- It will also help deepen the capabilities of the cyber security community here.

INFRASTRUCTURE for an innovation ecosystem

The second key thrust of Singapore's FinTech agenda is to facilitate the infrastructure necessary for an innovation ecosystem and the adoption of new technologies.

- We need an ecosystem where people can connect and collaborate, and ideas can flow and multiply.

- We need common standards and inter-operable systems so that innovations can be scaled up quickly and their potential benefits fully realised.
- We want a hundred flowers of innovation to bloom but also want to ensure they make a garden.

To facilitate such an ecosystem, MAS started with itself:

- Last year, we formed within MAS a new FinTech & Innovation Group under a Chief FinTech Officer — probably the first regulator in the world to do so. The Group's task is to work with the financial industry and FinTech players and help foster a conducive ecosystem for innovation.
- MAS has committed S$225 million (or US$160 million) over five years to support the development of a vibrant FinTech ecosystem.
- Earlier this year, MAS and the National Research Foundation (NRF) set up a FinTech Office to provide a one-stop point-of-contact for all FinTech matters.
    - If you are a FinTech company interested in finding out what are the grants and assistance schemes available in Singapore or connecting with relevant government agencies to expedite approvals — this is the Office to go to.

Creating the infrastructure for an innovation ecosystem is a shared responsibility and joint effort. MAS plays the role of a facilitator, the real work is done by the financial industry and the FinTech community coming together to collaborate and create.

Let me highlight the exciting infrastructure initiatives underway:

- Physical spaces for collaboration and experimentation.
- Infrastructure for electronic payments.
- A national "know-your-customer" utility.
- A blockchain infrastructure for cross-border inter-bank payments.
- An open API architecture.

Physical spaces for collaboration and experimentation

A basic element of the FinTech infrastructure is having physical spaces that facilitate collaboration and partnerships among different players.

Just last week, we saw the launch of LATTICE80, Singapore's first FinTech innovation village.

- LATTICE80 offers dedicated physical space in the heart of Singapore financial district for FinTech start-ups to work, connect, and co-create with the financial industry and VC investors.

More than 20 global FIs have set up innovation centres here. You would have seen during the Innovation Lab Crawl earlier this week some of the exciting things they are experimenting with:

- digital health solutions tapping on wearable devices;
- telematics for motor insurance;
- blockchains to streamline payments;
- big data to produce customised service offerings.

MAS itself has set up an innovation lab — called Looking Glass. It aims to:

- spur collaboration among MAS, FIs, start-ups, and technologists; and
- facilitate consultations for start-ups by industry experts on legal, regulatory, and business-related matters.

Infrastructure for electronic payments: UPOS, CAS

We have a world-class infrastructure for electronic payments.

- It is a 24/7, real-time inter-bank fund transfer system.
- We call it FAST; short for Fast and Secure Transfers.
- But FAST is grossly under-utilised and Singapore is still heavily dependent on cash and cheques as means of payments.

The Association of Banks in Singapore is working on two key initiatives to make electronic payments seamless and convenient for everyone.

- First, a *Central Addressing Scheme* (CAS) that will allow you to pay anyone using that person's mobile number, national ID number, email address, or any other social media address, without the need to know the recipient's bank or bank account number.

- <u>Second</u>, a *Unified Point-of-Sale* (UPOS) terminal that will allow a merchant to accept all major card brands, including those that are contactless or embedded in smartphones.

A national KYC utility

Knowing the identity of a customer — or KYC — is one of the biggest pain points in the financial industry.

- The process is costly and laborious, and hugely duplicative.
- The pain is pervasive because KYC and identity authentication are involved in so many financial services, from opening a bank account to making a payment to making an insurance claim.
- We need an infrastructure solution to this problem.

Singapore is in the process of creating a national KYC utility.

- Now, obviously this involves several layers of identity verification depending on the purpose of the transaction, the extent of information involved, and the degree of rigour required.

The basic building block is the *MyInfo* service, jointly developed by the Ministry of Finance and GovTech, the lead agency for digital and data strategy in Singapore.

- MyInfo is a personal data platform, containing government-verified personal details, e.g. the national ID number, residential address, and so on.
- MyInfo enables residents to provide their personal data just once to the government, and retrieve their personal details for all subsequent online transactions with the government.

MAS is partnering MOF and GovTech to embark on a pilot that will expand the MyInfo service to the financial industry for more efficient KYC using trusted government collected personal data.

- No more tedious form-filling and providing hardcopy documents for manual verification by the FI.

- No more data entry errors. Higher productivity for the FI and greater convenience for customers.
- The government will run a MyInfo pilot with two banks in Q1 2017, before scaling it up to other FIs progressively.
- And beyond MyInfo, we have to think of more advanced forms of KYC for more sophisticated use cases.

A blockchain infrastructure for cross-border interbank payments

Another big pain point is cross-border interbank payments.

- Today, banks have to go through correspondent banks to intermediate these payments. It takes time and adds to cost.

MAS, the Singapore Exchange, and eight banks have embarked on a proof-of-concept project to use blockchain technology for inter-bank payments, including cross-border transactions in foreign currency.

- This effort is supported by the R3 blockchain research lab and BCS Information Systems.

Under the pilot system, banks will deposit cash as collateral with the MAS in exchange for MAS-issued digital currency. The banks can later redeem the digital currency for cash.

- Participating banks can pay each other directly with this digital currency instead of first sending payment instructions through MAS.
- This is an improvement over current large-value payment systems that are centrally operated. It strengthens resilience and lowers cost.

The banks also have the option of using the existing common payments gateway provided by BCS Information Systems to transact on the blockchain.

- The banks need not rewrite their back-end systems.
- This practical capability rides on the advances made by OCBC Bank in its recently announced inter-bank payments pilot.

This project marks the first step in MAS' exploration of ways to harness the potential of central bank issued digital currency.

- The next phase of the project will involve transactions in foreign currency, possibly with the support of another central bank.

An open API architecture

And saving the best for the end: creating an API *economy*.

- APIs, or Application Programming Interfaces, are likely to be one of the most important building blocks for innovation in the future economy.

APIs are basically a set of protocols that define how one system or application interacts with another, usually from the perspective of information exchange.

- They allow systems to interact with one another without the need for human intervention.
- Publishing these APIs allows FIs to collaborate with external users to:
  - — seamlessly merge multiple data sets from different sources into an integrated rich data set; and
  - — deliver more functional and customised solutions faster and cheaper.

MAS aims to establish Singapore as a centre of excellence for APIs on financial services.

- We are actively pushing FIs to develop and adopt APIs, and to offer as many of them as possible to the broader community.
- APIs are the essential 'plumbing' — the pipes — that enable the connections and collaborations that foster innovation.

The financial industry has come together, in partnership with MAS and the Association of Banks in Singapore, to develop guidance on APIs.

- I am pleased to announce that we will publish today what we call the "Finance-as-a-Service API Playbook".

The API Playbook provides guidance on common and useful APIs that FIs could make available. For instance:

- Many of us struggle today to track and use our rewards points on our credit cards issued by various banks before they expire.
- Imagine if the banks publish their 'rewards points' suite of APIs, a single aggregator app could be developed that allows us to enquire and redeem points directly with merchants and service providers.

The Playbook also provides guidance for the standardisation of APIs.

- The industry has come up with standards for information security, data exchange, and governance mechanisms.
- Having common standards will help promote greater data sharing and interoperability.

The API Playbook is an important milestone in our FinTech journey.

- Some of our FIs are announcing their API initiatives over the course of this week. So watch this space.
- Not to be outdone, MAS published last week 12 APIs for its most heavily used data sets. We will progressively expand the list.

Conclusion

Let me conclude by saying a few words about the larger picture behind what we are trying to do in FinTech.

We talk a lot about technology but it is really about fostering a culture of innovation.

- In an industry facing the headwinds of lower economic growth and heavier regulatory burdens, innovation must be the way to refresh and re-energise the business model.
- And innovation is not always about high-tech. It is about seeking newer and better ways to do things, about a spirit of enterprise. It is about hope in the future. The financial industry needs that.

And let us not forget the purpose of innovation. We want to create a Smart Financial Centre:

- because we want to *increase efficiency* — to do things cheaper, better, faster;
- because we want to *manage our risks better* — to keep our system safe and sound;
- because we want to *create new opportunities* — to generate growth and good jobs;
- and most of all, because we want to *improve people's lives* — to provide them better services, to help them realise their goals.

Innovative finance must be purposeful finance.

Thank you and I wish you all the best.

Appendix 8.4

List of Clusters and Industries in the Committee of Future Economy (February 2017)

Manufacturing	Energy & Chemicals and Process Construction & Maintenance
	Precision Engineering
	Marine & Offshore EDB
	Aerospace EDB
	Electronics EDB
Built Environment	Construction (including Architecture and Engineering Services)
	Real Estate CEA24
	Environmental Services NEA25
	Security MHA26
Trade and Connectivity	Logistics
	Air Transport CAAS27
	Sea Transport MPA28
	Land Transport (including Public Transport)
	Wholesale Trade IES30

Essential	Healthcare
Domestic	
Services	Education (Early Childhood, and Training & Adult Education)
Modern Services	Professional Services
	ICT and Media MCI33
	Financial Services MAS34
Lifestyle	Food Services
	Retail SPRING
	Hotels STB36
	Food Manufacturing

Agencies involved: Singapore Economic Development Board, Building and Construction Authority, 24 Council for Estate Agencies, National Environment Agency, Ministry of Home Affairs, Civil Aviation Authority of Singapore, Maritime and Port Authority of Singapore, Land Transport Authority, International Enterprise Singapore, Ministry of Health, Ministry of Education, Ministry of Communications and Information, Monetary Authority of Singapore, SPRING Singapore and 36 Singapore Tourism Board.

Source: www.futureeconomy.sg

Appendix 8.5

MAS Clarifies Regulatory Position on the Offer of Digital Tokens in Singapore

1. Singapore, 1 August 2017... The Monetary Authority of Singapore (MAS) clarified today that the offer or issue of digital tokens in Singapore will be regulated by MAS if the digital tokens constitute products regulated under the Securities and Futures Act (Cap. 289) (SFA). MAS' clarification comes in the wake of a recent increase in the number of initial coin (or token) offerings (ICOs) in Singapore as a means of raising funds.
2. A digital token is a cryptographically-secured representation of a token-holder's rights to receive a benefit or to perform specified functions. A virtual currency is one particular type of digital

token, which typically functions as a medium of exchange, a unit of account or a store of value.

3. ICOs are vulnerable to money laundering and terrorist financing (ML/TF) risks due to the anonymous nature of the transactions, and the ease with which large sums of monies may be raised in a short period of time. MAS' media release of 13 March 2014 had communicated that while virtual currencies per se were not regulated, intermediaries in virtual currencies would be regulated for ML/TF risks. MAS is currently assessing how to regulate ML/TF risks associated with activities involving digital tokens that do not function solely as virtual currencies.

4. MAS' position of not regulating virtual currencies is similar to that of most jurisdictions. However, MAS has observed that the function of digital tokens has evolved beyond just being a virtual currency. For example, digital tokens may represent ownership or a security interest over an issuer's assets or property. Such tokens may therefore be considered an offer of shares or units in a collective investment scheme[27] under the SFA. Digital tokens may also represent a debt owed by an issuer and be considered a debenture under the SFA.

5. Where digital tokens fall within the definition of securities in the SFA, issuers of such tokens would be required to lodge and register a prospectus with MAS prior to the offer of such tokens, unless exempted. Issuers or intermediaries of such tokens would also be subject to licensing requirements under the SFA and Financial Advisers Act (Cap. 110), unless exempted, and the applicable requirements on anti-money laundering and countering the financing of terrorism. In addition, platforms facilitating secondary trading of such tokens would also have to be approved or recognised by MAS as an approved exchange or recognised market operator respectively under the SFA.

---

[27]Examples of schemes falling under the revised definition of a collective investment scheme are found in Section 3 of the Consultation Paper on Proposals to Enhance Regulatory Safeguards for Investors in the Capital Markets, July 2014.

6. The types of digital tokens offered in Singapore and elsewhere vary widely. Some offers may be subject to the SFA while others may not be. All issuers of digital tokens, intermediaries facilitating or advising on an offer of digital tokens, and platforms facilitating trading in digital tokens should therefore seek independent legal advice to ensure they comply with all applicable laws, and consult MAS where appropriate.

Source: http://www.mas.gov.sg/News-and-Publications/Media-Rele ases/2017/MAS-clarifies-regulatory-position-on-the-offer-of-digital-tokens-in-Singapore.aspx

Appendix 8.6

Consumer Advisory on Investment Schemes Involving Digital Tokens (Including Virtual Currencies)

The CAD and the MAS advise consumers to be mindful of potential risks of digital token and virtual currency-related investment schemes.

Singapore, 10 August 2017... The Commercial Affairs Department (CAD) and the Monetary Authority of Singapore (MAS) have observed the emergence of initial coin (or token) offerings (ICOs), and other investment schemes involving digital tokens, in Singapore. Members of the public are advised to exercise due diligence to understand the risks associated with ICOs and investment schemes involving digital tokens.

What is a digital token?

2. A digital token is a cryptographically-secured representation of a token-holder's rights to receive a benefit or perform specified functions. One particular type of digital token is virtual currency. Virtual currencies are typically used as a means to purchase goods or services. Examples of virtual currencies include Bitcoin and Ether.
3. However, the function of digital tokens has evolved beyond a virtual currency. For example, these digital tokens may represent

ownership or a security interest over the token seller's assets or property, or a debt owed by the seller. Such digital tokens have been marketed as investment opportunities.

How do ICOs and investment schemes involving digital tokens work?

4. Digital tokens may be offered through an ICO or other investment schemes. Digital tokens offered through an ICO are usually specific to the seller, and such tokens are typically sold to consumers in exchange for a widely-used virtual currency (such as Bitcoin or Ether) or cash. These sellers often set out their business proposal in a so-called "whitepaper" which is published online.

5. ICOs and other investment schemes involving digital tokens may be structured in many ways with different business propositions. For example, they may seek to develop a new digital platform. Others may offer an opportunity to invest in a property, business, and assets, or with a promise of certain benefits or monetary returns.

What risks should consumers look out for?

6. Consumers should make it a point to understand the product. Where sellers of digital tokens fail to highlight the risks, consumers should make the effort to find out more information about the underlying project, business or assets. The risks highlighted below are worth considering but they are not exhaustive.

Risks relating to foreign and online operators

7. A consumer is exposed to heightened risk of fraud when investing in schemes that operate online or outside Singapore. As these operators do not have a presence in Singapore, it would be difficult to verify their authenticity. Should the scheme collapse, it would also be difficult to trace the scheme's operators. The recovery of invested monies may also be subject to foreign laws or regulations, which may not be the same as Singapore's.

Risks relating to sellers without a proven track record

8. The seller of digital tokens may not have a proven track record, making it hard for consumers to establish its credibility. As with all start-ups, the failure rate tends to be high.

Risks relating to insufficient secondary market liquidity

9. Even if digital tokens are tradable in a secondary market, in practice, there may not be enough active buyers and sellers or the bid-ask spreads may be too wide. Consumers may not be able to exit their token investments easily. In the worst case scenario where no secondary market develops, a consumer may not be able to liquidate his token holdings at all. The exchanges or platforms that facilitates secondary trading of digital tokens may not be regulated by MAS.

Risks relating to highly speculative investments

10. The valuation of digital tokens are usually not transparent, and highly speculative. Where digital tokens do not hold any ownership rights to the seller's assets, the digital tokens would not be backed by any tangible asset. Such tokens would be merely speculative investments and their traded price can fluctuate greatly within a short period of time. There is a high risk that a consumer could lose his entire investment amount. In the worst case scenario, the digital tokens could be rendered worthless.

Risks relating to investments promising high returns

11. Consumers should be wary of investment schemes involving digital tokens that promise high returns. The higher the promised returns, the higher the risks. High returns could come in the form of high referral commissions, i.e. promising consumers benefits for referring additional participants. In fact, such commissions would increase operating costs, which could lower the chances of achieving the returns.

Risks of money laundering and terrorist financing

12. Funds invested into investment schemes involving digital tokens are prone to being misused for illegal activities due to the

anonymity of transactions, and the ease with which large sums of monies may be raised in a short period of time. Consumers would be adversely affected if law enforcement agencies investigate any alleged illicit activities related to the token investment scheme.

Check if the person or entity is regulated by the Monetary Authority of Singapore (MAS)

13. The laws administered by MAS require disclosure of information on investment products being offered to consumers. MAS-regulated entities are also subject to conduct rules, which aim to ensure that they deal fairly with consumers. If consumers deal with entities that are not regulated by MAS, they forgo the protection afforded under laws administered by MAS.

14. To find out whether an entity is regulated by MAS, consumers can check the MAS' Financial Institutions Directory on the MAS website. Consumers can also look up the MAS' Investor Alert List for a non-exhaustive list of entities that may have been wrongly perceived to be regulated by MAS. Consumer Alerts on the MoneySENSE website also has tips on avoiding scams.

15. Consumers who suspect that an investment scheme involving digital tokens could be fraudulent should report such cases to the Police.

In a nutshell — what consumers should do before making any investment decision

1. Make sure they fully understand the benefits and risks of the product or service before committing.
2. Assess whether the features of the product or service offered meets their needs.
3. Before committing to an investment, consumers should ASK, CHECK and CONFIRM

   a. ASK the seller as many questions as they need to fully understand the investment opportunity.
   b. CHECK if the information provided by the seller on itself or its scheme is true.

c. CONFIRM before investing, the seller or its representative's credentials by using resources such as

   i. MAS' Financial Institutions Directory
  ii. MAS' Register of Representatives
 iii. Investor Alert List

Source: http://www.mas.gov.sg/News-and-Publications/Media-Rele ases/2017/Consumer-Advisory-on-Investment-Schemes-Involving-Di gital-Tokens.aspx

Appendix 8.7

Reply to Parliamentary Question on the Prevalence Use of Cryptocurrency in Singapore and Measures to Regulate Cryptocurrency and Initial Coin Offerings

QUESTIONS NO 658

NOTICE PAPER 874 OF 2017

FOR WRITTEN ANSWER

Date: For Parliament Sitting on 3 October 2017

Name and Constituency of Member of Parliament

Miss Cheng Li Hui, MP, Tampines GRC

Question:

To ask the Prime Minister (a) whether the Government is keeping track of the use/investment of crypto currencies such as bitcoin in Singapore; (b) how do crypto currencies affect our finance industry; (c) whether studies are being conducted to assess the problems and risks of using/investing in crypto currencies; and (d) whether regulatory frameworks are necessary in the future.

Answer by Mr Tharman Shanmugaratnam, Deputy Prime Minister and Minister in charge of MAS:

1. We are familiar with money, i.e., notes and coins, as a medium of exchange — an intermediary instrument use to facilitate transactions. I make a TV, sell it for money, and then use it to buy a pair of shoes. Money becomes a medium of exchange because

all of us put our trust in its reliability. The Central Bank issues these notes and coins, and makes them legal tender. Legal tender means that the medium of exchange is recognised by law to be valid for meeting a financial obligation.

2. With advancement in technology, new virtual means of payment have emerged, such as cryptocurrency, which is a form of digital token secured by cryptography. They are not legal tender. But some people put their trust in them and use them as a means of payment. Hence, Bitcoin and Ether have been adopted by people in some communities to pay one another or to pay for goods and services.

3. MAS has been monitoring the use of such virtual currencies. Their use is not prevalent in Singapore — about 20 Singapore retailers like restaurants and online shops currently accept Bitcoins.[28] This is unlike places like Japan, where the use is more popular. Likewise, in the Singapore financial industry, use of virtual currencies as a mode of payment is not significant. Trading is generally for speculative investment purposes, and the volume is low[29] compared to other countries such as US, Japan and Hong Kong.

4. Similar to most jurisdictions, MAS does not regulate such virtual currencies per se. However we regulate the activities that surround them if those activities fall within our more general ambit as financial regulator. Let me give two examples.

5. First, virtual currencies, due to the anonymous nature of the transactions, can be exploited for money laundering and terrorism financing risks. MAS is working on a new payment services regulatory framework that will address these risks.

6. A second example is fund-raising. Virtual currencies can go beyond being a means of payment, and evolve into "second generation" tokens representing benefits such as ownership in assets, like a share or bond certificate. The sale of such "second

---

[28]This is based on the directory maintained by Coin Republic of bitcoin-related businesses in Singapore (http://coinrepublic.com).
[29]Based on virtual currency exchanges data.

generation" tokens to raise funds is commonly known as an initial coin offering or ICO ("ICO"). A number of ICOs have been structured out of Singapore in recent months.

7. These are financial activities that falls under MAS' regulatory ambit. Hence, on 1 August 2017, MAS clarified that if a token is structured in the form of securities, the ICO must comply with existing securities laws aimed at safeguarding investors' interest. So the requirements of having to register a prospectus, obtain intermediary or exchange operator licences, will apply. These intermediaries must also comply with existing rules on anti-money laundering and countering terrorism financing.

8. MAS has not issued new legislation specifically for ICOs. We will continue to monitor the developments of such offers, and consider more targeted legislation if necessary.

9. Some consumers may be attracted to invest in virtual currencies and digital tokens due to their recent exponential rise in value. However, as a financial regulator, our focus is securitised interests in assets — such as shares in a company. MAS does not and cannot regulate all products that people put their money in thinking that they will appreciate in value. But recognising that the risks of investing in virtual currencies are significant, MAS and the Commercial Affairs Department have published an advisory alerting consumers to these risks, and are working together to raise public awareness of potential scams.

Source: http://www.mas.gov.sg/News-and-Publications/Parliament ary-Replies/2017/prevalence-use-of-cryptocurrency.aspx

Appendix 8.8

Project Ubin: Central Bank Digital Money Using Distributed Ledger Technology

Project Ubin is a collaborative project with the industry to explore the use of Distributed Ledger Technology (DLT) for clearing and settlement of payments and securities. DLT has shown potential in making financial transactions and processes more transparent, resilient and at lower cost. The project aims to help MAS and the industry better understand the technology and the potential benefits it may bring through practical experimentation. This is with the eventual goal of developing simpler to use and more efficient alternatives to today's systems based on digital central bank issued tokens.

Phase 1: Domestic inter-bank payments using a central bank issued SGD equivalent

MAS announced on 16 November 2016 that it is partnering R3, a Distributed Ledger Technology company, and a consortium of financial institutions on a proof-of-concept project to conduct inter-bank payments using Blockchain technology. The consortium includes Bank of America Merrill Lynch, Credit Suisse, DBS Bank, The Hongkong And Shanghai Banking Corporation Limited, J.P. Morgan, Mitsubishi UFJ Financial Group, OCBC Bank, R3, Singapore Exchange, UOB Bank, and BCS Information Systems as a technology provider to the project.

The successful conclusion of Phase 1 was announced on 9 March 2017. Deloitte was commissioned to produce a report that covers the aspects of DLT that are most suited to settlement systems and details the design principles used for the prototype. The report "Project Ubin: SGD on Distributed Ledger" will serve as an introduction to Distributed Ledger Technology (DLT), and provide an understanding of the prototype developed.

Phase 2 and beyond

MAS and its partners will be conducting research and development on queuing and gridlock resolution mechanism.

MAS plans to make available the prototypes developed, and provide opportunities for students and working professionals to gain practical experience in developing real-world applications on DLT. This could be through Hackathons organised in collaboration with Tertiary Institutions.

There will also be two spin-off projects that will leverage the lessons of the Phase 1 domestic inter-bank payments project. The first project, driven by the Singapore Exchange (SGX), focuses on making the fixed income securities trading and settlement cycle more efficient through DLT. The second project focuses on new methods to conduct cross border payments using central bank digital currency.

Source: http://www.mas.gov.sg/Singapore-Financial-Centre/Smart-Financial-Centre/Project-Ubin.aspx

http://www.mas.gov.sg/~/media/ProjectUbin/Project%20Ubin%20%20SGD%20on%20Distributed%20Ledger.pdf

References and Further Readings

Fintechnews Singapore. (November 14, 2016). First bank in Southeast Asia to use blockchain technology for payment services. Fintechnews Singapore. Retrieved from http://fintechnews.sg/6726/blockchain/first-bank-southeast-asia-use-blockchain-technology-payment-services/

TenX Whitepaper, https://www.tenx.tech/whitepaper/tenx_whitepaper_draft_v04.pdf

Chapter 9

FinTech in ASEAN

9.1 Introduction to ASEAN

For the Association of Southeast Asian Nations (ASEAN), this Chapter will cover Brunei, Cambodia, Indonesia, Laos, Malaysia, Myanmar, the Philippines, Thailand, and Vietnam. We discussed the FinTech scene in Singapore in the previous Chapter.

Historically, the original ASEAN members formed ASEAN-5 (spearheaded by Thailand, which also included Indonesia, Malaysia, the Philippines, Singapore, and Thailand) with the signing of the ASEAN or Bangkok Declaration on 8 August 1967. Brunei joined on 7 January 1984, when it got its independence from the UK.

Vietnam was the first of the remaining newer states to join ASEAN in July 1995. Laos and Myanmar joined in July 1997 and Cambodia in April 1999, completing ASEAN-10. Understandably a wide gap in economic growth and development, hence also of FinTech is evident for ASEAN-5 and the rest. Even among ASEAN-5, Brunei is strictly an oil economy without much emphasis on industrialisation and financial development. Among the CLMV,[1] Vietnam is closer to Indonesia and the Philippines in macroeconomic performance with Myanmar opening a tad faster than Cambodia and Laos. Figures 9.1 to 9.4 provide some snapshots of ASEAN as a group.

---

[1]CLMV is referred to ASEAN-4 as distinguished from older members as ASEAN-6, together forming ASEAN-10.

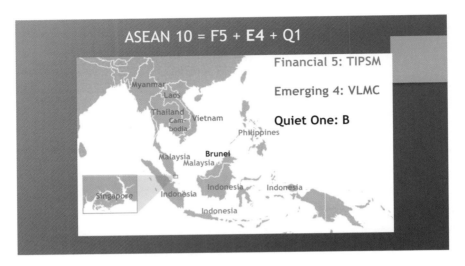

Figure 9.1. Map of ASEAN-10.

Source: By authors.

Country	Total land area	Total population	Gross domestic product at current prices	Gross domestic product per capita at current prices	
	km²	thousand	US$ million	US$	US$ PPP
	2013	2013	2013	2013	2013
Indonesia	1,860,360	248,818.1	860,849.5	3,459.8	9,467.1
Thailand	513,120	68,251.0	387,573.8	5,678.7	14,131.6
Malaysia	330,290	29,948.0	312,071.6	10,420.5	23,089.0
Singapore	716	5,399.2	297,941.3	55,182.5	78,761.9
Philippines	300,000	99,384.5	269,024.0	2,706.9	6,403.8
Viet Nam	330,951	89,708.9	171,219.3	1,908.6	5,314.7
Myanmar	676,577	61,568.0	54,661.2	887.8	3,464.4
Brunei Darussalam	5,769	406.2	16,117.5	39,678.7	73,775.0
Cambodia	181,035	14,962.6	15,511.1	1,036.7	3,081.8
Lao PDR	236,800	6,644.0	10,283.2	1,547.7	4,531.6
ASEAN	**4,435,618**	**625,090.5**	**2,395,252.5**	**3,831.8**	**9,389.8**

89% ($2.13 Tril) of GDP in Top 5

Fairly rich neighbours that are willing to help growing neighbours!

Figure 9.2. ASEAN Basic Statistics.

Source: By authors; national accounts.

USD2.15Tri of GDP for F5

	SG	MY	ID	TH	PH
Reserves (effective, USD bn)					
end-2012	364	134	104	195	87
end-2013	340	125	83	182	84
2014	309	116	97	173	79
GDP (USD bn)					
total 2012	287	305	877	366	250
total 2013	298	313	870	387	272
est total 2014	309	330	850	377	286

As a Group, they can do and grow a lot more than other Debtor Nations!

Figure 9.3. ASEAN-5 GDP.

Source: By authors; DBS Research Reports 2014.

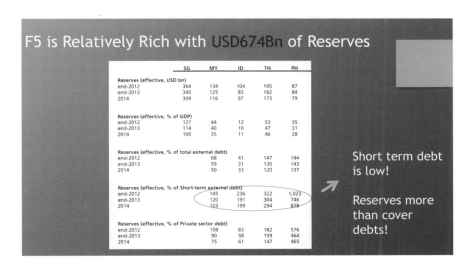

Figure 9.4. ASEAN-5 Official Reserves.

Source: By authors; DBS Research Reports 2014.

9.1.1 *ASEAN growth by inclusion*

There are great prospects for ASEAN growth by inclusion, beginning with the ASEAN Capital Markets Forum (ACMF). Formed in 2004, comprising by capital market regulators from the 10 ASEAN jurisdictions under the auspices of the ASEAN Finance Ministers, the ACMF initially focused on harmonisation of rules and regulations before shifting towards more strategic issues to achieve greater integration of ASEAN capital markets. This aim is under the ASEAN Economic Community (AEC) Blueprint 2015.

The ACMF meets twice a year, with the objective of integrating ASEAN Stock Exchanges to compete with International Stock Exchanges. In particular, it encompasses Mutual Recognition of Disclosure Standards, which aims to harmonise and equal of ASEAN Standards. Mutual Recognition of Collective of Investment Scheme (CIS) also aims to harmonise all regulations in ASEAN with its purpose to facilitate cross-border offers of retail ASEAN funds. The CIS is the manager in member jurisdictions and can offer locally constituted and authorised funds to retail investors in other member jurisdictions under a streamlined process. The initial signatories to Framework Memorandum of Understanding of CIS included Singapore (USD1.12 trillion), Malaysia (USD1.5 billion) and Thailand (USD700 million).

Since the 1997 Asian Financial Crisis which hit Thailand first before impacting Malaysia and Indonesia as the three most affected in ASEAN, the Chiang Mai Initiative was established and has been the swap arrangement among the members. It started operations as the ASEAN+3 Macroeconomic and Research Office (AMRO) in Singapore in May 2011, with the three being China, Japan and South Korea. It performs a key regional surveillance function as part of the USD120 billion of Chiang Mai Initiative Multilateralisation (CMIM) currency swap facility as established in December 2009 by the respective Finance Ministers and Central Bank Governors of ASEAN countries plus China, Japan and South Korea. On 3 May 2012, ASEAN+3 Finance Ministers agreed to double emergency reserve fund to USD240 billion.

The ASEAN Swap Arrangement (ASA) has spread to include all 10 ASEAN countries with an expanded facility of USD1 billion (reserve USD1 trillion). It has two components, namely, an expanded ASEAN Swap Arrangement and a network of bilateral swap arrangements among ASEAN countries, China, Japan and South Korea.

9.1.2 *ASEAN 2020: ASEAN banking intergration*

By 2015, the ASEAN Economic Community (AEC) with its goal of regional economic integration including, a single market and production base; a highly competitive economic region; a region of fair economic development; and a region fully integrated into the global economy, is completed. The AEC's areas of cooperation include human resources development; recognition of professional qualifications; closer consultation on macroeconomic and financial policies; trade financing measures; enhanced infrastructure and communications connectivity; development of electronic transactions through e-ASEAN; integrating industries across the region to promote regional sourcing; and enhancing private sector involvement. AS AEC 2015 concluded, ASEAN's gross domestic product (GDP) has reached USD2.5 trillion. The average GDP per capita had grown some 80% to USD4,000 in the period 2007–2014.

With the 2020 ASEAN Banking Integration Framework (ABIF) still to be completed, as the flow of goods, services, investment, capital and skilled labour between countries are liberalised with the ASEAN Economic Integration in 2015, the need arises for ASEAN banking institutions to accommodate and expand their services to a greater intra-ASEAN market.

9.1.3 *ASEAN 2025: An ASEAN currency payment system*

The AEC 2015 is followed by ASEAN 2025 aimed at one vision, one identity and one community. The ASEAN vision of integrated, peaceful, stable community with shared prosperity is to be achieved by completing the ASEAN Political-Security Community and ASEAN Economic Community, together with a Master Plan for ASEAN

Connectivity. There are ample opportunities for finance, especially
for FinTech activities to grow and develop across ASEAN-10. More
to develop would be non-banking institutions providing banking
services as FinTech implies.

Finance and monetary integration, in summary, includes capital
market development, capital account liberalisation, financial services
liberalisation and ASEAN currency co-operation. Specifically, capital
market development entails promoting institutional capacity, including the legal and regulatory framework, as well as the facilitation
of greater cross-border collaboration, linkages and harmonisation
between capital markets in the region. Orderly capital account
liberalisation will be promoted with adequate safeguards against
volatility and systemic risks. Currency co-operation would involve
exploration of possible currency arrangements, including an ASEAN
currency payment system for trade in local goods to reduce the
demand for US dollars and help promote stability of regional
currencies, such as by settling intra-ASEAN trade using regional
currencies.

Given the geographical spread as shown in Figure 9.1, we can
see the potential of ASEAN in e-commerce and therefore FinTech.
With 1% or less in e-commerce penetration as at March 2015,
there is a lot more upside in the market for FinTech. In November
2016, seven angel networks from ASEAN countries (Cambodia,
Indonesia, Malaysia, the Philippines, Singapore, Thailand, and Vietnam) formed the ASEAN Angel Alliance to promote cross-border
syndication and co-investment support, as well as intra-ASEAN
investment in start-ups, particularly tech-based companies and high
growth businesses.

9.1.4   *ASEAN financial inclusion*

At the 18th ASEAN Finance Ministers Meeting in 2015, there was
an agreement to enhance the financial inclusion system aimed to
help all people in the region to get access to financial services.
The government can play an important role to e-payments and
promote access and usage and partnership with the private sector
is the fastest and most efficient route. ASEAN will have to pay

attention to a reduction in remittance costs as they continue to stay above 7.32% globally but 8.12% for East Asia and Pacific. Remittances are defined as a cross-border person-to-person payments of relatively low value according to the World Bank. The public policy objectives may have to be in enabling safe and efficient remittance services with the payment market being contestable, transparent, accessible and sound. In January 2007, the Committee on Payment and Settlement System (CPSS) and the World Bank issued a report entitled General Principles for International Remittance Services. The report contains five general principles covering: transparency and consumer protection; payment system infrastructure; the legal and regulatory framework; market structure and competition; and governance and risk management.

Remittances can be expensive and ASEAN have many migrant workers. Lowering the cost of remittances will move more money into the hands of senders and recipients, typically migrant workers and their families. The cost of sending remittances is, therefore, an indicator of safe and efficient international remittance services and markets. Instruments such as e-money accounts, debit cards and low-cost regular bank accounts can significantly increase access for those who are now excluded from the financial system. ASEAN's gender disparity is lower than the worldwide average of 8% gap. Besides the Philippines where there are more bank accounts for female than male (34%, 19%) at a formal financial institution, the rest of ASEAN are fairly even except for Malaysia (63%, 69%), Vietnam (19%, 24%) and Myanmar (2%, 4%).

However, what is clear is that mobile payment will reduce delivery costs and expand reach into remote areas at costs well below traditional branch-based banking. Furthermore, electronic payments can enhance supply chain efficiencies through digitalisation of working capital, payment, business and global settlement. Better receivables management will bring significant benefits to small and medium-sized enterprises (SMEs) by reducing financing and processing costs of up to 5%. Interoperability is important for financial inclusion to reduce cost and inconvenience. Interoperability can be achieved through established ASEAN standards recognised globally with best practices. An open and competitive payment system is key to encouraging investment and innovation to bring about the much-needed financial integration.

In ASEAN, consumers rely on informal financial services with low financial literacy and consumers. As the number of products and complexity increase, bad decisions and bad actors can hurt financially uneducated consumers. FinTech and especially blockchain can provide another avenue to protect consumers with transparency and big data collected and reported by the central banks. With the Belt and Road Initiative (BRI), ASEAN presents great potential for inclusive FinTech that promotes greater access to financial services. Inclusive FinTech has become an enabler for economic development and will propel the financial inclusion vision. There are certainly a lot of low-hanging fruits as shown in Figures 9.5 to 9.7. Banking services are not well established in ASEAN, neither is e-commerce as the statistics show.

9.2   Indonesia

By and large, Indonesia is the largest economy and state in ASEAN, with over 14,000 islands as an archipelago and the fourth-largest population in the world. Indonesia has had impressive growth since the 1997 Asian financial crisis followed by the Global Financial Crisis of 2008–2009. While there was a decline in the poverty rate, inequality was the highest in the last half-century. The government understood that higher inequality and poverty tend to have a lower and less durable growth. According to official statistics, there are more than 11% or 28 million of the population below the poverty line. The national vision of financial inclusion in Indonesia is to achieve a financial system that is accessible by all layers of the community to promote economic growth, poverty reduction and income equality. Indonesia has a very structured financial inclusion framework that targets the very poor, working poor and near poor. They work through two channels: financial products and services (savings, credit, insurance, remittance, pension fund, mutual fund and others), as well as public finance (subsidy, fiscal incentives,

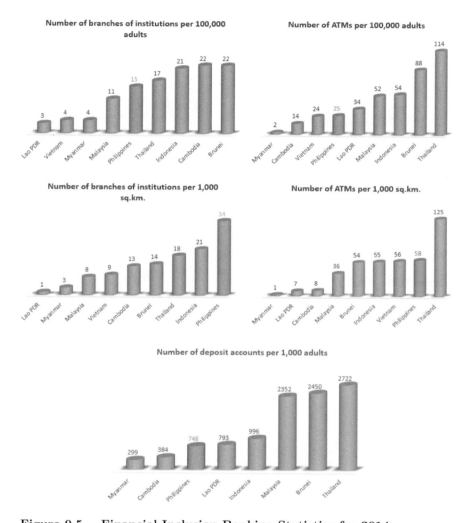

Figure 9.5. Financial Inclusion Banking Statistics for 2014.

Source: By authors; World Bank Financial Inclusion Data/Global Index.

social welfare, cash transfer health coverage "Jamkesmas" and other). The National Strategy for Financial Inclusion seeks to increase the financial inclusion index from 36% in 2014 to 75% in 2019.

President Joko "Jokowi" Widodo rolled out the 14th economic reform package including a presidential decree on e-commerce

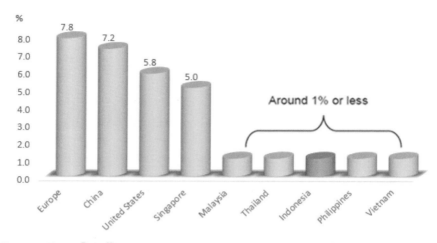

Source: Frost & Sullivan, A.T. Kearney, Macquarie Research, March 2015

Figure 9.6.   Online Retail.

Source: By authors; Frost & Sullivan; A. T. Kearney; Macquarie Research.

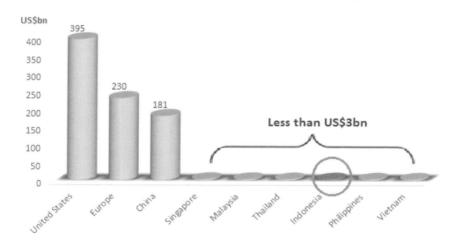

Source: Frost & Sullivan, A.T. Kearney, Macquarie Research, March 2015

Figure 9.7.   Online Retail Sales.

Source: By authors; Frost & Sullivan; A. T. Kearney; Macquarie Research.

roadmap. Similar to other ASEAN countries, funding for start-ups is a major pain point. The six solutions put forth by the Indonesian government were Crowdfunding, Micro Credit, Grants for Business Incubators, Universal Service Obligation (USO) Funds for Digital-Based SMEs, Angel Investment, and Seed Capital from Venture Capital. The USO, started on 2005 and halted in 2015, was originally provided for telco infrastructure in the rural areas charged at 1.25% (0.75% in the beginning) of telco companies' gross revenue.

The funds reached USD150 million annually with only 41% of the collected used for the core purpose of building base transceiver stations (BTSs). These were suggestions to use these funds to support the start-up industry. Indonesia's comparative role and position are clear in the following figures as self-explanatory. In Figures 9.8 and 9.9, we can see the number of Internet users and online shoppers increasing over time. They show that there are great potential for e-commerce and FinTech.

FinTech deals had picked up substantially in 2017 to 53 as compared to previous years of 21 in 2016, 11 in 2015 and only 3 in 2014 according to CBInsights. Peer-to-Peer (P2P) lending platforms have taken off with 80% of the unbanked population. The statistics for Indonesia present the most interesting picture for inclusive FinTech:

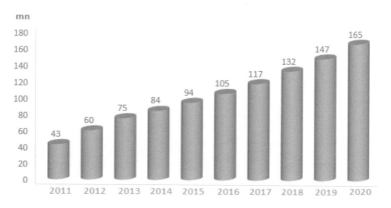

Source: eMarketer, Statista, Macquarie Research, March 2015

Figure 9.8.   Number of Internet Users in Indonesia.

Source: By authors; eMarketer; Statista; Macquarie Research.

SMEs account for 99% of enterprises, 41 million small economic units, 60,000 medium-sized enterprises, and more than 2,000 large enterprises according to Bali International Consulting Group. The loan-to-GDP ratio of 37% was the lowest in Asia-Pacific according to EY 2014 numbers due mainly to the banks being located in Java.

According to Indonesia's FinTech Association (or Asosiasi FinTech Indonesia), there were more than 140 FinTech companies by end 2016. Majority of the companies were in the areas of Payment (43%), Lending (17%) and Aggregator (13%). Personal Financial Planning and Crowdfunding form around 8% of the start-ups. Indonesia's FinTech market is booming and grew by 78% from 2015 to 2016 with 20 foreign venture capital firms buying stakes in the local FinTech scene. There were already eight FinTech start-ups officially registered with the Financial Services Authority (OJK) by June 2017. Figures 9.10 to 9.15 presents a summary of FinTech start-ups in Indonesia.

As Indonesia shifts from its old economy alongside new emerging and ASEAN as young and forward-looking in the digital economy, telecom finance in Indonesia is already appearing. Three companies in this area are Blanja with Telkom owning 60% and Ebay 40%; Elevenia with co-ownership by XL Axiata (50%) and SK Planet

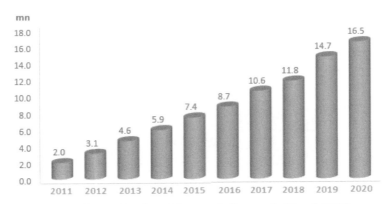

Source: eMarketer, Statista, Macquarie Research, March 2015

Figure 9.9.   Number of Shoppers in Indonesia.

Source: By authors; eMarketer; Statista; Macquarie Research.

Figure 9.10. FinTech Start-Ups in Indonesia.

Source: Fintech Singapore, http://fintechnews.sg/

Figure 9.11. Indonesia FinTech Players: Crowdfunding, Financial Aggregator/Marketplace, and Lending.

Source: Indonesia's Fintech Association; Crunchbase; Daily Social; Tech in Asia.

Figure 9.12.   Indonesia FinTech Players: Payment.

Source: Indonesia's Fintech Association; Crunchbase; Daily Social; Tech in Asia.

(50%); and Cipika, owned wholly by Indosat. These have great implications for telecom-based financial inclusion in the future.

On 6 October 2016, Financial Services Authority or Otoritas Jasa Keuangan (OJK) made the following announcement:

> In order to support the FinTech sector's development, soon the OJK will implement several plans, including:
>
> (1) Launching FinTech Innovation Hub as development and one-stop contact center for the national FinTech industry where FinTech companies can network and cooperate with institutions and agencies that support digital financial ecosystem.
> (2) Following up its agreement with the Ministry of Communication and Information Technology. For this plan, the OJK has prepared a certificate authority (CA) for the financial services sector. As the issuer of certificates that attest to digital signatures of financial services companies, CA can guarantee that digitally-signed electronic transactions are secure and have legal status that complies with the applicable provisions in Indonesia.

Figure 9.13. Indonesia Fintech Player: Personal Financial Planning and Support.

Source: Indonesia's Fintech Association; Crunchbase; Daily Social; Tech in Asia.

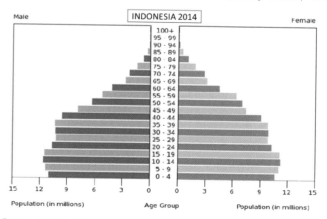

Figure 9.14. Indonesia Population Pyramid.

Source: CIA World Factbook, Macquarie Research.

Source: TechinAsia, Macquarie Research, March 2015

Figure 9.15.   Indonesia's Low Internet Penetration as Compared to Other ASEAN Countries.

Source: By authors; Tech in Asia; Macquarie Research.

(3) Providing Sandbox Regulatory for the FinTech industry. Regulations concerning this tool specify the minimum requirements that need to be satisfied, so the industry's development will be supported by the legal grounds essential for attracting investments and protecting consumer interests towards efficient and sustainable growth.

(4) Reviewing implementation of data and information security standards in relation to FinTech industry management and the need for a Reporting Center for Information Security Incidents in the financial services industry.

(5) Reviewing a Centralized Vulnerability Assessment (VA) system in the financial services industry in order to make sure that posture on, and sophistication of, dealing with information security are maintained at all times to minimize risks and threats against it.

Indonesia is huge, and standardisation will remain difficult. The plan was to introduce identity verification using digital signature methods in 2017, but few FinTech companies were ready to implement except the banks. The Debt Information System (SID) is currently not accessible to non-bank financial institutions, and the data collection capability of start-ups has also not reached the technical level of their Chinese counterparts. The red tape in implementing Financial Information Service System (SILK) by

FSA to replace SID may also present an obstacle to start-ups. The experience in China in having easy compliance for the P2P in its initial stage of developments may be something that Indonesia can benefit. As identity and credit data are collected, FinTech companies are growing in tandem.

Asosiasi Fintech Indonesia is legally registered as a non-profit industry association working to advance a technology-centric financial services future in Indonesia. Its roles are to:

(1) Act as a policy research and government relations body which helps advance an equitable and technology-centric financial services sector in Indonesia for their members;
(2) Engage actively in the financial services and technology communities in Indonesia through education, sharing, and awareness to promote and advance a FinTech agenda; and
(3) Connect with other international FinTech bodies to link Indonesia's FinTech community with the global FinTech community, ensuring best-practice, cross-pollination of ideas, and skills-sharing.

Other FinTech start-ups in cryptocurrency and blockchain are starting to grow. There are at least 11 cryptocurrency exchanges that one can have access to purchase cryptocurrencies in Indonesia. Asosiasi Blockchain Indonesia (Blockchain Association of Indonesia, or idBitcoin) appears as a special form of association for all the Bitcoin users in Indonesia with a vision to legalising the use of cryptocurrency and ensure it to be used positively in the country.

9.3 Malaysia

In Malaysia, the Central Bank Act 2009 made financial inclusion a primary function. More than 99% or half a million of business entities in Malaysia were SMEs with fewer than 13% indicating financial institutions were their main source of financing according to data in 2005. The microfinance industry grew as a result of the comprehensive sustainable microfinance institutional framework introduced in 2006. The Central Credit Reference Information System, complemented by Credit Bureau Malaysia, was the key enabler for efficient and reliable data collection and dissemination of credit information. The vision for the Financial Sector Blueprint for 2011–2020 is to enhance financial inclusion. In particular, it strives for "an inclusive financial system that best serves all members of society, including the underserved, to have access to and usage of quality, affordable essential services to satisfy their needs towards shared prosperity."

The desired outcomes are convenient accessibility, high take-up, responsible usage and high satisfaction with four broad strategies of innovative channels, innovative products and services, effective financial institutions and infrastructure, and well informed and responsible underserved. Areas underserved and unserved were mapped, and agent banking enhanced the outreach of basic financial services to rural areas. Within three years from end 2011, close to 100% of all areas were served by at least one physical financial services access point according to Bank Negara's report.

Among the middle-income countries, Malaysia recorded the highest innovation performance. There has been a strong drive to grow the FinTech sector in Malaysia. The high levels of digital adoption and Internet penetration in Malaysia also make it a potential FinTech market. Ranked fourth in global financial market development by the World Economic Forum (WEF), Malaysia has positioned itself as a future major financial centre by its proximity to a large potential customer base of international financial institutions and end users. For instance, the global Islamic financial market, which is worth about USD2 trillion, is tightly connected to Malaysia. Also, Malaysia's ambitions to develop its FinTech sector is also a reflection of the growing need to reduce its economy's reliance on energy, given that the global oil prices would remain at a lower level within a period. So it is little wonder that in 2015, Malaysia became the first nation in the Asia-Pacific countries (APAC) to regulate for equity crowdfunding.[2]

---

[2] http://www.austrade.gov.au/EventViewBookingDetails.aspx?Bck=Y&EventID =14508&m=0|0

Figure 9.16.   FinTech Start-Ups in Malaysia.

Source: Fintech Singapore, http://fintechnews.sg/

Regarding regulation, the Securities Commission Malaysia (SC) launched the "Alliance of FinTech Community" or "aFINity@SC" in September 2015 to impulse a network of FinTech stakeholders to accelerate growth and innovation in this sector.[3] At the beginning of this initiative, the SC would call for a gathering of FinTech stakeholders such as entrepreneurs, investors, innovators and relevant institutions to discuss and set FinTech agenda together. Further, FinTech start-ups could get advice and support to adapt to the current regulatory environment. Effective discussions between enterprises and relevant authorities would be guaranteed to resolve regulatory and risk concerns.

In the capital Kuala Lumpur, in 2003, the Malaysian government launched Cradle Fund to provide financial support for start-ups. Three years later, Malaysia Pre-Seed Fund was launched for the same goal. By 2014, these two funding programmes had supported more than 800 start-ups in Malaysia.[4] At this stage, the emergence and growth of FinTech start-ups are continuously backed by the

---

[3]http://www.sc.com.my/post_archive/sc-launches-afinitysc-at-world-capital-markets-symposium-2015/

[4]http://www.techtalks.ph/wp-content/uploads/2015/12/Philippine-Roadmap-for-Digital-Startups-FinalDraft_launch.pdf

funding programmes. Table 9.1 shows the three largest banks and their partners in Malaysia with various FinTech initiatives.

Maybank has cooperated with Malaysian Global Innovation and Creativity Centre (MaGIC) to boost FinTech start-ups not only in Malaysia but also in ASEAN.[5] MaGIC provides start-up services including legal advice, intellectual property consultations, company secretarial services, and visa application via its own platform. Also, Maybank serves as an advisory partner to MaGIC's Accelerator Programmes and Academy to help start-ups build viable propositions. This cooperation could boost social enterprise initiatives and also the development of FinTech start-ups in Malaysia and even the whole region.

Set up in 2016, FinTech Association of Malaysia aims to be the key enabler and a national platform to support FinTech innovation and investment. The association plays the role of creating a national platform and building an ecosystem. ACCESS Malaysia, affiliated to ACCESS Singapore, was set up in 2017 to connect with the Malaysian blockchain community. It promotes blockchain technology, fosters cooperation, conducts talks, consults government agencies and intends to set up a blockchain centre. It is clear that Malaysia has been very successful in financial inclusion and there are scopes for P2P lending and crowdfunding sectors to grow further. Its cryptocurrency and blockchain scene is beginning to come to take shape.

9.4 Thailand

The poverty rate in Thailand was 10.5% in 2014 with close to 45% of the adults with no formal bank accounts. Special financial institutions (SFIs) play a special role in Thailand as they service close to 20% of the adults. According to 2011 data, the SFIs provided 56.2% of the microfinancing with cooperatives and village funds provided 31.4%. Eight SFIs were serving mainly the middle-income group while 13,000 cooperatives and 27,000 village funds were serving

---

[5]http://FinTechranking.com/2016/01/06/maybank-magic-collaborate-to-boost-start-up-businesses-in-malaysia/

Table 9.1. **Three Largest Malaysia Banks and Their FinTech Activities.**

Banks	Partners	Programmes/ Measures	Goals	Focuses
Maybank (The Largest Bank In Malaysia)	L337 Ventures	Maybank FinTech: Aspiring innovators to showcase their ideas, and help grow and support entrepreneurs, by providing them with an avenue to connect directly with the financial industry.	To harness the start-up's ecosystem regionally, to acquire the best innovation ideas in financial technology.	Mobile Banking Payments Lending Blockchain Asset Management Humanising Financial Services Security IoT Islamic Finance Big Data
CIMB Bank (The 2th Largest Bank)	Multimedia Development Corporation, Start-upboot camp (in Singapore)	Innochallenge: Mentoring the FinTech start-ups to generate new FinTech solutions.	Aimed at the ideation and creation of new FinTech solutions.	Loyalty & Rewards Identity, Security & Document Management Using Blockchain Remittances Mobile Payments P2P Digital Wallets
RHB Bank (The 4th Largest Bank)	Start-upboot-camp (in Malaysia)	Evaluating, funding, mentoring and also organising hackathons in Kuala Lumpur. Spending 20% of their Capital Expenditure this year to execute new digital strategies.	To bring digital innovations to the banking market in Malaysia.	

Source: By authors.

the low income and poor. The regulators for the SFIs and non banks are the Ministry of Finance and Bank of Thailand with less than international standard prudential regulation, while the regulators for the cooperatives and village funds are the Ministry of Agriculture and Cooperatives of Thailand (MOAC) and National Village and Urban Community Funds Office (NVFO) with non-prudential regulation. Despite high levels of formal access to financial services, substantial pockets of unmet demand remain such as the utilisation of formal credit products, insurance, and mobile money transfers.

Like many other ASEAN countries, the challenges facing Thailand are:

(1) lack of credit information;
(2) non-comprehensive regulatory approach;
(3) financial literacy;
(4) distance barriers;
(5) government sector being the major provider;
(6) lack of private sector participation;
(7) the existence of informal sector;
(8) the fragmentation of regulatory oversight;
(9) inadequate or absence of deposit insurance; and
(10) in need of a more balance approach to prudential regulations and promoting access to finance.

There has been limited expansion by commercial banks to low-income or rural households despite the issuance of the Microfinance Guidelines for Commercial Banks by the Bank of Thailand in 2011. The 38 commercial banks are still unwilling to play a more active role leaving the SFIs to service the middle income. The demand for microfinancing remains strong, but quality microfinance services are lacking. Loan shark problems and financial literacy remain the priority, and hopefully, new regulatory bodies can be set up to spearhead the efforts to amend related laws to facilitate quality microfinance services and to implement.

However, all these challenges present great opportunities for FinTech companies such as Ant Financial, Omise and many others that serve the underserved. Both direct and indirect costs for sending money via the banking system are high, particularly for smaller amounts. Thailand's mobile phones and Internet penetration are 99% and 26%, respectively, with 99% of the population using a mobile phone and 50% for a mobile broadband-based phone (smart phone). This is likely to drive new business models for financial service delivery but will require a concerted effort in conjunction with the government-driven/affected entities (SFIs). Formal credit and insurance products include features and requirements that are inappropriate for low-income households, and these are all opportunities for FinTech start-ups.

According to United Nations Development Programme (UNDP), there are more observations regarding consumers:

(1) Proximity of access and opening hours for customers in non-municipal areas.
(2) Price sensitivities to formal credit products and high use of informal credit services.
(3) Difficulty complying with formal financial institutions' requirements, vis-à-vis proof of income, proof of residence, etc.
(4) Lack of financial literacy and financial management ability, especially in regards to debt.
(5) Lack of cheap, efficient money transfer services for both domestic and international remittances.
(6) Overly complex loan application procedures and documentation requirements which many households cannot easily provide.
(7) Lack of any legal documentation for the approximately 2.5 million undocumented migrants from Cambodia, Lao PDR, and Myanmar.

First, regarding talent, Thailand has potential raw talent that can be developed into high-performing FinTech start-ups. They have won innovative awards in some accelerator programmes. Specifically, Bangkok Entrepreneurs Co. Ltd. is an Event Management Start-up based in Bangkok. Its mission is to help SMEs and Start-ups do business, connect fellow professionals and facilitate business partnerships.[6]

---

[6]https://e27.co/3-ways-to-attract-thai-FinTech-talents-against-stiff-regional-competition-20160519/

Universities that are represented are those with natural strengths in computer science, digital disciplines and engineering (i.e., King Mongkut University of Technology Thonburi, Sripatum University). Other universities are getting into the action through developing in-house innovation hubs (i.e., Chulalongkorn University Innovation Hub) and innovation entrepreneurship partnerships with foreign universities (i.e., University of the Thai Chamber of Commerce partnership with Massachusetts Institute of Technology (MIT)).

Enough anecdotal evidence of a talent shortage in the start-up scene has prompted the launch of Getlinks — a curated hiring marketplace focused on Tech (i.e., primarily for Developers, Designers and Digital Marketers). This is further evidence of Thailand's start-up ecosystem maturation.

On capital development,[7] the Thai government endeavours to create an ecosystem that will foster sources of support and funding including incubators, venture capital, and crowdfunding. The setting up of the National Start Centre by the Ministry of Finance to compile all the start-ups, venture capitals and incubators under one roof. There are also some tax incentives or some guarantees to encourage investors.

Thai banks are also endeavouring to create new subsidiaries internally that focus on developing innovative FinTech solutions for their banks. Externally, these banks invest in local Thai FinTech start-ups through their corporate venture capital (CVC) firms.

Two local crowdfunding platforms launched in 2015: Dreamaker and Dreamaker Equity; and SinWattana. Dreamaker is a Thai-based crowdfunding platform that allows individuals or start-up companies to raise fund for their project and give back products or services in return. SinWattana is a local platform with regional ambitions, launched by the "Crowdfunding Asia" team.

---

[7]https://www.linkedin.com/pulse/startup-thailand-2016-edtech-glance-paul-api vat-hanvongse; http://embedslide.net/slide-thailand-startup-ecosystem-q1-2016-s56c2b0c558e6935e3314fea7.html; and http://www.slideshare.net/Bangkok- Ent repreneurs/thailand-startup-ecosystem-q4-2015/34-ThailandStartupEcosystemQ 42015Five_VC_Venture_Capital_Firms

The five venture capital (VC) firms based in Thailand are 500 Start-ups, ARDENT Capital, InVent, Galaxy Ventures and Inspire Ventures. The six foreign VC firms investing in Thailand are Digital Media Partners, Golden Gate Ventures, East Ventures, Red Dot Ventures, CyberAgent Ventures and Jungle Ventures. Five Thai-based incubators and accelerators are dtac Accelerate, True incube, AIS Start-up, Expara i4-x and Tech Grind.[8]

As at December 2015, there were 19 commercial banks, 12 full branch foreign banks, two finance companies and three credit foncier[9] companies registered in Thailand. The past decade has seen an influx of foreign investment in the sector, and foreign banks accounted for 22.2% of total lending at the end of 2014, compared to 12.5% in 2009. Within the commercial banking industry, corporate loans comprise 68.4% of total lending and consumer loans 31.6%.

For regulation,[10] the overall regulatory environment is good. Through its political storms, Thailand climbed two places in 2015, ranking an impressive 26th on the World Bank's "Doing Business Index". The implication is that local firms can start and operate with ease. Furthermore, in 2013 and 2014, the government made the payment of taxes less costly for companies through the reduction of the profit tax and the social security contribution rates, respectively.

At the end of 2014, the Thai Minister of Information and Communication Technology announced that the ministry would be renamed as the Digital Economy and Society Ministry. The recruitment of 700 additional employees is also part of this restructuring process.

---

[8]http://embedslide.net/slide-thailand-startup-ecosystem-q1-2016-s56c2b0c558e6 935e3314fea7.html; and http://www.slideshare.net/Bangkok-Entrepreneurs/thai land-startup-ecosystem-q4-2015/34-ThailandStartupEcosystemQ42015Five_VC_ Venture_Capital_Firms

[9]"Credit foncier" relates to real estate mortgage or a loan for a fixed period with regular repayments where each repayment includes components of both principal and interest, such that at the end of the period the principal will have been entirely repaid.

[10]http://www.oxfordbusinessgroup.com/overview/steadying-course-government-strategies-aim-keeping-sector-attractive; and https://home.kpmg.com/xx/en/ho me/insights/2016/03/tnf-thailand-foreign-business-license-no-longer-required-ban king-and-insurance.html

Thai financial regulators including the SEC and the Bank of Thailand (BOT) are moving forward with supporting FinTech initiatives and equity crowdfunding specifically. The BOT, Securities and Exchange Commission (SEC) and Office of Insurance Commission are each looking to amend rules and provide channels for new market entrants within diverse areas of the financial industry. Simultaneously, the government has launched an SME private equity trust fund to help drive capital to SMEs. The fund has been capitalised with THB2 billion.

In 2016, the new financial transactions law was then being considered by the National Legislative Assembly, and the new act will allow the BOT to supervise all business transactions of commercial banks, non-banks, and FinTech instead of having them monitored by several other ministries.

To catch up with the new trend in FinTech development in other countries, the SEC is preparing to change the landscape of business licenses within the capital markets based on four amendments. These include the structure of the business licenses, the minimum capital requirement, the qualifications of the applicant, and other monitoring regulations where further details regarding the changes will be provided in the near future.

In 2015, under the subsidiary license system, foreign banks can open up to 20 branches and 20 off-site Automatic Teller Machines (ATMs), although they must meet more stringent capital requirements than local banks. Banks are eligible if they come from countries having "significant business relations with Thailand" or those who have signed free trade agreements with Thailand. Countries offering reciprocal access to their home markets for Thai banks are also eligible.

Foreign banks in Thailand have grown their market position sharply, with notable deals including the acquisition of Thailand's fifth-largest commercial lender, Bank of Ayudhya, by the Mitsubishi UFJ Financial Group, which paid USD5.31 billion for a 72% share in 2013. Under the new licensing system implemented by the Financial Sector Master Plan Phase II (FSMP2), Australia's ANZ Bank and Sumitomo Mitsubishi Trust Bank both obtained subsidiary licenses in July 2014 and June 2015, respectively. In April 2015, Fitch Ratings announced that it expected foreign banks to continue expanding their presence in Thailand's commercial banking sector, the majority of which will be banks based in the Asia-Pacific region.

Thailand's Ministry of Commerce in February 2016 issued a regulation providing that foreign companies conducting certain banking and insurance services are no longer required to obtain a "foreign business license" from the government. The guidance is known in English as Ministerial Regulation Prescribing Service Business Not Requiring Foreign Businesses License (No. 2) B.E. 2559 (2016). Under this regulation, a foreign business license is not required for foreign companies seeking to operate:

- Commercial banking business,
- Service business as representative offices of banks,
- Life insurance business, and
- Non-life insurance business.

Still, Thai regulation does not provide an exemption from the requirements under specific laws governing commercial banking and insurance service businesses. Thus, foreign companies are still required to comply with those specific laws before operating the subject service businesses in Thailand.

Thai government's further efforts continued as in January 2016, the Thai Bankers' Association (TBA) announced it was developing a new five-year strategy emphasising five themes, including digitisation and next-generation payment infrastructure, financial inclusion, contribution to society, regional integration, and legal and regulatory enabling.[11] Under the digitisation theme, the TBA hopes to facilitate integrated development of next-generation payment infrastructure, with the target of seeing between 50% and 60% of transactions become cashless by 2020 — up from January 2016 levels of 25% — and for electronic payments to comprise between 60% and 70% of the total — up from the current 30%. Three initiatives have been planned

---

[11]http://www.oxfordbusinessgroup.com/analysis/going-digital-digitalisation-beco ming-norm-banking-sector

to help meet these targets: the development of a payment system roadmap, publication of common standards, and establishment of shareable payment infrastructure.

In February 2016, Thai financial regulators, including the SEC and the BOT, moved forward with supporting FinTech initiatives, specifically equity crowdfunding. TechSauce, a Thai start-up website, reported that regulators plan to embrace FinTech, with the BOT, the SEC and the Office of Insurance Commission planning to amend existing regulations and provide channels for new market entrants across the financial services sector.

Consider the initial undersupply of infrastructure for FinTech start-ups, it is improving a lot. For the hard infrastructure, the Thai government has started the national fibre optic broadband network, which will provide Gigabit bandwidth fibre coverage nationwide in three years. The government not only contributes to the expansion of Wi-Fi coverage nationwide but also to the public and private sector data centre and cloud infrastructure development. On the soft infrastructure side, the E-payment and E-transaction standards have been established, so as the data privacy protection and cyber-security laws.

On the demand side, according to the country's National Broadcasting and Telecommunications Commission, there were 97 million mobile subscribers in 2014 and 26 million Internet users in 2013, representing penetration rates of 144.8% and 38.8%, respectively (in a population of 67 million).[12] With mobile connections as 97 million, the mobile penetration rate is 150%. Consumers have a large appetite for online shopping and payments. Studies recommended banks increase their digital offerings through the introduction of mobile wallets, which enable smaller transactions, after which institutions can introduce more complex products.

Figure 9.17 illustrates the trend of FinTech in Thailand.

Even though FinTech is still at an early stage in Thailand, some companies have backed or launched initiatives to increase their

---

[12]http://embedslide.net/slide-thailand-startup-ecosystem-q1-2016-s56c2b0c558e 6935e3314fea7.html

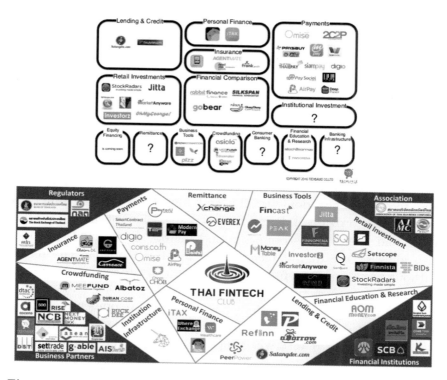

Figure 9.17.   Trend of FinTech in Thailand.

Source: Fintech Singapore, http://fintechnews.sg/; Thai FinTech Club.

interactions with the FinTech start-up ecosystem. Banks are taking a closer look at how to promote synergies, accelerate innovation opportunities and provide more digital banking services. The new technology also underlines the need for regulators to keep up with an ever-changing banking landscape. To respond to this shift in financial technology, Thai regulators, such as the BOT, the SEC, and the Office of Insurance Commission of Thailand are sharing the same concerns. Thailand's financial landscape is transforming, with FinTech a potential game changer.

The expectation from Thailand's FinTech start-ups is high with transaction value in the FinTech market amounting to USD6,464.7 million in 2016. The transaction value is expected to show an annual growth rate (compound annual growth rate (CAGR) 2016–2020) of

19.99% resulting in the total amount of USD13,401.8 million by 2020. The market's largest segment is the segment "Digital Payments" with a total transaction value of USD6,440.9 million in 2016.

On the driver of innovation, the government attaches great importance to introducing foreign banks and developing FinTech. The banking sector is also involving actively to expand its reach and digital service. FinTech start-ups are also flourishing to take advantage of the trend.

Companies like TrueMoney are licensed by the BOT to issue e-money, and their services enable customers to pay bills, send and receive money domestically, and buy TrueMove airtime. The organisation provides a digital "smart wallet" for consumers to store value and spend on e-commerce and digital products. TrueMoney also aims to use digital technologies to give people in the region without bank accounts full access to financial services to undertake transactions such as bill payment.

Another company is Mergepay involved in mobile payment and MergePay Pulse, which tracks cash flow, receipts, and other bookkeeping data points. Yet another company called Omise allows e-commerce merchants to accept credit card payments via its mobile and web interface and a suite of APIs (application programming interfaces). As seed capital, USD300,000 was raised as USD2.6 million Series A; undisclosed amount for Series B in October 2015, also for Series C in November 2015. Advantages include Mergepay being the only one that is PCI 3.0 compliant in Thailand which allows it to tokenise cards for one-click payments and ongoing subscriptions, as well as enable merchants to start their online business and facilitate trade and business, a large demand, indeed.

The star performer of Thailand has to be crypto-token OmiseGO, a token launched in 2017. Founded in 2013, Omise is a venture-backed payments company operating in Thailand, Japan, Singapore, and Indonesia, with rapid expansion plans to neighbouring countries across Asia-Pacific. In November 2016, Omise was featured on Forbes as Fintech Rockstar. OmiseGO, on the other hand, is a public Ethereum-based financial technology for use in mainstream digital wallets, that enables real-time, P2P value exchange and payment services agnostically across jurisdictions and organisational silos, and across both fiat money and decentralised currencies. Designed to enable financial inclusion and disrupt existing institutions, access would be made available to everyone via the OmiseGO network and digital wallet framework, starting in the fourth quarter of 2017.

FinTech Association of Thailand was set up with the objectives of reducing the cost of financial transactions in Thailand, increasing accessibility to financial products and services for Thai people, and supporting Thai FinTech start-ups to compete and expand to global market. It intends to set up a National FinTech Sandbox and build an ecosystem for globalisation.

9.5   Vietnam

The Central Bank or The State Bank of Vietnam has partnered the World Bank Group to implement a national financial inclusion strategy since 2016. Digital finance is the focus with an emphasis on shifting government payments digital and providing financial services to the rural, agriculture and ethnic minorities. Financial literacy and consumer protection are keys to financial inclusion. Only one-third of the population has access to formal banking according to Global Findex database. According to the World Bank, these are now the priorities of the Vietnamese government with the State Bank of Vietnam being the lead agency for financial inclusion:

(1) The Ministry of Finance (MOF) to facilitate the transformation of overall government payments and reform of the Vietnam Bank for Social Policies (VBSP) towards more market-based principles.

(2) The Ministry of Information and Communications (MIC) to facilitate the development and regulation of mobile payment solutions.

(3) The Ministry of Labor, Invalids and Social Affairs (MOLISA) for government to people payments.

(4) The Ministry of Agriculture and Rural Development (MARD) for extending financial services to rural and agricultural communities.

(5) The Vietnam Women's Union (VWU) to leverage their strong network of women's groups and micro-loan programs.

(6) The Ministry of Education and Training (MOET) for financial education in the school curriculum to produce a new generation of more financially savvy and confident consumers.

(7) Representatives of the private sector, including FinTech companies and agribusinesses.

Among the ASEAN-4 as CLMV, Vietnam since its *doi moi* has caught up almost as fast and well as some in ASEAN-6. FinTech start-ups in Vietnam are among the most dynamic in synchrony given its strong entrepreneurial base and environment. Bitcoin, crowdfunding, mobile phones and all other features of FinTech are among its many applications with a relatively young cohort of millennials. The country is as large and diverse for the growing expansion of innovative financial services (see Figure 9.18)

Vietnam is a land of promising potential with many mobile payments start-ups (see Figures 9.18, 9.19 and 9.20). The features of such Vietnamese FinTech start-ups are

(1) It serves a large and young population of over 90 million people with the majority of the population living in rural and remote

Digital Vietnam - Jan. 2017

Population	94.93 M
Internet users	50.05 M
Social media users	46.00 M
Mobile connections	124.7 M
Mobile social users	41.00 M

Source: We Are Social, Hootsuite, Jan 2017

ASEAN^{up} *Empowering business in Southeast Asia - aseanup.com*

Figure 9.18. Vietnam with a Large Internet and Social Media Population.

Source: We Are Social; Hootsuite.

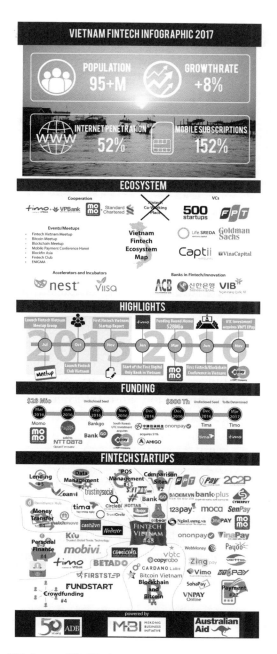

Figure 9.19. Vietnam FinTech.

Source: Fintech Singapore, http://fintechnews.sg/

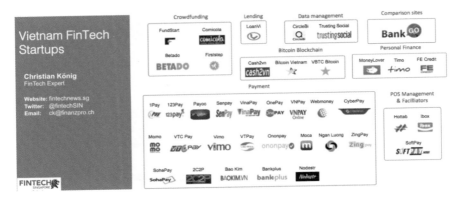

Figure 9.20.   Fintech Start-Ups in Vietnam.

Source: Fintech Singapore, http://fintechnews.sg/

areas. With little or no access to banks, or financial services
mean the infrastructure as in information and communications
technology (ICT) for mobile phones have to be a prerequisite.

(2) It follows that with the concomitant low penetration of banking
and financial services, much education and publicity for the
proper use of FinTech services have to be launched.

(3) It is the availability and affordability of mobile phones, and
access to telecommunication and Internet services require as
much investment, both hard and soft. With a high penetration
of mobile phones, relatively good and reliable Internet access is
as important as all be affordable.

Vietnam has a good number of cryptocurrency and blockchain
companies (see Figures 9.19 and 9.20) and in terms of developers,
it has a good base that many have tapped from the region. Given
its large population, underdeveloped financial inclusion space with
qualified technology professionals, the potential is understated.

9.6   Philippines

The Office of the President issued Executive Order No. 208 on
2 June 2016 to institutionalise the Financial Inclusion Steering
Committee (FISC), the governing body that provides strategic

direction, guidance and oversight of the National Strategy for Financial Inclusion (NFI). The Central Bank or the Bangko Sentral ng Pilipinas drives the NSFI with 14 other government agencies. The aims are to align various financial inclusion policies and programmes; to ensure effective monitoring of the progress of initiatives; and to collaborate with public and private sector stakeholders on various agenda that fall under its focus areas. The approach is very systematic with a tactical plan to facilitate the identification of complementarities and synergies, measurement of progress and results, and partnerships and stakeholder support. The Philippines views on financial inclusion can be summarised as follows.

(1) Financial inclusion is a state wherein there is effective access to a wide range of financial products and services by all.
(2) Effective access does not only mean that there are financial products and services that are available. These products and services must be appropriately designed, of good quality, and relevant to lead to actual usage that can benefit the person accessing the said product or service.
(3) Wide range of financial products and services refers to a full suite of products and services (savings, credit, insurance, payment, remittance, investment) for different market segments, particularly those that are traditionally unserved and underserved.

Besides the interbank account-to-account fund transfer system enabled by the Electronic Payment and Clearing System, a new interoperability system allows consumers to pay anyone with a bank account or e-money account electronically. I-SIP (Financial Inclusion, Financial Stability, Financial Integrity and Consumer Protection) research methods were applied in selected financial inclusion-related policy to determine whether positive linkages were optimised and negative linkages or trade-offs were managed. New research on virtual currencies, crowdfunding, big data analytics and digital customer identification were initiated.

In the Philippines, the use of micro-banking offices (MBOs) is important to serve the rural areas. There were 540 MBOs operating in 338 local government units in 2015, of which 66 cities and

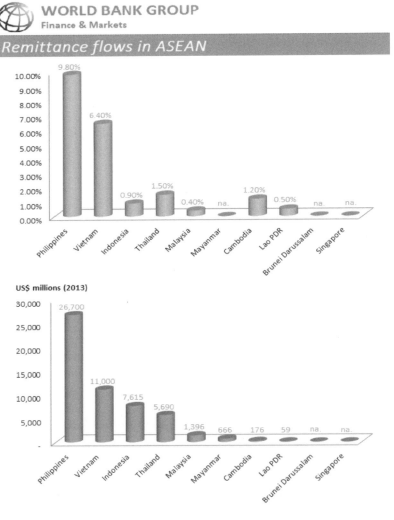

Figure 9.21.   The Philippines Top Remittance Flows in ASEAN.

Source: World Bank Group.

municipalities were being served by MBOs alone. Out of 652 banks, 39 banks are using a non full-blown bank MBOs. MBOs have been growing at annual rate of 22% since 2011.

The Philippines is top in remittances as shown in Figure 9.21.

With the experiences of both Spanish and American colonisation, the Philippines can reach its potential economic growth and FinTech development when the government picks up speed with reforms and job creation. There are more than remittances which flow back home. The Filipino returnees will bring along their experiences working overseas, from the Middle East to other ASEAN states, as well as Hong Kong, together with business and social networks. FinTech definitely is part and parcel of that package to jumpstart the Philippines.

Figure 9.22 shows the depth of the FinTech start-up ecosystem with many well-known names. Payment is one area that the Phillipines had a head start because of its large population of migrant workers. The cryptocurrency and blockchain start-ups started to flourish in 2013 in line with payments and other financial inclusion needs.

Figure 9.22.   The FinTech Start-Ups in the Philippines.

Source: Fintech Singapore, http://fintechnews.sg/

9.7   Myanmar

Figures 9.23, 9.24 and 9.25 show the financial scene in Myanmar with ample opportunities for payments, savings, credit and insurance as FinTech activities. However, problems in Myanmar are well known: capital constrained regulated the retail sector and product constrained low-quality financial product sector. Access to financial services is low as only 30% have access to formal financial services. The vision of the Central Bank of Myanmar is "By 2020, Increase Financial Inclusion in Myanmar from 30% to 40%, More than one product from 6% to 15%, with full range of affordable, quality, effective and responsible financial services by getting all stakeholders to work together in an integrated manner."

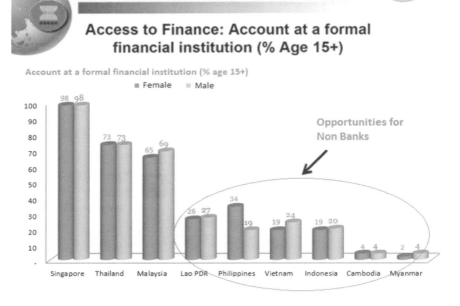

Figure 9.23.   Central Bank of Myanmar: Access to Finance in 2014.
Source: By authors.

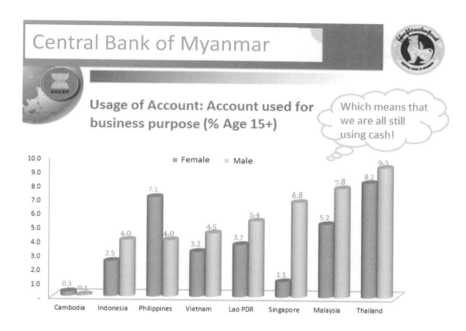

Figure 9.24. **Usage of Account in Myanmar in 2014.**

Source: By authors.

Myanmar faces many challenges such as a weak regulatory environment, cash-based economy, weak saving culture, low trust in the formal system, inappropriate and insufficient products, capital constraints, limited accessibility, weak institutions, absence of infrastructure and lack of hard infrastructure. However, these challenges can be viewed as opportunities as this is one country that has few legacy systems and historical silo structure that plague other well-developed financial centres. More than half the debts are sourced informally, and that presents an opportunity for digital finance for more transparency. According to UNDP's 2015 report, 42% of the 5 million farmers used credit to deal with agri-related risk.

Given that agriculture forms the backbone of the economy with half the population in agriculture, micro, small, medium enterprises (MSMEs) are critical for economic development, and low-income households are important for poverty reduction, the priorities are

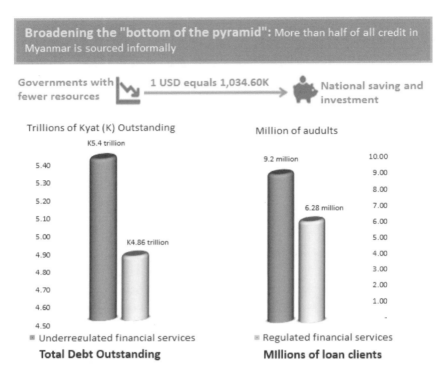

Figure 9.25.   Broadening the Bottom of Pyramid in Myanmar.
Source: By authors.

in these three areas. These present great opportunities for FinTech to facilitate efficient payments, micro-savings, as well as responsible credit and micro-insurance. Most people use informal ways to save (e.g., gold), to borrow (e.g., friends and money lenders) and to transfer money (e.g., traditional agents).

The trend of FinTech in Myanmar and its general landscape may revive with its banking system having long existed, but behind a wall.[13] Many of its largest banks are internationally blacklisted due to the economic sanctions. Further, 97% of the population has no

---

[13]https://www.linkedin.com/pulse/yes-you-can-FinTech-change-what-tradition al-burmese-banks-gueguen-1

bank accounts. Great opportunities exist for FinTech in Myanmar, but that is still at a very initial stage.

There have been many improvements in the regulation, with the announcement of the rules for mobile money operators. However, so far, there is no policy regulating the overall payment ecosystem. There are a lot of grey areas, which give space to unregulated activities such as hundi (unofficial remittance system). Another issue is talent. There is limited local know-how in Myanmar, and it is still difficult to attract foreign talents. Capital is also limited. There is the Myanmar VC Club but funding is still coming from Foreign VCs and Singapore. Last, the financial system in itself is still under development: KYC is still not mandatory for telcos and money providers for instance. Myanmar has, since the beginning of 2016, its clearance system, a stock exchange market and a payment system. However, these infrastructures take time to be fully constructed.

Regarding expectation of Myanmar's FinTech start-ups, its financial services industry has begun a significant transformation with the explosive growth of mobile and Internet penetration. Mobile operators, partnering with banks, are best placed to expand the reach of financial services in Myanmar to those that are unbanked today, leveraging the significant distribution networks that are already in place.

As Myanmar continues its transition, it is critical that financial inclusion remains a priority and that industry-wide collaboration occurs to develop business models that will be sustainable and beneficial to the financially excluded. The government is playing an important role in ensuring that the right regulatory model is put in place to allow for mobile operators and subsidiaries to provide these services.

Agent banking has been identified as an effective vehicle to drive true financial inclusion driven by rapid mobile penetration rate with telcos expecting to cover 90% of the population within the next three years compared to 10% in 2013, along with innovative financial technologies. The country is in the middle of a positive economic transition and its market widely regarded as the last true frontier filled with real opportunities.

Challenges have been identified as follows, awaiting the right responses. There is a lack of basic infrastructure in general, and

FinTech infrastructure, in particular, to kick-start in a country with at least five power cuts per day and low Internet connectivity. There is also a lack of customer awareness and trust in technology where education will be key. Also, FinTech should be simple, at least initially, as better to walk before the industry can run.

A nascent financial system is where Western FinTech has been built on top of existing old systems. Burmese FinTech has to start everything from scratch. Equally lacking is a limited talent pool. Burmese FinTech talent is, so far, a scarce resource. However, some "tech hubs", such as the Yangon MICT Park (and to a lesser extent the Mandalay's one) might well be the future hubs for appealing fresh and innovative spirits.

On the financial side, a limited capital pool is where VC funds are popping up in the US and family offices are investing in the Indian FinTech scene, but funds are still limited in Myanmar. However, foreign investment, through local partnerships or joint ventures (JVs) might be a good solution.

Accordingly, Myanmar must rid itself of strong regulatory barriers.[14] The Central Bank of Myanmar is working to regulate e-money providers. However, the regulation regarding digital currencies, crowdfunding, or even outbound international remittance is still to be debated. The strict regulation of foreign investments might also limit the entry of successful foreign start-ups.

A driver of innovation responding to a real need for efficient payment solutions and financial inclusion is missing. Also, the fast development of mobile penetration which is being seen as opportunities for telcos, global banks and investors needs to be reckoned with.

As for companies,[15] there is Telenor Myanmar which is partnering with Yoma Bank to offer mobile banking, with the aim of providing

---

[14] https://www.linkedin.com/pulse/yes-you-can-FinTech-change-what-traditional-burmese-banks-gueguen-1

[15] http://crossroadsmyanmar.com/focus/future-banking-myanmar-online-banking-and-challenges-lie-ahead; http://qz.com/48250/creating-online-banking-in-myanmar-a-country-with-little-of-either/; https://e27.co/FinTech-myanmar-gets-boost-new-e-commerce-payments-platform-20150224/; http://www.leotech.com.sg/

basic financial services. While the sector was dominated by a state-owned monopoly Myanma Posts and Telecommunications, two international mobile operators — Norway's Telenor and Qatar's Ooredoo — have been issued licenses. They will compete with two state-owned operators — Myanma Posts and Telecommunications (MPT) and Yatanarpon Teleport Co. Ltd. (YTP). Mobile networks enable customers to use their mobile wallets to gain access to basic banking services. The launch of Wave Money to drive financial services for the unbanked is welcomed, since it will start with money transfer, an important on-ramp feature to raise active usage in a nascent country. Other innovative payment models in the works include Myanmar mobile money and myKat, as well as local app MyCHAT, which is planning to enable mobile payment on its social chat.

Since 2013, more than 177 microfinance institutions (MFIs) had received a license from the Myanmar Microfinance Supervisory Enterprise to operate and this number has continued to increase. These are likely partners for FinTech companies that utilise blockchain and other Internet of Things and devices on the ground. Most of them are tiny organisations with less than a thousand clients, and MFIs have a chance to reach significant scale if the technology is available to them. The largest operator, PACT Global MFIs, is serving over 500,000 clients and has worked in Myanmar since 1997. ACLEDA Bank has also received licenses to operate as MFIs with other global champions such as BASIX and ASA Microfinance are expected to follow soon.

In July 2013, the Central Bank of Myanmar became autonomous from the Ministry of Finance after the Law of the Central Bank was passed in government. A key responsibility of the central bank is overseeing payments and mobile banking. The priorities are probably in the areas of electronic payments, low-cost savings products, agriculture input credit, unsecured credit, insurance products for

---

myanmar-FinTech-collaborations-no-exclusives/; http://www.FinTechasia.net/why-mobile-financial-services-matter-for-myan/; http://blogs.accion.org/features/FinTech-in-myanmar-leapfrogging-to-mobile-money/; http://FinTechnews.sg/FinTech-events-singapore/

health and funeral, as well as insurance products for credit, especially in the agriculture sector.

According to the Consultative Group to Assist the Poor (CGAP), UNDP started funding microfinance projects in the mid-1990s and was followed by several other agencies through the Livelihoods and Food Security Trust Fund (LIFT). Bilateral agencies such as Department for International Development (DFID) and United States Agency for International Development (USAID) are supporting financial inclusion. The World Bank Group (International Finance Corporation (IFC) and the World Bank) are supporting the regulatory framework and good practices in the industry. United Nations Capital Development Fund (UNCDF) has been present in Myanmar since 2012 with MicroLead Expansion, CleanStart and Shaping Inclusive Finance Transformation focusing on Green Energy, Financial Inclusion and Women. In Chapter 8, we mentioned Sentinel Chain and Infocorp that has operation in Myanmar to tokenise livestocks. Since most farmers have digital devices and livestocks, blockchain is a promising technology for financial inclusion. This may be a viable token project to leapfrop the Myanmar financial sector. Making unregulated activities transparent using inclusive blockchain technology will enable the sector to take off. All these are catalysts for inclusive FinTech!

9.8   Cambodia, Laos, and Brunei

9.8.1   *Cambodia*

In 2016, only 13% of adults in Cambodia had bank accounts with less than 4% with savings, a situation very similar to Myanmar as a new emerging player. However, it has 100% of the population with mobile phones with 4G coverage with 70% having a National ID. So far, none of the mobile money service providers offer saving products, and none of the MFIs have been able to develop an extensive network of agents to facilitate micro-deposits. Wing, Metfone, BanhJi, Bongloy, Smart Axiata and Asia Wei Luy are some notable FinTech companies in Cambodia.

Wing (Cambodia) Limited Specialised Bank provides mobile banking services such as local money transfer, phone top-ups, bus payment, bill payment and remittances. It has more than 5,000 Wing Cash Expresses. ANZ (Australia and New Zealand Banking Group Limited) launched Wing commercially in 2009 with a support of AUD1.5 million from the Australian government's Enterprise Challenge Fund. ANZ sold Wing to Logistics, the parent company of Refresh Mobile, in November 2011. With 7,000 airtime voucher sales agents, these became the Points of Sales. Wing Mobile is the leading mobile payment provider in Cambodia. Associations with ANZ and Refresh Mobile have enabled Wing to grow. With an established retailer, trust and brand building have been much easier for growth. There are 600,000 transactions per month and 600,000 registered accounts. Hoffman (2013) provides an excellent perspective of the success factors and lessons from Wing in her report for the Enterprise Challenge Fund.

MePhone is telecom operator with 50% market share with e-money as the platform for money transfer, payments, phone top-ups and payroll services. Metfone and MB Bank jointly operate e-money.

BanhJi Accounting is a free open platform that allows third-party localised accounting applications. It helps customers comply with local accounting, tax, and other related regulations for SMEs. BanhJi offers API to partners to develop a vertical solution for industry-specific needs that is fully integrated with their core accounting modules. Nine core accounting modules (Customer, Suppliers, Inventory, Employee, Cash, General Ledger, Service, Management Report and Tax Module) are offered free to SMEs to perform all related accounting transactions and prepare financial reports by a country-specific accounting standard. The software uses standard HTML5, Javascript, and CSS with Amazon Web Service providing scalability for its application. Data storage by Amazon RDS MySQL and PHP accesses data from AWS RDS. It provides the data back to front end application via AJAX in the form of JSON. The front end consumes and displays the data via Javascript, CSS and HTML.

Bongloy is a flexible API-based payment solution for merchants and works with most Stripe's open source plugins. It allows for local and international payments and is flexible enough for building marketplace, mobile app, online storefront or subscription service.

Smart Axiata is a mobile service provider with 8 million subscribers that provides payment, insurance, loan and other services with Smart Pay, Smart Hospital, Smart Insurance, Smart Music and other mobile services. Smart Axiata is part of Axiata Group Berhad, one of the largest telecommunications groups in Asia with over 300 million customers across 10 countries. Since September 2016, its 4G+ or LTE Advanced covers more than 98% of the population in 25 key provincial capitals in Cambodia.

Asia Wei Luy is a mobile payment service provider that allows individuals and businesses to transfer, settle bill payment, top up phone credits and provide loan services. TrueMoney is a mobile payment provider in Cambodia that enables customers, who are typically "un-banked", to access financial services using their mobile phone and/or the TrueMoney agent network (Terminal POS). Figure 9.26 is the FinTech start-up map of Cambodia.

9.8.2   *Laos*

Laos has a small and young population of 7 million but its GDP growth is over 7%. Half its population is under the age of 25, with one-third of the population living in urban areas. According to We Are Social's statistics, Internet penetration stands at 20% with an unbanked population of close to 60%. Penetration of cell phones is at 85%. The only FinTech solution is offered by Banque Pour Le Commerce Exterieur Lao (BCEL) with a secure online payment system for its merchant customers. It has developed a mobile application, BCEL One, to facilitate cardholders' payments and transaction inquiry through mobile or the Internet. The commercial bank, BCEL, and a mobile network operator, Unitel, are working to start mobile money operations in which people can deposit money to a network of agents of Unitel who will convert it into e-money and send it to distant locations. Thailand's Superrich currency

Figure 9.26.   Cambodia FinTech Start-Up Map.

Source: Fintech Singapore, http://fintechnews.sg/

exchange platform is attempting to offer a digital platform for foreign exchange, cash transfers and payment services.

Farming remains the main source of income, and all financial activities are conducted through the informal network of friends and family. Financial literacy, insurance coverage, savings, transactions, and remittances are keys to financial inclusion. As for FinTech, the small population is a major disadvantage for Laos.

9.8.3   *Brunei*

In February 2017, Autoriti Monetari Brunei Darussalam (AMBD) had undertaken several initiatives to encourage the growth of FinTech companies and launched AMBD's FinTech Sandbox or a virtual facilitation office. The FinTech Regulatory Sandbox Guidelines was also introduced during the event, a guideline which will allow FinTech companies to test their financial products or solutions safely and efficiently while receiving regulatory support from AMBD.

9.9   Stability and Financial Inclusion

There have been various articles written about the negative correlation between financial stability and financial inclusion. FinTech, if applied successfully with the transparency of data and new credit rating methods, may just turn the correlation to positive.

Lagua (2017) has argued:

> Basel III, for example, will provide regulations by way of stricter standards on banks on the levels of capital they maintain. The regulations will improve the quantity and quality of bank capital through mandated capital ratios. It will also redefine what constitutes core (or Tier 1) bank capital and redefine bank liabilities and risk management standards. Liquidity coverage and funding ratios are tweaked to increase capital and improve liquidity, problems that were encountered in previous financial crises.

> While stability is enhanced, the cost of raising capital for small business could be affected. The higher capital ratios and compliance costs, together with the higher cost of capital, will impact the viability of smaller banks. Small banks are more inclined to serve and lend to small business entrepreneurs. This is attested to by the banking community's compliance with the mandatory lending provisions of the Magna Carta for SMEs, where the thrift banks and rural banks are reported to be most compliant in the micro and small business segment. Regulations that will require banks to assign higher risk weights to small businesses will serve as a disincentive to servicing this sector. Customization of loans to a small business' unique needs also suffers in the process because of the higher costs of doing business. In general, Basel III effects on lending to small businesses are generally expected to be disproportionally negative.

The argument put forth is that a liberal approach to financial inclusion ignoring the moral hazard issue will eventually lead to a crisis because there is a tradeoff between stability and inclusion. Cihak, Mare and Malecky (2016) further comment that financial stability and financial inclusion are negatively correlated and thus are linked more through tradeoffs than synergies. They also argue that rapid increases in credit to previously informal firms that enter the formal sector should be monitored for potential threats to financial stability. The argument hinges heavily on the issue of borrower's creditworthiness as well as the relaxed attitude towards granting credit rapidly. However, these arguments did not take into account what has been achieved in China where many of the technology-based firms are based. Ant Financial has employed artificial intelligence (AI), cloud, and data to achieve a low default rate of less than 1%. Big data, facial recognition, and AI have changed the business of lending. Default rates vary across female versus male, consumer versus business, and many other factors. Some new digitised concepts such as those of Infocorp.io that digitises cows using chips and blockchain may be a cheap way to securitise livestock with access to global capital. This will lower the borrowing rates as previously MFIs had difficulties in securing the livestocks for low-risk lending. Working hand in hand with MFIs, there is also a better chance of ensuring the digital identity of borrowers which will reduce moral hazard issues. Whatever, these are new areas of inclusive FinTech that can change behaviour and perhaps can address the moral hazard issues that plague the microfinancing industry. While for the individual borrower's perspective of better behaviour leading to lower borrowing rates, the supplier of credit is not merely a supplier of single financial services as he or she may be able to move beyond a single product to take advantage of the economies of scope.

The technology start-ups may view the digitalisation for financial inclusion in a very different way as written in InfoCorp's website:

> There are 5 elements in addressing the financial inclusion problem. Firstly, there must be a way to create safe and secure store of value, i.e. an account. Secondly, there must be a secure and trusted way for funds to be transferred between accounts. Most mobile payment wallet applications are designed to address the first two elements. The next two elements are the ability to borrow without credit history, and the ability to grow their money through savings and investments. The final element is the ability to protect one's assets through insurance. The key to achieving these goals is driving adoption of technologies that enable these 5 elements and InfoCorp aims to create a financial service delivery mechanism that can unlock financial access for the unbanked.

Economies of scale with economies of scope raise the profitability and margin. Digitalisation and tokenisation reduce the risk of both borrowers and lenders. Disintermediation, democratisation and decentralisation increase reach globally and liquidity. It may worth thinking whether technology improvement can solve some of the pain points that traditional financial inclusion approaches cannot. We have no verdict but it is worth thinking out of the box as technology is available for such applications:

> Despite obvious poverty in the informal sector, even those who live in slums possess far more capital than anyone realizes. These possessions, however, are not represented in such a way as to make them fungible assets. "Dead capital" therefore cannot create value for the poor. For instance, the rural population mainly consists of agricultural micro-entrepreneurs and smallholder farmers whose only asset could be a single cow in their farm. But with titles, shares and property laws, people can go beyond looking at their assets as they are — livestocks locked up as an illiquid asset — to imagining what they could be: things like security for credit to start or expand a business.[16]

> Blockchain gives us a set of tools to begin building solutions, because one of the most powerful features of this technology is that it enables us to recapture "dead capital" — for example, a farmer's cow.

> Blockchain technology has the ability to provide asset tokenization, which means that ownership of illiquid asset can be fractionalized and partially traded for liquidity and also give the unbanked the ability to manage livestock assets, because it is decentralized by nature. In addition, blockchain provides an unparalleled framework to improve the system of property right registrations for such assets. The key factor to achieving a flawless execution of managing livestock assets must first address the problem of provenance and attestation of ownership. The word "provenance", when applied to livestock, refers to the ability to provide an authentic trail of ownership history of the livestock. Attestation refers to the ability to provide evidence to support a claim, for instance, that the livestock truly belongs to that particular individual. The best path to resolving this is setting up an appropriate incentive model and tracking method for the transaction process.

9.10   Conclusion and the Growth Pyramid

ASEAN-10 is a diverse grouping comprising a relatively more developed and mature set as ASEAN-6, with the rest which joined later as emerging and transitional economies. With its equally vast and

---

[16]It is Hernando de Soto's term for an asset that cannot easily be bought, sold, valued or used an investment (de Soto, 2000).

diversified population and demography, ASEAN-10 is as propitious for FinTech activities. The long-term prospects are well identified in various ASEAN plans from the AEC2015 to ASEAN2025.

Even the short-term catalysts for ASEAN-5 (excluding Brunei) are clear. There is relatively abundant cheap money in the region with loose monetary policy. Even for oil dependent Indonesia or Brunei, weak oil prices prompt going into FinTech activities with low interest rate. Policy shifts to economic inclusion including wealth distribution and social safety nets are as evident as many consumer financial staples to be served. The policy shift to social inclusion requires infrastructure building and construction. With the policy shift to financial inclusion, shadow banking needs to be reckoned with care. The newer ASEAN members have the luxury of growing their economies by serving the 70% underserved in their own countries and others in the rest of ASEAN-10. Figure 9.27 highlights some recent analysts' calls for the key drivers of ASEAN markets indicating that inclusive growth may be coming from the bottom of the pyramid.

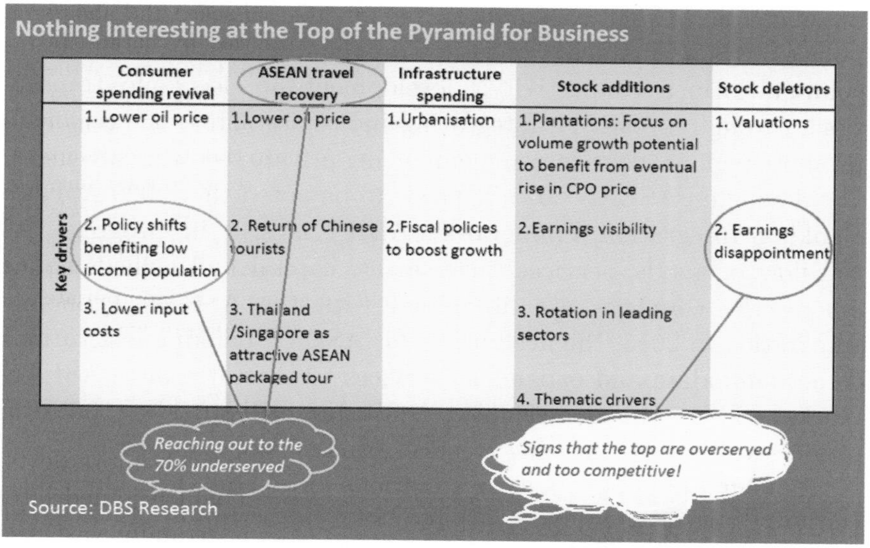

Nothing Interesting at the Top of the Pyramid for Business

	Consumer spending revival	ASEAN travel recovery	Infrastructure spending	Stock additions	Stock deletions
Key drivers	1. Lower oil price	1. Lower oil price	1. Urbanisation	1. Plantations: Focus on volume growth potential to benefit from eventual rise in CPO price	1. Valuations
	2. Policy shifts benefiting low income population	2. Return of Chinese tourists	2. Fiscal policies to boost growth	2. Earnings visibility	2. Earnings disappointment
	3. Lower input costs	3. Thailand /Singapore as attractive ASEAN packaged tour		3. Rotation in leading sectors	
				4. Thematic drivers	

Reaching out to the 70% underserved

Signs that the top are overserved and too competitive!

Source: DBS Research

Figure 9.27. Signs That Sustainable Growth for Business Is at the BoP.

Source: By authors.

Over the longer term, ASEAN-5 will be strengthening their relationships beyond ASEAN-10 to reach out to other parts of the Asian region like China, India, Taiwan, Korea and Hong Kong but excluding Japan. Of course, Japan is a traditional and active partner, and as Japan climbs out of its recession, it will be much welcomed. ASEAN-10 has a lot more going at the bottom, that is, the newer ASEAN members as CLMV to grow. By the way, Vietnam wants to tout itself as part of the growth cohort comprising Philippines and Indonesia abbreviated as VIP rather than as CLMV as the former projects faster growth, having joined ASEAN in 1995 and is more dynamic than CLM.

From AEC2015 to ASEAN2025, it is an achievement by itself. The ASEAN Economic Community as the goal of regional economic integration by 2015 is characterised by having a single market and production base; a highly competitive economic region; a region of balanced economic development; and a region fully integrated into the global economy. The areas of co-operation include human resources development; recognition of professional qualifications; closer consultation on macroeconomic and financial policies; trade financing measures; enhanced infrastructure and communications connectivity; development of electronic transactions through e-ASEAN; integrating industries across the region to promote regional sourcing; and enhancing private sector involvement.

Moving on ASEAN 2025, it needs to be noted that 2020 ASEAN Banking Integration Framework (ABIF) is still in progress. As the flow of goods, services, investment, capital and skilled labour among the countries are liberalised with the ASEAN Economic Integration in 2015, the need arises for ASEAN banking institutions to accommodate and expand its services to a greater intra-ASEAN market. Thus, the non-banking institution as providing banking services will be an emerging trend as FinTech companies.

As China puts out its clear ambitions in its One Belt, One Road (OBOR)[17] project, coupled with its Asian Infrastructure Investment

---

[17]We shall use OBOR and BRI interchangeably here. OBOR has now been renamed as BRI (Belt Road Initiative).

Bank (AIIB) policy, ASEAN-10 will not only have more businesses, including FinTech with China, both OBOR and AIIB can be tied up with ASEAN's Master Plan on ASEAN Connectivity (MPAC).

In ASEAN-10, the governments and private sectors are working on the Internet Plus policy with China's FinTech companies as WeChat and Alipay, as well as the emergence of the electronic Renminbi using blockchain. The three Ma's, Peter Ma (马明哲) of PingAn Insurance, Pony Ma (马化腾) of Tencent and Jack Ma (马云) of Alibaba, formed the ZhongAn Insurance Company way back in 2013. They have not only succeeded in disrupting the banks, insurance companies, credit rating agencies and supply chain financing but have also begun to have their presence felt in ASEAN and beyond. Now, Jack Ma has also accepted Indonesia's invitation to be the e-commerce advisor. The Chinese are good at scaling and serving people in remote areas and expanding their businesses in ASEAN.

To most people, technology is about the disruption of brick and mortar businesses; it is about displacing existing jobs; it is about confrontations with policy makers; it is about causing chaos in a well-behaved society; it is about getting rid of centralised control. However, to China, it is an Internet Plus policy. Thus, ASEAN leaders must mull over three essential questions.

First, with the growth of the likes of Wechat, ZhongAn, Ant Financial and other scalable technology companies, how can we change the mindset of our people so that we can also embrace digital openness, inclusiveness, decentralisation, lighter regulation and especially China's Internet Plus ways of doing business?

Second, how would ASEAN take advantage of China's OBOR and AIIB, including their related technology impact to grow the ASEAN economy and jointly and severally? These questions are food for thought as we probe in this volume.

A third issue which may or may not bear much rumination as politically sensitive, but has immense implications as opportunities within ASEAN is clearly the pace of economic development and financial technology development. This reflects the original ASEAN-6 (Brunei, Indonesia, Malaysia, Philippines, Singapore and Thailand) and the rest ASEAN-4 (Cambodia, Laos, Myanmar and Vietnam) as joining to make ASEAN-10. Even within ASEAN-4, Vietnam is noticeably ahead.

The implication is that while financial technology and all forms of modern information communications technology (ICT) are the digital way forward in the 21st century when it comes to money matters, trust is imperative. How the more rural sectors and financial transactions may still be based on trust and face-to-face interactions have to be carefully and conscientiously brought into all gimmicky and modern digital devices and paperless ways of doing business. That ASEAN still has large rural areas and population to exploit must be in tandem with financial technology as in vogue in their urban counterparts. Time will tell if the ambitious experiments using latest inclusive technology, such as those of InfoCorp's Sentinel Chain, can leapfrog the developing economies in ASEAN.

Finally, what is more interesting is the recent comment by Nobel Laureate and State Counsellor of Myanmar Aung San Suu Kyi. In her speech in November 2016, she said that "In 20 year's time, Myanmar will have overtaken Singapore." (See Figure 9.28.) Such a statement will only make sense if Myanmar can bypass all the hard infrastructure and political issues and leapfrog (see Figure 9.29).

At the beginning of Singapore's independence, the then Prime Minister Lee Kuan Yew said that in 20 years' time, Singapore would have caught up with Burma

"I think we have to change that a bit and say: In 20 years' time, Myanmar will have overtaken Singapore."

Aung San Suu Kyi,
30 Nov 2016,
IE Singapore's Global Conversations business dialogue
http://www.channelnewsasia.com/news/singapore/myanmar-hopes-to-overtake-singapore-economically-in-20-years/3330330.html

Figure 9.28.   A Bold Statement by a Nobel Laureate.

Source: Channel NewsAsia, http://www.channelnewsasia.com/news/singapore/myanmar-hopes-to-overtake-singapore-economically-in-20-years/3330330.html

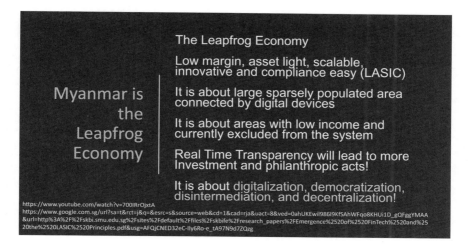

The Leapfrog Economy

Low margin, asset light, scalable, innovative and compliance easy (LASIC)

Myanmar is the Leapfrog Economy

It is about large sparsely populated area connected by digital devices

It is about areas with low income and currently excluded from the system

Real Time Transparency will lead to more Investment and philanthropic acts!

It is about digitalization, democratization, disintermediation, and decentralization!

https://www.youtube.com/watch?v=700IRrOjxtA
https://www.google.com.sg/url?sa=t&rct=j&q=&esrc=s&source=web&cd=1&cad=rja&uact=8&ved=0ahUKEwiI986I9KfSAhWFqo8KHUi1D_gQFggYMAA&url=http%3A%2F%2Fskbi.smu.edu.sg%2Fsites%2Fdefault%2Ffiles%2Fskbife%2Fresearch_papers%2FEmergence%2520of%2520FinTech%2520and%2520the%2520LASIC%2520Principles.pdf&usg=AFQjCNED32eC-IIy6Ro-e_tA97N9d7ZQzg

Figure 9.29.   The Leapfrog Economy.

Source: By authors; Google, https://www.youtube.com/watch?v=700IRrOjxtA; https://www.google.com.sg/url?sa=t&rct=j&q=&esrc=s&source=web&cd=1& cad=rja&uact=8&ved=0ahUKEwiI986I9KfSAhWFqo8KHUi1D_gQFggYMAA& url=http%3A%2F%2Fskbi.smu.edu.sg%2Fsites%2Fdefault%2Ffiles%2Fskbife%2 Fresearch_papers%2FEmergence%2520of%2520FinTech%2520and%2520the%252 0LASIC%2520Principles.pdf&usg=AFQjCNED32eC-IIy6Ro-e_tA97N9d7ZQzg

Thus the term Leapfrog Economy for ASEAN has a special meaning in the China's Belt and Road Initiative. With Singapore as the Chair of ASEAN in 2018, financial inclusion and leapfrog economy may just be the uniting factors for the 10 countries.

References and Further Readings

Channel NewsAsia. (November 30, 2016). Myanmar hopes to overtake Singapore economically in 20 years' time: Suu Kyi. Retrieved from http://www.channel newsasia.com/news/singapore/myanmar-hopes-to-overtake-singapore-econom ically-in-20-years/3330330.html

Cihak, M., Mare, D., & Melecky, M. (2016). The Nexus of Financial Inclusion and Financial Stability: A Study of Trade-offs and Synergies. Policy Research Papers, World Bank Group. http://documents.worldbank.org/curated/en/ 138991467994676130/pdf/WPS7722.pdf

De Soto, H. (2000). The Mystery of Capital: Why Capitalism Triumphs in the West and Fails Everywhere Else." New York: Basic Books.

Fintech Singapore. http://fintechnews.sg/

Lagua, T. B. D. (2017). Financial inclusion and financial stability. BusinessWorld Online. Retrieved from http://www.bworldonline.com/content.php?section =Opinion&title=financial-inclusion-and-financial-stability&id=139313

Mariano, T. (2016, August 22). How Bitcoin is disrupting Southeast Asia's remittance industry. Inc. Southeast Asia. Retrieved from http://inc-asean.com/editor-picks/bitcoin-disrupting-southeast-asias-remittance-industry/?utm_so urce=newsletter&utm_medium=email&utm_campaign=newsletter_fintech

Chapter 10

Regional Trends
and FinTech Future

10.1 Introduction

Generally and globally, the big actors are the US and China,
perhaps India due to its sheer population base and accelerating
digitalisation outpacing that of Japan. Even small, open Singapore
establishing as a FinTech hub is a necessity as noted by the
speeches from Minister for Trade and Industry (Industry) S Iswaran
and Monetary Authority of Singapore (MAS) Managing Director
Ravi Menon, Budget announcements, as well as the report by the
Committee on the Future Economy which identified the economy as a
growth node.

As noted in Japan, FinTech as evolving in creative innovations
is not the problem holding innovative Japanese banks. Instead, the
issue lies with regulation and the culture of consumption based
on cash-on-delivery. In sharp contrast, China with its Alipay and
WeChat is taking FinTech like a duck to water. Whether Chinese
consumers will be big spenders like the Americans or remain savers
as in traditional Japanese psyche and culture, has much to morph
with demographic changes — keeping in mind China and Japan both
as ageing.

10.2   Regulation and Monetary Policy

Government legislation and regulations can be viewed from two perspectives as quite diametrically opposing. On one hand, various countries have shown that it is not any fear of FinTech as an innovation that is the cause for any slow take-up or progress. It is more to do with changing mindset, existing laws and regulations to enable FinTech to develop and grow.

On the other hand, given the nature and characteristics of FinTech as seen in its decentralised payments as opposed to existing centralised systems of payments as in credit cards issued by banks, is there a need for regulations pertaining to FinTech? With bitcoin and other cryptocurrencies in circulation, how would their usage affect monetary policy upheld by central banks and MAS in Singapore? Other challenges like money laundering using physical cash and FinTech cryptocurrencies also enter the fray of the legality of transactions, safety and security.

Since the Global Financial Crisis, with interest rates as zero or even negative as in Japan, monetary policy as a tool for macroeconomic stabilisation is obfuscated. In fact, as the world awaits economic recovery to some positive economic growth to allow interest rates to be raised to some positive figures, it is as prescriptive as also to enable monetary policy to return as a policy tool.

As the FinTech/financial cluster expands, what are the other regulatory challenges? Business models, banking and financial models change in parallel. Serving the unbanked with greater financial inclusion remains an imperative, both economically and as noble as it gets. On the flipside, would there be more occurrences of financial globalisation and financial crises?

10.3   Digital Disruption Revisited

What can FinTech Venture Capital (VC) investments tell us about a changing industry and indeed, a changing way of payments and way of life? Very telling is a finding that China roared while the rest of the West continued to evolve in FinTech in 2016. Have Western FinTech leaders wilted as the Chinese dragon roared and what this portends?

As important is China in the first Digital Disruption GPS report in March 2016, would its financial earthquakes be worth watching and minding? In a follow-on report in January 2017,[1] Citi GPS followed the money trail of VC and corporate investments to revisit the theme of the Chinese FinTech as Chinese dragons roar at home and expand overseas. The main conclusion is that the rise of the Chinese dragons reflects a unique combination over the past decade. Into the mix is incredibly rapid digitisation, simultaneous rise of the Chinese mass middle class, plus poorly prepared incumbent financial institutions (as well as regulations). All are facing off against entrepreneurial e-commerce and social media ecosystems. Thus, unsurprisingly, China accounted for over 50% of total FinTech investments globally in the first nine months of 2016. It was the only major region where FinTech investments increased in 2016 (in fact doubling in China in the first nine months of 2016 versus the same period in 2015).[2]

More than a "new kid on the block", there are ways as different the Western FinTech evolution versus China's roar of FinTech dragons. In essence, the West had the US pivoted to InsurTech in 2016 with two of the largest US FinTech VC funding rounds in the health insurance space for that year. The emergence of Big Data, the Internet of Things (IoT) and wearable devices, among other trends, will help insurance companies use FinTech to be more creative and customised. The InsurTech focus remains more to improve distribution efficiency and user experience, as with applications of Business-to-Consumer (B2C) FinTech in general. As lending remains, including Peer-to-Peer (P2P) lending as a vast opportunity, the lines defining financial and non-bank financial activities become more blurred or in a word, inclusive.

That the trend is especially rapid and heady in China and emerging markets where financial inclusion remains the key driver, concerns are as global and across all interlinking industries. Whereas

---

[1]Study by Citi GPS: Global Perspectives & Solutions, January 2017 (pdf file). https://www.privatebank.citibank.com/home/fresh-insight/citi-gps-digital-disruption-revisited.html

[2]https://www.itwire.com/business-it-news/business-intelligence/76564-china-ove rtakes-us-in-fintech-investment-report.html

China and elsewhere in ASEAN, Latin America and Africa require accessing underserved clients, the contrast is sharp as in the US about serving others as sub-prime/near-prime with credit card debt consolidation plan. Lending accounts for about 80% of 9 million 2016 VC FinTech investments ex-US, but if Asia is excluded (basically China data), then the share of lending drops to sub-30%. Moreover, in the developed world, Europe remains a laggard for start-ups/VC investing at about 10% of global FinTech VC investment in 2015–2016.

China is again the forerunner in the B2C world. From 2017, we have seen many Chinese FinTech companies expanding outside their home market. Whether strategic or like Chinese budget hotels[3] following their compatriots travelling abroad to better serve and cater to Chinese tastes, this is indeed the "Blue Ocean" for Alipay and WeChat to tap, just as China was a decade ago as the factory of the world in goods.

Not to be dismal, as the Chinese dragon roars, would these dragons also in and of themselves be a source of financial disruption and crisis, just as the made-in-US subprime mortgage turned Global Financial Crisis was, with the Renminbi getting as globalised too? This will happen even if by default as more Renminbi entering the global system with China kick-starting its very ambitious One Belt, One Road (OBOR) or renamed as Belt and Road Initiative (BRI) together with its Asian Infrastructure Investment Bank (AIIB) as similar to the World Bank and Asian Development Bank in finessing infrastructure.

The BRI covers the whole continental length from China to Europe, traversing Central Asia and the Middle East and also reaching the tip of North Africa. It covers ASEAN too connecting roads as well as ports in its maritime section. China makes it clear that the BRI and AIIB are two separate projects, though in practice it is a brilliant two-in-one idea. While the AIIB's role in the financing of BRI is only growing with other Chinese SOE banks in a larger dominant role, the potential for AIIB in BRI is equally clear.

---

[3]Financial Times, 7 February 2017. https://www.ft.com/content/a87defcc-e36f-11e6-8405-9e5580d6e5fb.

What about Jack Ma's idea of building a huge Hinternet across the entire world? A Hinternet that consists of sticky customers on the net is the ultimate for any FinTech company. A Hinternet that collects all data and has access to all information of those "residing" on it.

In the words of Jack Ma:

> The greatest difference between the Belt and Road Initiative and general globalisation lies in the inclusion of young people, women, smaller enterprises and developing countries. It aims to reach more people. This is both a responsibility and an opportunity.

> Last year I spent more than 820 hours travelling all across the globe to gain insight into the world. It is important to be there, observe and think. We want to do something different. Instead of simply selling our products to Belt and Road countries or importing cheap labour and raw materials, we want to create jobs, stimulate overseas economies and improve people's livelihoods.

Ma's words echo those of Chinese President Xi Jinping who spoke at the economic forum in Beijing, saying:

> We have no intentions to meddle in the internal affairs of other countries via bringing our social system and the development model, or by imposing our will (on other states).[4]

With the slowdown and clamping down on Internet finance companies in China, these companies may have to grow more aggressively with BRI, and it will be interesting to see how FinTech will change the livelihood and societal structure of the region.

10.4 Are ASEAN Banks Ready to Be Digitally Disrupted?[5]

Whereas Automated Teller Machine (ATM) created a financial buzz in the 1960s, it was only introduced in Asia in the 1980s as in Singapore in 1979, Malaysia early 1980s, Indonesia 1979, Thailand

---

[4]https://www.sott.net/article/351158-Jack-Ma-highlights-difference-between-One-Belt-One-Road-and-western-trade-schemes

[5]DBS Group Research. Equity Regional Industry Focus: ASEAN Banks, 14 April 2015.

1983 and the Philippines 1981. Then came Internet banking catching up in the 1990s.

With FinTech it is next phase of mobile banking, a smartphone. Aided and abetted by ICT, with near field communication (NFC) speed and ease will further be pushed up. In ASEAN, Singapore and Malaysian banks have been leading, with banks in Indonesia, Thailand and the Philippines as slower and more traditional.

More to the point is that FinTech is quintessentially a disruptive technology, way of payments and way of life as FinTech goes into non-bank financial services including insurance as a start. The whole FinTech cluster is morphing with financial inclusion as the all-purpose aim as well as territorial confines to conquer in all forms of P2P, Business-to-Business (B2B), B2C and other decentralised modalities and business models.

10.5   Technology and Education for the Future

While this book has aimed and tried to tease out the evolving FinTech scenes by country and ASEAN as a region, there are still more uncharted and evolving areas to be done as future research. A more ready and needy area is in technology and education for the future with FinTech in mind.

For the millennials defined as the new generation since the new millennium in the 2000s (21st century) as one equipped with technology, mobility and seeped as never before, already some USD2.2 billion were raised for Millennials Fintech in the form of start-ups, SMEs and others as financial inclusion across the board. FinTech enterprises as Level Money, Homeslice, Hello Digit, Acorns, Even, Qapital, Moven, Osper, Loyal3, Motif, Robinhood, Kapitall, Tip's Off, DriveWealth, Openfolio, eToro, Stox, TradeHero Venmo , Square, CommonBond, SoFi, Upstart, Affirm, Earnest, Vested, Vouch, Pave, Tuition.io, Valorie, Wealthfront, Betterment, LearnVest, Sigfig, Personal Capital, WiseBanyan, Rebalance IRA, FutureAdvisor and their kind, may not yet possess Technology and Education for the Future and be household names as big banks.[6]

---

[6]https://www.cbinsights.com/blog/fin-tech-startups–millennials/

In the US, FinTech start-ups located in Silicon Valley were discussed (Chapter 5). Putting that together with the massive hoards of Chinese students studying all levels and all fields in US universities, they are bound to pick up the Silicon Valley's flavour of FinTech incommensurate. With China already powering ahead in FinTech, the second-largest economy by GDP after the US, one wonders whither China goes, whither the US goes even if this is not a direct game or competition between the two economic superpowers?

Figure 10.1 speaks for itself. If there were 100 million Chinese between ages 18–23, roughly 500–700 million from this age group as a cohort would demand for education. About 523,700 Chinese

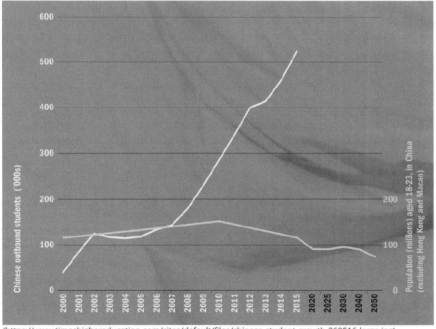

(https://www.timeshighereducation.com/sites/default/files/chinese-student-growth-260516-large.jpg)

Sources: National Bureau of Statistics of China, British Council, United Nations

Figure 10.1. Chinese Student Growth.

Source: National Bureau of Statistics of China; British Council; United Nations.

students were studying abroad in 2015.[7] Of the over half a million students studying abroad, 25,900 were funded by the government, 16,000 by employers and 481,800 by their own expenses (parents). Equal percentages were in business and management (20.2%) and engineering (20.2%) with agriculture at the lowest (1.3%).

Chinese students form the largest foreign group in both the US and the UK (as top 10 countries). Australia has an even higher concentration of Chinese students. In time, Chinese returnees will outnumber outbound students and the former will demand jobs, at home or abroad.

In contrast, US universities and colleges are shrinking with budget cuts. FinTech firms are not the subject of the US Fed's student loan rules. They offer crowdfunded loans at lower-than-average rates as FinTech firms make up an economic industry using technology to make financial services more efficient. Even Amazon has teamed up with Wells Fargo Bank in student loan business. Other FinTech companies in the business include Student Loan Hero, Gradible, Achieve Lending, LendKey, and Credible.

On the flipside, student debt may be the next crisis facing elderly American parents, in contrast to Chinese parents' ability to afford their children's overseas education. However, the number of international students mainly from China0 may be nearing its peak to impact US universities' enrolment and finance — another form of disruption.

10.6   Rivalry, Cooperation or Competition?

Traditional sectors and companies, including high technology ones in the Silicon Valley, are facing new relationships with their FinTech counterparts.[8] Just as Silicon Valley has disrupted or even upended some traditional industries within the US, a flurry of FinTech start-ups as seen together with other related technology entrepreneurs are the "new kids on the block". To pose some threat to even a

---

[7]Reported in Xinhua, 17 March 2016.
[8]See for instance, https://www.nytimes.com/2017/02/22/business/dealbook/silicon-valley-tried-to-upend-banks-now-it-works-with-them.html?src=me

part of the business of the big banks can be considered as some form of cannibalism. For instance, old jobs disappear as robotics and digitalisation take over as counter staff.

Such challenges, including those from financial start-ups, are not uniformly faced across the global landscape. As noted China seems to be leading in FinTech, where the technology company Ant Financial has grown to 450 million users since it was spun off from the e-commerce giant Alibaba in 2014. Ant Financial dominates in the processing of a majority of online payments in China as it is an electronic, phone-based wallet serving other financial business services for Chinese consumers. It offers online loans, insurance and investment advice to China's hundreds of millions of customers.

By 2017, CB Insights noted that China had four of the five most valuable financial technology start-ups in the world. Ant Financial led with a market share of USD60 billion. For China, its investments in financial technology rose 64% in 2016 in contrast to a fall of 29% in the US (CB Insights, 2017).

Even Africa's financial industry has been shaken up by the rise of new forms of mobile phone-based payment systems as in M-PESA in Kenya (Chapter 1). M-PESA was started by a local mobile phone operator instead of a bank. It has risen to become the dominant form of payment in Africa, that is, jumping some steps compared to others as in China or ASEAN. Nonetheless, compared to the US with the majority of Americans with access to many financial products over time, financial start-ups in Africa and China have not attained the same level of American growth.

Whether such start-ups evolve into banks is yet another matter. For the time being, banks with the ability to create money, accept deposits and disburse loans, coupled with the money multiplier effect, are vital tools for monetary policy. Increasing or decreasing money supply by this crucial role of banks enables central banks to implement expansionary and contractionary monetary policies accordingly. Unless otherwise changed and regulated, payment companies do not perform this money creation or destruction role in monetary policy. This is an important point and distinction to note.

FinTech as cryptocurrency is by nature not part of monetary policy as money supply.

How, when and why the financial landscape may or should change is beyond mere speculation. What matters is the government's role as the gatekeeper in affecting macroeconomic stabilisation as well as the microeconomics of the nature of certain firms and industries.

Online banks and payment companies can play their complementary and supplementary roles or establish some partnerships as the nature of FinTech continues to morph. They can be as differentiated as serving different market segments and customers in different areas as rural or urban, and at different stages of growth and development of countries. All juggle with operating costs, economies of scale and scope and what governments ultimately want. Managing financial crises with financial globalisation as lethal has been proven as hard and challenging in the Asian and global financial crises.

In conclusion, the following may serve as some policy directions:

(1) **FinTech payment companies currently cannot do without banks** as banks collect deposits from people and lend out money for investment as part of money creation and monetary policy. Central bank's policy such as the one in China to allow for payment companies to be part of the system will take away the monopoly of the banks to control who should own an account with central banks having more information of FinTech customers.

(2) **Governments around the world will not let FinTech companies be unregulated**, no matter what benefits of decentralisation may offer as against traditional centralised banking. However, central banks need to have a grip on what can and what cannot be regulated. Decentralised system, while can be controlled through shutting down power or slowing down access, is inherently difficult to monitor, let alone to control and regulate. In the case of P2P with disintermediation with smart contract, it is challenging for the regulator to control the Internet or white spaces. WWW that may now stand for the Wild Wild West and control may have been lost without regulators

even knowing. Net neutrality remains a contentious issue for governments. The war between setting up a Great Firewall to block access and the use of VPN (Virtual Private Network) will be more intense, and the war between centralised authority (in governance, technology and services) versus decentralised network (in storage, transaction, privacy, legality) will escalate.

(3) **China and Africa have taken off in FinTech via smartphones because they did not have the institutional setting** as traditional banks evolving in the US and elsewhere have.

(4) **Accidents are always waiting to happen**, including in the financial sector and managing a financial crisis by central banks, whether centralised or decentralised financial systems will remain imperative with financial globalisation happening apace with FinTech.

(5) **Least of all, with heady FinTech in China, its tools for handling any financial crisis may be sorely tested**, with detritus littered globally just like the Global Financial Crisis. This is a sobering thought.

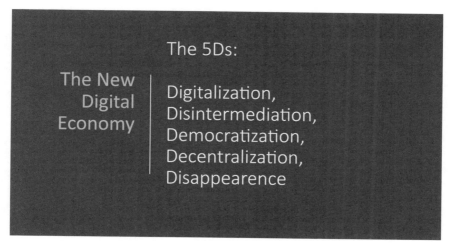

Figure 10.2.   The 5D's.

Source: By authors.

It is only through Diminshing oneself that a well prepared community will grow into a much bigger pie for all including the orginal facilitator!

Figure 10.3.   Diminishing Oneself: The Fifth D.

Source: By authors.

Finally, in Figures 10.2 and 10.3, the 5D's of FinTech is what makes blockchain companies and projects different. The first 3D's, Digitalisation, Disinternmediation and Democratisation are practised by many Chinese FinTech companies. But without the fourth D, they find it difficult to cross border. Of course, without the fifth D, they have great problems retaining good talents. It is through diminishing oneself that FinTech companies and projects really scale with the community taking over while the pie grows. Therefore, blockchain which is very inclusive, may be the driver for the Fourth Industrial Revolution with untrusted partners working together.

References and Further Readings

CB Insights. (February 15, 2017). The Global FinTech Report 2016 in Review.

Appendix

Interviews, Podcasts and Videos

A.1 Alternative Investments and the Burmese Cow[1]

As alternative investments such as hedge funds lose their ability to differentiate or deliver sustainable outperformance, the new frontier will move to digital assets — with new digital asset classes being created in emerging markets.

February 7, 2017

A cow in rural Myanmar seems an unlikely place to imagine the future of alternative investments.

The cow belongs to a farmer who has no formal title to his land. He has no bank account: there isn't a branch within easy reach, and the bank wouldn't give him a loan anyway. His daily life is one of manual labor and scraping by, and his children seem destined to either become farmers or scrape a living in the city doing manual labor; if they are boys, they might get a religious education at the local monastery.

All he's got is that cow ... and, now, a mobile phone. And that's enough to turn that cow into an asset that can be digitized, securitized, and traded among the nascent breed of alternative investment managers.

David Lee Kuo Chuen, a former long/short arbitrage hedge fund manager and now professor at the Singapore Institute of

---

[1]http://www.digitalfinancemedia.com/blog/2017/02/07/alternative-assets/

Management (SIM University), says digital technology will put people and things, currently outside the formal financial system, into the mix of alternative investors' future portfolios.

"We should look for asset classes that aren't in the portfolio."

Myanmar's cows aren't quite there yet. A lot needs to be done before they win the attention of global hedge-fund managers. But they symbolize an emerging asset class based on crypto-currency, scalable technology, rising wealth in emerging markets, and the expansion of high-speed data networks to previously remote locations (what Lee calls the development of the 'hinternet').

Those developments will attract investors looking for new asset classes. "We should look for asset classes that aren't in the portfolio, and that don't correlate with others," Lee said at a recent talk in Hong Kong hosted by the Chartered Alternative Investment Analyst (CAIA) Association.

Escaping the crowded trade

That search will be spurred by the increasingly same-same nature of many alternative asset classes. Correlations are rising among traditional and alternative assets, from long-only stocks and bonds to hedge funds, private equity and commodities.

Although individual investors and firms can still stand out from the crowd, as an asset class, alternatives no longer provide exciting risk-adjusted returns. That's partly because there is too much money chasing too few opportunities, itself a reflection of the institutionalization of the investor base.

The new true alternatives, Lee says, are digital assets. Investing in Bitcoin (or Bitcoin-denominated assets) today, for example, has parallels to investing in hedge funds in the 1990s. It was viewed as dangerous and destabilizing, and frowned upon by most governments and big money managers. But those were the heydays of outsized returns.

Financial technology pioneers such as China's Ant Financial are not just disrupting incumbent institutions, but are creating new businesses by going into markets that were previously underserved, Lee says.

Digital businesses thrive in low-margin, high-volume businesses that are asset-light, scalable, innovative and regulated lightly or not at all. The best examples of such opportunities are found in emerging markets with a rising middle class and little service from traditional financial institutions.

"Technology makes what was previously uninvestible into the new investible digital asset class," Lee said. This will benefit companies that can create connections among this giant population, quickly and cheaply.

Frontier markets such as Myanmar may not have much in the way of roads and bridges, or fiber-optic cable. But they can deploy 'hinternet' technologies relatively cheaply. Moreover, some of these governments will be eager to do so, because they are eager to move people out of underground cash economies and tax them.

"The hinternet is what's important," Lee said. "It means you get a lot of sticky customers."

"The new alternative investment class involves going to a remote area and monetizing all of its agriculture and livestock."

This is where the Burmese cows come home. A farmer in Myanmar can afford a very cheap microchip that can tag the cow. That enables the farmer to prove his ownership. Once all the farmers in his village create these digital assets, they can use their new smartphones to register them via blockchain technology. That lets the village mutually own livestock, or trade them.

The data allows the farmers to keep track of the cows, and to monitor their health. Therefore they can use the cows as collateral, so they can expand their business. A blockchain permits them to trade the cows with anyone in the world, or securitize the cows' output.

"The new alternative investment class involves going to a remote area and monetizing all of its agriculture and livestock," Lee said.

From the point of view of an investor in Singapore or New York, the means to trade in these new areas will be through crypto-currencies such as Bitcoin.

But, he said, it's the expansion of digital finance to the previously ignored populations of the world that will generate new asset classes — types of debt, equity and structured products — unrelated to their current versions based on fiat money.

A.2 How the Internet Is Democratising Global Finance[2]

David Lee and Christopher Dula
Published
Feb 13, 2016, 5:00 am SGT

The modern banking system is in doubt.

Despite US$11 trillion (S$15.4 trillion) in quantitative easing since 2007, economic growth has been persistently sluggish. The money isn't going where it should be. Growing compliance costs and shrinking margins will push banks towards greater consolidation. Fewer banks mean less competition, potentially more fragility and therefore greater dependency on governments to underwrite their lending practices — which further distorts the financial system. This is all made worse by widespread uncertainty, which favours hedging activity versus real investment.

Meanwhile, alternative banking and financial services operating on the FinTech frontier are chipping away at banking's traditional revenue streams. If banks are to survive, they will need to rethink the ways in which they acquire, transact and engage with customers.

Acquiring new customers is key to growing new business for banks and stimulating the global economy. More than two billion people in the world remain unbanked or under-banked. This represents a lost opportunity. Without access to banking and financial services, these people are hard pressed to grow businesses and engage in new ventures.

Banks have been reluctant to cater to this segment given the unknown risk profile, low income, limited wealth and geographic dispersion of their potential customers. They are simply too expensive to service.

Information technology, big data and mobile penetration have changed everything. The reach and scalability necessary to service those at the bottom of the pyramid is now not only economically

---

[2]http://www.straitstimes.com/opinion/how-the-internet-is-democratising-global-finance

possible — but profitable. The market potential is huge, and it's not limited to emerging markets. There is significant latent demand in the advanced economies as well.

Inclusivity is the next growth frontier in banking and finance. But by ignoring those neglected by the financial system, banks left room for tech companies to make financial inclusion a viable and sustainable business model. They've since innovated alternative, more efficient systems to provide banking and financial services at scale to the unbanked. Starting with payments, they have moved into financial services like savings, loans, micro insurance and investments. Ant Financial, Lending Club and M-Pesa are just a few notable companies in this space.

Global investment in FinTech has mushroomed in the past few years. Banks have taken notice, and are now vigorously acquiring FinTech start-ups to get in on the action. But this approach may not work for banks. Alternative banking and financial services have far fewer compliance obligations and lower operational costs because they do not operate on a traditional banking model. FinTech alternatives instead operate on small facilitation fees and volume, which would be insufficient to cover a bank's business costs.

Banks also suffer from massive legacy systems that make it difficult to incorporate new technology into their infrastructure. Even if a bank acquires a FinTech company for its technology, it may lack the tools to quickly and successfully integrate that technology into its system. Although several large banks have invested billions of dollars in digital, they still lack the culture, speed and scalability that have made tech companies, such as Alipay, so successful.

Internet companies in the social media, e-commerce and logistics space are much better poised to incorporate FinTech into their digital infrastructure. What's more, these companies already have millions of active users and are at an advantage in how they interact and engage with them. Internet companies are completely immersed in consumer lifestyles and can better understand customer context given the depth of their data. They're also well positioned for payments, peer-to-peer lending and integrating into new media and the sharing economy. There are thus hitherto unknown business models that could usurp traditional banking and finance in ways not yet imagined.

The most exciting applications are found in FinTech platforms built on cryptocurrencies like bitcoin and other blockchain technologies. Blockchain is a new way to store and record transactions. It is like a traditional database but the blocks are linked cryptographically in order to make sure they are tamper-proof.

Blockchain technologies operate on distributed peer-to-peer networks. These are open-access platforms with extraordinary potential to automate banking services while improving security and transparency.

Cyptocurrencies can also be programmed to represent anything of value: a company share, tax credits, vouchers, cash, votes ... whatever. Embedded instructions can be programmed to perform any transaction determining how, when and where the ransaction can take place. This has extraordinary implications for streamlining banking systems and easing compliance costs.

Banks, however, have been reluctant to adopt technologies like bitcoin, given its nefarious press and association with illicit money transfers. Although this sentiment is changing, distributed ledger technologies and peer-to-peer lending is alien to the banks' middle-man mentality and centralised nature.

A distributed ledger allows people to produce a tamper-proof record of transactions that is public. The idea behind it is to get rid of the middleman.

Attempts by more Wall Street-friendly Fintech firms to engage banks and other financial institutions with "permissioned blockchain" technology, which would establish a closed private network of distributed ledgers amongst banks, is interesting, but misses the point.

Such a collaborative consortium would likely result in non-competitive behaviour, leading to even greater market consolidation.

Blockchain adoption is more likely to originate in a decentralised trustless environment through the sharing of initially low value assets before scaling exponentially — not through a centralised financial market that transacts in high-value "smart" contracts, such as those from the derivative market.

There is a lot of uncertainty here, and perhaps some overselling by blockchain advocates, but if the hype is to be believed, and the massive investments in FinTech pay off, the global financial system could become indistinguishable from the Internet itself: an open-access distributed network of computer systems built on communication protocols with no centralised ownership or governance.

This level of democratisation could decouple the money supply from regulators — its fate thus influenced purely by market forces.

- David Lee is Practice Professor of Quantitative Finance at the Lee Kong Chian School of Business at Singapore Management University and, Christopher Dula is Senior Case Writer at the Centre for Management Practice at Singapore Management University and a Contributing Writer for Asian Management Insights.

A version of this article appeared in the print edition of The Straits Times on February 13, 2016, with the headline 'How the Internet is democratising global finance'.

A.3 In Conversation with Professor David Lee[3]

Professor David Lee is exceptionally extraordinary. He is not only effectively bilingual and tech savvy, but also has a strong bent for applied research that has been perceptibly shaped by his extensive management experience from managing large enterprises and finance companies, as well as his intense desire in serving the underserved. He has a knack of "finding the next big thing" as shown by his illustrious career.

Graduating with a PhD in Mathematical Economics and Econometrics from the London School of Economics in 1990, Professor Lee began his career as a lecturer in econometrics and public policy in the National University of Singapore. Subsequently, with the development of Singapore as a financial centre, he left academia to become a stock broker, and later became the managing director of Fraser Asset Management. Riding on an increase in interest in hedge fund strategies in this country, he founded his own hedge fund company Ferrell Asset Management in 1999 and was involved in property REITs (real estate investment trusts), mergers and acquisitions, and then property development.

As he widened his interest horizons, he concurrently took on the appointment of the Group Managing Director of Auric Pacific Group, and later the Group Managing Director and Chief Executive Officer of Overseas Union Enterprise Limited. In 2010, he was appointed non-executive Chairman of a listed company that specialised in manufacturing disk drive component, enterprise management services (EMS) for the Passport external disk drive and plastic medical supplies. Driven by his love for applied research and a desire to share his knowledge and experience in an ever-changing environment in the financial sector, he returned to the academia as a Professor of Quantitative Finance and an Advisor to the Provost in Singapore Management University. In 2014, he also assumed the position of the Director of the Sim Kee Boon Institute for Financial Economics

---

[3]http://www.econsandsociety.com/volumes/2017/Conversation.pdf

in addition to taking charge of the Global Master of Finance Programme with Washington University.

After finishing his appointment as a Visiting Fulbright Fellowship in Stanford University in 2015/2016, he now spends his time teaching in the Singapore University of Social Sciences. Recently, one of his books entitled "Handbook of Digital Currency: Bitcoin, Innovation, Financial Instruments and Big Data" was nominated to be one of the year's most outstanding business reference sources by the Reference and User Services Association (RUSA). Economics & Society interviewed Professor David Lee to find out his interests and views on the value of technology in our society.

Hi Professor Lee, in your opinion, what is the biggest issue we are currently facing in the study of Economics?

I am most concerned about the failure of Economics in addressing wealth and income inequality, as there has been no theory propounded so far to solve the problem. I rejoined academia in 2012 in the hope of finding answers to the many questions that have been troubling me, such as those relating to the widening wealth and income divide and the continuing existence of a huge segment at the bottom of the pyramid that remains underserved. I want to find out the next big thing and see where I can contribute most to a better and more equitable world. Currently, I am working on FinTech (Financial services or products built upon technology) and scalable technology for inclusion. I believe digital finance can change the economic landscape via digital asset sharing using blockchain. With a fall in business cost through scalable technology and decentralisation, we can increasingly reach out to the underserved. With blockchain technology, the large number of underserved in remote areas of agricultural economies can now have a digital identity. They can register their interest of ownership using digital means without having to form a company, which is expensive. A handphone with a blockchain is sufficient to register and own whatever assets, including digitised livestock located miles away. A chip worn on a livestock will be able to locate, identify and verify the cows, goats, or horses to be owned via smartphone. The poor remain poor because it is costly to own assets and borrowing is difficult without a digital identity. Decentralised digital revolution will be one of the most powerful means to reduce inequality working through the asset sharing economy.

In this case, what is the most important asset in the new economy?

With the advent of the fourth industrial revolution, we have now moved from steam engine to data and computing power. With smart data, the entire supply chain can be transparent to those with computing power. For instance, companies can detect their clients' problems before the clients are aware that they have problems. We are used to owning wealth through cash, bond, equities, and other complex instruments using a legal entity and a custodian. But all these arrangements and structures are inherently expensive to operate and owned. If we think in terms of data and computing as an investable asset class that need no intermediaries, the cost of owning such digital assets will be reduced tremendously without the middlemen. There will be more transparency. It will lead to decentralisation and disintermediation allowing for Peer-to-Peer transactions that are affordable to the poorest among us. The lowest denomination of a digital value will be smaller than one cent and can be divisible up to 16 decimal places if needed. This low-cost asset ownership blockchain technology will be able to serve a large population across all borders. With data and computing power, this would also provide autonomy for individuals to own very cheap assets which were not viable previously.

Going forward, our traditional factors of production will now include data and computing power: land, labour and capital would become relatively less important. Labour will be replaced by robots/machines, land is not in short supply as we could operate in remote areas 24/7 with scalable technology and renewable energy. When almost everything can be digitised and decentralised, digital assets will play an important role in transforming the way the entire society is organised. Data and computer power will be one of the most important asset classes and valuable resources.

Are there any threats that we should be cognisant of?

Yes, we must be mindful not to end up with a few centralised digital empires that control the entire world. If a few companies own all the data and computing power, it will lead to a concentration of ownership of digital assets, which will lead to a concentration of power and wealth. Inequality will be worsened with greater uneven distribution of wealth.

Moreover, there is a danger of artificial consciousness beyond just intelligence whereby machines have the capability to decide for themselves what is right or wrong. I highly recommend the movie West World to the readers. In this show, we can see the danger of androids malfunctioning. Hence, we cannot have only a few centralised empires. The digital world should be decentralised with on demand encryption. If it is decentralised and encrypted, humans can still have dignity when machines take over. Hence, blockchain technology with encryption is so significant. When we talk about ZCash as an experiment, many will view it negatively as it permits anonymous transactions. But the technology in ZCash, just like the first blockchain technology Bitcoin, has tremendous implications as artificial intelligence becomes an important part of the digital world.

How would these new technologies transform the lives of people?

Scalable technology includes drones that can connect Wi-Fi with people within a radius of over thousands of miles. Drones can deliver data and physical goods over sparsely populated areas. Augmented and Virtual Reality (AR/VR) can transport 3D images making our virtual "physical" presence felt all over the world at the same time. As cities become crowded, people now have the incentive to move away from crowded areas to enjoy clean air and water without affecting their career aspirations. They can have meetings and move around in Augmented Reality (AR) and Virtual Reality (VR) settings. They have more autonomy now and have access to cheaper accommodation and regenerative energy in a healthier environment. Cities may hollow out with fewer jobs and lower standard of living. But not all countries, however, can transform themselves because of legacy issues.

Of course, we should also expect incumbents to put on a fight and resist changes. Hence, this new industrial revolution is biased for countries which are sparsely populated with no incumbents. Myanmar is a case in point. We should expect Myanmar to benefit the most from these technological advancements. Within five to 10 years, Myanmar would be able to leapfrog many other economies as the underserved would become the engine of growth for the future in the "Hinternet" as opposed to Hinterland. If Myanmar successfully builds a "Hinternet" full of sticky customers, initially underserved, its economic growth will accelerate as more services are created at a fraction of the cost to the same customers on the net. A leapfrog economy like Myanmar can overtake financial cities such as Hong Kong and Singapore with economies of scale over a large and sparsely populated area. New digital economy services may be introduced, some of which we have not even thought of at this moment.

How should Singapore get ready for the new industrial revolution that you have just mentioned?

Mindset is more important than skillset. Singapore has been focusing too much on skillset. In today's fast-changing world, skills become obsolete much faster than before. We need to focus more on mindset: mindset to embrace failures, mindset to do good, mindset to create ecosystems and communities to collaborate, mindset that engenders compassion and mercy.

Often, young people are not aware of the onslaught of the fourth industrial revolution, which brings with it a new society and economic order with the characteristics of sharing of services and assets, thriving with the on-demand economy, rewarding suppliers with bounty reward and not salary. More importantly, there will hardly be any lifelong jobs. Even if the young people are aware of the challenges, they may not be able to participate in or join a start-up with its attendant high risks due to parents' disapproval. We need to have a supportive environment before we start talking about acquiring relevant skillsets.

Educators are only beginning to realise that knowledge and content are not as valuable as experience. So, learning is about experiencing actual life situations rather than merely acquiring skills per se. Policymakers need to understand that it is the speed of innovation that is important. Knowing how to be creative is just one dimension. We need to learn how to scale our innovation exponentially in the shortest possible time in the global economy. With the internet and digitisation, we can reach out to billions of people in a very short time span. Ultimately, man will need to decide what they want to do with technology. Technology can do good but technology can also do harm. An economy without a sense of mission to serve others will eventually lead to a digital world where machines will dominate humans and take away the dignity of mankind. Singapore with its huge reserves and talents must decide if the regional sharing of asset strategy with the underserved enabled by technology is what it wishes to pursue! If it is, then being conversant in scalable technology and infrastructure such as AI, smart data, blockchain, drones, AR/VR and holoportation will be the best defence against disruption!

A.4   An Interview with David Lee Kuo Chuen[4]

Position:

Singapore Management University

Singapore Management University's Professor of Quantitative Finance (Practice) speaks with FST Media about how digital currencies will shape the payments space in 2020.

FST Media: Where do you see the future of crypto-currencies like Bitcoin and how will this change the financial services sector over the next 5 years?

Lee: My research involves understanding the key issues faces by ASEAN and beyond. I feel that Singapore has been growing for many years and inclusion has always been the key policy that they are looking into. One key development that has arisen from the growth of bitcoin and cryptocurrency is actually its use as a new technology and the Monetary Authority of Singapore (MAS) is very interested in this. There is a lot of interest in doing further research in the area and there seems to be a consensus that new technologies like bitcoin can help the financial institutions to further their business especially in terms of lowering their business costs. As a consequence, there is the possibility of servicing new customers who possibly could not have been serviced before.

The key here is that the focus has been on the technology rather the currency itself. However, I think the currency bitcoin and cryptocurrency in general will see a lot more clarity going forward from a tokenisation point of view because there are a lot of possibilities to have your own cryptocurrency — either as a country, organisation or business enterprise. We are still in the early stages but the technology itself has proven to be groundbreaking and a very interesting creation.

FST Media: Does Bitcoin represent a threat to banks or an opportunity for innovation in financial services?

---

[4]http://fst.net.au/features/interview-david-lee-kuo-chuen

Lee: Bitcoin is one of the biggest experiments that we have seen so far in the financial world. We have had other innovations like eCash which the public has resisted. Many of them run into compliance problems and stop operating, but bitcoin is in some ways decentralised, so it is a lot harder for the regulators to examine it closely. Because there is no legal entity behind bitcoin, it is harder to regulate it. The only way we can regulate it is through the financial intermediaries, and a lot of countries have set out rules and regulations for intermediaries and for the technology authorities to look at whether it is a currency or asset for trading.

As far as the banks are concerned, what I am observing is that the banks have a lot of compliance procedures to abide by. When they are regulating the intermediaries, they have to ensure that the intermediaries would all have the same standard of compliance so that they could be responding to the authorities. In some cases, the cost of compliance is a lot higher than the profit that they can generate from these enterprise so it is not surprising to me that some banks are not so keen to engage with these bitcoin companies. However, this does not apply to all banks as there are a lot of other banks who are keen to work with bitcoin companies, it is just a matter of getting the right standard of compliance for the intermediaries. I think it is not an unsolvable problem, it is just a process that any enterprise has to go through especially where if you are deemed to be a financial intermediary, you need more time to convince the banks and financial institutions that you are running a genuine business.

FST Media: What will be the next big innovation in contactless payments?

Lee: The next big innovation will be cybersecurity-related. I think bitcoin has come out with this groundbreaking idea of blockchain technology, providing a decentralised ledger that can potentially save a lot of operational cost for financial services institutions as well as many other industries. The real contribution that bitcoin has made has been with this consensus ledger, and I think this will change the way that we look at accounting and the way we store data, as well as how we form consensus on register. If the technology can successfully penetrate the market and the industry comes to the consensus that this is the way to move forward, then we could see the technology being used in a way that not only saves costs but also, in terms of cybersecurity, may help mitigate the [problem] of hacking. From a cybersecurity perspective, the consensus ledger will be a very interesting innovation that many financial institutions and institutions in other industries will embrace for cost-effectiveness.

I am not undermining the tokenisation of the decentralised system [of bitcoin]. However, when the regulations catch on, bitcoin currency will be a major force. Though, it is still too early to see bitcoin as a world currency because we are not there yet but we should not undermine the tokenisation of digital currency as well.

FST Media: How will digital currencies shape the payments space in 2020?

Lee: The first thing that you notice is that cash is not cheap; it is inefficient. Most of the central banks eventually will come to the consensus that digital currency is the way to move forward for various reasons: taxation is much clearer, you have a greater knowledge of money flows through available data and analysis, and you have a real control of money supply. I think digital currency has a lot of potential to give us a lot more information than cash itself. Those benefits will eventually be used by most of the government and in the collection of taxation, it is also much more efficient as you can trace where the money is going. It makes perfect sense to have digital currency and I see that this is a natural progression going forward — it is just a matter of how long it takes for us to reach that conclusion.

FST Media: In your novel, *Handbook of Digital Currency*, you discuss how crypto-currency was traditionally thought to possess "the characteristics of a currency that can impose fiscal discipline on the government." What are the key challenges that governments face with regulating crypto-currencies like Bitcoin?

Lee: One of the ideas of Satoshi is that by having constant growth rates of your money, you are able to have more discipline. It also makes a lot of sense in terms of looking at digital currency — it is the issue of debt. By having a constant growth rate, the ability to trim and pay off your debt is a lot more challenging because of the [nature of] the modern debt system. There are no restrictions on a government when it comes to printing currency, provided that there is enough confidence in that particular currency. I think that will reach a point where debt is so huge and when your consistent budget deficit will signal to the rest of the world that your debt cannot be repaid.

In this situation, the confidence in the currency will be shaken and that is where we will have a major issue. However, it does not mean that a new financial system will not be a form of innovation. One area that you can look at is the Chinese way of internationalising their currency through bilateral agreements. The establishment of the AIIB is another very interesting development in the sense that more money which is needed now for raising debt is no longer used for consumption but rather for infrastructure building. You now have a world organisation that focuses on infrastructure building for borrowing and consumptive use within a country. You will see the whole financial architecture changing over time and there will be fears surrounding the question of whether those countries who are in huge debt will increase their taxation for foreign investors, as well as whether they have the ability to redeem and return their debt as this will have ripples in the entire monetary system. Government discipline imposed on how much you bring and borrow is important because it affects the interests and confidence in that currency and can have an effect on the rest of the world.

The implications that this may have on cryptocurrency is very interesting, particularly when we look at how this unfolds in years to come. My own view is that cryptocurrency has an advantage over digital currency because it has no central storage, is more transparent and also provides you with the opportunity to be in control of the growth of this currency. With cryptocurrency, you may not be able to create as much debt as you wish to have.

FST Media: In your novel, you also discuss how the authenticity of Bitcoin transactions can be determined using digital signatures and public-key cryptography. How significant is the problem of cybercrime with bitcoin transactions and what are the key security issues that need to be addressed?

Lee: I think the problem we have here is one of perception. Bitcoin has been seen to be used for transactions surrounding activities like money laundering, drugs and online casino games. Our research has shown that there is a lot of speculation on the future of bitcoin and many believe that it will not be a world currency because generally people are wary that it is being used for the wrong purpose. In addition, it is designed in such a way that it is very difficult to regulate because there is no legal entity to make anyone responsible and this makes it hard. The only way it can be regulated is through the intermediaries such as enterprises all over the world. Compared to cash, you have a lot more transparency with bitcoin as it leaves a trace whereas cash does not leave any public record. Given the kind of technology we have for tracing where the money is located or where it is going, it is unwise to use bitcoin for the dark side of cybercrime.

FST Media: What are your thoughts on payment platforms like Google's Android Pay and Alibaba's Alipay and how can banks learn from them?

Lee: I think the disruption of banks is a very interesting area, particularly when we consider how banks can use some of these technologies (like a consensus ledger) to lower costs and enhance their operational ability. The major challenge for banks is not from bitcoin or cryptocurrency, but from the centralised non-financial institutions and e-commerce firms like Alibaba. There is no point in having e-wallet [capabilities] and then hoping the public will use this. However, introducing certain business activities can help to create customer retention.

For businesses to buy and sell their goods, e-commerce firms like Alibaba create retention by forging a sense of trust between buyer and seller through Alipay. Subsequently, it becomes a lending platform for people who want to buy more goods to sell online and you then create a retentive population who will use your platform. Even though your payment app is given as a freebie, you can actually increase your profit margins by providing fund management services, micro-insurance business, crowdfunding for movies and many other similar business ventures. This is what separates Alibaba as a business organisation backed by an e-commerce platform that has extended its services to lending platforms, big data credit analysis and other platforms because essentially data itself is being monetised. This is the greatest challenge for financial institutions: how do you create customer retention?

We are seeing challenges to banks, not only from e-commerce platforms like Alibaba or telecommunications platforms like M-Pesa, but also a lot of other alternative platforms that are creating consumer retentiveness. Disruptive companies like Uber and Airbnb could all be challengers to financial institutions in the future.

In this sense, the challenge does not revolve around bitcoin or cryptocurrency, but from the centralised businesses focusing on consumer retention. Going forward, I think cryptocurrency will play a significant role in financial services because you will need to tokenise your services and if regulation allows this, then it can create a lot of loyalty through these tokens. Once companies like Alibaba have your data, they can record your behaviour using this data and then use it for monetising solutions. As a result, the incumbents are increasingly being disrupted.

FST Media: What is the 'holy grail' that is yet to be delivered in financial services?

Lee: The next big thing in financial services is about 'connectivity inclusion'. This is more than just financial inclusion, it is about being connected by smartphones, wearables and across all radio signals. They connect you to more than just economy — this is the amalgamation of social inclusion, financial inclusion and collectively I term this to be 'connectivity inclusion'. Previously, it has been very expensive for banks to service people who are not in the system because of high compliance and operational costs. Now, with the latest technology this has become viable and this is where cryptocurrency comes into the picture. I think the consensus ledger is one of the cheapest and most secure ways to overcome this problem. For connectivity inclusion, banks need to look at these new technologies and cryptocurrencies to lower their costs. Inclusion is the key word here, if you want the economy to grow and businesses to continue to advance, then this is the opportunity to see sustainable growth. This is how I came up with my 'LASIC model': low barriers of entry for business, asset line, sociability, innovation, and then compliance-ready. All the new disruptive models will conform to these LASIC principles.

The most advanced country in the world for digital banking and financial inclusion is China. We have seen some digital banks being set up in Kenya, the US and Europe but the sustainable model for growth rests with China because it has a social agenda behind digital banking.

FST Media: Every leader has a legacy they wish to be remembered for, what is yours?

Lee: I would not say that I am a leader. I study economics because my inclination is to do research to improve the welfare of people. To advance your knowledge is something that is very appealing to me but that was not my mission. I have been in the industry for a long time; I have been in the financial industry and an academic for close to 30 years now. I want to do research that has an impact on the welfare of people and I hope that the things I do will help address certain issues in the financial industry which to me are unreasonable. I want to take it a step further and discover solutions which are a win-win for enterprises and regulators, as well as the people who will benefit from this. At the end of the day, we need to make sure that whatever research we do, we are improving the welfare of people in the world at large. We have a very unbalanced economic system in place and it is unreasonable to have so many people not included in the financial, economic and social system globally.

I want to look at how an ecosystem can be initiated and studied so that we can solve the problem of 'connectivity exclusion'. I hope that all of us can create an ecosystem to make the world a better place.

Professor David Lee Kuo Chuen will be speaking at FST Media's 6th annual ASEAN Technology & Innovation — the Future of Banking & Financial Services conference in Singapore, in addition to a distinguished panel of executives across financial services from July 22–23, 2015. For more insights and information about the event, register for your complimentary pass here.

A.5 David Lee: Served the Underserved[5]

Professor David Lee Kuo Chuen, author of 'Handbook of Digital Currency', shares his views on the country's cryptocurrency scene.

By April *Zara Chua*

Cryptocurrency has been slowly building momentum since its introduction in 2009, and investors who saw its potential then are reaping its rewards now. According to CoinDesk's Bitcoin Price Index, a bitcoin was valued at less than US$1 in early 2011, but has now skyrocketed to about US$2,000 to 3,000. It's only a matter of time before cryptocurrency hits the mainstream in Singapore.

But what is cryptocurrency exactly? Simply put, it's money in a purely digital form. To keep it safe and secure, transactions are encrypted and cross-audited by a decentralised network. Examples include Bitcoin, Litecoin, Ethereum, Zcash, Dash and Ripple.

IMpact spoke to David Lee Kuo Chuen — entrepreneur, professor at the Singapore University of Social Sciences, and author of *Handbook of Digital Currency* — to get his thoughts on the cryptocurrency scene in the country.

How has cryptocurrency affected Singapore's trading economy?

Cryptocurrency currently has a limited impact on the Singapore's trading economy. However, the cryptocurrency community has created a good number of startup jobs and has put Singapore on the map as one of the best destinations for cryptocurrency and blockchain startups.

Is cryptocurrency a threat to banks and other financial institutions?

Successful cryptocurrency companies are not competing for the same business areas or clients as the financial institutions; they are trying to complete the imperfect financial ecosystem. The underserved

---

[5]https://www.imda.gov.sg/infocomm-and-media-news/in-conversation-with/2017/8/david-lee-serve-the-underserved

segments, such as immigrant workers and small- and medium-sized enterprises (SMEs), are the ones that benefit from the services offered by some cryptocurrency companies.

How long do you think before Bitcoin filters down to consumer level?

Bitcoin is not in the mainstream in Singapore yet even though it has been around since 2009. However, it has become a legal payment system in Japan since 1 April this year. Many are expecting that about 260,000 merchants would use the network, making it the highest volume of trading of cryptocurrencies outside China and Korea.

While you can purchase air tickets, book hotel rooms and buy goods by Bitcoin online, there are a few places in Singapore where you can do that physically. Bitcoin vending machines and cafés using Bitcoin as a form of payment have mostly been tourist attractions. You can find those vending machines in Chinatown, Tiong Bahru (by Bitcoin Exchange) and soon in Orchard Road (by DZL).

What can companies do to build a more inclusive digital currency ecosystem?

Companies should have the mindset to serve the underserved. Building a blockchain ecosystem to reach out to needy in the region can be sustainable and profitable. Blockchain is successful because it is created to benefit the users rather than squeezing the next cent out from them. It is by serving the underserved and providing free services that value is created.

To transform, companies should consider the following: how to complete rather than to compete, open source rather than chasing IP, benefitting rather than squeezing consumers, being inclusive rather than being exclusive, having a global mindset rather than thinking local, and building new business models rather than protecting incumbents.

Companies also need to watch and plug into China, which has mastered the skills of scaling, financial inclusion, and user experience. It will dominate the blockchain industry because of its size and capital expenditure on research and development.

What can companies learn from current successful interoperability schemes? Any example of this in Singapore?

The most powerful feature of blockchain is the sharing of asset ownership. No amount of capital or technology can do what blockchain does: enhancing collaboration and enabling parties to work efficiently together in a decentralised and innovative environment.

In Singapore, a startup called COMIT does cryptographically-secured multi-asset instant transaction network. Their product, TenX card, takes the form of a physical card or a mobile debit e-wallet card. It can be funded with Bitcoin, Ether or other blockchain assets.

TenX payment facilities can be used in Singapore and in approximately 200 countries. Users and businesses can exchange their blockchain assets seamlessly from one user to another in a decentralised manner, removing any risk that is usually associated with current centralised solutions.

Where do you see Singapore's digital payment economy moving into?

Singapore is a small country and the only way it can grow is to be as open, inclusive and global as it can be. Cross-border payment is where the growth is but payment itself is just a service that does not yield good returns. That's why Singapore's digital payment strategy must be one that provides additional services, such as wealth management, insurance and investment banking.

The largest growing online market will be Southeast Asia, as it is relatively new to the payment scene and has a young population. Grab, Alipay, WeChat, and other global payment companies are all eyeing this region, which has 660 million people with smartphones — most of which are unbanked. If Singapore can capitalise on its position as a supplier of capital to the underserved and unbanked, and as a provider of assurance and wealth management service to the needy, it can be a service centre to the region.

A.6   An Interview with David LEE Kuo Chuen, Professor of FinTech and Blockchain at the Singapore University of Social Science[6]

Recently, we sat down with David LEE Kuo Chuen, Professor of FinTech and Blockchain at Singapore University of Social Sciences. As an industry leader and subject matter expert, David provides strategic direction and advice on the design, technology and inclusiveness behind our cryptocurrency solution. With that in mind, we asked David for his thoughts on the industry, our product and why cryptocurrency has a role to play in equalizing the future of finance.

FINTECH, IN THIS HEAVILY REGULATED AND HIGH-COST ENVIRONMENT, CAN PERHAPS BE RE-DEFINED AS AN ACTIVITY THAT CHANGES THE MINDSET AND BREAKS DOWN THE SILOS FOR THE BENEFIT OF ALL.

DAVID LEE KUO CHUEN
PROFESSOR FOR FINTECH AND BLOCKCHAIN,
SINGAPORE UNIVERSITY OF SOCIAL SCIENCES
ADVISOR, STK GLOBAL PAYMENTS

STACK | STK

STK: Hi David, thanks for chatting with us today. You've just published two books on Blockchain, Digital Finance and Inclusion recently. You were one of the academics that started research early in bitcoin, and you published the America award-winning book on digital currency in 2015. You were also an early founding investor in Zcash, Qtum, Netki, Bloq, TenX, InfoCorp, and many others. To get things started, tell us what is top of mind for you these days about inclusion.

David: There are many things that I have been focusing on as of late, and my goal is always to generate open and constructive discourse

---

[6]https://medium.com/@STKtoken/an-interview-with-david-lee-kuo-chuen-professor-of-fintech-and-blockchain-at-the-singapore-34358564bda5

on these topics. The world of finance is rapidly changing, driven largely by an industry that didn't even have a label until just a few years ago — FinTech. Successful financial institutions have never been short of capital or new technology. FinTech, in this heavily regulated and high-cost environment, can perhaps be re-defined as an activity that changes the mindset and breaks down the silos for the benefit of all. It is therefore inconceivable to conjecture that the best and most valuable form of FinTech is one that focuses on the original purposes of banking services, i.e., to serve those in need of banking services.

I am specifically interested in FinTech innovations with a focus on inclusiveness, accessibility, community orientation, creativity and collaboration.

Financial Inclusion

FinTech has enhanced the ability to innovate freely, to collaborate and to serve low profit margin customers. I have a particular interest in those focusing on serving the entire pyramid of customers and completing the financial eco-system. In modern days, this means having the infrastructure for digital finance. It is even more interesting to observe that the successful FinTech companies are closely linked to serving the underserved segments of the economy and payment is almost always the conduit and first step. These companies are serving many supposedly "insignificant" customers or businesses. My efforts recently are to assist some of these inclusive payment companies to reach out to the segment as a first step followed by fractional ownership of digital assets. OmiseGo, InfoCorp, TenX and HelloGold are all working in this space but providing different types of technologies and services through serving different segments to complete the ecosystem. In particular, InfoCoprp serves the migrants and farmers through payments, certification and ownership. HelloGold allows for fractional ownership for financial inclusion. I observe that more than 80% of the people without bank accounts in some ASEAN countries and there is room for many digital financial services projects.

Decentralization and Blockchain

The other area that I am interested in is decentralisation. Many ask me why decentralisation is important as an area of research and investment. Open and inclusive blockchain has a lot of socially beneficial properties besides being auditably secure and transparently accountable. It can restore faith and increase resilience in the financial system by enabling cross-border economic cooperation and integration. Secure cross-border Peer-to-Peer (P2P) payment wallet is the first step in achieving this goal and critical in helping economies leapfrog, bypassing all the pains points faced by developed economies. Decentralisation plays an important role because it allows for frictionless cross-border P2P activities. Most of the successful decentralised projects are open source experiments that encourage mass participation and contribution, has a benevolent economic incentive structure that embodies the interest of all, and global in nature to source for markets, talents and resources. Decentralisation also prevents an extreme concentration of power and inequality of wealth that have proven to impede economic growth and is the cause of social instability. Decentralisation can build economic resilience with more even distribution of wealth. For a just, prosperous and asset sharing global economy, decentralisation and the spirit of diminishing oneself and furthering the network's interest are vital. I have an investment interest in Least Authority, Cybex, Scry and few others because decentralised encryption, decentralised privacy, decentralised exchange of value, decentralised storage, and decentralised access are keys to ensure dignity for humans in an AI world. These projects and experiments will hopefully reduce the pain points of cross-border net neutrality with secure privacy and ensure mass adoption and usage.

STK: There's been a lot of buzz and hype around blockchain and decentralized financial systems lately. Recently, Christine Lagarde, Managing Director of the IMF stated that cryptocurrency could be the future of money. Despite that, cryptocurrency is still in its infancy in terms of mainstream adoption. Why do you think more people are not using cryptocurrency and decentralized financial systems?

David: There are 4 distinct challenges with cryptocurrencies like Bitcoin including technical limitations, difficulties of onboarding and accessing or buying into cryptocurrencies, merchant acceptance, and delays in verifying transactions:

1. Technical limitations

Bitcoin has been around for eight years and many are surprised at its resilience in terms of technology, financial and adoption. However, it is still in its infancy and has all the signs of a project with great potential. Its influences are not limited to the mindset change of a generation. However, contrary to most people think, volatility is not a significant reason why it is not widely adopted. There are many technical reasons such as transaction per second, blocksize, storage of blockchain, privacy, legality surrounding the use of smart contracts and Oracle. With only seven transactions per second, bitcoin cannot compete with private blockchain and payment companies such as Alipay that can reach more than 100,000 transactions per second. However, these issues are being looked into and I do not think technology will be stagnant. It is just a matter of time that a decentralised secure cross-border payment system will dominate. With smart contracts and more open blockchain, I am optimistic that it is not a question of whether there will be mass adoption, but when. Japan has declared its leadership in the adoption of cryptocurrency, and that signal is enough to give comfort to merchants and users. Bitcoin, Ether, Zcash and a few others are clear market anchors and leaders, but there are many other respectable ones in the 1200 cryptocurrencies space. I am sure we will hear more about them.

2. Difficulties in onboarding and getting access/buying into cryptocurrencies like Bitcoin

For those of us who were involved since the early days, we noticed that hardly any energy was spent on improving UI, UX or KYC in the beginning. Open blockchain was created to bypass regulation, and also research has shown that cryptocurrency is not the best medium for money laundering, tax evasion or terrorist financing. Forensic science can identify a user based on the pattern of usage with more than 80% success rate. It was also too early to talk about interoperability and being inclusive in the protocol standards. However, since 2016, the efforts have been concentrating on the issue of identity, onboarding and user experience. In 2017, the community is beginning to look at improving the standard for integration and interoperability in the name of inclusive blockchain. Once the community understands the value of the blockchain is the degree of inclusiveness, the issues of UX and UI will become the focus. It takes time, and I have seen vast improvement over the past six months. Furthermore, for financial inclusion, it is not the standard KYC or ATF procedures that are important but facial recognition, GPS positioning, and other modern techniques. I believe user-friendly wallet will be the winning formula and easy access to cryptocurrencies are more important factors for mass adoption outside the financial centres.

3. Lack of merchant acceptance

Before Japan declared that bitcoin is a legal payment system, the efforts of the community have been on building the base layer of technology. The industry is short of app developers, and it is only since April 2017 that there is a focus on merchant acceptance. Without having to understand the backend of the app or cryptocurrency, mass adoption is just a matter of time. Earlier ventures into this area have been challenging with negative sentiments towards bitcoin. However, that has changed from misunderstanding to fear of missing out. Many governments and incumbents will be keen to promote cryptocurrency payment as technology advances to solve the last mile problem. It is the most cost-effective way for cross-border payments, and I believe the World Bank and IMF will push for it to lower remittance charges.

4. Delays in verifying transactions

This is an issue for bitcoin, but recent BIPs are trying to address some of these issues using lightning, sidechains and other methods. I do not think it will be a major issue in a year's time.

STK: As you know, those are some of the challenges we have designed our token to solve. Using our STK token utility, we hope to facilitate ubiquitous merchant acceptance and address delays of blockchain transactions so that it can be used for real-time point-of-sale transactions. By creating a solution that lets you spend your cryptocurrency at almost any point-of-sale that accepts major debit and credit cards, we hope to overcome some of these obstacles that other cryptocurrencies are facing today. Why did this type of project appeal to you?

David: The idea of a bridge between the traditional financial and payment systems, and the new world of FinTech and blockchain is both new and necessary. The cryptocurrency technology is still in its infancy, and it takes time to evolve. However, what bitcoin and other cryptocurrencies have achieved over the last few years have been amazing. My primary interest lies in the development of distributed technology to ensure that human dignity is not compromised when AI machines take over the world. In the meantime, the main problem is financial exclusion because of the way the society is organised. Blockchain will be the catalyst for the 4th industrial revolution because it enables untrusted parties, especially if they have no access to capital to improve their infrastructure, to collaborate. Familiar breeds behaviour. This project can potentially distribute a point of sales via smartphones into the hands of all those that have been excluded from the system in remote areas. At the same time, it is inclusive that it potentially allows the cryptocurrency system to be complete in providing an avenue for P2P transactions.

I'm also behind the mission of providing people with access to "their money" whether it was fiat or cryptocurrency

Eventually, two types of digital currencies will have mass support. One that is backed by trade and reserves, and another that is cryptographically secured. This project not only plays a role in completing the cryptocurrency system, but it is also inclusive and forward-looking in allowing everyone to have access to his or her money anytime, anywhere.

More importantly, the team has strong technical background and proven execution track record. Given their business experience, they will be able to find more collaborations. Collaborations are essential to be successful in the borderless blockchain world because the identified market is more than half the world population of above 15 years old with few incumbents ready to venture into those areas.

STK: Is there anything else that excites you about the project?

David: One of the areas of financial services and financial technology that I'm most passionate about is the idea of financial inclusion. People around the world face many barriers when it comes to accessing, spending or saving their money. A universally accessible solution that provides advanced financial services to people regardless of country or currency is something I am excited to be a part of.

How successful a project will be will depend not on how much it will rule the market or compete in the ecosystem, but rather how it is going to serve the underserved and how it positions itself to complete the fiat and cryptocurrency ecosystem. The team is fascinating and technically very competent. Their sense of mission is what inspires me in sharing with them my views and direction of where the world is heading. I believe the project focuses on inclusiveness and completeness, and that philosophy is in full alignment with the crypto community.

STK: David, thank you again for letting us interview you.

A.7 List of Other Interviews and Podcasts and Youtube

Other Interview

https://www.smu.edu.sg/sites/default/files/smu/news_room/BT_20 160323.pdf?kui=_nEa-yiTMKO-YEXsXSpfxA

Podcasts and YouTube

http://internalconsulting.com/global-thought-leaders/clients/prof-david-lee-kuo-chuen

https://www.youtube.com/watch?v=700IRrOjxtA

http://ink.library.smu.edu.sg/podcasts/28

http://ink.library.smu.edu.sg/podcasts/24

https://soundcloud.com/nextmoney/episode07

References

Preface

Merle, R. (May 20, 2017). Once considered the titans of Wall Street, hedge fund managers are in trouble. Retrieved from https://www.washingtonpost.com/ business/economy/once-considered-the-titans-of-wall-street-hedge-fund-man agers-are-in-trouble/2017/05/29/61049f1e-34ce-11e7-b373-418f6849a004_sto ry.html?noredirect=on&utm_term=.5eccc0655a44

Chapter 1

Accenture (2015). The Future of FinTech and Banking: Digitally disrupted or reimagined?. Retrieved from http://www.FinTechinnovationlablon don.net/media/730274/Accenture-The-Future-of-FinTech-and-Banking-digit allydisrupted-or-reima-.pdf

Alt, R., & Puschmann, T. (2012). The rise of customer-oriented banking — electronic markets are paving the way for change in the financial industry. Electronic Markets, 22(4), 203–215.

BOC News. http://www.boc.cn/en

CBInsights. https://www.cbinsights.com/

Communications Commission of Kenya (CCK). http://ca.go.ke/index.php/ statistics

Demirrguc-Kunt, A., & Klapper, L. (2012). Measuring Financial Inclusion: The Global Findex Database. Policy Research Working Paper 6025, The World Bank Development Research Group. http://documents.worldbank.org/ curated/en/453121468331738740/pdf/WPS6025.pdf

EY. (2016a). Defining FinTech. Retrieved from https://FinTechauscensus.ey. com/Home/Defining-FinTech

EY. (2016b). UK FinTech: On the cutting edge. Retrieved from https://www. gov.uk/government/uploads/system/uploads/attachment_data/file/502996/ UK_FinTech_-_On_the_cutting_edge_-_Exec_Summary.pdf

Fidor Bank. https://www.fidor.com

Lee, D. K. C. (2015a). Handbook of Digital Currency. Elsevier.

Lee, D. K. C. (2015b). Handbook of Digital Currency: Bitcoin, Innovation, Financial Instruments, and Big Data. Academic Press ISBN: 0128023511, 9780128023518. Retrieved from http://store.elsevier.com/Handbook-of-Digital-Currency/isbn-9780128021170/

Lee, D. K. C. (2015c). On the edge of disruption. Asian Management Insights, 2(2), 78–83. Retrieved from http://www.emeraldgrouppublishing.com/learn ing/ami/vol2_iss_2/disruption.pdf

Lee, D. K. C. (2017). Decentralisation and Distributed Innovation. Paper presented to Stanford Asia-Pacific Innovation Conference, Stanford.

Lee, D. K. C., & Teo, E G. S. (2015) Emergence of FinTech and the LASIC Principles Journal of Financial Perspectives, (Vols. 33) Retrieved from https://www.gfsi.ey.com/the-journal-x.php?pid=18&id=122

Lee, D. K. C., & Teo, E (2017) The Game of Dian Fu: The Rise of Chinese Finance: Handbook of Blockchain, Digital Finance and Inclusion (Vol. 1). Elsevier.

National Bureau of Statistics of China. http://data.stats.gov.cn/

People's Bank of China. http://www.pbc.gov.cn/publish/zhifujiesuansi/4263/index.html

Piketty, T. (2014). Capital in the Twenty-First Century. (Goldhammer. A., Trans.). Belknap Press.

Statista. https://www.statista.com/

The Global Findex Database. (2014). World Bank. Retrieved from http://www.worldbank.org/en/programs/globalfindex

Zen, S. (2016, December 6). TechFin: Jack Ma coins term to set Alipay's goal to give emerging markets access to capital. South China Morning Post. Retrieved from http://www.scmp.com/tech/article/2051249/TechFin-jack-ma-coins-term-set-alipays-goal-give-emerging-markets-access

Chapter 2

Andresen, G. (2015). BIP101: Increase maximum block size. Retrieved from https://githumb.com/bitcoin/bips/blob/master/bip-0101.mediawik

Androulaki, E., Karame, G. O., Roeschlin, M., Scherer, T., & Capkun, S. (2013, April). Evaluating user privacy in bitcoin. In International Conference on Financial Cryptography and Data Security (pp. 34–51). Berlin, Heidelberg: Springer. Retrieved from http://fc13.ifca.ai/proc/1-3.pdf

Back, A. (1997). A partial hash collision based postage scheme, s.l.: s.n. Retrieved from http://www.hashcash.org/papers/announce.txt. Accessed on January 25, 2015.

Back, A. (2002). Hashcash — A denial of service counter-measure, s.l.: s.n. Retrieved from http://www.hashcash.org/papers/hashcash.pdf. Accessed on January 25, 2015.

BBC News. (2013, May 27). Liberty Reserve digital money service forced offline. Retrieved from http://www.bbc.co.uk/news/technology-22680297

BitcoinCash. (2017). Bitcoin Cash — Peer-to-peer electronic cash. Retrieved from https://www.bitcoincash.org/

Bitcoin.org. (2014). Choose your bitcoin wallet. Retrieved from https://bitcoin.org/en/choose-your-wallet

Bitcoin Project. (2014). Frequently asked questions. Retrieved from https://bitcoin.org/en/faq

Bitcoin Unlimited. (2017). Retrieved from https://www.bitcoinunlimited.info/

Blockgeeks. (2017). What is Segwit? Retrieved from https://blockgeeks.com/guides/what-is-segwit/

Brito, J. (2013). The top 3 things I learned at the bitcoin conference. Mercatus Center. Retrieved from http://mercatus.org/expert_commentary/top-3-things-i-learned-bitcoin-conference

Brito, K. & Castillo, A. (2013). Bitcoin: A primer for policymakers. Mercatus Center. Retrieved from http://mercatus.org/publication/bitcoin-primer-policymakers

Buterin, V. (2017). On sharding blockchains. Retrieved from https://github.com/ethereum/wiki/wiki/Sharding-FAQ

Caffyn, G. (2015). What is the Bitcoin block size debate and why does it matter? Retrieved November 9, 2017, from https://www.coindesk.com/what-is-the-bitcoin-block-size-debate-and-why-does-it-matter/

Chaum, D. (1983). Blind signatures for untraceable payments. In Chaum, D., Rivest, R. L., & Sherman, A. T. (Eds.), Advances in Cryptology. In Proceedings of Crypto, vol. 82. Springer, 199–203. Retrieved from http://link.springer.com/chapter/10.1007%2F978-1-4757-0602-4_18

Chaum, D., Fiat, A., & Naor, M. (1990). Untraceable electronic cash. Adv. Cryptol CRYPTO' 88 (403), 319–327.

Chen, A. (2011, June 1). The undergroundwebsite where you can buy any drug imaginable. Gizmodo. Retrieved from http://gawker.com/5805928/the-underground-website-where-you-can-buy-any-drug-imaginable

CoinDesk. (2014, July 22). How to store your bitcoins. CoinDesk. Retrieved from http://www.coindesk.com/information/how-to-store-your-bitcoins/

Dai, W. (1998). b-money, s.l.: s.n.

Decker, C. & Wattenhofer, R. (2014). Bitcoin transaction malleability and MtGox. Cryptography and Security.

Doherty, S. (2011, June 16). All your bitcoins are ours ... Symantec Blog. Retrieved from http://www.symantec.com/connect/blogs/all-your-bitcoins-are-ours

Finney, H. (2004). RPOW — Reusable Proofs of Work, s.l.: s.n. Retrieved from http://cryptome.org/rpow.htm. Accessed on January 25, 2015.

Hileman, G. (2014). From bitcoin to the Brixton pound: History and prospects for alternative currencies (poster abstract). In Böhme, R., Brenner, M., Moore, T., Smith, M. (Eds.), Berlin: Springer, 163–165.

Hughes, E. (1993). A Cypherpunk's Manifesto. Retrieved from https://w2.eff.org/Privacy/Crypto/Crypto_misc/cypherpunk.manifesto

Kaminsky, D. (2013, April 12). I tried hacking bitcoin and I failed. Business Insider. Retrieved from http://www.businessinsider.com/dan-kaminsky-highlights-flaws-bitcoin-2013-4

Kaplanov, N. M. (2012). Nerdy money: Bitcoin, the private digital currency, and the case against its regulation. Retrieved from http://ssrn.com/abstract1/42115203

Lam, P. N. & Lee, D. K. C. (2015). Introduction to Bitcoin. Handbook of Digital Currency. Elsevier.

Lau, J. & Wuille, P. (2016). BIP143: Transaction Signature Verification for Verstion 0 Witness Program. Retrieved from https://github.com/bitcoin/bips/blob/master/bib-0143.mediawiki

Lee, D. K. C. (2015). Handbook of Digital Currency. Elsevier.

Lee, D. K. C. (2017). Decentralised and Distributed Innovation. Paper presented at the Stanford APARC Innovation Concerence.

Lee, D. K. C., & Deng R. (2017). Handbook of Blockchain, Digital Finance and Inclusion. Elsevier.

Levey, S. (1993). Crypto Rebels. Wired. Retrieved from https://www.wired.com/1993/02/crypto-rebels/

LocalBitcoins. (2014). Buy and sell bitcoins near you. Retrieved from https://localbitcoins.com/

Lombrozo, E., & Wuille, P. (2016). BIP144: Segregated Witness (Peer Services). Retrieved from https://github.com/bitcoin/bips/blob/master/bip-0144.mediawiki

Lombrozo, E., Lau, J., & Wuille, P. (2015). BIP141: Segregated Witness (Consensus Layer). Retrieved from https://github.com/bitcoin/bips/blob/master/bip-0141.mediawiki

Madeira, A. (2017, September 28). What is the block size limit. Retrieved from CryptoCompare, https://www.cryptocompare.com/coins/guides/what-is-the-block-size-limit/

Matonis, J. (2013). Bitcoin gaining market-based legitimacy as XBT. Retrieved from http://www.coindesk.com/ bitcoin-gaining-market-based-legitimacy-xbt/

May, T. (1992). The Crypto Anarchist Manifesto. s.l.: s.n. Retrieved from http://www.activism.net/cypherpunk/crypto-anarchy.html. Accessed on January 25, 2015.

Nakamoto, S. (2008). Bitcoin: A P2P electronic cash system. Retrieved from https://bitcoin.org/bitcoin.pdf

Ober, M., Katzenbeisser, S., & Hamacher, K. (2013). Structure and anonymity of the bitcoin transaction graph. Future Internet 5(2), 237–250. Retrieved from http://www.mdpi.com/1999-5903/5/2/237

Pacia, C. (2013). Bitcoin mining explained like you're five: part 2 — mechanics. Escape Velocity. Retrieved from http://chrispacia.wordpress.com/2013/09/02/bitcoin-mining-explained-like-youre-five-part-2-mechanics/. Accessed on September 2, 2013.

Poon, J. & Buterin, V. (2017). Plasma: Scalable autonomous smart contracts. Retrieved from https://plasma.io/plasma.pdf

Poon, J., & Dryja, T. (2016). The Bitcoin Lightning Network: Scalable off-chain instant payments. Retrieved from https://lightning.network/lightning-network-paper.pdf

Raiden Network. (2017). Retrieved from http://raiden-network.readthedocs.io/en/stable/spec.html

Reid, F., & Harrigan, M., 2013. An analysis of anonymity in the bitcoin system. In Altshuler, Y. et al, (Eds.), Security and Privacy in Social Networks. New York: Springer. Retrieved from http://arxiv.org/pdf/1107.4524v2.pdf

Romano, D., & Schmid, G. (2017). Beyond Bitcoin: A critical look at blockchain-based systems. Cryptography, 1(15), 1–31.

Shirky, C. (2000). The case against micropayments. O'Reilly Media, Inc. Retrieved from http://www.openp2p.com/pub/a/p2p/2000/12/19/micropayments.html. Accessed on January 25, 2015.

Shirriff, K. (2014). Bitcoin transaction malleability: Looking at the bytes. Retrieved November 8, 2017, from http://www.righto.com/2014/02/bitcoin-transaction-malleability.html

Song, J. (2017). Understanding Segwit block size. Retrieved from https://medium.com/@jimmysong/understanding-segwit-block-size-fd901b87c9d4

Szabo, N. (1999). The God Protocols. IT Audit, 15 November.

Szabo, N. (2002). Shelling Out — The origins of money, s.l.: s.n. Retrieved from http://szabo.best.vwh.net/shell.html. Accessed on January 25, 2015.

Szabo, N. (2008). Bit gold, s.l.: s.n. Retrieved from http://unenumerated.blogspot.com/2005/12/bit-gold.html. Accessed on January 25, 2015.

The Economist. (2016, January 26). Known unknown: Another cryto-currency is born. Retrieved from http://www.economist.com/news/finance-and-economics/21709329-another-crypto-currency-born-known-unknown

Tindell, K. (2013). Geeks love the bitcoin phenomenon like they loved the internet in 1995. Business Insider. Retrieved from http://www.businessinsider.com/how-bitcoins-are-mined-and-used-2013-4. Accessed on April 5, 2013.

Van Wirdum, A. (2015a). Chinese exchanges reject Gavin Andresen's 20MB block size increase. Retrieved from https://cointelegraph.com/news/chinese-exchanges-reject-gavin-andresens-20-mb-block-size-increase/

Van Wirdum, A. (2015b). Segregated Witness, Part 1: How a clever hack could significantly increase Bitcoin's potential. Retrieved from https://bitcoinmagazine.com/articles/segregated-witness-part-how-a-clever-hack-could-significantly-increase-bitcoin-s-potential-1450553618/

Wallace, B. (November 2011). The rise and fall of Bitcoin. Wired (23).

Chapter 3

Allison, I. (2016). Ethereum reinvents companies with launch of The DAO. Retrieved from http://www.ibtimes.co.uk/Ethereum-reinvents-companies-launch-dao-1557576

Breber, D. (August 20, 2016). On tokens and crowdsales: How startups are using blockchain to raise capital. Coindesk. Retrieved from https://www.coindesk.com/tokens-crowdsales-startups/

Chwierut, M. (2017a). Token Rights: Key considerations in designing a token economy. Smith + Crown. Retrieved from https://www.smithandcrown.com/token-rights/

Chwierut, M. (2017b). Token sale market performance. Smith + Crown. Retrieved
    from https://www.smithandcrown.com/token-sale-market-performance/

Coindesk. https://www.coindesk.com/ico-tracker/

CoinSchedule. https://www.coinschedule.com/

El-isa, M. (2017). The difference between protocol tokens and traditional asset
    tokens. Retrieved from https://medium.com/melonport-blog/the-difference-
    between-protocol-tokens-and-traditional-asset-tokens-89e0a9dcf4d1

Goodman, L. M. (2014). Tezos — A self-amending crypto-ledger. White paper.
    Retrieved from https://www.tezos.com/static/papers/white_paper.pdf

Hajdarbegovic, N. (2013). Mastercoin Foundation lets virtual currencies use
    Bitcoin protocol. Retrieved from https://www.coindesk.com/mastercoin-
    foundation-virtual-currencies-bitcoin-protocol/

Kastelein, R. (2017). What Initial Coin Offerings are, and why VC firms care.
    Retrieved from https://hbr.org/2017/03/what-initial-coin-offerings-are-and-
    why-vc-firms-care

Keane, J. (2017). The state of ICO regulation? New report outlines legal status
    in 6 nations. Retrieved from https://www.coindesk.com/state-ico-regulation-
    new-report-outlines-legal-status-6-nations/

Lea, T. (2016). An introduction to Initial Coin Offerings (ICO's) — The
    venture capital disrupters. Retrieved from https://www.linkedin.com/pulse/
    introduction-initial-coin-offerings-icos-venture-capital-tim-r-lea

Lee, K. C. D., Guo, L., & Wang, Y. (2017). Cryptocurrency: A New Investment
    Opportunity? Working paper. Retrieved from https://ssrn.com/abstract=29
    94097

Lewis, A. (2017). A gentle introduction to Initial Coin Offerings (ICOs).
    Retrieved from https://bitsonblocks.net/2017/04/25/a-gentle-introduction-
    to-initial-coin-offerings-icos/

Lex, S. (2017). Token mania. Autonomous NEXT. Retrieved from https://
    autonomous.app.box.com/v/tokenmania

Reuben, B. (2017). The perfect token sale structure. Retrieved from https://
    blog.gdax.com/the-perfect-token-sale-structure-63c169789491.

RIALTO.AI. (2017). Understanding RIALTO.AI Crowdsale. Retrieved
    from https://medium.com/ico-brief/understanding-rialto-ai-crowdsale-ce106
    16e3033

Skinner, C. (2017). The crazy world of crypto currencies and ICOs. Retrieved from
    https://thefinanser.com/2017/06/crazy-world-crypto-currencies-icos.html/

Smith + Crown. https://www.smithandcrown.com/wp-content/uploads/2017/
    05/Token-Sale-Market-Overview.png

Tomaino, N. (2017). On token value. Retrieved from https://thecontrol.co/on-
    token-value-e61b10b6175e

Vincent, J. (2017). China bans all ICOs and digital currency launches as "ille-
    gal public financing". Retrieved from https://www.theverge.com/2017/9/4/
    16251624/china-bans-ico-initial-coin-offering-regulation

Voshmgir, S. & Kalinov, V. (2017). What is an ICO? Initial Coin Offering —
    Blockchain tokens. Retrieved from https://blockchainhub.net/ico-initial-
    coin-offerings/

Xie, L. (2017). A beginner's guide to Tezos. Retrieved from https://medium.com/@linda.xie/a-beginners-guide-to-tezos-c9618240183f

Zysman, L. (September 30, 2016). DAOs and securities regulation. Smith + Crown. Retrieved from https://www.smithandcrown.com/daos-securities-regulation/

Chapter 4

Anderson, W. (2017a). The Legends Room Token Sale: Tokenized Membership to a Private Las Vegas Lounge. Working paper, Smith + Crown. Retrieved from https://www.smithandcrown.com/legends-room/

Anderson, W. (2017b). Zrcoin: Crypto-Tokens Backed by a Zirconium Oxide Factory. Working paper, Smith + Crown. Retrieved from https://www.smithandcrown.com/sale/zrcoin/

Chwierut, M. (2016a). A History of Bitcoin. Working paper, Smith + Crown. Retrieved from https://www.smithandcrown.com/a-history-of-bitcoin/

Chwierut, M. (2016b). DECENT "Software Sale". Working paper, Smith + Crown. Retrieved from https://www.smithandcrown.com/sale/decent/

Chwierut, M. (2016c). First Blood Token Sale. Working paper, Smith + Crown. Retrieved from https://www.smithandcrown.com/sale/first-blood/

Chwierut, M. (2017a). Token rights: Key Considerations in Designing a Token Economy. Working paper, Smith + Crown.

Chwierut, M. (2017b). Token Sales Market Performance. Working paper, Smith + Crown. Retrieved from https://www.smithandcrown.com/token-sale-market-performance/

CoinDesk. Bitcoin venture capital. Retrieved from http://www.coindesk.com/bitcoin-venture-capital/

The Economist. (2017, April 27). The market in the Initial Coin Offerings risk becoming a bubble. Retrieved from http://www.economist.com/news/finance-and-economics/21721425-it-may-also-spawn-valuable-innovations-market-initial-coin-offerings. Accessed on June 9, 2017.

Glaser, F., & Bezzenberger, L. (2015). Beyond Cryptocurrencies — A Taxonomy of Decentralized Consensus Systems. 23rd European Conference on Information Systems (ECIS), Münster, Germany. Retrieved from https://ssrn.com/abstract=2605803

Hull, C., Chwierut, M., Lio, B., & Anderson, W. (2017). Cryptocurrency, Digital Innovation, and the Digital Entrepreneur: How Blockchain Technology and ICOs (Initial Coin Offerings) Facilitate Digital Entrepreneurship and Innovation. (Forthcoming).

Investopedia. (2017). http://www.investopedia.com/terms/i/initial-coin-offering-ico.asp. Accessed on March 30, 2017.

Kalla, S. (2016). What Is an ICO?. Working paper, Smith + Crown. Retrieved from https://www.smithandcrown.com/what-is-anico. Accessed on March 6, 2017.

Kastelein, R. (2017). What Initial Coin Offerings are, and why VC firms care. Harvard Business Review. Retrieved from https://hbr.org/2017/03/what-initial-coin-offerings-are-and-why-vc-firms-care. Accessed on June 9, 2017.

Laurent, L. (2017, April 18). Want to be a VC just flip a Bitcoin. Bloomberg. Retrieved from https://www.bloomberg.com/gadfly/articles/2017-04-18/beating-vc-funds-is-as-easy-as-flipping-a-bitcoin. Accessed on June 9, 2017.

Lee, D. K. C. (2017). The Deep Skill of Business Blockchain. Retrieved from April 25, 2017. Presentation.

Lio, B. (2016). Introduction to Decentralized Autonomous Corporations (DACs). Working paper, Smith + Crown. Retrieved from https://www.smithand crown.com/introduction-decentralized-autonomous-corporations-dacs/

Metz, C. (2017). The Initial Coin Offering, the Bitcoin-y stock that's not stock — But definitely a big deal. Wired. Retrieved from https://www.wired.com/2017/03/initial-coin-offering-stock-thats-not-stock/. Accessed on June 9, 2017.

Nakamoto, S. (2008). Bitcoin: A Peer-to-Peer Electronic Cash System. Working paper. Retrieved from http://www.cryptovest.co.uk/resources/Bitcoin%20 paper%20Original.pdf. Accessed on March 30, 2017.

Smith + Crown. (2016). Daos Securities Regulation. Retrieved from https://www.smithandcrown.com/daos-securities-regulation/

Smith + Crown. (2017a). Bitcoin. Retrieved from https://www.smithandcrown.com/currency/bitcoin/. Accessed on March 30, 2017.

Smith + Crown. (2017b). Ethereum. Retrieved from https://www.smithand crown.com/currency/ethereum/

Weiler, A. (2017). Matchpool Token Sale (ICO): Curated Dating Communities with the Security of a Blockchain. Working paper, Smith + Crown. Retrieved from https://www.smithandcrown.com/matchpool-token-sale-ico-curated-dating-communities-security-blockchain/

Chapter 5

Bloq. (2017a). Retrieved from http://bloq.com/#team

Bloq. (2017b). Retrieved from http://bloq.com/bloq-and-pwc-australia-launch-vulcan-to-accelerate-global-adoption-of-digital-money.html

Buldas, A., Kroonmaa, A., & Laanoja, R. (2013). Keyless Singatures' Infrastructure: How to build global distributed has-tress. Retrieved from https://eprint.iacr.org/2013/834.pdf

Factom. (2017). Retrieved from https://www.factom.com/about/team

Fink, B. (2017, June 22). Antshares rebrands, introduces NEO and the new smart economy. Retrieved from https://bitcoinmagazine.com/articles/antshares-rebrands-introduces-neo-and-new-smart-economy1/

Handler, J. (2015, July 28). Addressimo: Making BIP 0032 & BIP 0070 easy for developers. Retrieved from https://blog.Netki.com/2015/07/

Irrera, A. (2017, May 23). BofA, HSBC, Intel, others invest $107 mln in blockchain startup R3. Retrieved from https://finance.yahoo.com/news/bofa-hsbc-intel-others-invest-123000543.html

Lee, D. K. C. (2016a). Blockchain as an enabler. Retrieved from https://www.slid eshare.net/DavidLee215/blockchain-as-an-enabler16-july-2016david-leefinal

Lee, D. K. C. (2016b). The future of FinTech and blockchain. Retrieved from https://www.slideshare.net/WanfengChen/the-future-of-FinTech-and-blockchain-63339789

Libra. (2017). Retrieved from http://www.libra.tech/

Medium. (2016). Blockchain applications beyond the financial services industry. Retrieved from https://medium.com/@LetsTalkPayments/blockchain-applications-beyond-the-financial-services-industry-ef7fcce216d6

Moh-Rokib. (2016). Zcash — All coins are created equally. Retrieved from https://steemit.com/zcash/@moh-rokib/zcash-all-coins-are-created-equal

Nakamoto, S. (2008). Bitcoin: A peer-to-peer electronic cash system. Retrieved from https://bitcoin.org/bitcoin.pdf

Newton, A. (2017). Hype cycle for digital banking transformation. Retrieved from https://static1.squarespace.com/static/581ca875f5e2313c7cbad236/t/59c423157131a59f8b16b10a/1506026265604/hype_cycle_for_digital_banki_328 960.pdf

PwC. (2017). PwC's digital asset services: Powering the future of financial services. Retrieved from https://www.pwc.com.au/financial-services/FinTech/digital-asset-services.html

Reddit. (2016, March 12). What is Ethereum block size? https://www.reddit.com/r/ethereum/comments/4a3kqo/what_is_ethereums_block_size/

Samman, G. (2017). Sammantics. Retrieved from http://sammantics.com/

Scardovi, C. (2016). Restructuring and Innovation in Banking. Springer International Publishing.

UK Government. (2016). Distributed Ledger Technology: Beyond blockchain. UK Government, Office for Science. Retrieved from http://www.the-blockchain.com/docs/UK%20government%2088%20page%20Blockchain%20Report.pdf

Woobull. http://charts.woobull.com/bitcoin-risk-adjusted-return/

Zerocash. (2017). Retrieved from http://zerocash-project.org/

Chapter 6

All In Bits, Inc. (2017). Tendermint — Blockchain consensus. Retrieved from https://tendermint.com/

Androulaki, E., Karame G. O., Roeschlin M., Scherer T., & Capkun S. (2013). Evaluating user privacy in Bitcoin. In Sadeghi, A. R. (Ed.), Financial Cryptography and Data Security, Lecture Notes in Computer Science 7859 (pp. 34–51). Berlin, Heidelberg: Springer. Retrieved from https://link.springer.com/chapter/10.1007/978-3-642-39884-1_4

Atzei, N., Bartoletti M., & Cimoli T. (2017). A survey of attacks on Ethereum Smart Contracts (SoK). In Maffei, M., & Ryan, M. (Eds.), Principles of Security and Trust. In Proceedings of the 6th International Conference on Principles of Security and Trust, POST 2017. Springer, 164–186. Retrieved from https://link.springer.com/chapter/10.1007%2F978-3-662-54455-6_8

Bellare, M., Canetti, R., & Krawczyk, H. (1996). Keying hash functions for message authentication. In Koblitz, N. (Ed.), Advances in Cryptology —

CRYPTO' 96. In Proceedings of 16th Annual International Cryptology Conference, Santa Barbara, California, USA, August 18–22, 1996. Springer, 1–15. Retrieved from https://link.springer.com/chapter/10.1007%2F3-540-68697-5_1

Benet, J. (2014). IPFS — Content addressed, versioned, P2P file system. arXiv preprint arXiv:1407.3561. Retrieved from https://arxiv.org/pdf/1407.3561.pdf

Ben-Sasson, E., Chiesa, A., Tromer, E., & Virza, M. (2014). Succinct non-interactive zero knowledge for a von Neumann architecture. In Proceedings of the 23rd USENIX Conference on Security Symposium (SEC'14). USENIX Association, 781–796. Retrieved from https://www.usenix.org/system/files/conference/usenixsecurity14/sec14-paper-ben-sasson.pdf

Bernstein, D. J., Duif, N., Lange, T., Schwabe, P., & Yang, B.-Y. (2012). High-Speed High-Security Signatures. Journal of Cryptographic Engineering, 2(2), 77–89.

Brown, R. G., Carlyle, J., Grigg, I., & Hearn, M. (2016). Corda: An Introduction. White Paper.

Callas, J., Donnerhacke, L., Finney, H., Shaw, D., & Thayer, R. (2007). OpenPGP Message Format. Network Working Group RFC 4880, November 2007.

Chain Inc. (2016). Chain Protocol Whitepaper. White Paper.

Chain Inc. (2017). Chain | Enterprise blockchain infrastructure. Retrieved from https://chain.com/

Chen, C. (2014, May 21). Zeusminer delivers Lightning, Thunder and Cyclone Scrypt ASICs for Litecoin and Dogecoin mining. Retrieved from https://www.cryptocoinsnews.com/zeusminer-delivers-lightning-thunder-cyclone-scrypt-asics-litecoin-dogecoin-mining/

Coin Sciences Ltd. (2017). MultiChain | Open source private blockchain platform. Retrieved from https://www.multichain.com/

Coinprism. (2015). Openchain — Blockchain technology for the enterprise. Retrieved from https://www.openchain.org/

Dai, P., Mahi, N., Earls, J., & Norta, A. (2017). Smart-contract value-transfer protocols on a distributed mobile application platform. Retrieved from http://bit.ly/2vceYYW

DaxClassix. (2016). Ethereum Classic. Retrieved from https://ethereumclassic.github.io

Dell, I., Beddows, O., Meunier, L., & Kordek, M. (2017). The Lisk Protocol. Retrieved from https://docs.lisk.io/docs/the-lisk-protocol

DigixGlobal. (2016). Digix Global. Retrieved from https://www.dgx.io/

Disney. (2017). Dragonchain. Retrieved from https://dragonchain.github.io/

Douceur, J. R. (2002). The Sybil attack. In Druschel P., Kaashoek F., & Rowstron A. (Eds.), Peer-to-Peer Systems. In Proceedings of the 1st International Workshop on Peer-to-Peer Systems (IPTPS). Springer, 251–260. Retrieved from https://link.springer.com/chapter/10.1007%2F3-540-45748-8_24

Duffield, E., & Diaz, D. (2017). Dash: A Privacy-Centric Crypto-Currency. White Paper.

Dworkin, M. J. (2015). SHA-3 Standard: Permutation-Based Hash and Extendable-Output Functions. NIST Federal Information Processing Standard 202, 2015.

ElGamal, T. (1985). A public key cryptosystem and a signature scheme based on discrete logarithms. IEEE Transactions on Information Theory, 31(4), 469–472.

Ethereum Foundation. (2017). Ethereum Project. Retrieved from https://www. ethereum.org/

Factom. (2017). Factom — Making the world's systems honest. Retrieved from https://www.factom.com/

Ferguson, N., Lucks, S., Schneier, B., Whiting, D., Bellare, M., Kohno, T., Callas, J., & Walker, J. (2010). The Skein Hash Function Family. Submission to NIST (round 3) 7, 2010.

Fisher, M. J., Lynch, N. A., & Paterson, M. S. (1985). Impossibility of distributed consensus with one faulty process. Journal of the Association for Computing Machinery, 32(2), 374– 382.

Gauravaram, P., Knudsen, L. R., Matusiewicz, K., Mendel, F., Rechberger, C., Schläffer, M., & Thomsen, S. S. (2008). "Grøstl — A SHA-3 candidate. Retrieved from http://www.groestl.info

Gentry, C. (2009). A Fully Homomorphic Encryption Scheme. Working paper, Stanford University.

Goldreich, O., Micali, S., & Wigderson, A. (1991). Proofs that yield nothing but their validity or all languages in NP have zero-knowledge proof systems. Journal of the ACM (JACM), 38(3), 690–728.

Greenspan, G. (2015). MultiChain private blockchain — White paper. Retrieved from https://www.multichain.com/download/MultiChain-White-Paper.pdf

Gura, N., Patel, A., Wander, A., Eberle, H., & Shantz, S. C. (2004). Comparing Elliptic Curve Cryptography and RSA on 8-bit CPUs. In Joye, M., & Quisquater, J. J. (Eds.), Cryptographic Hardware and Embedded Systems — CHES, Lecture Notes in Computer Science 3156 (pp. 119–132). Berlin, Heidelberg: Springer.

Hankerson, D., Menezes, A. J., & Vanstone, S. (2006). Guide to Elliptic Curve Cryptography. NY: Springer Science & Business Media.

Hertig, A., & Rizzo. P. (2016, July 28). Ethereum's two Ethereums explained. Retrieved from http://www.coindesk.com/ethereum-classic-explained-block chain/

Higgins, S. (2017, April 26). Grayscale opens Ethereum Classic vehicle to accredited investors. Retrieved from http://www.coindesk.com/grayscale-ethereum- classic-vehicle/

Hopwood, D., Bowe, S., Hornby, T., & Wilcox, N. (2017). Zcash Protocol Specification. White Paper.

Intel. (2015). Hyperledger Sawtooth documentation. Retrieved from https:// intelledger.github.io/

Johnson, D., Menezes, A., & Vanstone, S. (2001). The Elliptic Curve Digital Signature Algorithm (ECDSA). International Journal of Information Security, 1(1), 36–63.

Josefsson, S., & Liusvaara, I. (2017). Edwards-Curve Digital Signature Algorithm (EdDSA). The Internet Engineering Task Force RFC 8032.

Kiraly, B. (2017, February 21). InstantSend. Retrieved from https://dashpay. atlassian.net/wiki/display/DOC/InstantSend

Kiraly, B. (2017, April 7). PrivateSend. Retrieved from https://dashpay.atlassian. net/wiki/display/DOC/PrivateSend

Kumar, A., Fischer, C., Tople, S., & Saxena, P. (2017). A Traceability Analysis of Monero's Blockchain. IACR Cryptology ePrint Archive 2017.

Ladha, A., Pandit, S., & Ralhan, S. (2016). The Ethereum scratch off puzzle. arXiv preprint arXiv:1612.04518, 2016.

Lai, R., & Lee, D. K. C. (2017). From public to private. In Lee & Deng. Handbook of Blockchain, Digital Finance and Inclusion. Elsevier.

Larimer, D., Scott, N., Zavgorodnev, V., Johnson, B., Calfee, J., & Vandeberg, M. (2016). Steem: An incentivised blockchain-based social media platform. Retrieved from https://steem.io/SteemWhitePaper.pdf

Lee, D. K. C. & Deng, R. (2017). Handbook of Blockchain, Digital Finance and Inclusion: Vol 1 and 2. Elsevier.

Li R. (2017, January 12). Blockchain software security report by China CERT, Ripple the worst. Retrieved from http://news.8btc.com/blockchain-software-security-report-by-china-cert-ripple-the-worst

Litecoin Project. (2011). Litecoin — Open source P2P digital currency. Retrieved from https://litecoin.org/

M'Raihi, D., Bellare, M., Hoornaert, F., Naccache, D., & Ranen, O. (2005). HOTP: An HMAC-Based One-Time Password Algorithm. The Internet Engineering Task Force RFC 4226.

Mao, W. (2013). Modern Cryptography: Theory and Practice. NJ: Prentice Hall Professional Technical Reference.

Maxwell, G. (2013). CoinJoin: Bitcoin privacy for the real world. Post on Bitcoin Forum.

Mazieres, D. (2016). The Stellar Consensus Protocol: A federated model for Internet-level consensus. Retrieved from https://www.stellar.org/papers/stellar-consensus-protocol.pdf

Merkle, R. C. (1988). A digital signature based on a conventional encryption function. In Pomerance, C. (Ed.), Advances in Cryptology — CRYPTO '87, Lecture Notes in Computer Science 293 (pp. 369–378). Berlin, Heidelberg: Springer.

Morabito, V. (2017). The security of blockchain systems. In Business Innovation through Blockchain. Cham: Springer International Publishing.

Moriarty, K., Ed., Kaliski, B., Jonsson, J., & Rusch, A. (2016). PKCS #1: RSA Cryptography Specifications Version 2.2. Internet Engineering Task Force RFC 8017.

Nakamoto, S. (2008). Bitcoin: A peer-to-peer electronic cash system. Retrieved from https://bitcoin.org/bitcoin.pdf

NIST. (2001). Federal Information Processing Standards Publication 197 — Announcing the Advanced Encryption Standard (AES). Retrieved from http://nvlpubs.nist.gov/nistpubs/FIPS/NIST.FIPS.197.pdf

NIST. (2015). Federal Information Processing Standards Publication 180-4 Secure Hash Standard (SHS). Retrieved from http://nvlpubs.nist.gov/nistpubs/ FIPS/NIST.FIPS.180-4.pdf

Pass, R., Seeman, L., & Shelat, A. (2017). Analysis of the blockchain protocol in asynchronous networks. In Coron, J. S., & Nielsen, J. (Eds.), Advances in Cryptology — EUROCRYPT 2017, Lecture Notes in Computer Science 10211 (pp. 643–673). Cham: Springer International Publishing.

Percival, C., & Josefsson., S. (2016). The Scrypt Password-Based Key Derivation Function. The Internet Engineering Task Force RFC 7914.

R3 Limited. (2016). Corda: Frictionless commerce. Retrieved from https://www. corda.net/

Rescorla, E. (2001). SSL and TLS: Designing and Building Secure Systems, Boston: Addison-Wesley Longman Publishing Co., Inc.

Ripple. (2013). Ripple — One frictionless experience to send money globally | Ripple. Retrieved from https://ripple.com/

Rivest, R. L., Shamir, A., & Tauman, Y. 2001. How to leak a secret. In Boyd, C. (Ed.), Advances in Cryptology — ASIACRYPT 2001, Lecture Notes in Computer Science 2248 (pp. 552–565). Berlin, Heidelberg: Springer.

Ron, D., & Shamir, A. (2013). Quantitative analysis of the full Bitcoin transaction graph. In Sadeghi, A. R. (Ed.), Financial Cryptography and Data Security, Lecture Notes in Computer Science 7859 (pp. 6–24). Berlin, Heidelberg: Springer.

Rosenfeld, M. (2014). Analysis of hashrate-based double spending. arXiv preprint arXiv:1402.2009.

Saarinen, M. J., & Aumasson, J. P. (2015). The BLAKE2 Cryptographic Hash and Message Authentication Code (MAC). The Internet Engineering Task Force RFC 7693.

Sandhu, R. S., & Samarati, P. (1994). Access control: Principle and practice. IEEE Communication Magazine, 32(9), 40–48.

Schoder, D., Fischbach, K., & Schmitt, C. (2005). Core concepts in peer-to-peer networking. In Subramanian, R., & Goodman, B. (Eds.), P2P Computing: The Evolution of a Disruptive Technology. Hershey: Idea Group Inc.

Schwartz, D., Youngs, N., & Britto, A. (2014). The Ripple Protocol Consensus Algorithm. Ripple Labs Inc White Paper 5.

Shoup, V. (2000). Practical threshold signatures. In Preneel B. (Ed.), Advances in Cryptology — EUROCRYPT 2000, Lecture Notes in Computer Science 1807 (pp. 207–220). Berlin, Heidelberg: Springer.

Stellar Development Foundation. (2014). Stellar — Develop the world's new financial system. Retrieved from https://www.stellar.org/

The Dash Network. (2017). Dash official website | Dash crypto currency — Dash. Retrieved from https://www.dash.org

The Linux Foundation. (2017). Hyperledger Fabric — Hyperledger. Retrieved from https://www.hyperledger.org/projects/fabric

The Monero Project. (2014). Monero — Secure, private, untraceable. Retrieved from http://getmonero.org/

van Saberhagen, N. (2013). CryptoNote v 2.0. White Paper.

Vasin, P. (2014). BlackCoin's Proof-of-Stake Protocol v2. White Paper.

Wood, G. (2017). Ethereum: A Secure Decentralised Generalised Transaction ledger. Ethereum Project Yellow Paper.

Yuen, T. H., Liu, J. K., Au, M. H., Susilo, W., & Zhou, J. (2013). Efficient linkable and/or threshold ring signature without random oracles. The Computer Journal, 56(4), 407–421.

ZECC. (2017). Zcash — All coins are created equal. Retrieved from https://z.cash

Zimmermann, P. R. (1995). The Official PGP User's Guide, MA: MIT Press.

Chapter 7

Alibaba. (2014). Alibaba Group Holding Limited IPO Prospectus, Form F-I Registration Statement Under the Securities Act of 1933, Securities and Exchange Commission. Retrieved from http://www.sec.gov/Archives/edgar/data/1577552/000119312514184994/d709111df1.htm

Allen, F., Demirguc-Kunt, A., Klapper, L., & Martinez Peria, M. S. (2012). The Foundations of Financial Inclusion: Understanding Ownership and Use of Formal Accounts. Development Research Group, World Bank.

Anson, J., Berthaud, A., Klappar, L., & Singer, D. (2013). Financial Inclusion and the Role of the Post Office. Development Research Group, World Bank.

Castillo, M. D. (2017). Bitcoin in the browser: Google, Apple and more adopting crypto-ready API. Coindesk. Retrieved from https://www.coindesk.com/bitcoin-browser-google-apple-move-adopt-crypto-compatible-api/

China Internet Watch. (2015). Weibo and Alipay's Hongbao Campaign Ggone viral. Retrieved from http://www.chinainternetwatch.com/12182/weibo-alipay-hongbao-2015/

CNNIC. (2015). China Internet Development Statistics (中国互联网络发展状况统计报告). Working paper in Chinese, CNNIC.

Demirguc-Kunt, A., & Klapper, L. (2012). Measuring Financial Inclusion: The Global Findex Database. Development Research Group, World Bank.

Ericsson. (2014). ICT & The Future of Financial Services. Networked Society Lab, Ericsson.

Federal Deposit Insurance Corporation. (2014). 2013 FDIC National Survey of Unbanked and Underbanked Households. Retrieved from https://www.fdic.gov/householdsurvey/

Federal Deposit Insurance Corporation. (October 29, 2014). FDIC releases National Survey of Unbanked and Underbanked. Retrieved from https://www.fdic.gov/news/news/press/2014/pr14091.html

Fingleton Associates. (2014). Data Sharing and Open Data for Banks. A Report for HM Treasury and Cabinet Office.

Herring, M. (2017). China's digital-payments giant keeps bank chiefs up at night: Ants in your pants. The Economist. Retrieved from https://www.economist.com/news/business/21726713-ant-financial-500m-customers-home-plans-expand-chinas-digital-payments-giant-keeps

Jingu, T. (2014). Risks and Opportunities in China's Growing P2P Lending Market. Nomura Research Institute.

LendingClub. (2014). LendingClub Corporation IPO Prospectus. Form S-1 Registration Statement Under the Securities Act 1933, Securities and Exchange Commission. Retrieved from http://www.sec.gov/Archives/edgar/data/1409970/000119312514428454/d766811ds1a.htm

People's Bank of China. (2012). China Payment System Development Report. Payment and Settlement Department of the People's Bank of China, China Financial Publishing House.

Safaricom Limited. (2014). Annual Report. Retrieved from http://www.safaricom.co.ke/annualreport_2014/public/downloads/Full%20Report.pdf

Chapter 8

Fintechnews Singapore. (November 14, 2016). First bank in Southeast Asia to use blockchain technology for payment services. Fintechnews Singapore. Retrieved from http://fintechnews.sg/6726/blockchain/first-bank-southeast-asia-use-blockchain-technology-payment-services/

TenX Whitepaper, https://www.tenx.tech/whitepaper/tenx_whitepaper_draft_v04.pdf

Chapter 9

Channel NewsAsia. (November 30, 2016). Myanmar hopes to overtake Singapore economically in 20 years' time: Suu Kyi. Retrieved from http://www.channelnewsasia.com/news/singapore/myanmar-hopes-to-overtake-singapore-economically-in-20-years/3330330.html

Cihak, M., Mare, D., & Melecky, M. (2016). The Nexus of Financial Inclusion and Financial Stability: A Study of Trade-offs and Synergies. Policy Research Papers, World Bank Group. http://documents.worldbank.org/curated/en/138991467994676130/pdf/WPS7722.pdf

De Soto, H. (2000). The Mystery of Capital: Why Capitalism Triumphs in the West and Fails Everywhere Else." New York: Basic Books.

Fintech Singapore. http://fintechnews.sg/

Lagua, T. B. D. (2017). Financial inclusion and financial stability. BusinessWorld Online. Retrieved from http://www.bworldonline.com/content.php?section=Opinion&title=financial-inclusion-and-financial-stability&id=139313

Mariano, T. (2016, August 22). How Bitcoin is disrupting Southeast Asia's remittance industry. Inc. Southeast Asia. Retrieved from http://inc-asean.com/editor-picks/bitcoin-disrupting-southeast-asias-remittance-industry/?utm_source=newsletter&utm_medium=email&utm_campaign=newsletter_fintech

Chapter 10

CB Insights. (February 15, 2017). The Global FinTech Report 2016 in Review.

Index